CASE CLOSED™

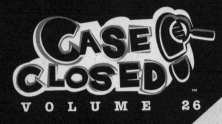

VOLUME 26

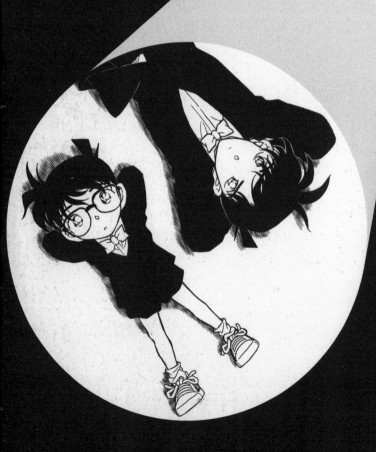

Gosho Aoyama

Case Briefing:

Subject:
Occupation:
Special Skills:
Equipment:

Jimmy Kudo, a.k.a. Conan Edogawa
High School Student/Detective
Analytical thinking and deductive reasoning, Soccer
Bow Tie Voice Transmitter, Super Sneakers,
Homing Glasses, Stretchy Suspenders

The subject is hot on the trail of a pair of suspicious men in black when he is attacked from behind and administered a strange substance which physically transforms him into a first grader. When the subject confides in the eccentric inventor Dr. Agasa, they decide to keep the subject's true identity a secret for the safety of everyone around him. Assuming the new identity of first-grader Conan Edogawa, the subject continues to assist the police force on their most baffling cases. The only problem is that most crime-solving professionals won't take a little kid's advice!

Table of Contents

ONFIDEN

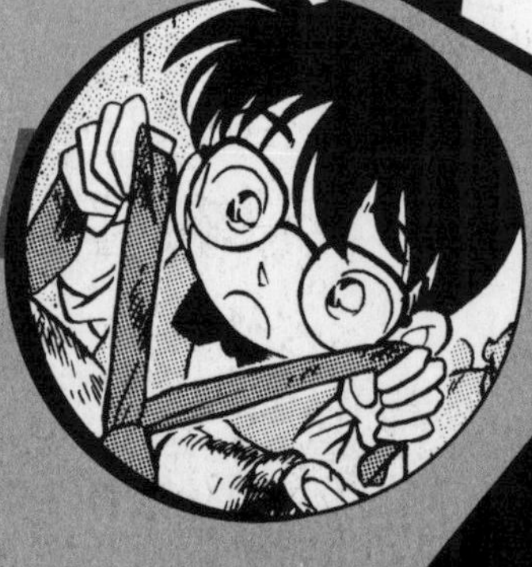

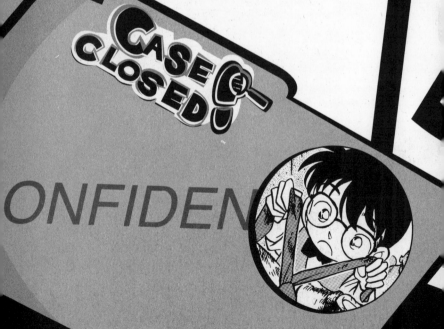

CASE CLOSED
Volume 26 • VIZ Media Edition

GOSHO AOYAMA

Translation
Tetsuichiro Miyaki

Touch-up & Lettering
Freeman Wong

Cover & Graphic Design
Andrea Rice

Editor
Shaenon K. Garrity

Editor in Chief, Books **Alvin Lu**
Editor in Chief, Magazines **Marc Weidenbaum**
VP, Publishing Licensing **Rika Inouye**
VP, Sales and Product Marketing **Gonzalo Ferreyra**
VP, Creative **Linda Espinosa**
Publisher **Hyoe Narita**

store.viz.com

viz
media
www.viz.com

Printed in the U.S.A.
Published by VIZ Media, LLC
P.O. Box 77010
San Francisco, CA 94107

10 9 8 7 6 5 4 3 2 1
First printing, November 2008

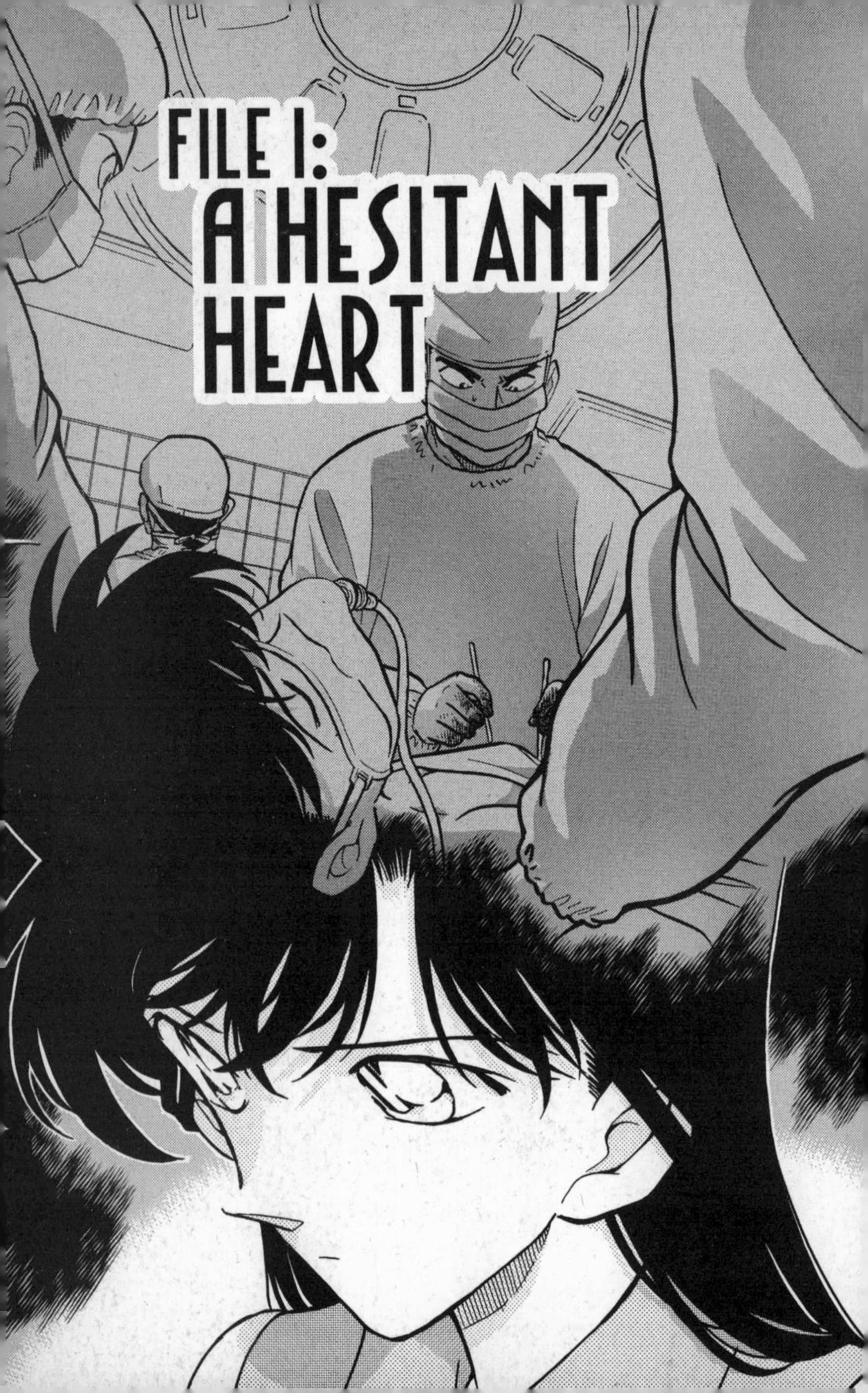
FILE 1:
A HESITANT HEART

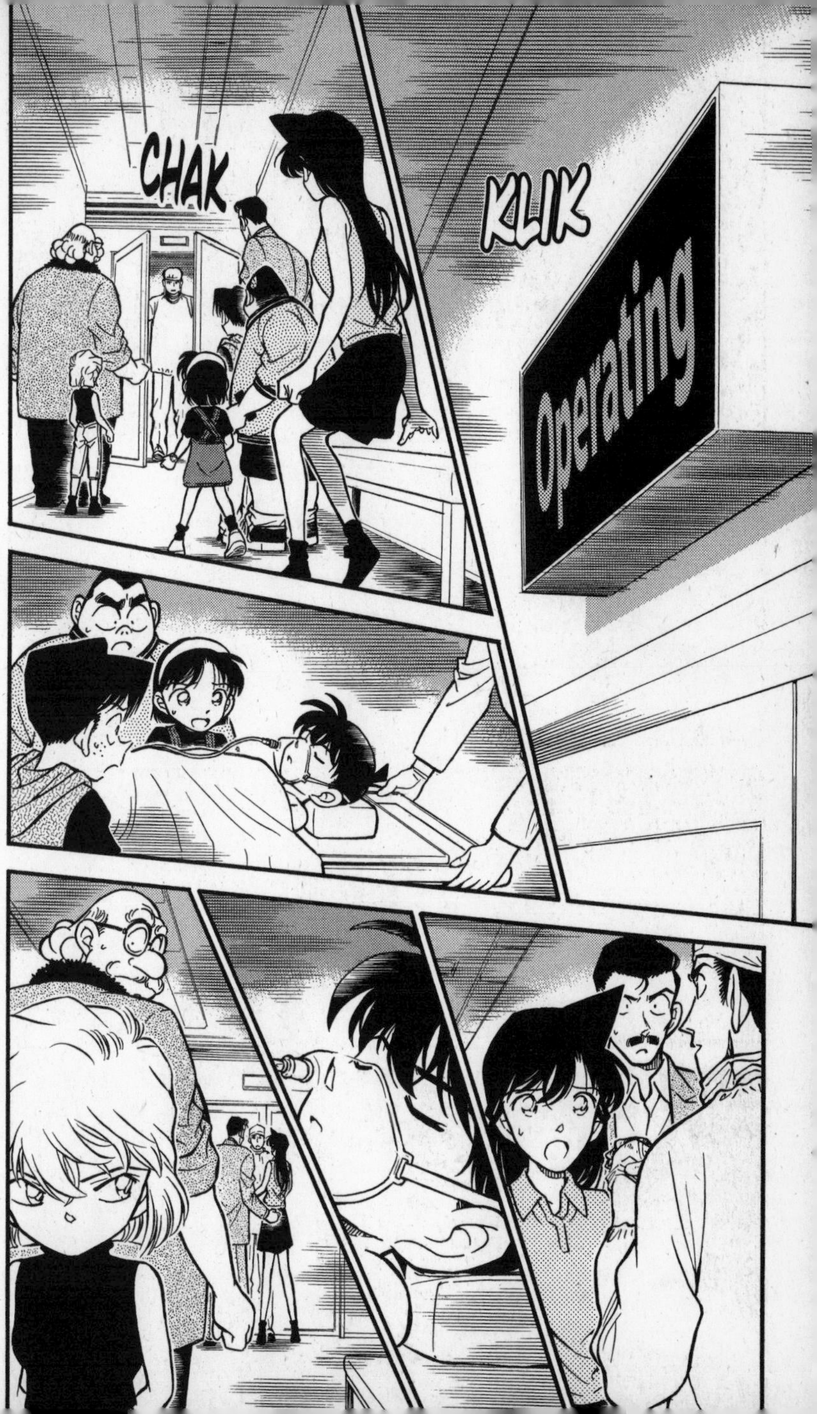
KLIK
CHAK
Operating

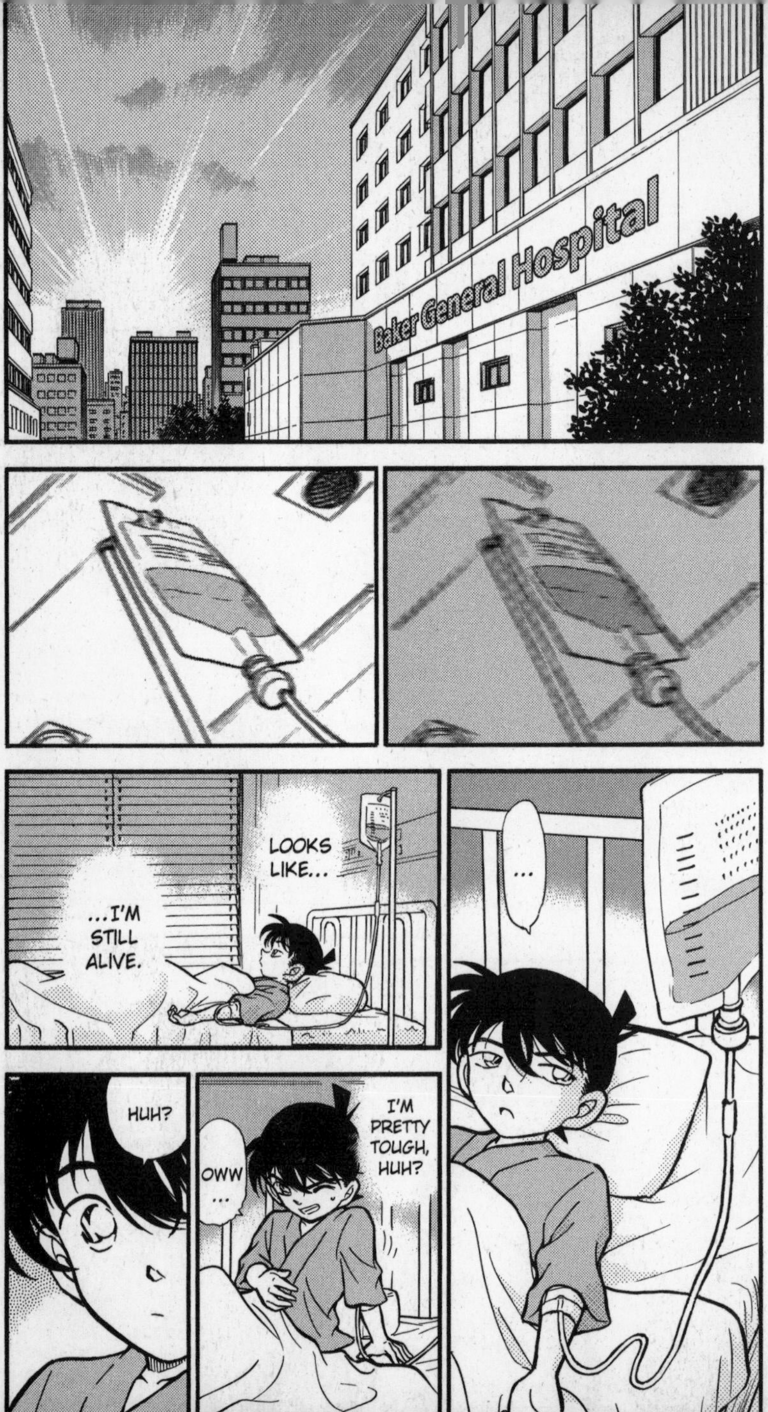
Baker General Hospital
...
LOOKS LIKE...
...I'M STILL ALIVE.
I'M PRETTY TOUGH, HUH?
OWW ...
HUH?

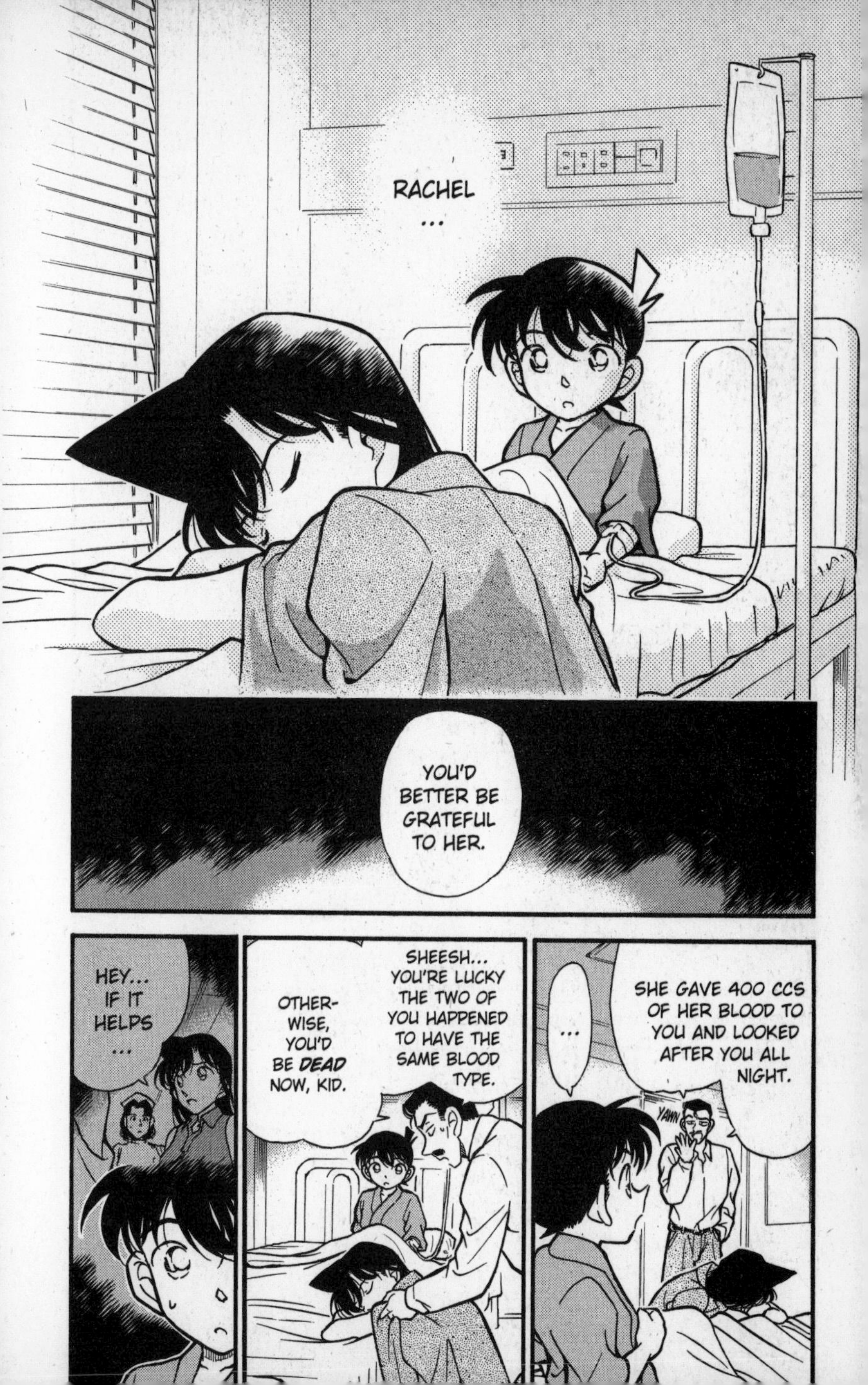
RACHEL ...
YOU'D BETTER BE GRATEFUL TO HER.
SHE GAVE 400 CCS OF HER BLOOD TO YOU AND LOOKED AFTER YOU ALL NIGHT.
...
YAWN
SHEESH... YOU'RE LUCKY THE TWO OF YOU HAPPENED TO HAVE THE SAME BLOOD TYPE.
OTHER-WISE, YOU'D BE ***DEAD*** NOW, KID.
HEY... IF IT HELPS ...

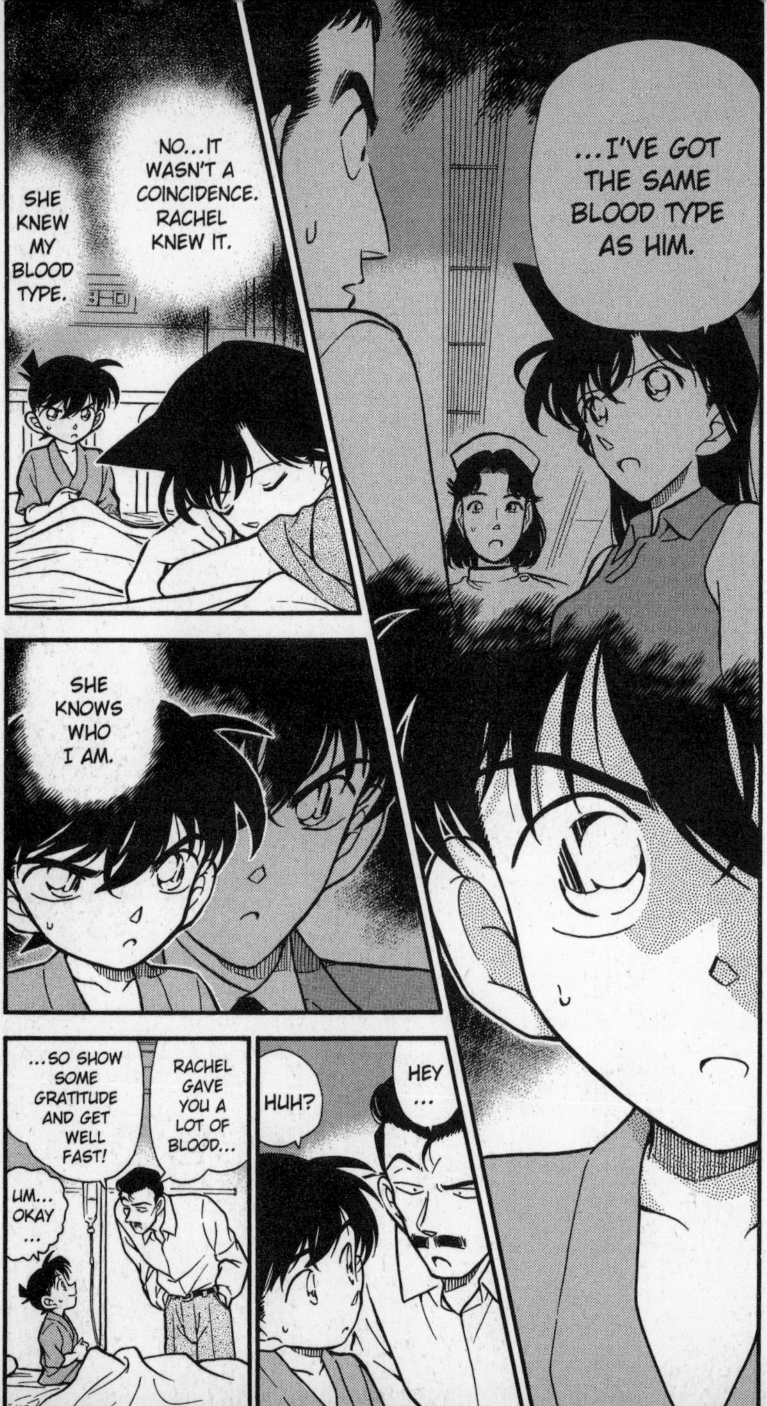
...I'VE GOT THE SAME BLOOD TYPE AS HIM.
NO...IT WASN'T A COINCIDENCE. RACHEL KNEW IT.
SHE KNEW MY BLOOD TYPE.
SHE KNOWS WHO I AM.
HEY...
HUH?
RACHEL GAVE YOU A LOT OF BLOOD...
...SO SHOW SOME GRATITUDE AND GET WELL FAST!
UM... OKAY...

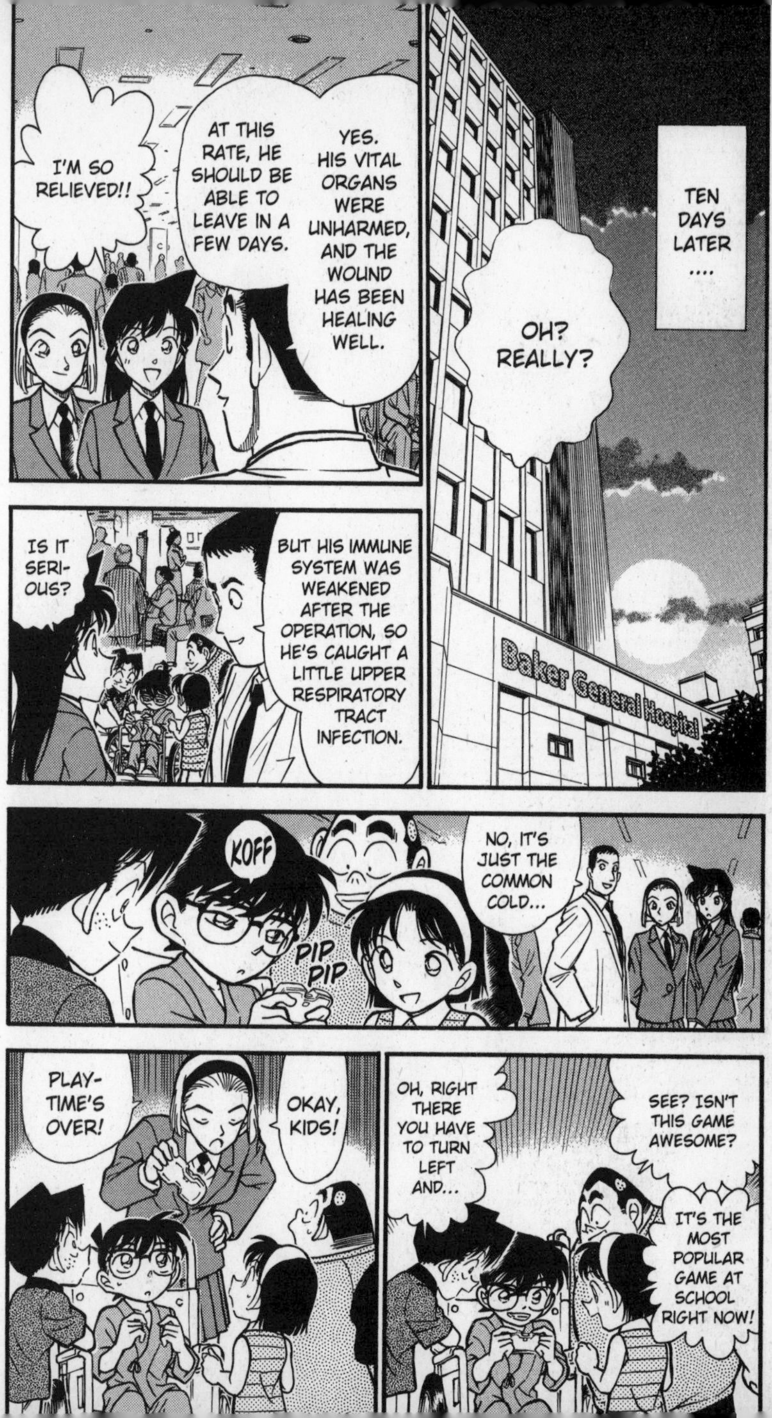
TEN DAYS LATER ....
OH? REALLY?
Baker General Hospital
YES. HIS VITAL ORGANS WERE UNHARMED, AND THE WOUND HAS BEEN HEALING WELL.
AT THIS RATE, HE SHOULD BE ABLE TO LEAVE IN A FEW DAYS.
I'M SO RELIEVED!!
BUT HIS IMMUNE SYSTEM WAS WEAKENED AFTER THE OPERATION, SO HE'S CAUGHT A LITTLE UPPER RESPIRATORY TRACT INFECTION.
IS IT SERI-OUS?
NO, IT'S JUST THE COMMON COLD...
KOFF
PIP PIP
SEE? ISN'T THIS GAME AWESOME?
IT'S THE MOST POPULAR GAME AT SCHOOL RIGHT NOW!
OH, RIGHT THERE YOU HAVE TO TURN LEFT AND...
OKAY, KIDS!
PLAY-TIME'S OVER!

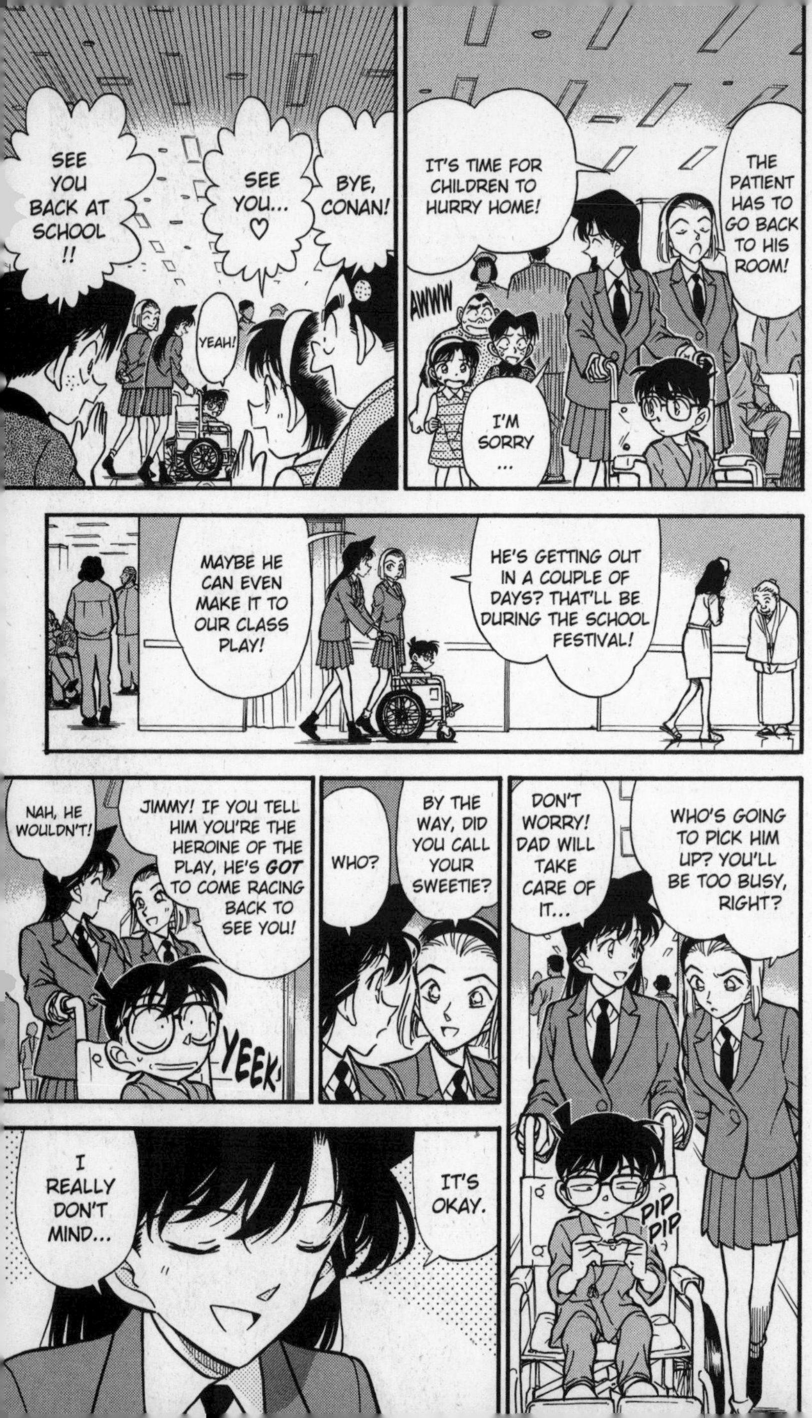
THE PATIENT HAS TO GO BACK TO HIS ROOM!
IT'S TIME FOR CHILDREN TO HURRY HOME!
AWWW
I'M SORRY ...
BYE, CONAN!
SEE YOU... ♡
SEE YOU BACK AT SCHOOL !!
YEAH!
HE'S GETTING OUT IN A COUPLE OF DAYS? THAT'LL BE DURING THE SCHOOL FESTIVAL!
MAYBE HE CAN EVEN MAKE IT TO OUR CLASS PLAY!
WHO'S GOING TO PICK HIM UP? YOU'LL BE TOO BUSY, RIGHT?
DON'T WORRY! DAD WILL TAKE CARE OF IT...
PIP PIP
BY THE WAY, DID YOU CALL YOUR SWEETIE?
WHO?
JIMMY! IF YOU TELL HIM YOU'RE THE HEROINE OF THE PLAY, HE'S **GOT** TO COME RACING BACK TO SEE YOU!
NAH, HE WOULDN'T!
YEEK!
IT'S OKAY.
I REALLY DON'T MIND...

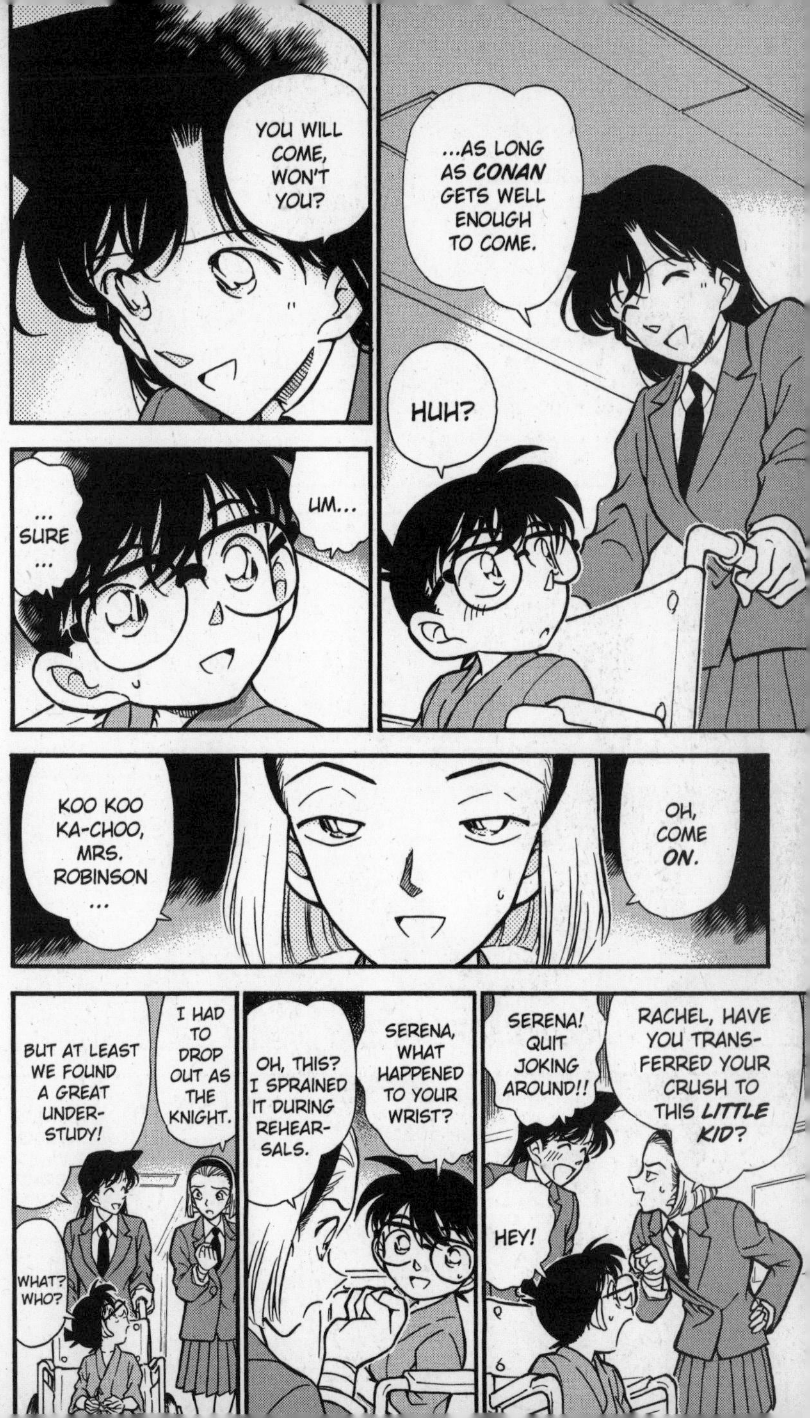

...AS LONG AS **CONAN** GETS WELL ENOUGH TO COME.
HUH?
YOU WILL COME, WON'T YOU?
UM...
... SURE ...
OH, COME **ON**.
KOO KOO KA-CHOO, MRS. ROBINSON ...
RACHEL, HAVE YOU TRANS-FERRED YOUR CRUSH TO THIS ***LITTLE KID***?
SERENA! QUIT JOKING AROUND!!
HEY!
SERENA, WHAT HAPPENED TO YOUR WRIST?
OH, THIS? I SPRAINED IT DURING REHEAR-SALS.
I HAD TO DROP OUT AS THE KNIGHT.
BUT AT LEAST WE FOUND A GREAT UNDER-STUDY!
WHAT? WHO?

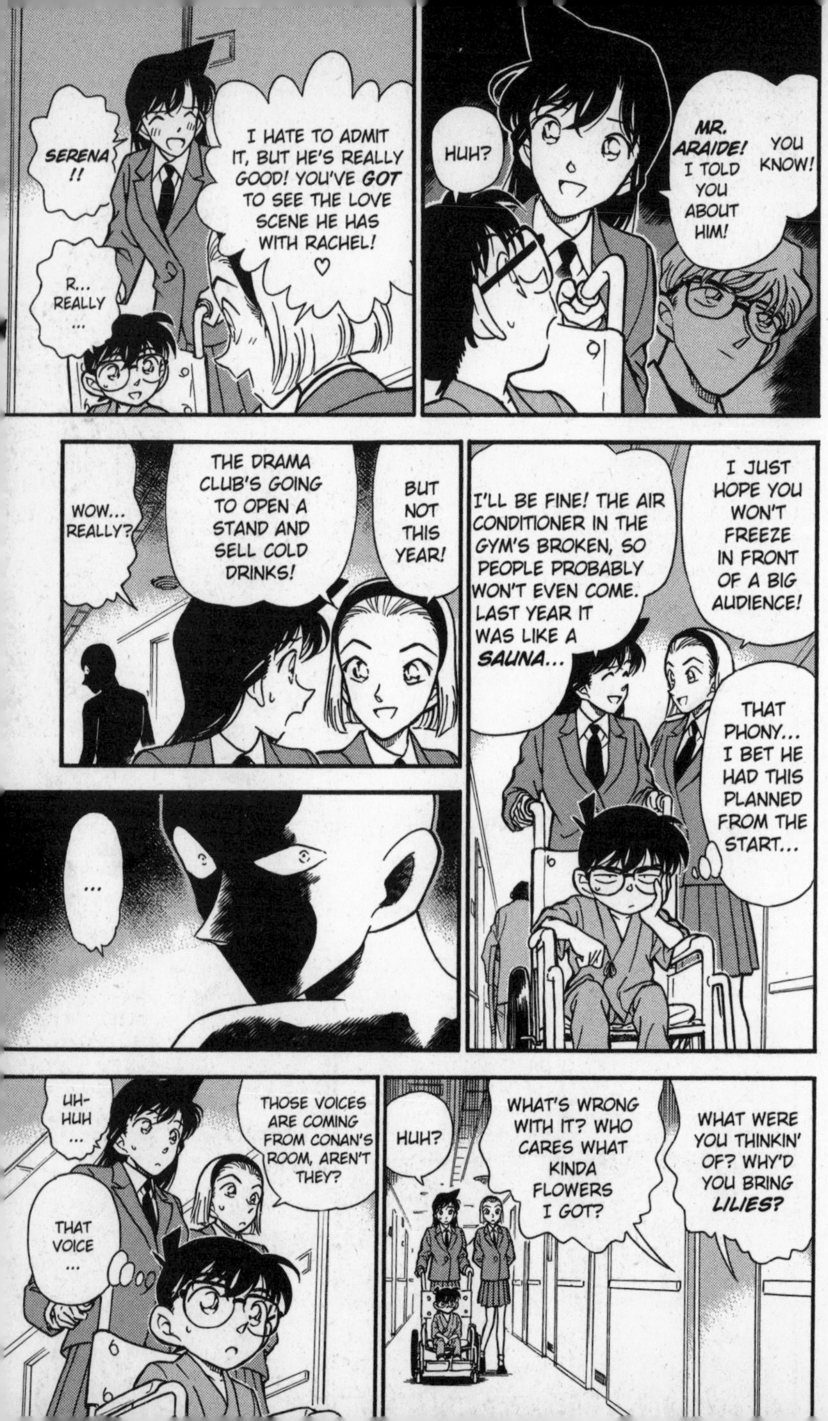
YOU KNOW!
MR. ARAIDE! I TOLD YOU ABOUT HIM!
HUH?
I HATE TO ADMIT IT, BUT HE'S REALLY GOOD! YOU'VE GOT TO SEE THE LOVE SCENE HE HAS WITH RACHEL! ♡
SERENA!!
R... REALLY...
I JUST HOPE YOU WON'T FREEZE IN FRONT OF A BIG AUDIENCE!
I'LL BE FINE! THE AIR CONDITIONER IN THE GYM'S BROKEN, SO PEOPLE PROBABLY WON'T EVEN COME. LAST YEAR IT WAS LIKE A SAUNA...
THAT PHONY... I BET HE HAD THIS PLANNED FROM THE START...
BUT NOT THIS YEAR!
THE DRAMA CLUB'S GOING TO OPEN A STAND AND SELL COLD DRINKS!
WOW... REALLY?
...
WHAT WERE YOU THINKIN' OF? WHY'D YOU BRING LILIES?
WHAT'S WRONG WITH IT? WHO CARES WHAT KINDA FLOWERS I GOT?
HUH?
THOSE VOICES ARE COMING FROM CONAN'S ROOM, AREN'T THEY?
UH-HUH...
THAT VOICE...

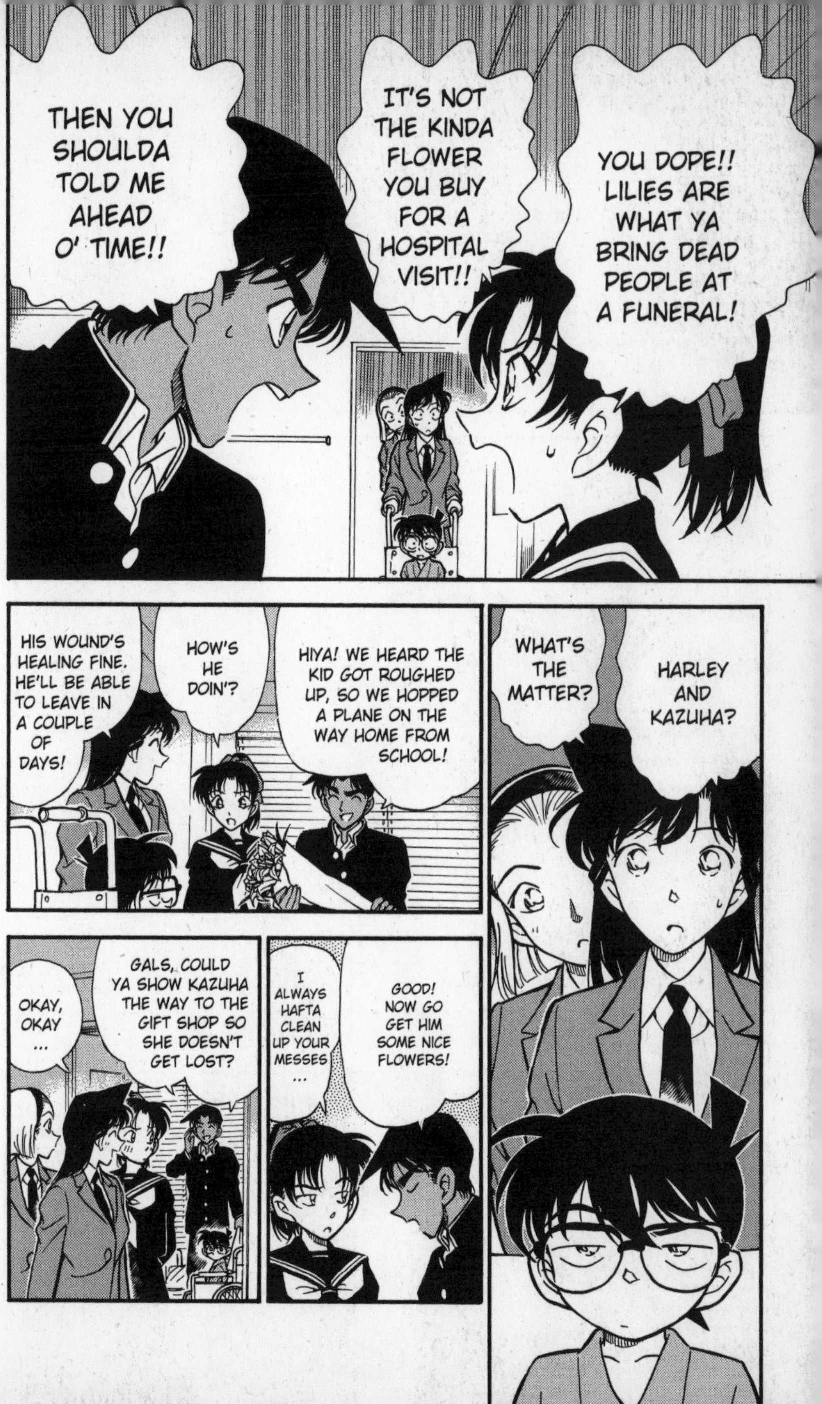
YOU DOPE!! LILIES ARE WHAT YA BRING DEAD PEOPLE AT A FUNERAL!
IT'S NOT THE KINDA FLOWER YOU BUY FOR A HOSPITAL VISIT!!
THEN YOU SHOULDA TOLD ME AHEAD O' TIME!!
HARLEY AND KAZUHA?
WHAT'S THE MATTER?
HIYA! WE HEARD THE KID GOT ROUGHED UP, SO WE HOPPED A PLANE ON THE WAY HOME FROM SCHOOL!
HOW'S HE DOIN'?
HIS WOUND'S HEALING FINE. HE'LL BE ABLE TO LEAVE IN A COUPLE OF DAYS!
GOOD! NOW GO GET HIM SOME NICE FLOWERS!
I ALWAYS HAFTA CLEAN UP YOUR MESSES ...
GALS, COULD YA SHOW KAZUHA THE WAY TO THE GIFT SHOP SO SHE DOESN'T GET LOST?
OKAY, OKAY ...

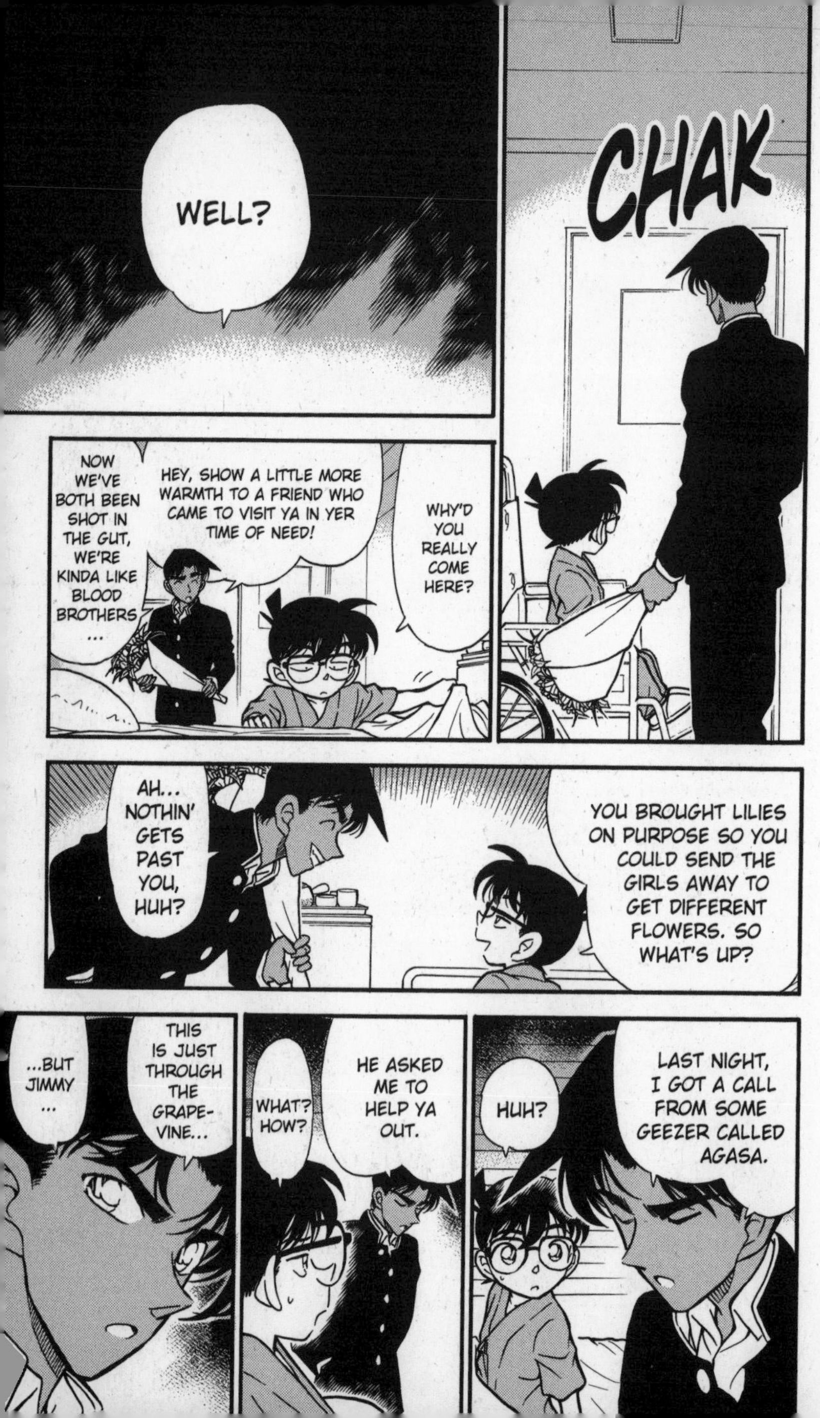
CHAK
WELL?
WHY'D YOU REALLY COME HERE?
HEY, SHOW A LITTLE MORE WARMTH TO A FRIEND WHO CAME TO VISIT YA IN YER TIME OF NEED!
NOW WE'VE BOTH BEEN SHOT IN THE GUT, WE'RE KINDA LIKE BLOOD BROTHERS ...
YOU BROUGHT LILIES ON PURPOSE SO YOU COULD SEND THE GIRLS AWAY TO GET DIFFERENT FLOWERS. SO WHAT'S UP?
AH... NOTHIN' GETS PAST YOU, HUH?
LAST NIGHT, I GOT A CALL FROM SOME GEEZER CALLED AGASA.
HUH?
HE ASKED ME TO HELP YA OUT.
WHAT? HOW?
THIS IS JUST THROUGH THE GRAPE-VINE...
...BUT JIMMY ...

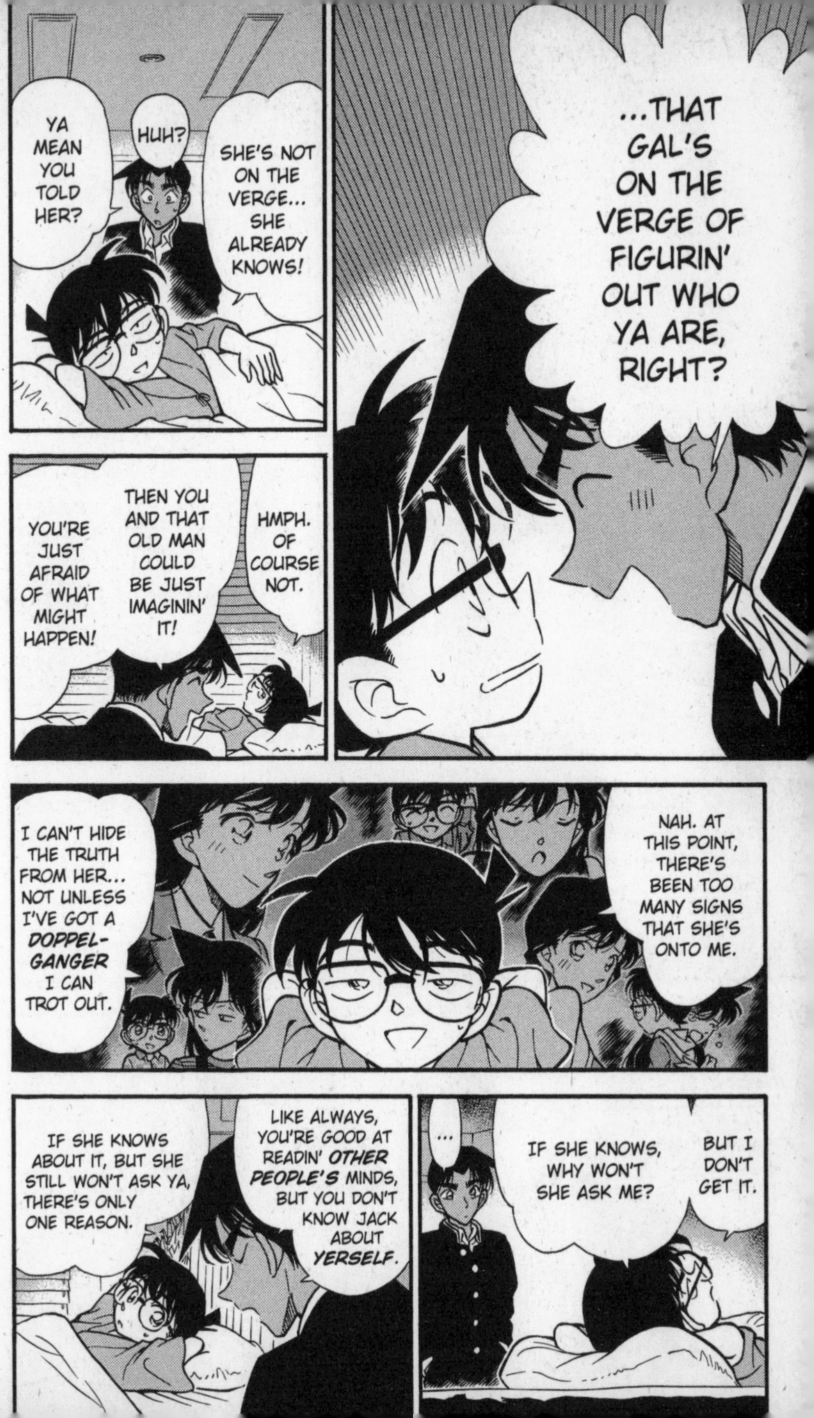
...THAT GAL'S ON THE VERGE OF FIGURIN' OUT WHO YA ARE, RIGHT?
SHE'S NOT ON THE VERGE... SHE ALREADY KNOWS!
HUH?
YA MEAN YOU TOLD HER?
HMPH. OF COURSE NOT.
THEN YOU AND THAT OLD MAN COULD BE JUST IMAGININ' IT!
YOU'RE JUST AFRAID OF WHAT MIGHT HAPPEN!
NAH. AT THIS POINT, THERE'S BEEN TOO MANY SIGNS THAT SHE'S ONTO ME.
I CAN'T HIDE THE TRUTH FROM HER... NOT UNLESS I'VE GOT A ***DOPPEL-GANGER*** I CAN TROT OUT.
BUT I DON'T GET IT.
IF SHE KNOWS, WHY WON'T SHE ASK ME?
...
LIKE ALWAYS, YOU'RE GOOD AT READIN' ***OTHER PEOPLE'S*** MINDS, BUT YOU DON'T KNOW JACK ABOUT ***YERSELF***.
IF SHE KNOWS ABOUT IT, BUT SHE STILL WON'T ASK YA, THERE'S ONLY ONE REASON.

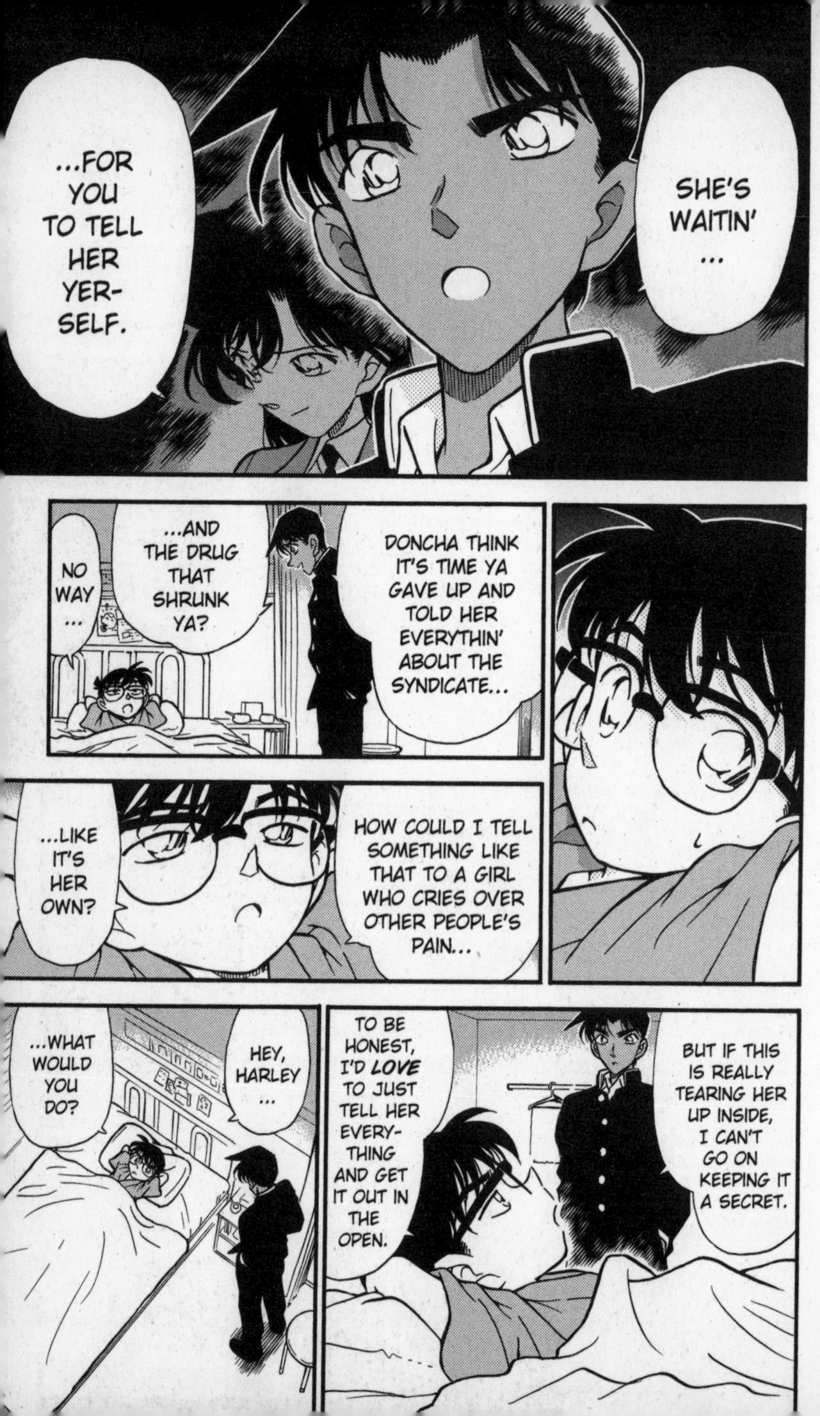
SHE'S WAITIN' ...
...FOR YOU TO TELL HER YER-SELF.
DONCHA THINK IT'S TIME YA GAVE UP AND TOLD HER EVERYTHIN' ABOUT THE SYNDICATE...
...AND THE DRUG THAT SHRUNK YA?
NO WAY ...
HOW COULD I TELL SOMETHING LIKE THAT TO A GIRL WHO CRIES OVER OTHER PEOPLE'S PAIN...
...LIKE IT'S HER OWN?
BUT IF THIS IS REALLY TEARING HER UP INSIDE, I CAN'T GO ON KEEPING IT A SECRET.
TO BE HONEST, I'D ***LOVE*** TO JUST TELL HER EVERY-THING AND GET IT OUT IN THE OPEN.
HEY, HARLEY ...
...WHAT WOULD YOU DO?

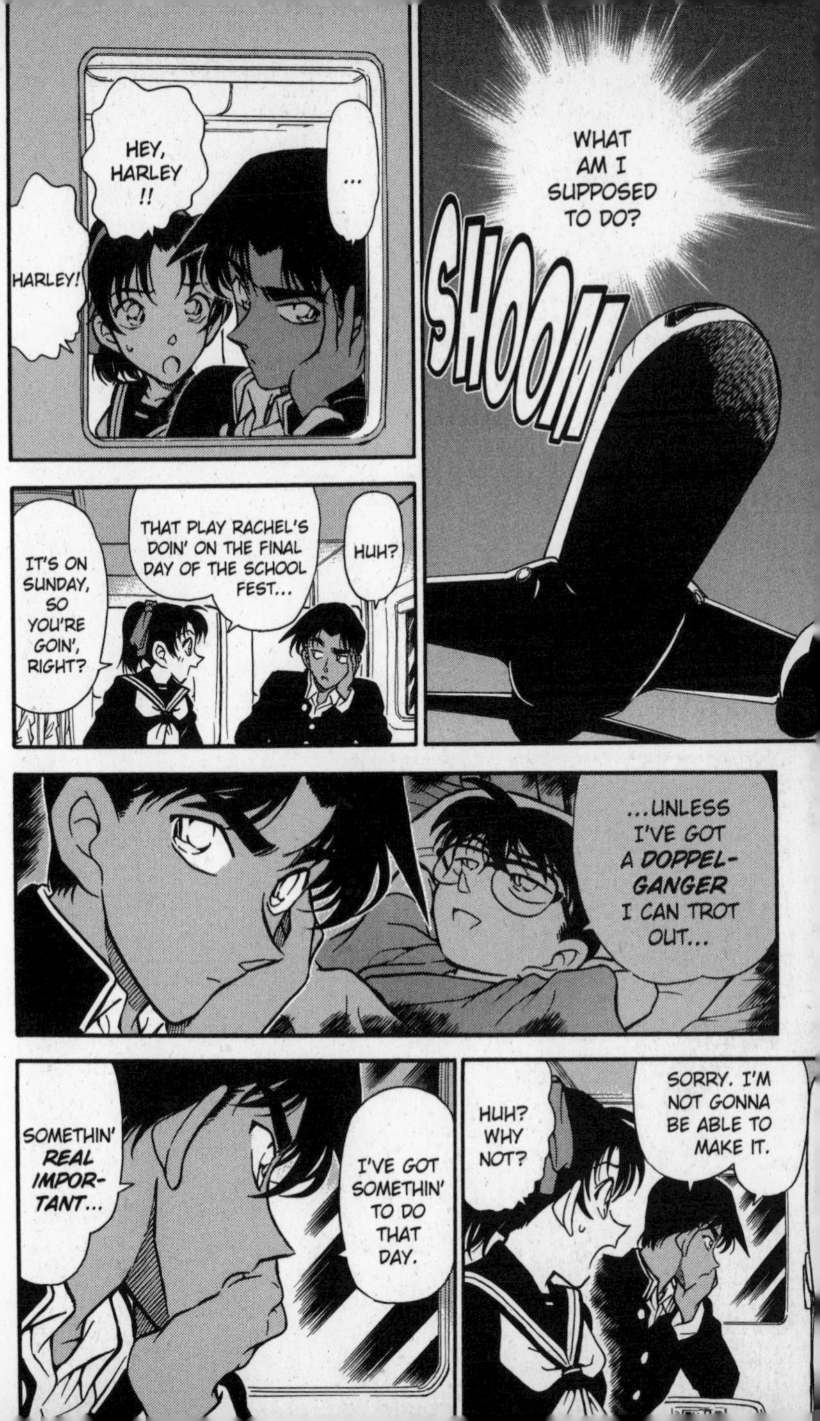
WHAT AM I SUPPOSED TO DO?
SHOOM
HEY, HARLEY !!
...
HARLEY!
HUH?
THAT PLAY RACHEL'S DOIN' ON THE FINAL DAY OF THE SCHOOL FEST...
IT'S ON SUNDAY, SO YOU'RE GOIN', RIGHT?
...UNLESS I'VE GOT A *DOPPELGANGER* I CAN TROT OUT...
SORRY. I'M NOT GONNA BE ABLE TO MAKE IT.
HUH? WHY NOT?
I'VE GOT SOMETHIN' TO DO THAT DAY.
SOMETHIN' *REAL IMPORTANT*...

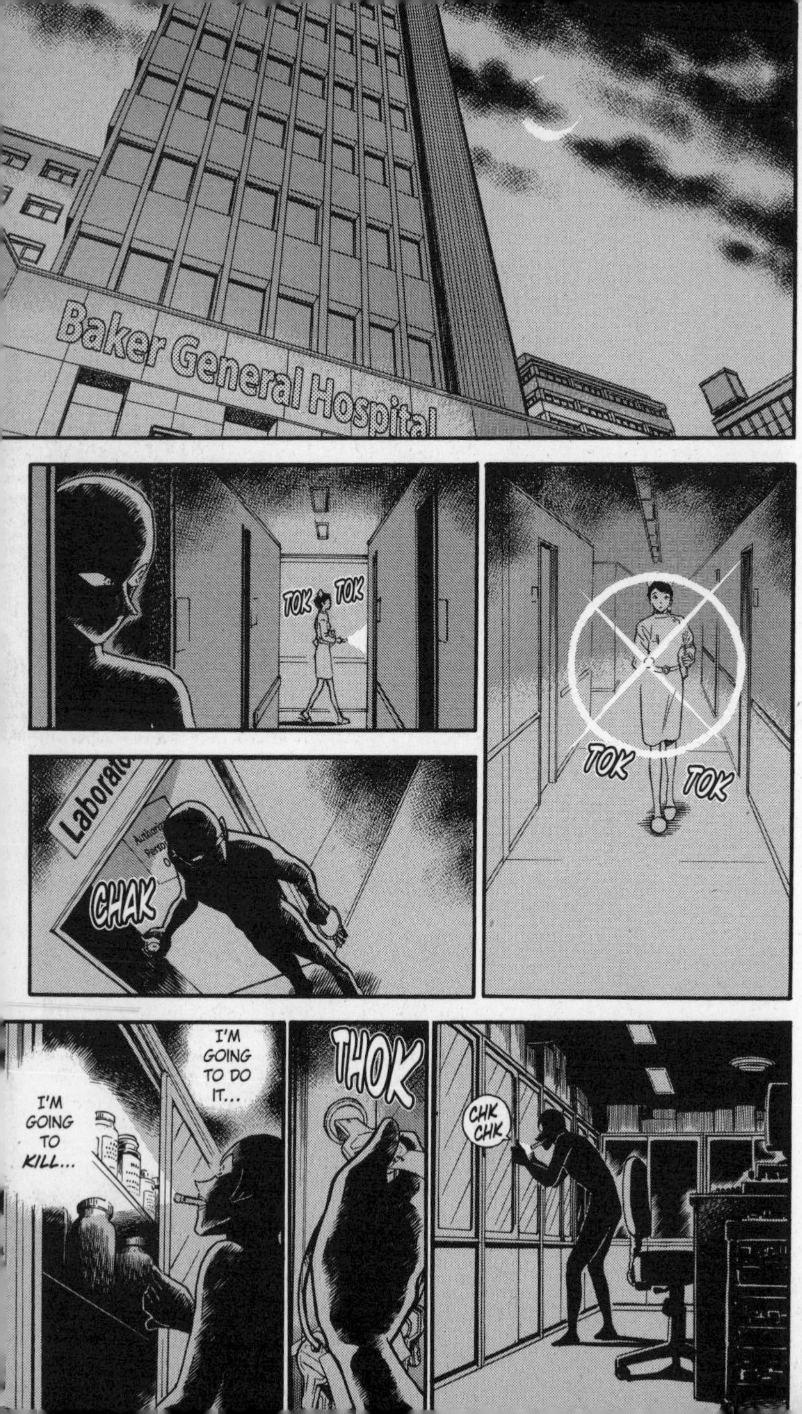
Baker General Hospital
TOK
TOK
TOK
TOK
CHAK
CHK CHK
THOK
I'M GOING TO DO IT...
I'M GOING TO KILL...

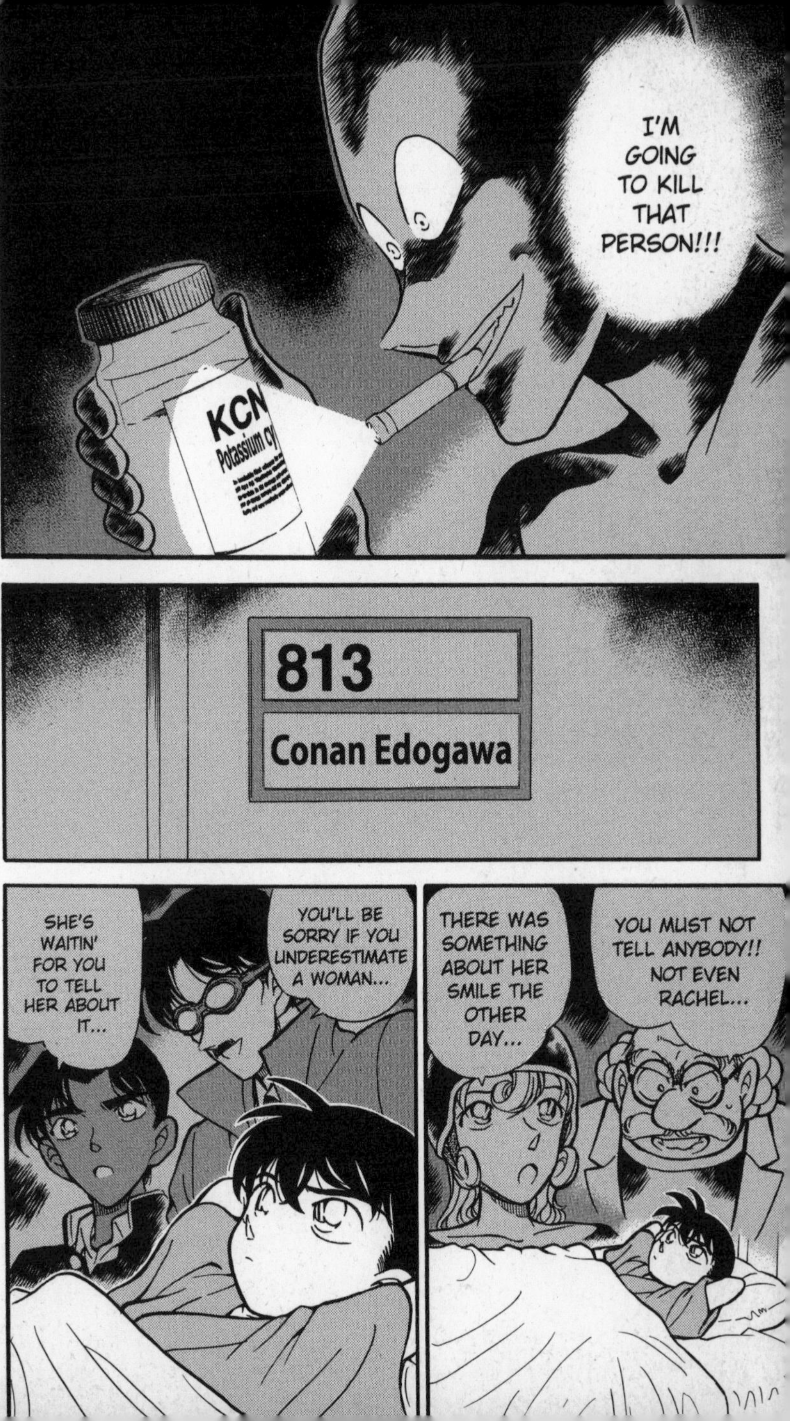
I'M GOING TO KILL THAT PERSON!!!
KCN
813
Conan Edogawa
YOU MUST NOT TELL ANYBODY!! NOT EVEN RACHEL...
THERE WAS SOMETHING ABOUT HER SMILE THE OTHER DAY...
YOU'LL BE SORRY IF YOU UNDERESTIMATE A WOMAN...
SHE'S WAITIN' FOR YOU TO TELL HER ABOUT IT...

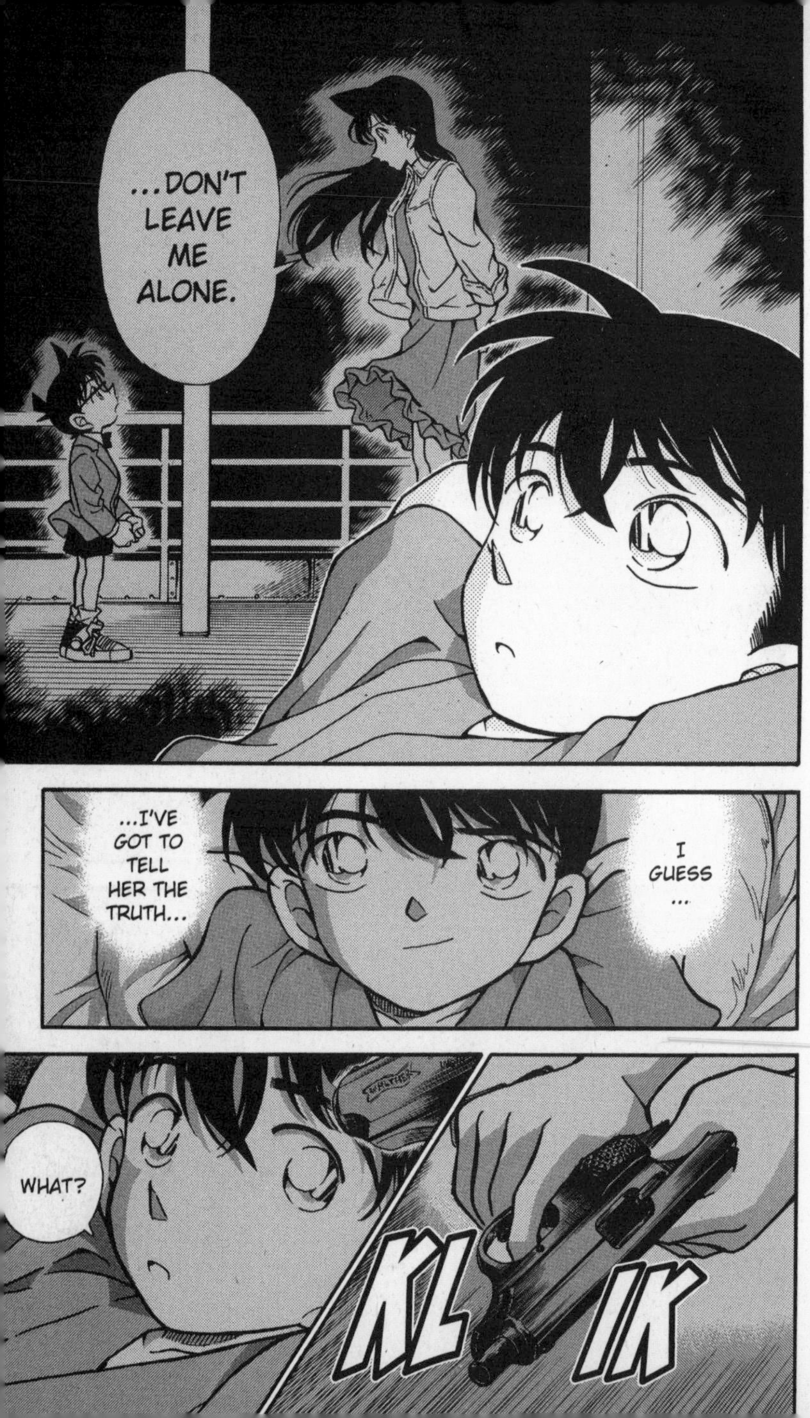
...DON'T LEAVE ME ALONE.
I GUESS ...
...I'VE GOT TO TELL HER THE TRUTH...
KL IK
WHAT?

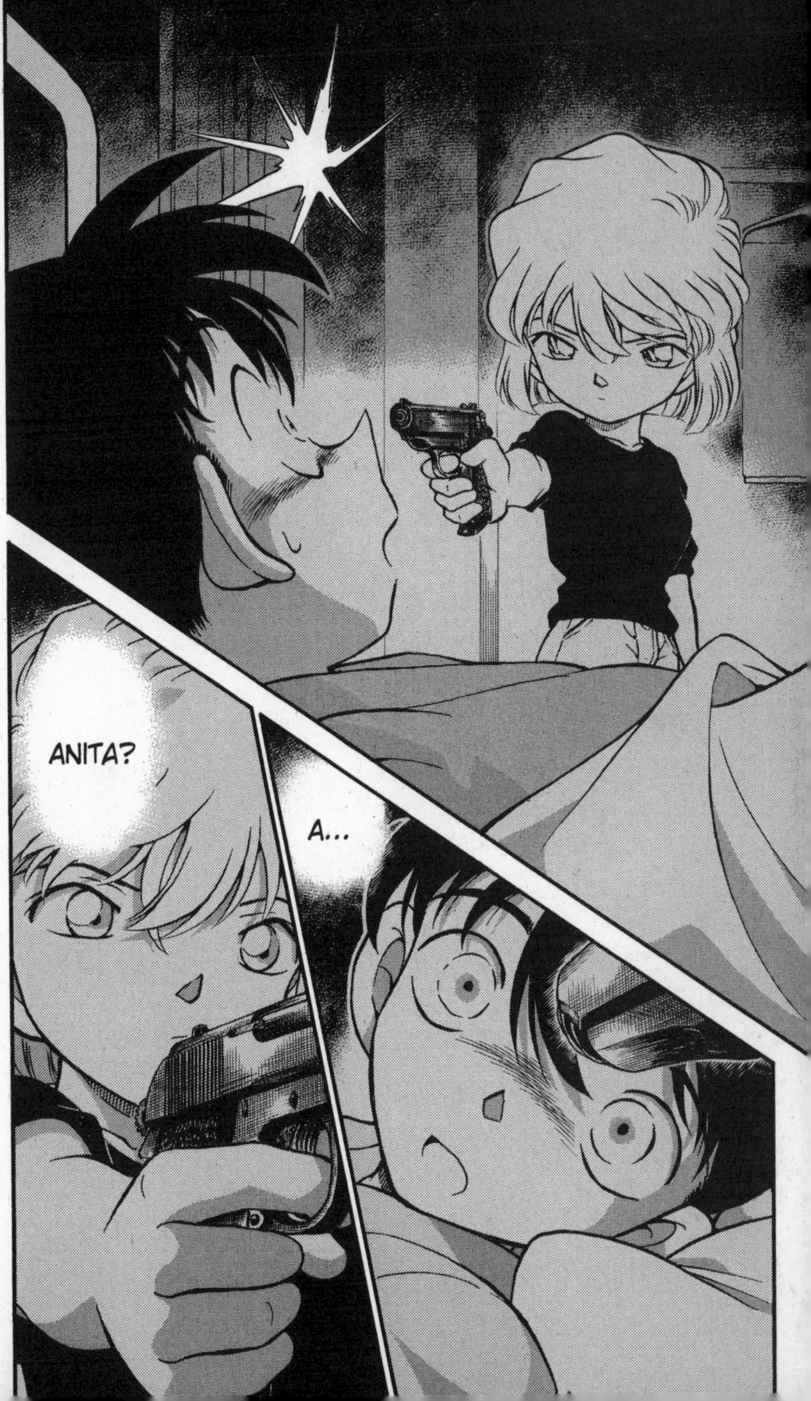
A...
ANITA?

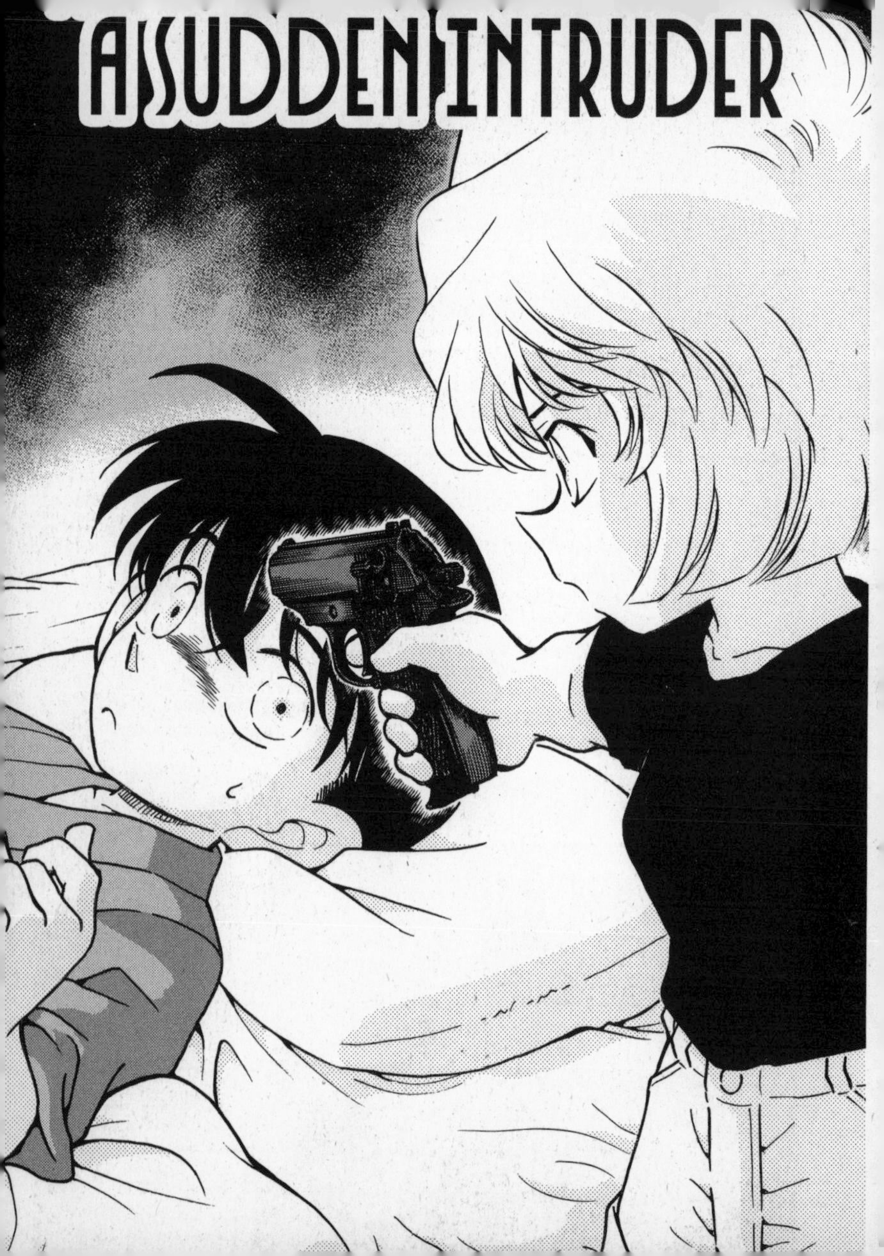
A SUDDEN INTRUDER

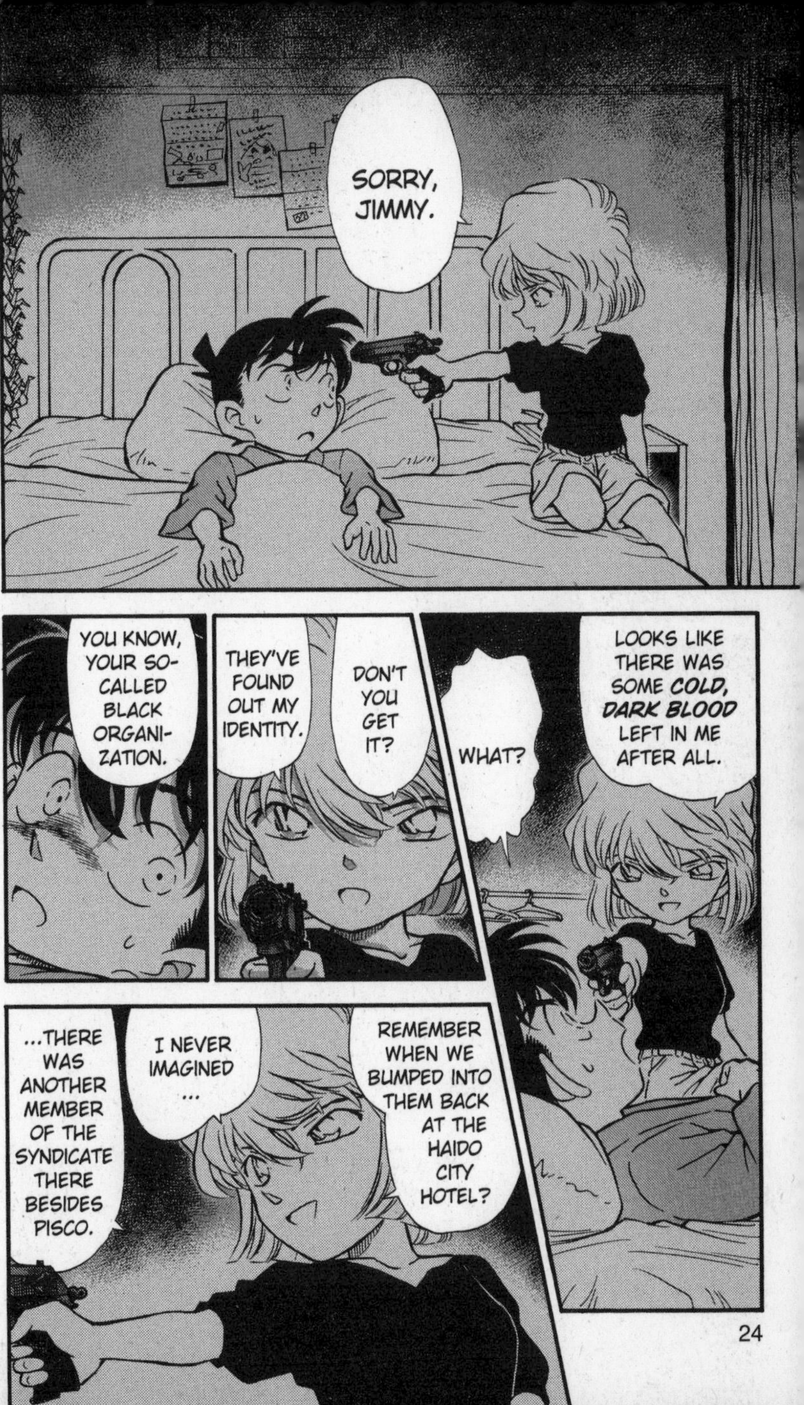

SORRY, JIMMY.
LOOKS LIKE THERE WAS SOME *COLD, DARK BLOOD* LEFT IN ME AFTER ALL.
WHAT?
DON'T YOU GET IT?
THEY'VE FOUND OUT MY IDENTITY.
YOU KNOW, YOUR SO-CALLED BLACK ORGANIZATION.
REMEMBER WHEN WE BUMPED INTO THEM BACK AT THE HAIDO CITY HOTEL?
I NEVER IMAGINED ...
...THERE WAS ANOTHER MEMBER OF THE SYNDICATE THERE BESIDES PISCO.

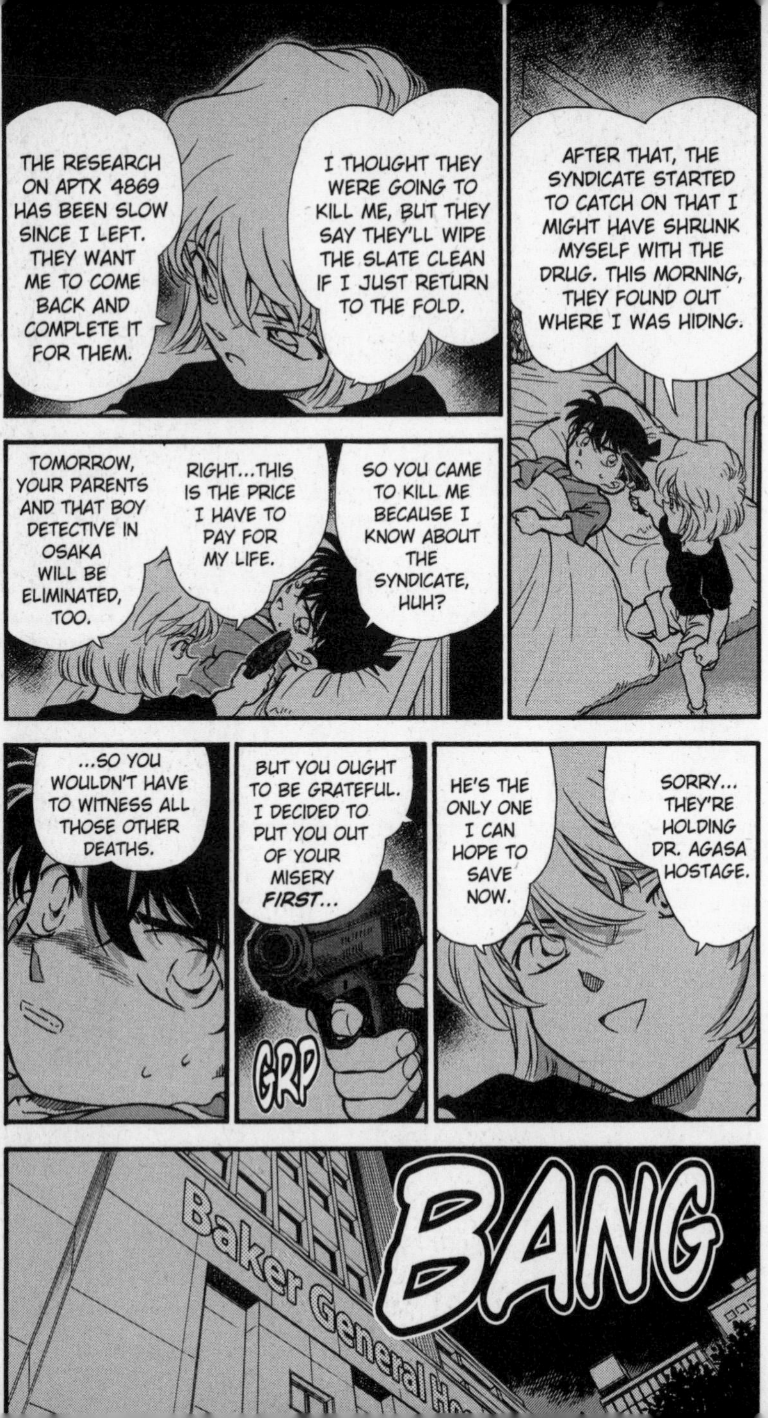
AFTER THAT, THE SYNDICATE STARTED TO CATCH ON THAT I MIGHT HAVE SHRUNK MYSELF WITH THE DRUG. THIS MORNING, THEY FOUND OUT WHERE I WAS HIDING.
I THOUGHT THEY WERE GOING TO KILL ME, BUT THEY SAY THEY'LL WIPE THE SLATE CLEAN IF I JUST RETURN TO THE FOLD.
THE RESEARCH ON APTX 4869 HAS BEEN SLOW SINCE I LEFT. THEY WANT ME TO COME BACK AND COMPLETE IT FOR THEM.
SO YOU CAME TO KILL ME BECAUSE I KNOW ABOUT THE SYNDICATE, HUH?
RIGHT...THIS IS THE PRICE I HAVE TO PAY FOR MY LIFE.
TOMORROW, YOUR PARENTS AND THAT BOY DETECTIVE IN OSAKA WILL BE ELIMINATED, TOO.
SORRY... THEY'RE HOLDING DR. AGASA HOSTAGE.
HE'S THE ONLY ONE I CAN HOPE TO SAVE NOW.
BUT YOU OUGHT TO BE GRATEFUL. I DECIDED TO PUT YOU OUT OF YOUR MISERY *FIRST*...
GRP
...SO YOU WOULDN'T HAVE TO WITNESS ALL THOSE OTHER DEATHS.
BANG
Baker General

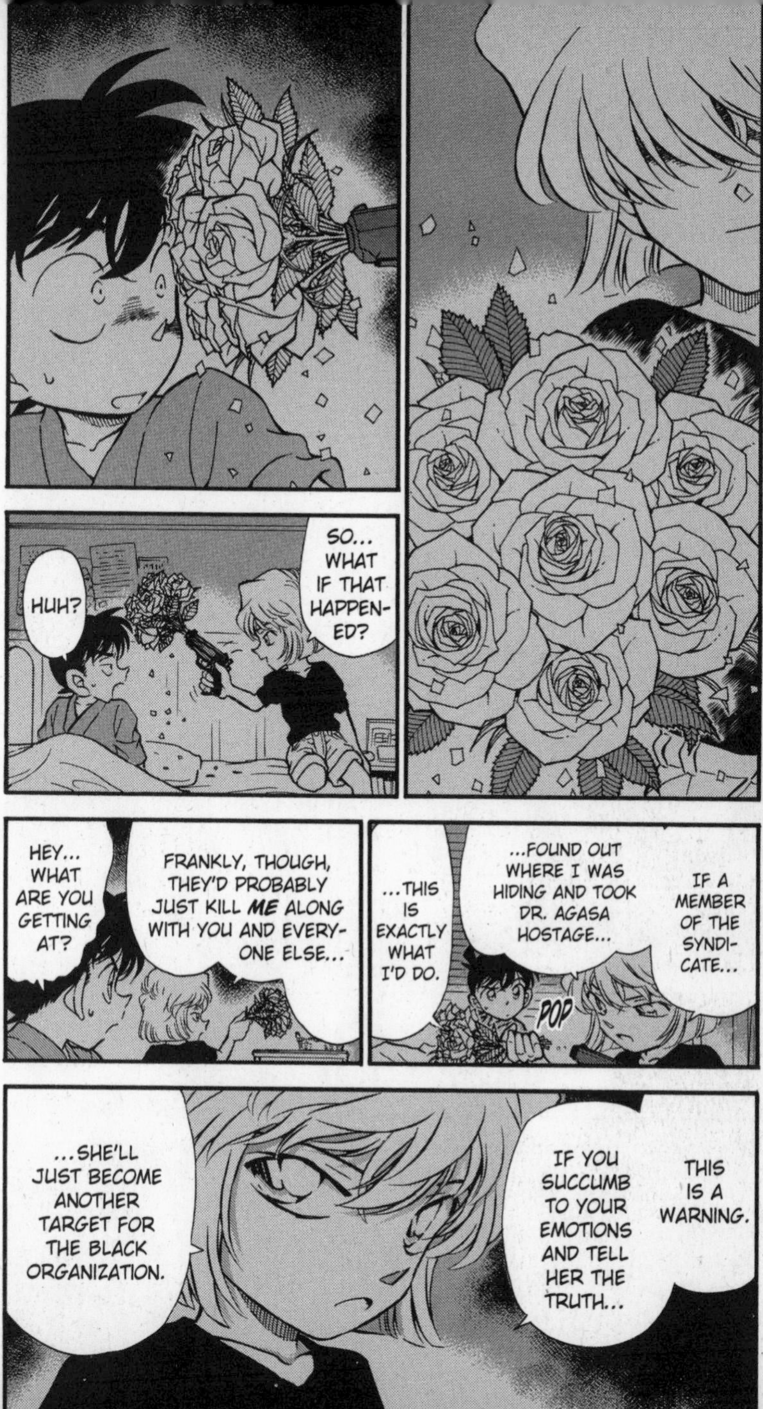
SO... WHAT IF THAT HAPPEN-ED?
HUH?
IF A MEMBER OF THE SYNDI-CATE...
...FOUND OUT WHERE I WAS HIDING AND TOOK DR. AGASA HOSTAGE...
POP
...THIS IS EXACTLY WHAT I'D DO.
FRANKLY, THOUGH, THEY'D PROBABLY JUST KILL *ME* ALONG WITH YOU AND EVERY-ONE ELSE...
HEY... WHAT ARE YOU GETTING AT?
THIS IS A WARNING.
IF YOU SUCCUMB TO YOUR EMOTIONS AND TELL HER THE TRUTH...
...SHE'LL JUST BECOME ANOTHER TARGET FOR THE BLACK ORGANIZATION.

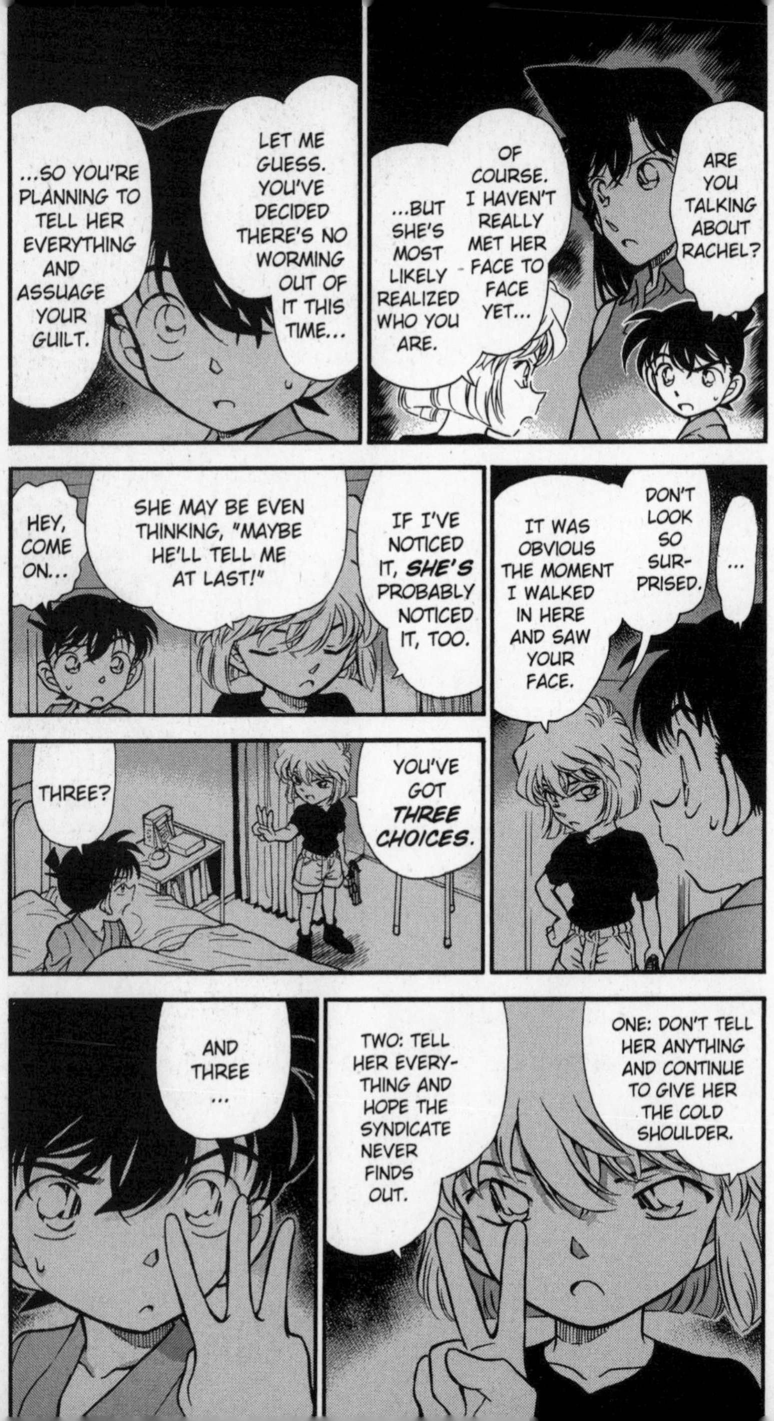
ARE YOU TALKING ABOUT RACHEL?
OF COURSE. I HAVEN'T REALLY MET HER FACE TO FACE YET...
...BUT SHE'S MOST LIKELY REALIZED WHO YOU ARE.
LET ME GUESS. YOU'VE DECIDED THERE'S NO WORMING OUT OF IT THIS TIME...
...SO YOU'RE PLANNING TO TELL HER EVERYTHING AND ASSUAGE YOUR GUILT.
...
DON'T LOOK SO SUR-PRISED.
IT WAS OBVIOUS THE MOMENT I WALKED IN HERE AND SAW YOUR FACE.
IF I'VE NOTICED IT, ***SHE'S*** PROBABLY NOTICED IT, TOO.
SHE MAY BE EVEN THINKING, "MAYBE HE'LL TELL ME AT LAST!"
HEY, COME ON...
YOU'VE GOT ***THREE CHOICES***.
THREE?
ONE: DON'T TELL HER ANYTHING AND CONTINUE TO GIVE HER THE COLD SHOULDER.
TWO: TELL HER EVERY-THING AND HOPE THE SYNDICATE NEVER FINDS OUT.
AND THREE ...

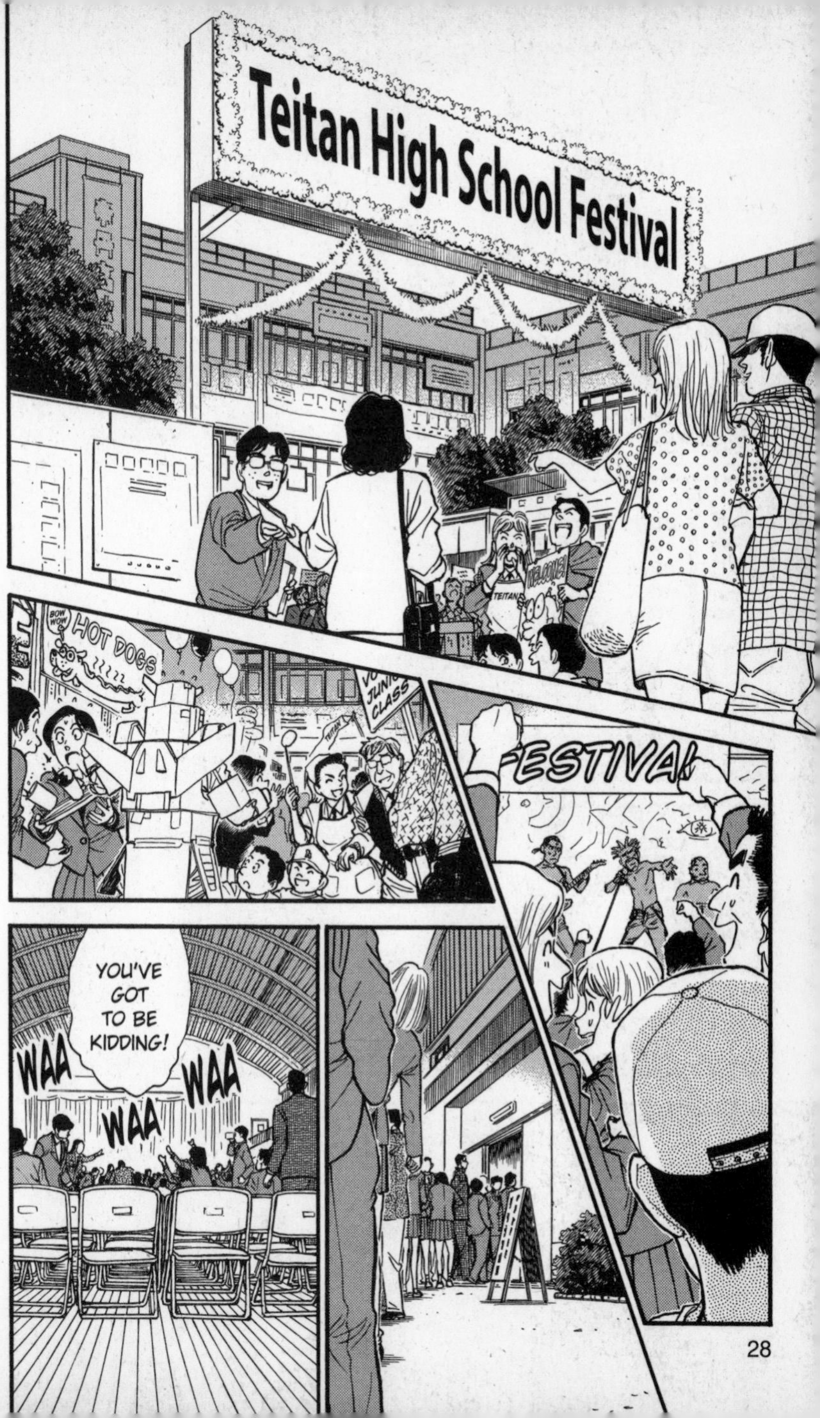
Teitan High School Festival
TEITAN
FESTIVAL
BOW WOW
HOT DOGS
YOU'VE GOT TO BE KIDDING!
WAA
WAA
WAA

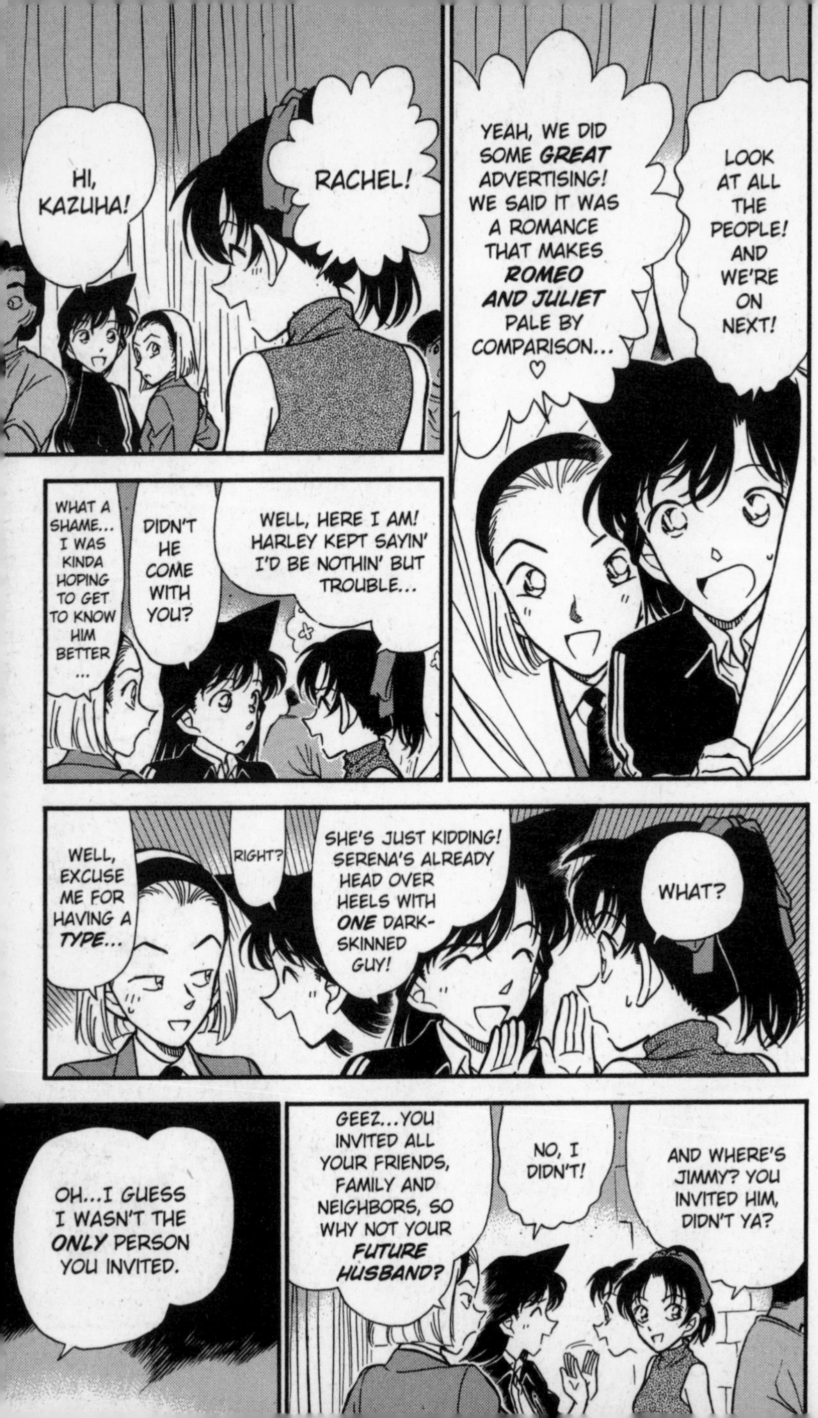
LOOK AT ALL THE PEOPLE! AND WE'RE ON NEXT!
YEAH, WE DID SOME GREAT ADVERTISING! WE SAID IT WAS A ROMANCE THAT MAKES ROMEO AND JULIET PALE BY COMPARISON... ♡
RACHEL!
HI, KAZUHA!
WELL, HERE I AM! HARLEY KEPT SAYIN' I'D BE NOTHIN' BUT TROUBLE...
DIDN'T HE COME WITH YOU?
WHAT A SHAME... I WAS KINDA HOPING TO GET TO KNOW HIM BETTER...
WHAT?
SHE'S JUST KIDDING! SERENA'S ALREADY HEAD OVER HEELS WITH ONE DARK-SKINNED GUY!
RIGHT?
WELL, EXCUSE ME FOR HAVING A TYPE...
AND WHERE'S JIMMY? YOU INVITED HIM, DIDN'T YA?
NO, I DIDN'T!
GEEZ...YOU INVITED ALL YOUR FRIENDS, FAMILY AND NEIGHBORS, SO WHY NOT YOUR FUTURE HUSBAND?
OH...I GUESS I WASN'T THE ONLY PERSON YOU INVITED.

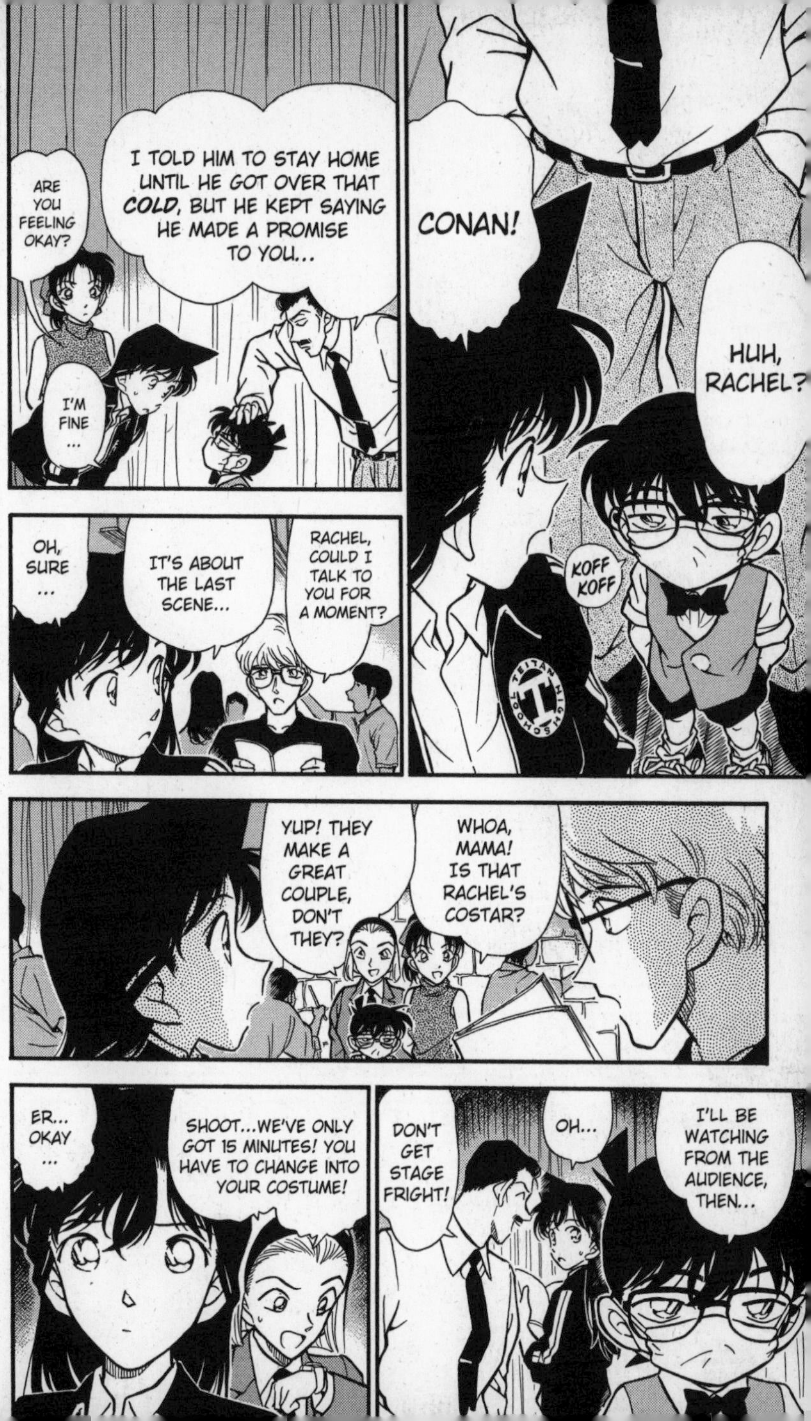
CONAN!
HUH, RACHEL?
KOFF KOFF
I TOLD HIM TO STAY HOME UNTIL HE GOT OVER THAT COLD, BUT HE KEPT SAYING HE MADE A PROMISE TO YOU...
ARE YOU FEELING OKAY?
I'M FINE ...
RACHEL, COULD I TALK TO YOU FOR A MOMENT?
IT'S ABOUT THE LAST SCENE...
OH, SURE ...
WHOA, MAMA! IS THAT RACHEL'S COSTAR?
YUP! THEY MAKE A GREAT COUPLE, DON'T THEY?
I'LL BE WATCHING FROM THE AUDIENCE, THEN...
OH...
DON'T GET STAGE FRIGHT!
SHOOT...WE'VE ONLY GOT 15 MINUTES! YOU HAVE TO CHANGE INTO YOUR COSTUME!
ER... OKAY ...

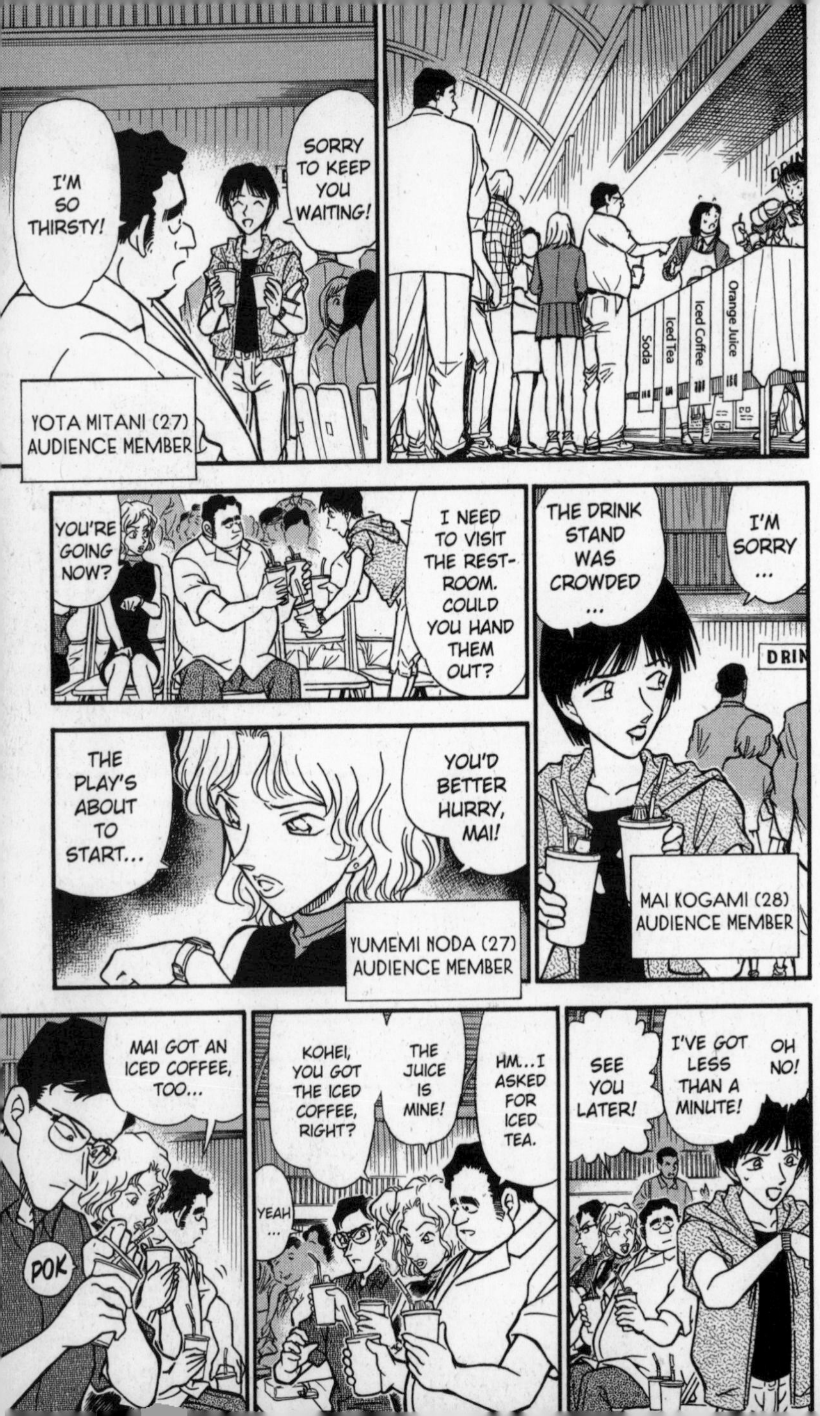
Orange Juice
Iced Coffee
Iced Tea
Soda
SORRY TO KEEP YOU WAITING!
I'M SO THIRSTY!
YOTA MITANI (27) AUDIENCE MEMBER
I'M SORRY ...
THE DRINK STAND WAS CROWDED ...
MAI KOGAMI (28) AUDIENCE MEMBER
I NEED TO VISIT THE REST-ROOM. COULD YOU HAND THEM OUT?
YOU'RE GOING NOW?
YOU'D BETTER HURRY, MAI!
THE PLAY'S ABOUT TO START...
YUMEMI NODA (27) AUDIENCE MEMBER
OH NO!
I'VE GOT LESS THAN A MINUTE!
SEE YOU LATER!
HM...I ASKED FOR ICED TEA.
THE JUICE IS MINE!
KOHEI, YOU GOT THE ICED COFFEE, RIGHT?
YEAH ...
MAI GOT AN ICED COFFEE, TOO...
POK

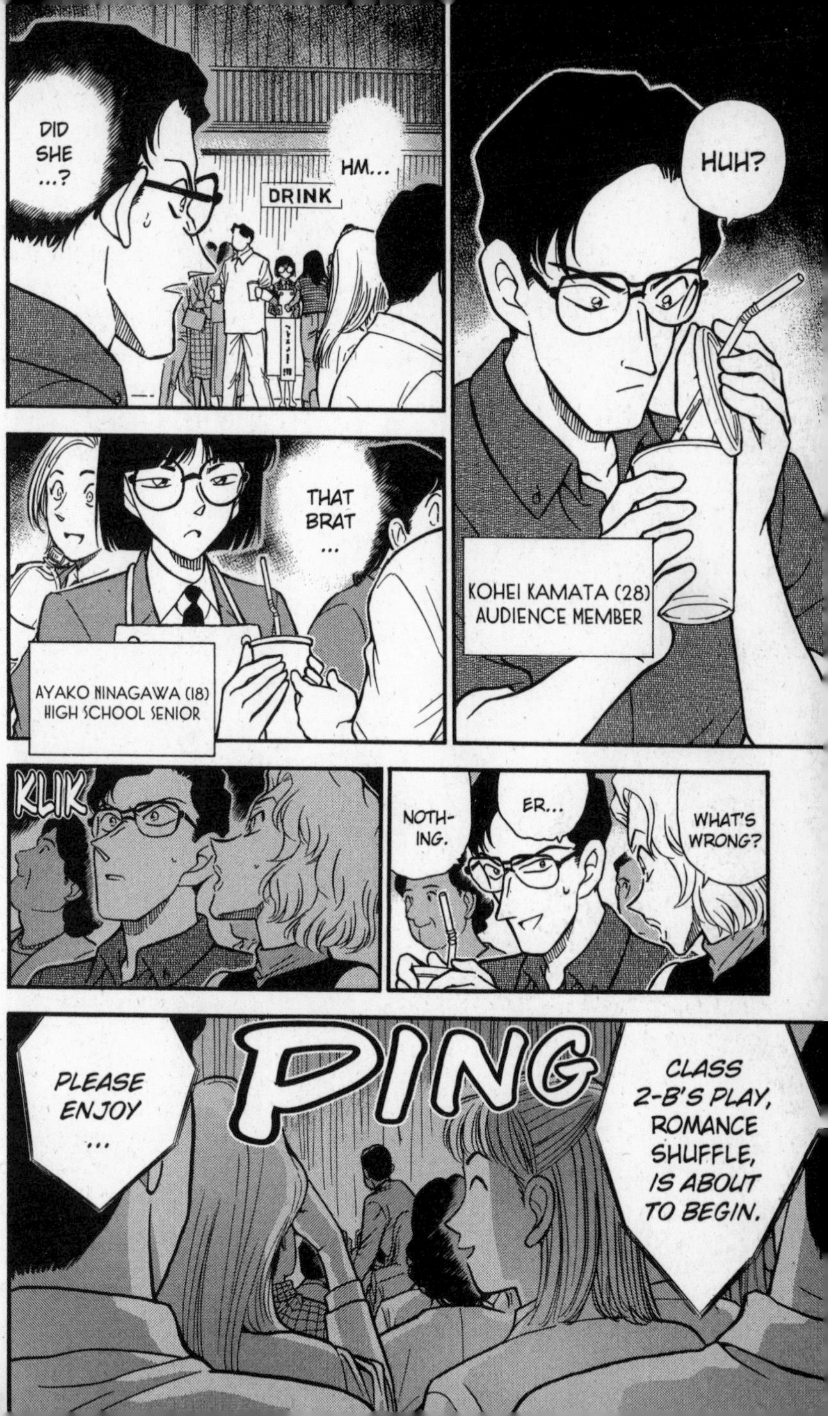
HUH?
KOHEI KAMATA (28)
AUDIENCE MEMBER
HM...
DRINK
DID SHE ...?
THAT BRAT ...
AYAKO NINAGAWA (18)
HIGH SCHOOL SENIOR
WHAT'S WRONG?
ER...
NOTH-ING.
KLIK
CLASS 2-B'S PLAY, ROMANCE SHUFFLE, IS ABOUT TO BEGIN.
PING
PLEASE ENJOY ...

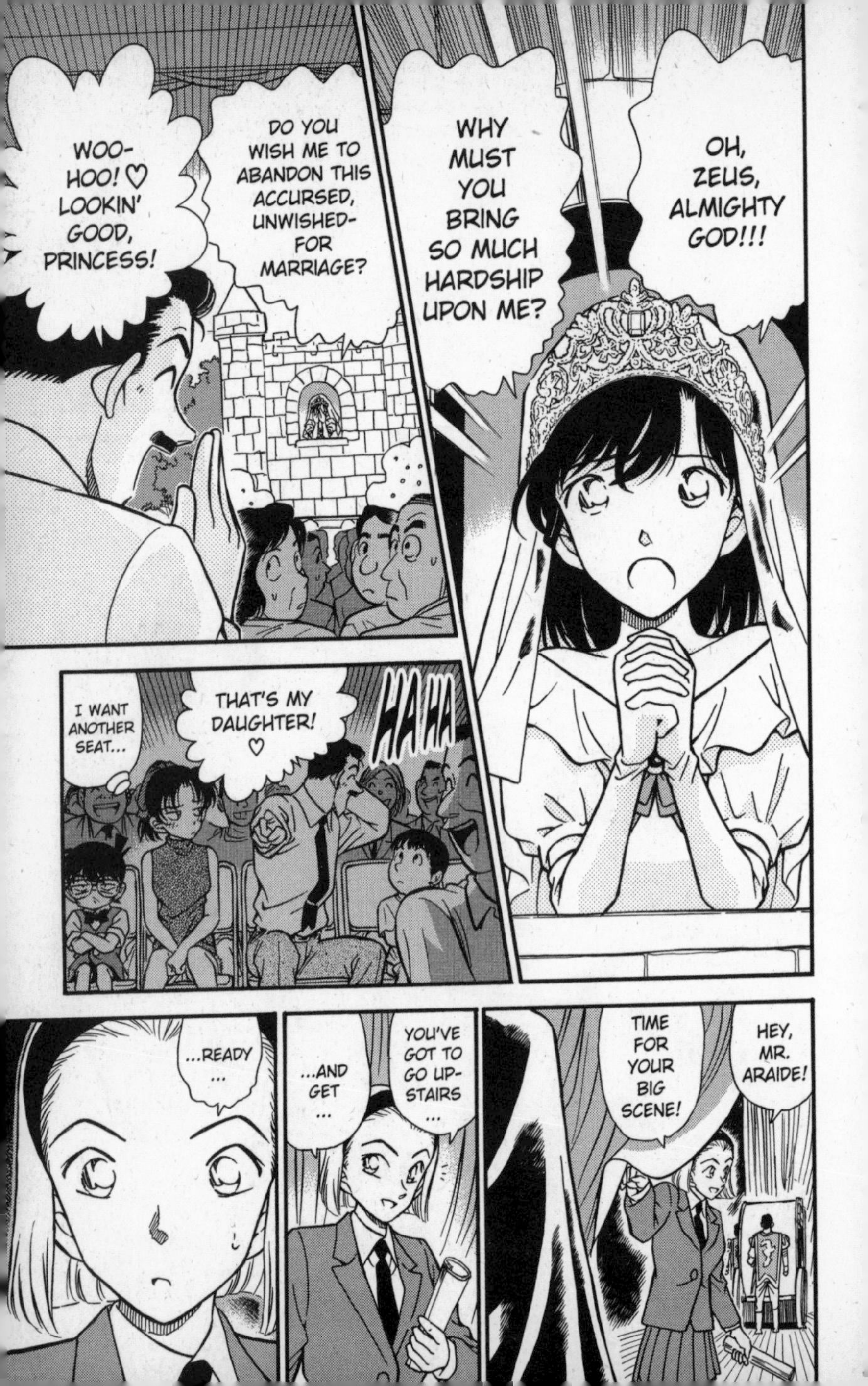
OH, ZEUS, ALMIGHTY GOD!!!
WHY MUST YOU BRING SO MUCH HARDSHIP UPON ME?
DO YOU WISH ME TO ABANDON THIS ACCURSED, UNWISHED-FOR MARRIAGE?
WOO-HOO! ♡ LOOKIN' GOOD, PRINCESS!
HA HA
THAT'S MY DAUGHTER! ♡
I WANT ANOTHER SEAT...
HEY, MR. ARAIDE!
TIME FOR YOUR BIG SCENE!
YOU'VE GOT TO GO UP-STAIRS ...
...AND GET ...
...READY ...

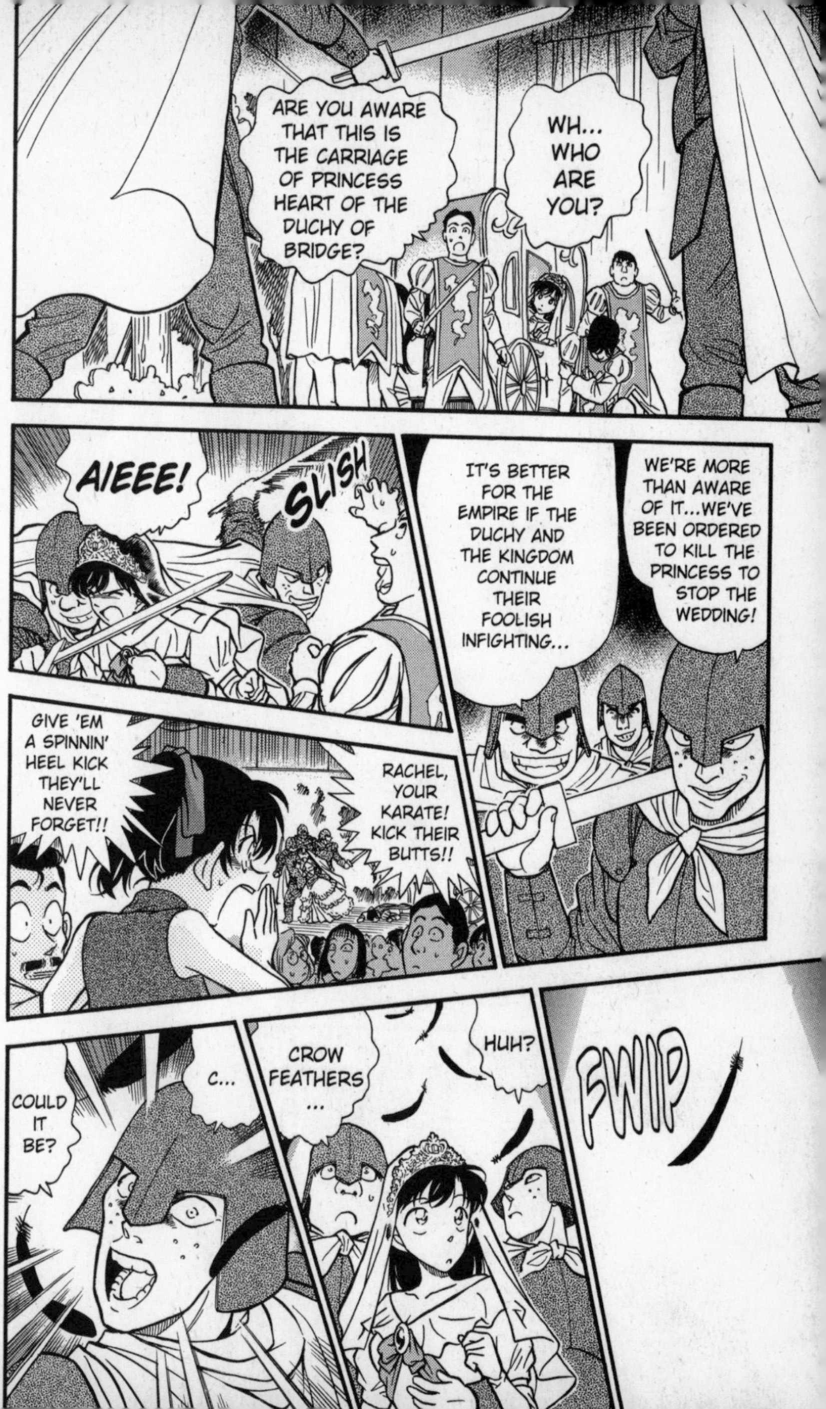
WH... WHO ARE YOU?
ARE YOU AWARE THAT THIS IS THE CARRIAGE OF PRINCESS HEART OF THE DUCHY OF BRIDGE?
WE'RE MORE THAN AWARE OF IT...WE'VE BEEN ORDERED TO KILL THE PRINCESS TO STOP THE WEDDING!
IT'S BETTER FOR THE EMPIRE IF THE DUCHY AND THE KINGDOM CONTINUE THEIR FOOLISH INFIGHTING...
SLISH
AIEEE!
RACHEL, YOUR KARATE! KICK THEIR BUTTS!!
GIVE 'EM A SPINNIN' HEEL KICK THEY'LL NEVER FORGET!!
FWIP
HUH?
CROW FEATHERS ...
C...
COULD IT BE?

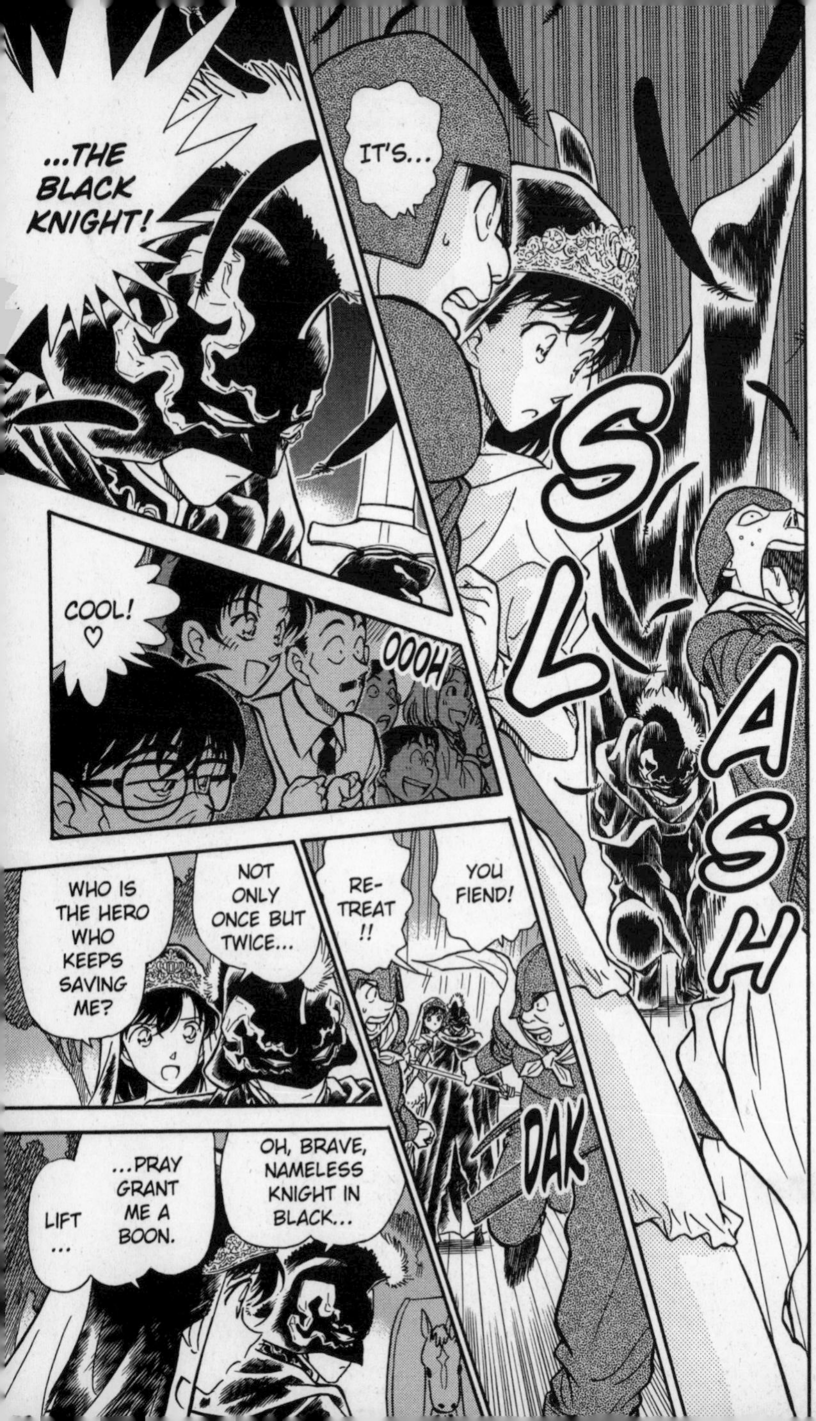
IT'S...
...THE BLACK KNIGHT!
SLASH
OOOH
COOL! ♡
YOU FIEND!
RE-TREAT !!
DAK
NOT ONLY ONCE BUT TWICE...
WHO IS THE HERO WHO KEEPS SAVING ME?
OH, BRAVE, NAMELESS KNIGHT IN BLACK...
...PRAY GRANT ME A BOON.
LIFT ...

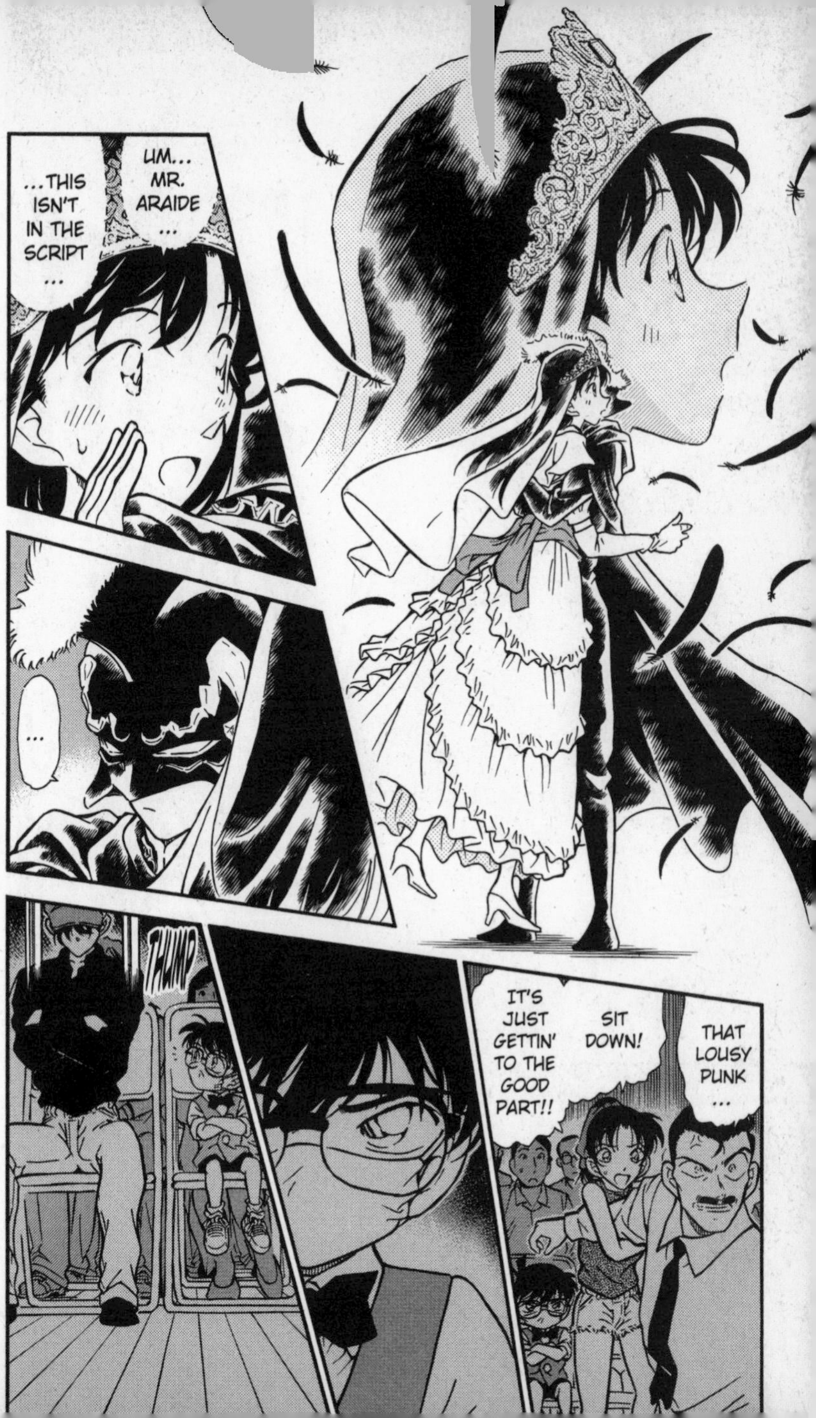
UM... MR. ARAIDE...
...THIS ISN'T IN THE SCRIPT...
......
THAT LOUSY PUNK...
SIT DOWN!
IT'S JUST GETTIN' TO THE GOOD PART!!
THUMP

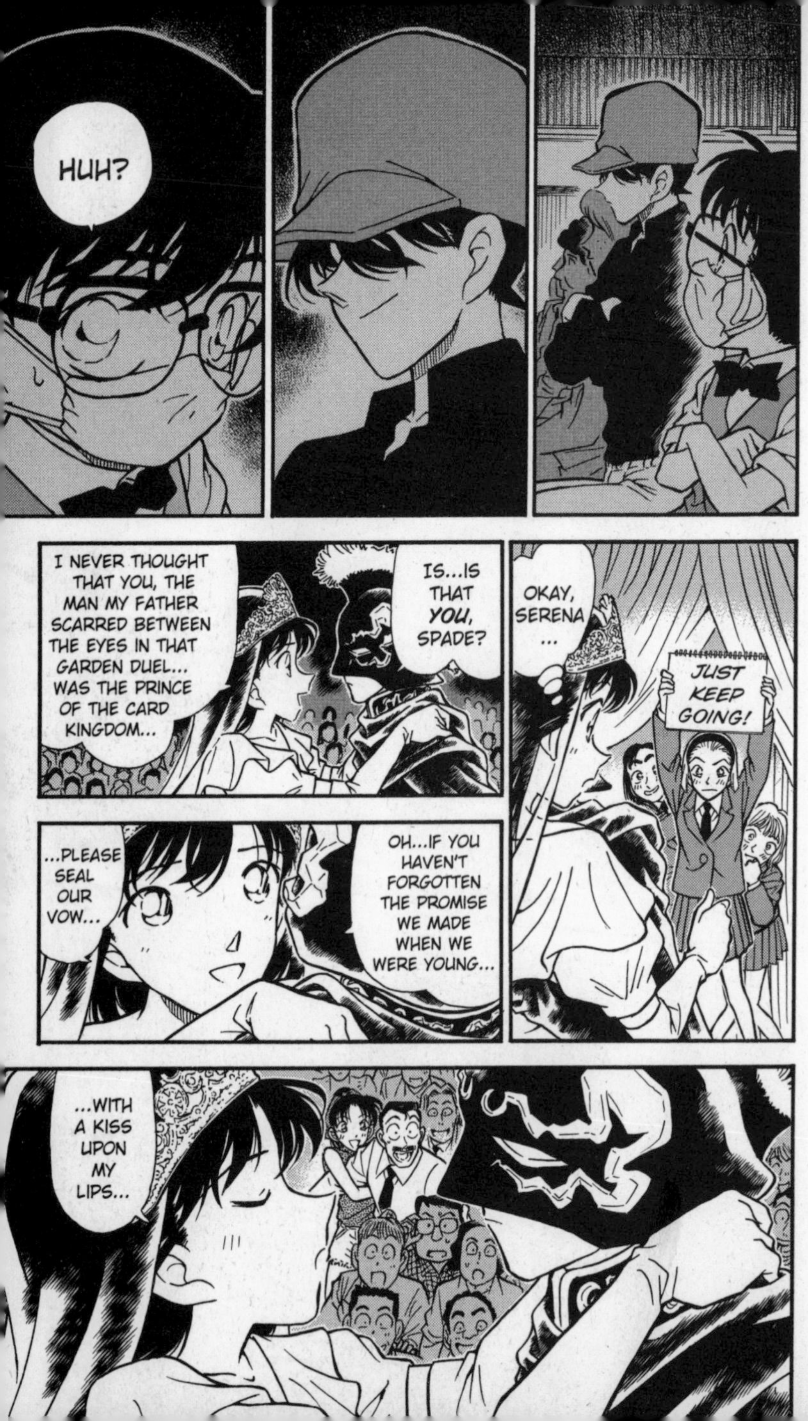
HUH?
OKAY, SERENA ...
JUST KEEP GOING!
IS...IS THAT *YOU*, SPADE?
I NEVER THOUGHT THAT YOU, THE MAN MY FATHER SCARRED BETWEEN THE EYES IN THAT GARDEN DUEL... WAS THE PRINCE OF THE CARD KINGDOM...
OH...IF YOU HAVEN'T FORGOTTEN THE PROMISE WE MADE WHEN WE WERE YOUNG...
...PLEASE SEAL OUR VOW...
...WITH A KISS UPON MY LIPS...

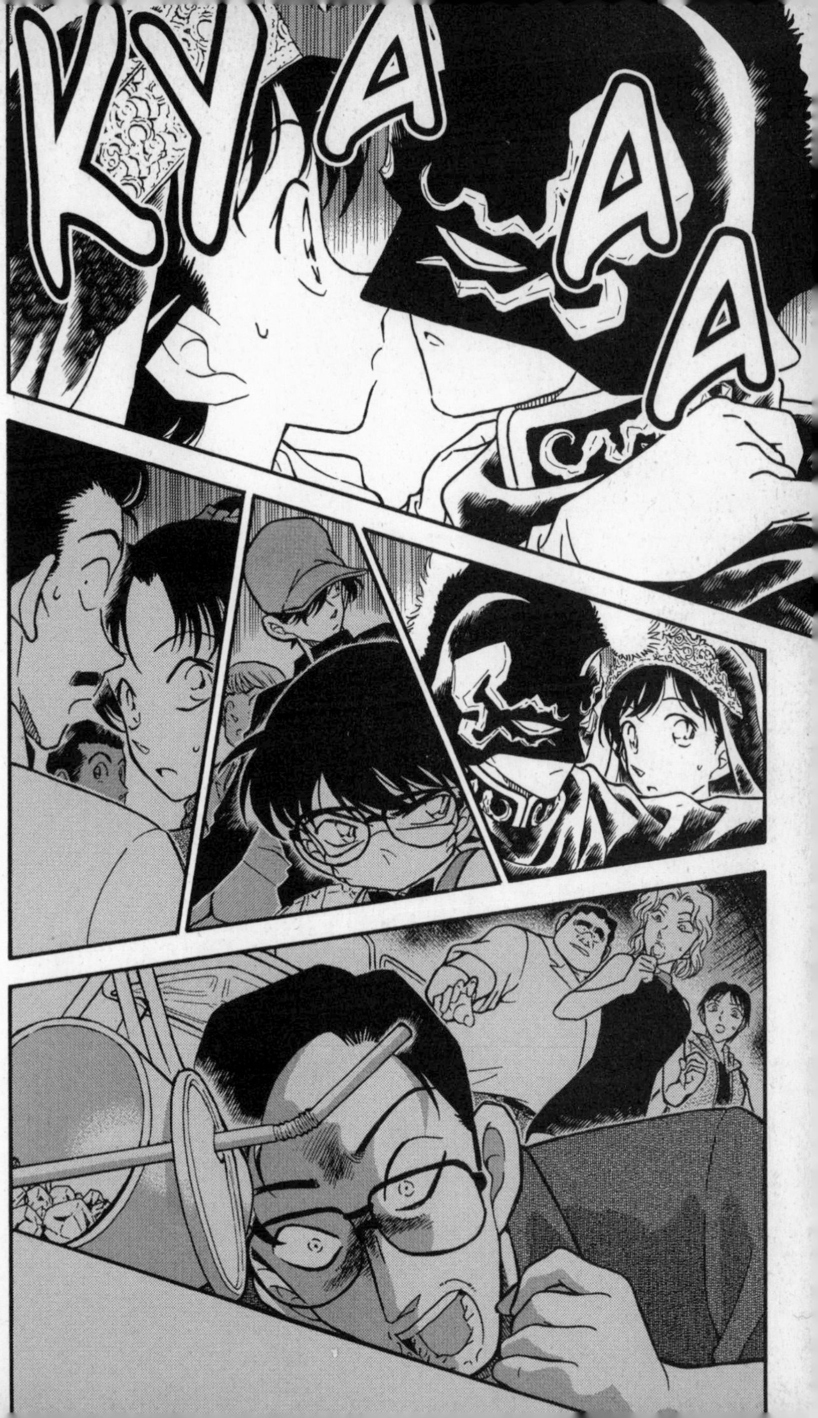
KYAAAA

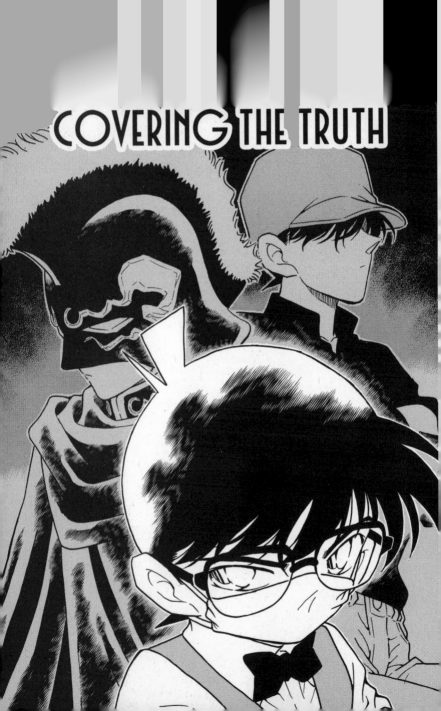

COVERING THE TRUTH

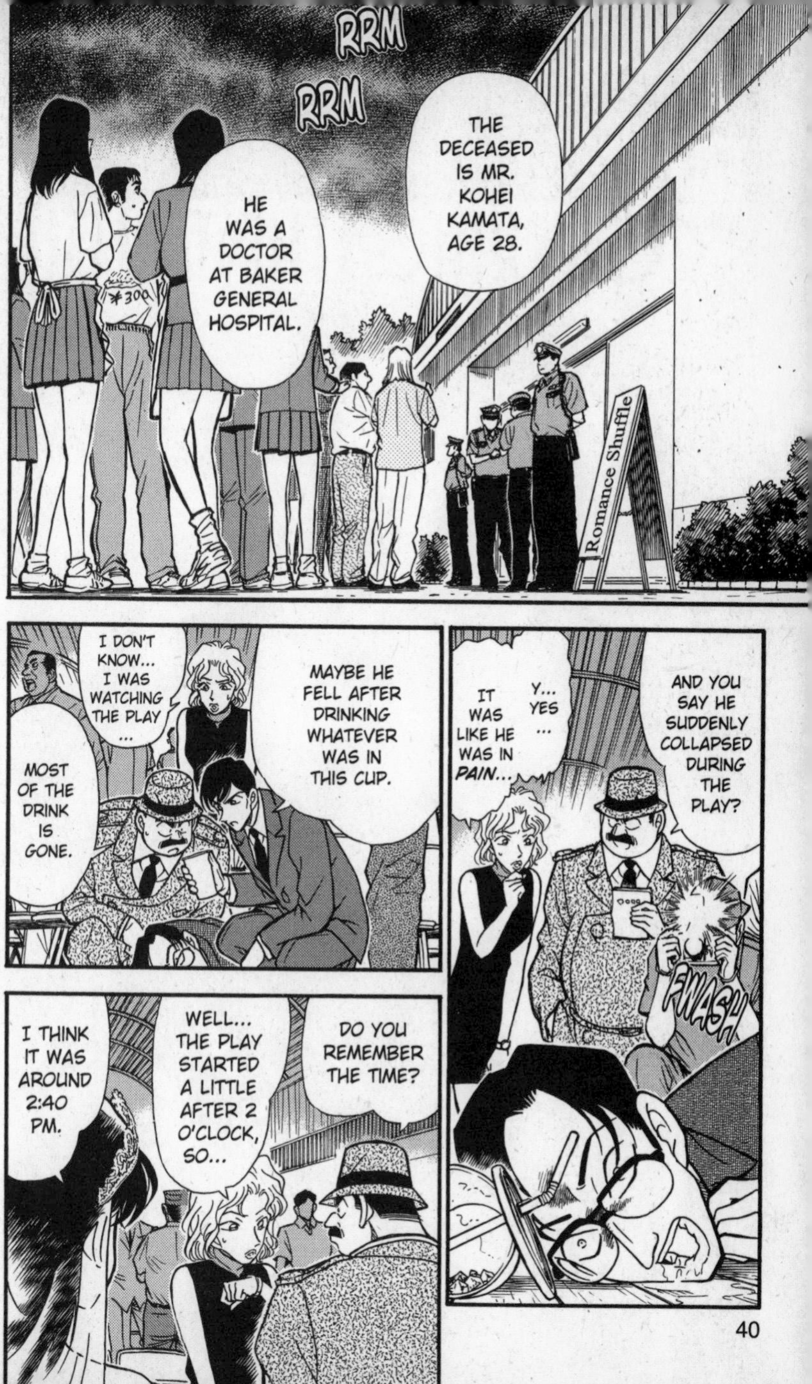
RRM
RRM
THE DECEASED IS MR. KOHEI KAMATA, AGE 28.
HE WAS A DOCTOR AT BAKER GENERAL HOSPITAL.
Romance Shuffle
AND YOU SAY HE SUDDENLY COLLAPSED DURING THE PLAY?
Y... YES ...
IT WAS LIKE HE WAS IN *PAIN*...
FWASH
MAYBE HE FELL AFTER DRINKING WHATEVER WAS IN THIS CUP.
I DON'T KNOW... I WAS WATCHING THE PLAY ...
MOST OF THE DRINK IS GONE.
DO YOU REMEMBER THE TIME?
WELL... THE PLAY STARTED A LITTLE AFTER 2 O'CLOCK, SO...
I THINK IT WAS AROUND 2:40 PM.

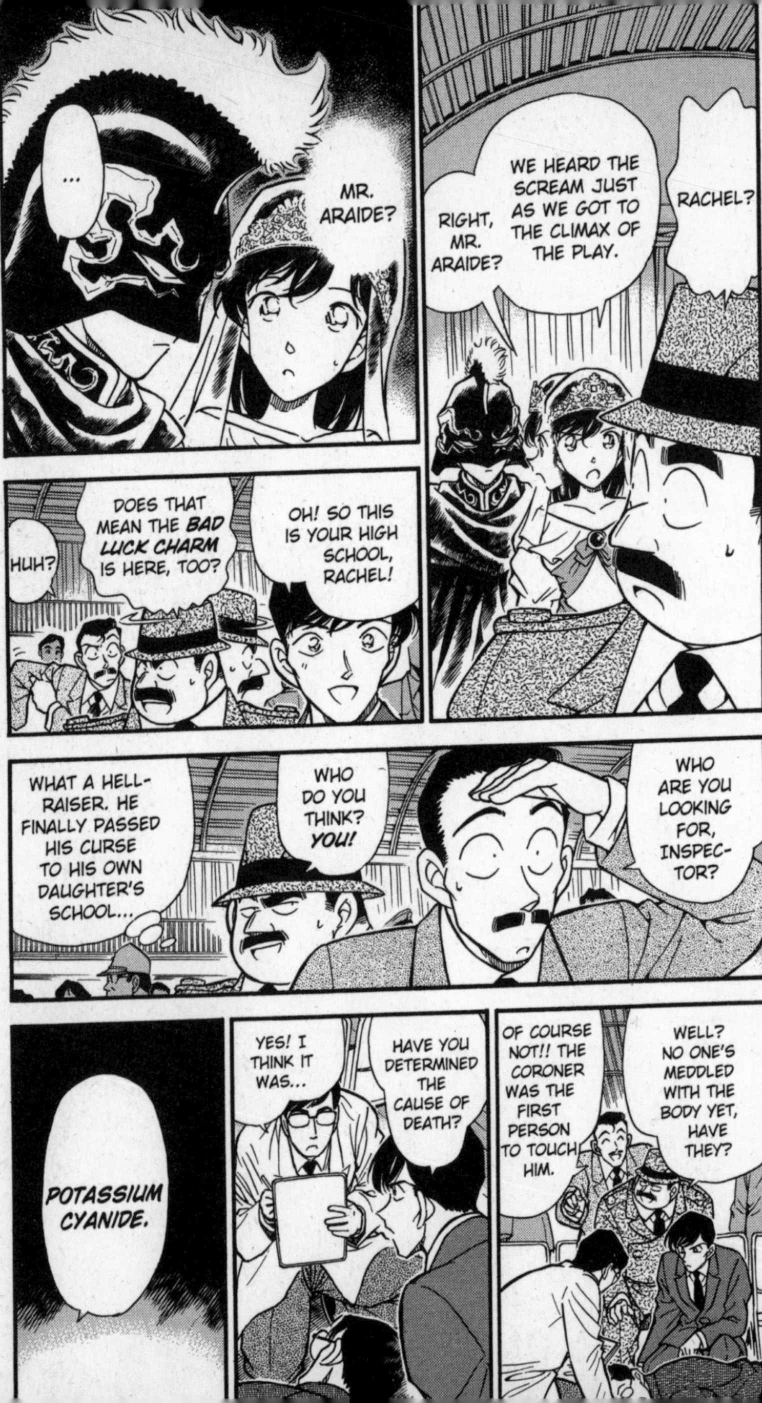
RACHEL?
WE HEARD THE SCREAM JUST AS WE GOT TO THE CLIMAX OF THE PLAY.
RIGHT, MR. ARAIDE?
MR. ARAIDE?
...
OH! SO THIS IS YOUR HIGH SCHOOL, RACHEL!
DOES THAT MEAN THE **BAD LUCK CHARM** IS HERE, TOO?
HUH?
WHO ARE YOU LOOKING FOR, INSPECTOR?
WHO DO YOU THINK? ***YOU!***
WHAT A HELL-RAISER. HE FINALLY PASSED HIS CURSE TO HIS OWN DAUGHTER'S SCHOOL...
WELL? NO ONE'S MEDDLED WITH THE BODY YET, HAVE THEY?
OF COURSE NOT!! THE CORONER WAS THE FIRST PERSON TO TOUCH HIM.
HAVE YOU DETERMINED THE CAUSE OF DEATH?
YES! I THINK IT WAS...
POTASSIUM CYANIDE.

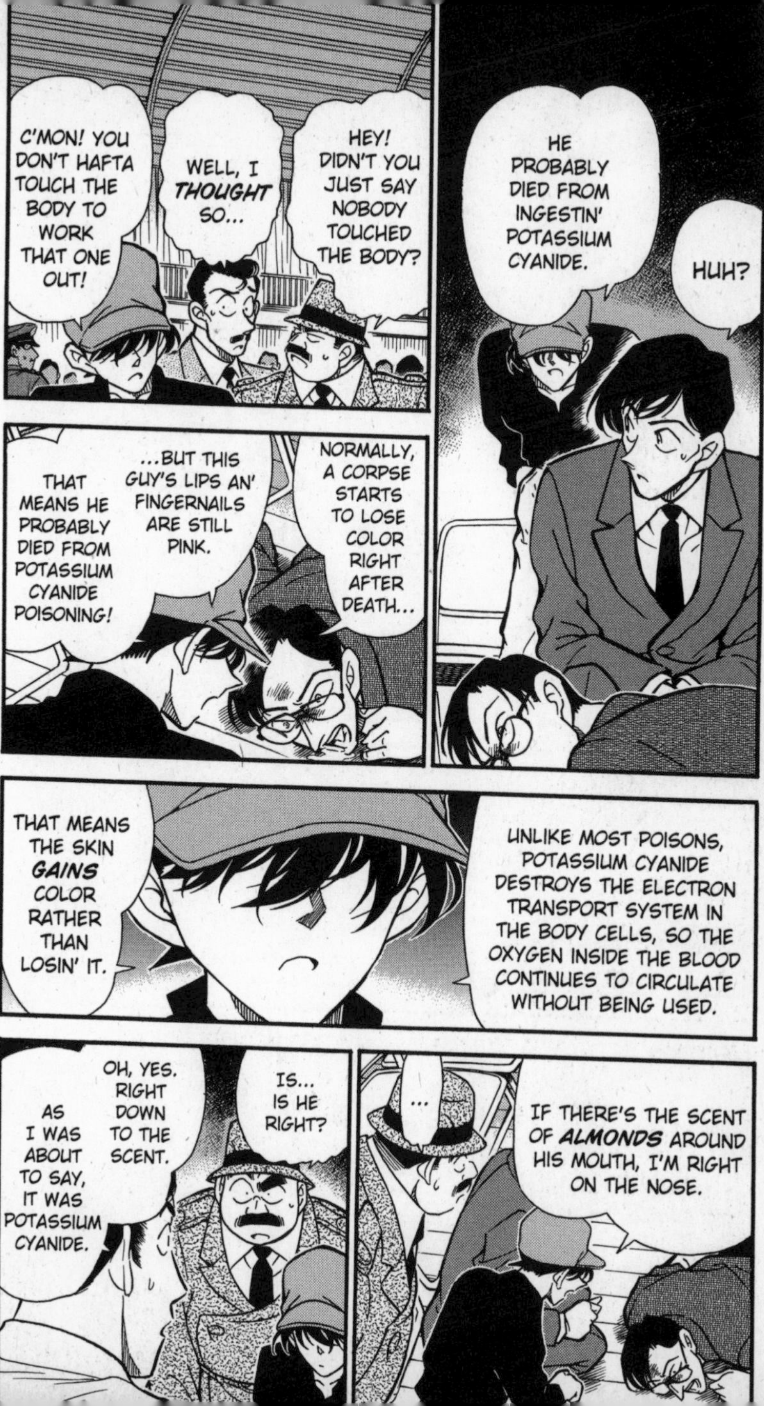
HE PROBABLY DIED FROM INGESTIN' POTASSIUM CYANIDE.
HUH?
HEY! DIDN'T YOU JUST SAY NOBODY TOUCHED THE BODY?
WELL, I *THOUGHT* SO...
C'MON! YOU DON'T HAFTA TOUCH THE BODY TO WORK THAT ONE OUT!
NORMALLY, A CORPSE STARTS TO LOSE COLOR RIGHT AFTER DEATH...
...BUT THIS GUY'S LIPS AN' FINGERNAILS ARE STILL PINK.
THAT MEANS HE PROBABLY DIED FROM POTASSIUM CYANIDE POISONING!
UNLIKE MOST POISONS, POTASSIUM CYANIDE DESTROYS THE ELECTRON TRANSPORT SYSTEM IN THE BODY CELLS, SO THE OXYGEN INSIDE THE BLOOD CONTINUES TO CIRCULATE WITHOUT BEING USED.
THAT MEANS THE SKIN *GAINS* COLOR RATHER THAN LOSIN' IT.
IF THERE'S THE SCENT OF *ALMONDS* AROUND HIS MOUTH, I'M RIGHT ON THE NOSE.
...
IS... IS HE RIGHT?
OH, YES. RIGHT DOWN TO THE SCENT.
AS I WAS ABOUT TO SAY, IT WAS POTASSIUM CYANIDE.

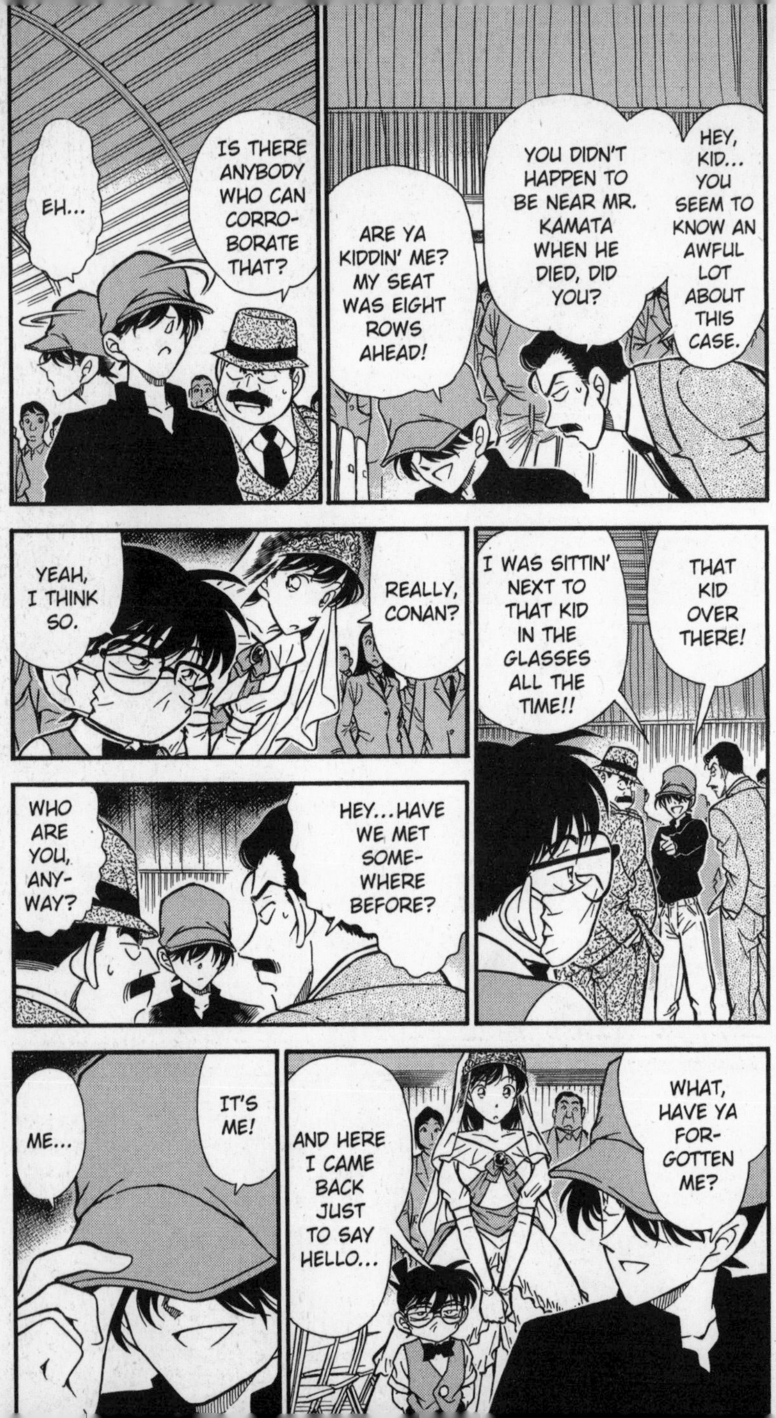
HEY, KID... YOU SEEM TO KNOW AN AWFUL LOT ABOUT THIS CASE.
YOU DIDN'T HAPPEN TO BE NEAR MR. KAMATA WHEN HE DIED, DID YOU?
ARE YA KIDDIN' ME? MY SEAT WAS EIGHT ROWS AHEAD!
IS THERE ANYBODY WHO CAN CORROBORATE THAT?
EH...
THAT KID OVER THERE!
I WAS SITTIN' NEXT TO THAT KID IN THE GLASSES ALL THE TIME!!
REALLY, CONAN?
YEAH, I THINK SO.
HEY...HAVE WE MET SOMEWHERE BEFORE?
WHO ARE YOU, ANYWAY?
WHAT, HAVE YA FORGOTTEN ME?
AND HERE I CAME BACK JUST TO SAY HELLO...
IT'S ME!
ME...

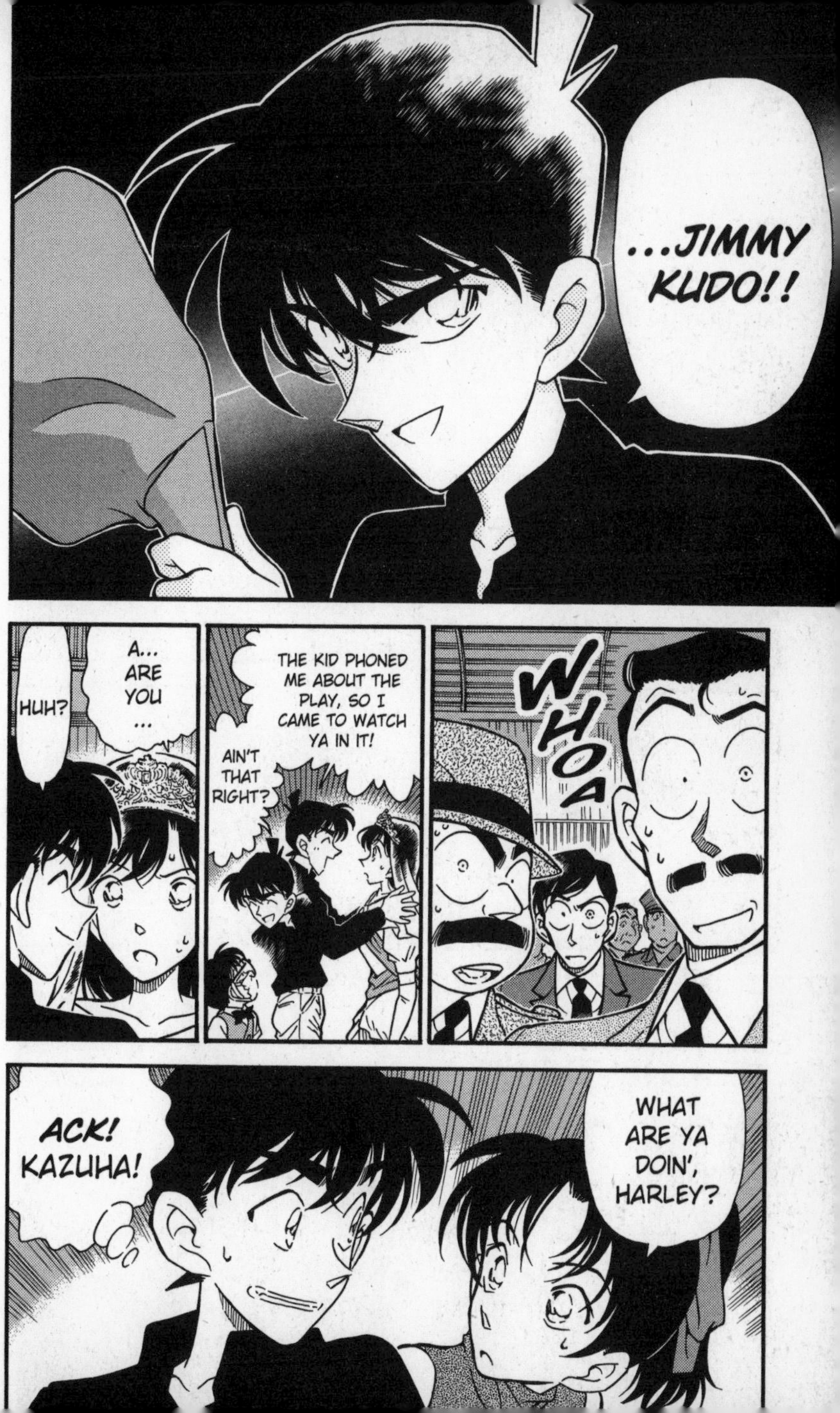
...JIMMY KUDO!!
WHOA
THE KID PHONED ME ABOUT THE PLAY, SO I CAME TO WATCH YA IN IT!
AIN'T THAT RIGHT?
A... ARE YOU ...
HUH?
WHAT ARE YA DOIN', HARLEY?
ACK! KAZUHA!

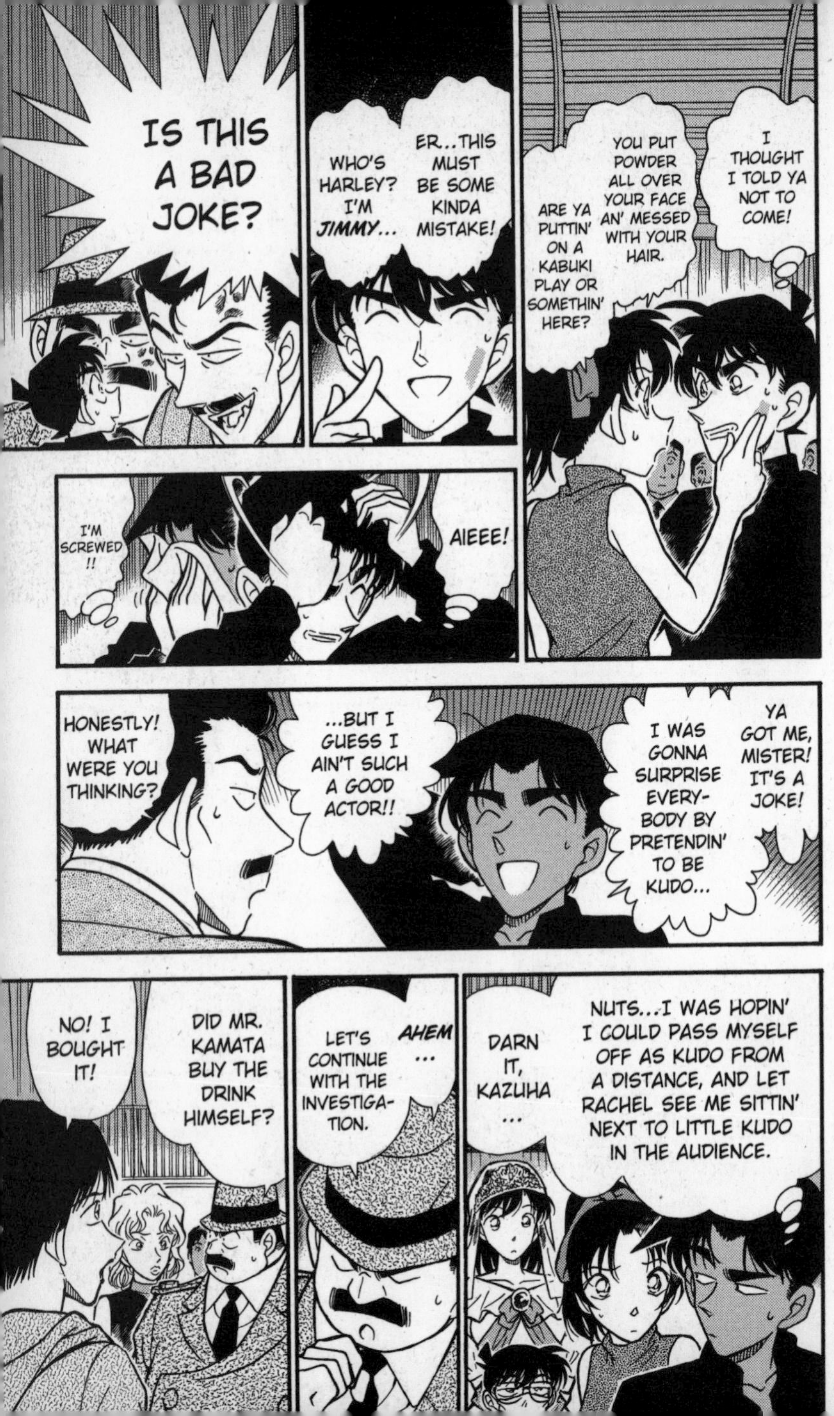
I THOUGHT I TOLD YA NOT TO COME!
YOU PUT POWDER ALL OVER YOUR FACE AN' MESSED WITH YOUR HAIR.
ARE YA PUTTIN' ON A KABUKI PLAY OR SOMETHIN' HERE?
ER...THIS MUST BE SOME KINDA MISTAKE!
WHO'S HARLEY? I'M *JIMMY*...
IS THIS A BAD JOKE?
AIEEE!
I'M SCREWED!!
YA GOT ME, MISTER! IT'S A JOKE!
I WAS GONNA SURPRISE EVERY-BODY BY PRETENDIN' TO BE KUDO...
...BUT I GUESS I AIN'T SUCH A GOOD ACTOR!!
HONESTLY! WHAT WERE YOU THINKING?
NUTS...I WAS HOPIN' I COULD PASS MYSELF OFF AS KUDO FROM A DISTANCE, AND LET RACHEL SEE ME SITTIN' NEXT TO LITTLE KUDO IN THE AUDIENCE.
DARN IT, KAZUHA...
AHEM...
LET'S CONTINUE WITH THE INVESTIGA-TION.
DID MR. KAMATA BUY THE DRINK HIMSELF?
NO! I BOUGHT IT!

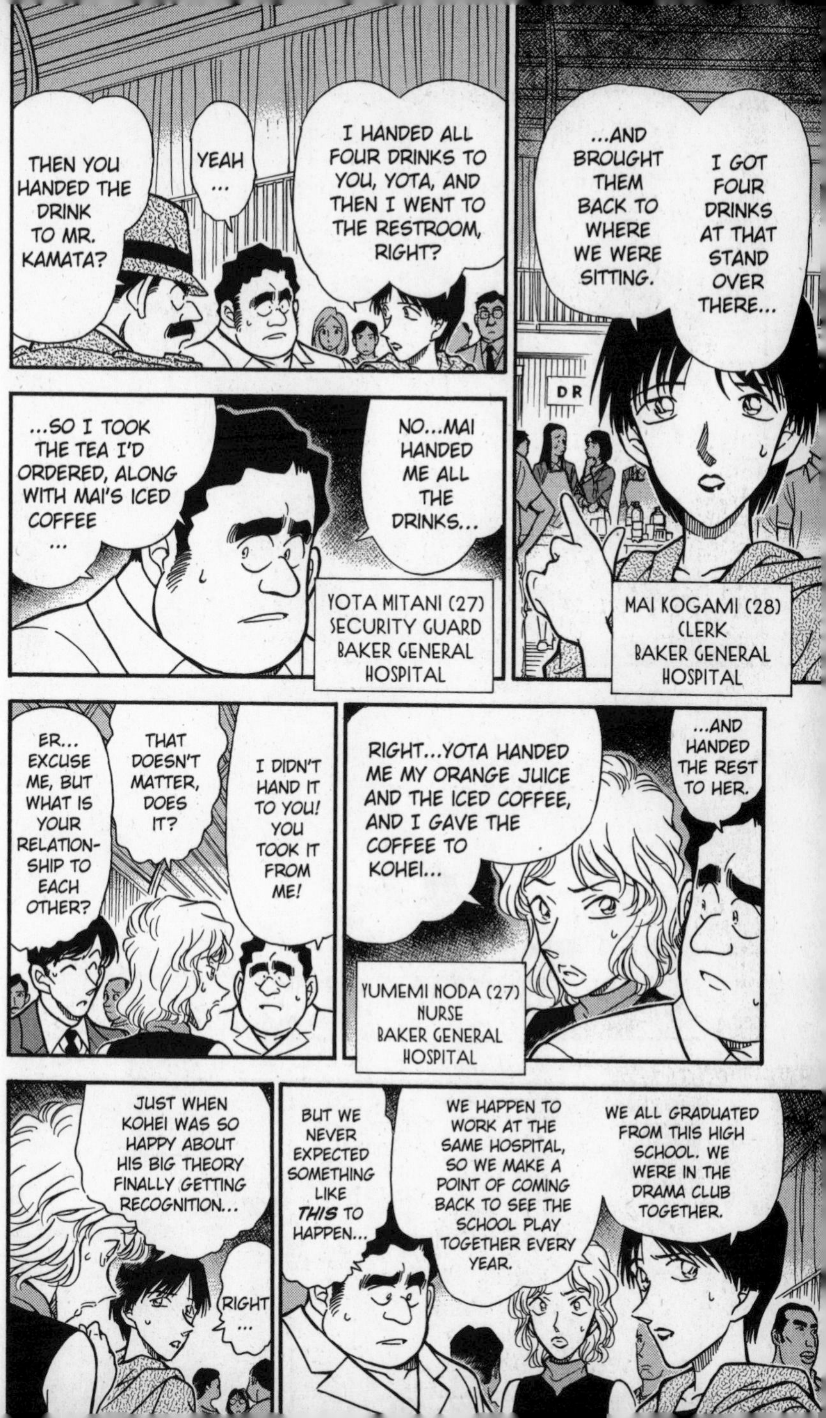
I GOT FOUR DRINKS AT THAT STAND OVER THERE...
...AND BROUGHT THEM BACK TO WHERE WE WERE SITTING.
DR
MAI KOGAMI (28) CLERK BAKER GENERAL HOSPITAL
I HANDED ALL FOUR DRINKS TO YOU, YOTA, AND THEN I WENT TO THE RESTROOM, RIGHT?
YEAH ...
THEN YOU HANDED THE DRINK TO MR. KAMATA?
NO...MAI HANDED ME ALL THE DRINKS...
YOTA MITANI (27) SECURITY GUARD BAKER GENERAL HOSPITAL
...SO I TOOK THE TEA I'D ORDERED, ALONG WITH MAI'S ICED COFFEE ...
...AND HANDED THE REST TO HER.
RIGHT...YOTA HANDED ME MY ORANGE JUICE AND THE ICED COFFEE, AND I GAVE THE COFFEE TO KOHEI...
YUMEMI NODA (27) NURSE BAKER GENERAL HOSPITAL
I DIDN'T HAND IT TO YOU! YOU TOOK IT FROM ME!
THAT DOESN'T MATTER, DOES IT?
ER... EXCUSE ME, BUT WHAT IS YOUR RELATIONSHIP TO EACH OTHER?
WE ALL GRADUATED FROM THIS HIGH SCHOOL. WE WERE IN THE DRAMA CLUB TOGETHER.
WE HAPPEN TO WORK AT THE SAME HOSPITAL, SO WE MAKE A POINT OF COMING BACK TO SEE THE SCHOOL PLAY TOGETHER EVERY YEAR.
BUT WE NEVER EXPECTED SOMETHING LIKE THIS TO HAPPEN...
JUST WHEN KOHEI WAS SO HAPPY ABOUT HIS BIG THEORY FINALLY GETTING RECOGNITION...
RIGHT ...

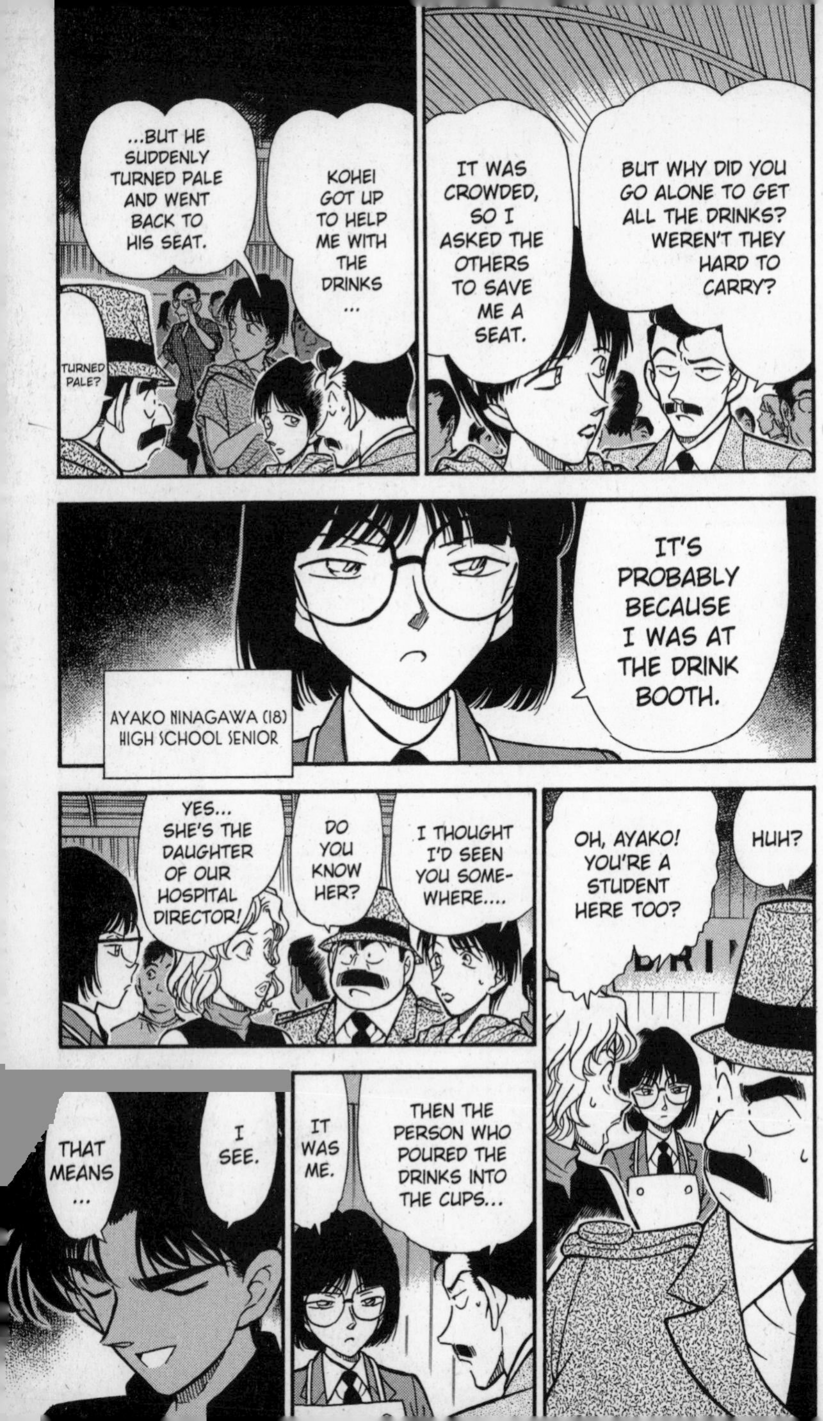
BUT WHY DID YOU GO ALONE TO GET ALL THE DRINKS? WEREN'T THEY HARD TO CARRY?
IT WAS CROWDED, SO I ASKED THE OTHERS TO SAVE ME A SEAT.
KOHEI GOT UP TO HELP ME WITH THE DRINKS ...
...BUT HE SUDDENLY TURNED PALE AND WENT BACK TO HIS SEAT.
TURNED PALE?
IT'S PROBABLY BECAUSE I WAS AT THE DRINK BOOTH.
AYAKO NINAGAWA (18) HIGH SCHOOL SENIOR
HUH?
OH, AYAKO! YOU'RE A STUDENT HERE TOO?
I THOUGHT I'D SEEN YOU SOME-WHERE....
DO YOU KNOW HER?
YES... SHE'S THE DAUGHTER OF OUR HOSPITAL DIRECTOR!
THEN THE PERSON WHO POURED THE DRINKS INTO THE CUPS...
IT WAS ME.
I SEE.
THAT MEANS ...

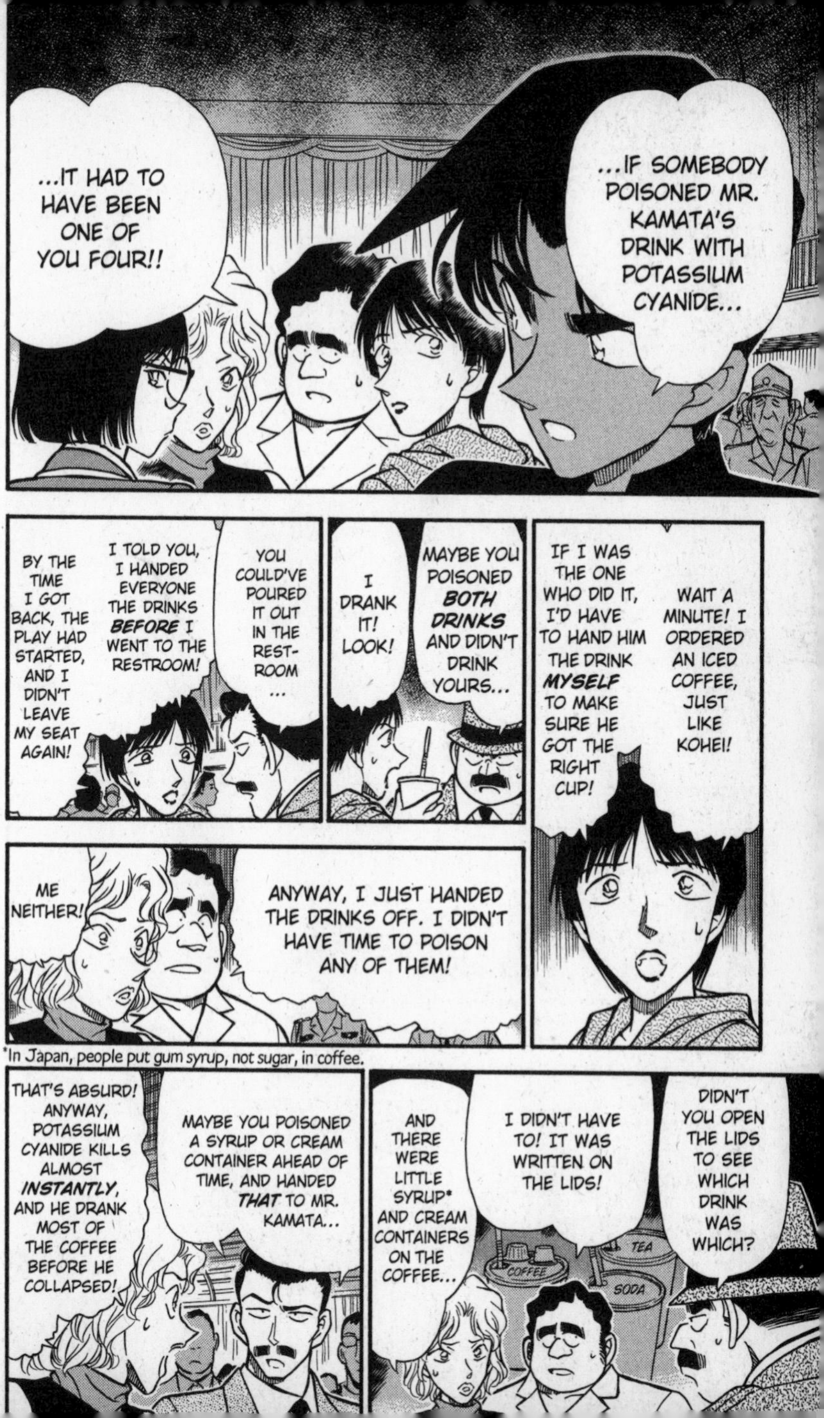
...IF SOMEBODY POISONED MR. KAMATA'S DRINK WITH POTASSIUM CYANIDE...
...IT HAD TO HAVE BEEN ONE OF YOU FOUR!!
WAIT A MINUTE! I ORDERED AN ICED COFFEE, JUST LIKE KOHEI!
IF I WAS THE ONE WHO DID IT, I'D HAVE TO HAND HIM THE DRINK *MYSELF* TO MAKE SURE HE GOT THE RIGHT CUP!
MAYBE YOU POISONED *BOTH DRINKS* AND DIDN'T DRINK YOURS...
I DRANK IT! LOOK!
YOU COULD'VE POURED IT OUT IN THE REST-ROOM...
I TOLD YOU, I HANDED EVERYONE THE DRINKS *BEFORE* I WENT TO THE RESTROOM!
BY THE TIME I GOT BACK, THE PLAY HAD STARTED, AND I DIDN'T LEAVE MY SEAT AGAIN!
ANYWAY, I JUST HANDED THE DRINKS OFF. I DIDN'T HAVE TIME TO POISON ANY OF THEM!
ME NEITHER!
DIDN'T YOU OPEN THE LIDS TO SEE WHICH DRINK WAS WHICH?
I DIDN'T HAVE TO! IT WAS WRITTEN ON THE LIDS!
TEA
COFFEE
SODA
AND THERE WERE LITTLE SYRUP* AND CREAM CONTAINERS ON THE COFFEE...
MAYBE YOU POISONED A SYRUP OR CREAM CONTAINER AHEAD OF TIME, AND HANDED *THAT* TO MR. KAMATA...
THAT'S ABSURD! ANYWAY, POTASSIUM CYANIDE KILLS ALMOST *INSTANTLY*, AND HE DRANK MOST OF THE COFFEE BEFORE HE COLLAPSED!

*In Japan, people put gum syrup, not sugar, in coffee.

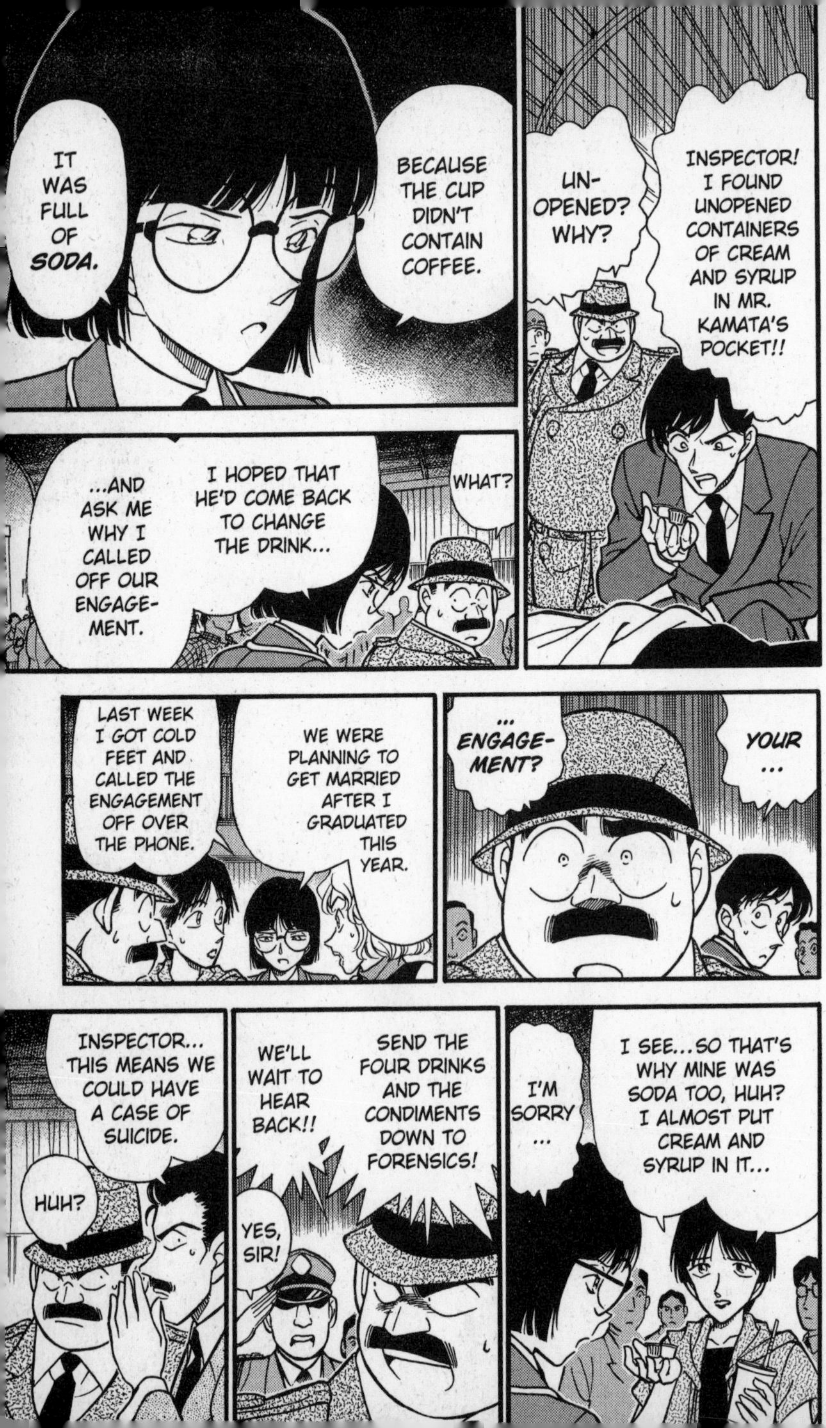
INSPECTOR! I FOUND UNOPENED CONTAINERS OF CREAM AND SYRUP IN MR. KAMATA'S POCKET!!
UN-OPENED? WHY?
BECAUSE THE CUP DIDN'T CONTAIN COFFEE.
IT WAS FULL OF SODA.
WHAT?
I HOPED THAT HE'D COME BACK TO CHANGE THE DRINK...
...AND ASK ME WHY I CALLED OFF OUR ENGAGE-MENT.
YOUR ...
... ENGAGE-MENT?
WE WERE PLANNING TO GET MARRIED AFTER I GRADUATED THIS YEAR.
LAST WEEK I GOT COLD FEET AND CALLED THE ENGAGEMENT OFF OVER THE PHONE.
I SEE...SO THAT'S WHY MINE WAS SODA TOO, HUH? I ALMOST PUT CREAM AND SYRUP IN IT...
I'M SORRY ...
SEND THE FOUR DRINKS AND THE CONDIMENTS DOWN TO FORENSICS!
WE'LL WAIT TO HEAR BACK!!
YES, SIR!
INSPECTOR... THIS MEANS WE COULD HAVE A CASE OF SUICIDE.
HUH?

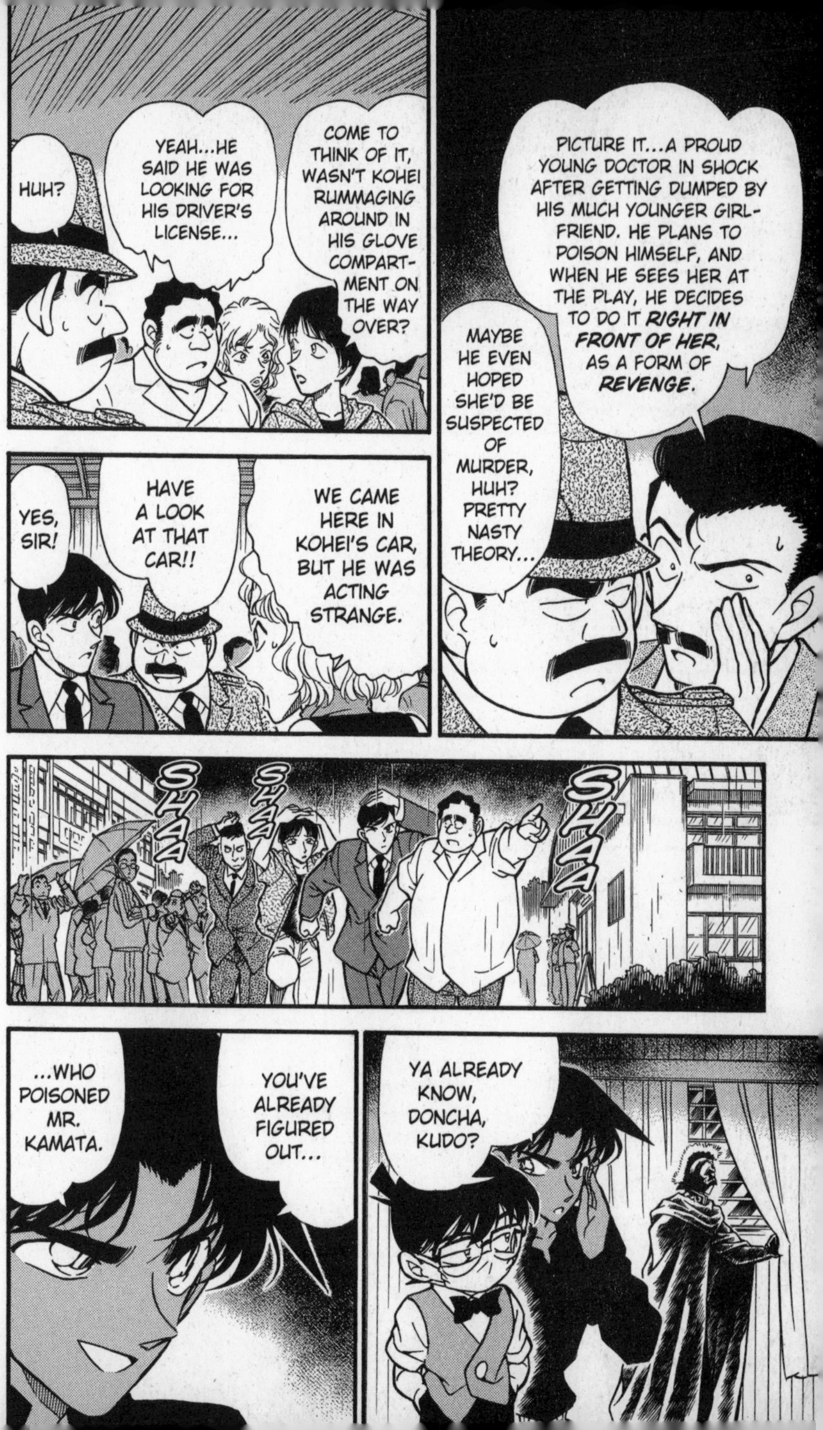
PICTURE IT...A PROUD YOUNG DOCTOR IN SHOCK AFTER GETTING DUMPED BY HIS MUCH YOUNGER GIRL-FRIEND. HE PLANS TO POISON HIMSELF, AND WHEN HE SEES HER AT THE PLAY, HE DECIDES TO DO IT **RIGHT IN FRONT OF HER**, AS A FORM OF **REVENGE**.
MAYBE HE EVEN HOPED SHE'D BE SUSPECTED OF MURDER, HUH? PRETTY NASTY THEORY...
COME TO THINK OF IT, WASN'T KOHEI RUMMAGING AROUND IN HIS GLOVE COMPART-MENT ON THE WAY OVER?
YEAH...HE SAID HE WAS LOOKING FOR HIS DRIVER'S LICENSE...
HUH?
WE CAME HERE IN KOHEI'S CAR, BUT HE WAS ACTING STRANGE.
HAVE A LOOK AT THAT CAR!!
YES, SIR!
SHAA
SHAA
SHAA
YA ALREADY KNOW, DONCHA, KUDO?
YOU'VE ALREADY FIGURED OUT...
...WHO POISONED MR. KAMATA.

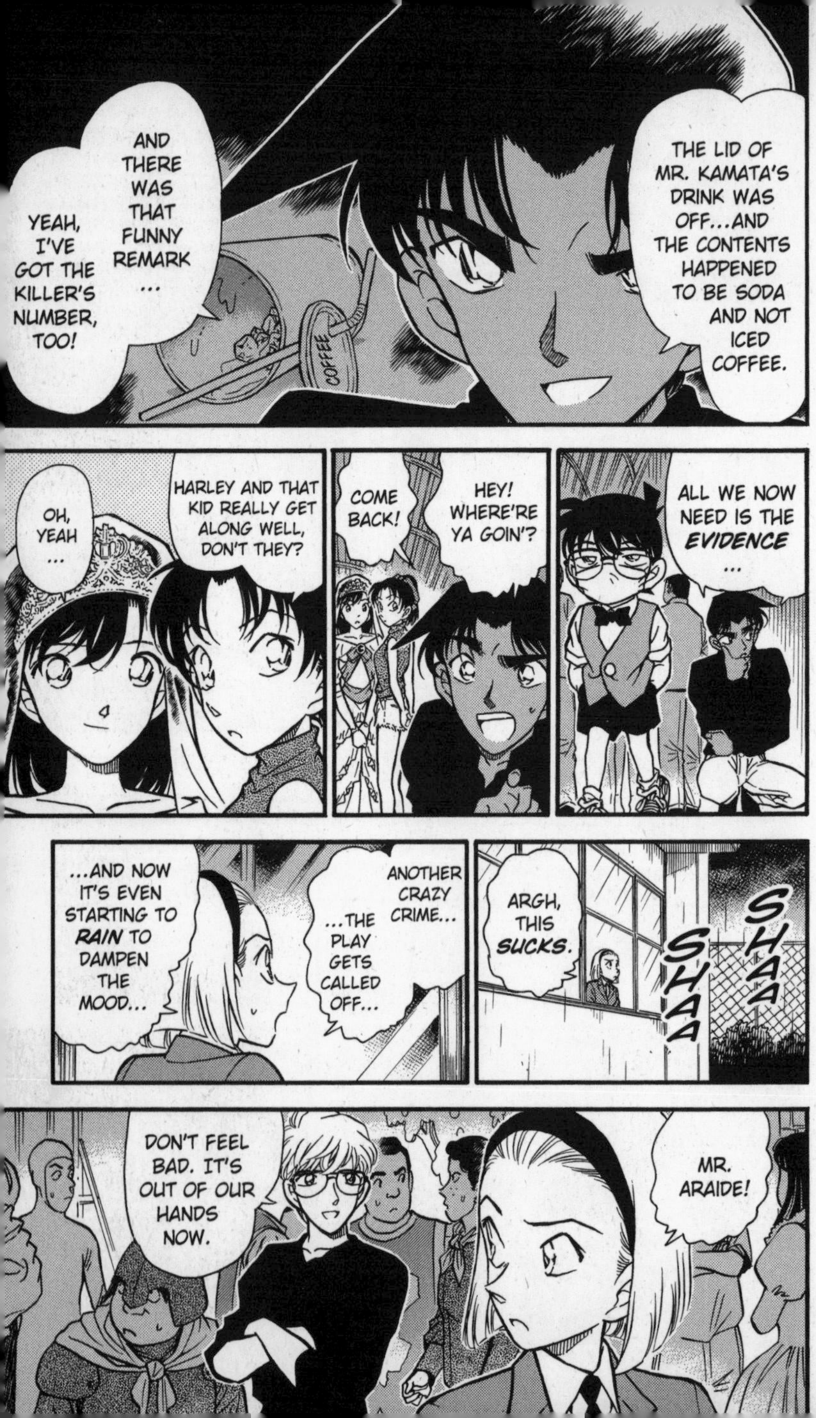
THE LID OF MR. KAMATA'S DRINK WAS OFF...AND THE CONTENTS HAPPENED TO BE SODA AND NOT ICED COFFEE.
COFFEE
AND THERE WAS THAT FUNNY REMARK...
YEAH, I'VE GOT THE KILLER'S NUMBER, TOO!
ALL WE NOW NEED IS THE *EVIDENCE*...
HEY! WHERE'RE YA GOIN'?
COME BACK!
HARLEY AND THAT KID REALLY GET ALONG WELL, DON'T THEY?
OH, YEAH...
ARGH, THIS **SUCKS**.
SHAA
SHAA
ANOTHER CRAZY CRIME...
...THE PLAY GETS CALLED OFF...
...AND NOW IT'S EVEN STARTING TO *RAIN* TO DAMPEN THE MOOD...
MR. ARAIDE!
DON'T FEEL BAD. IT'S OUT OF OUR HANDS NOW.

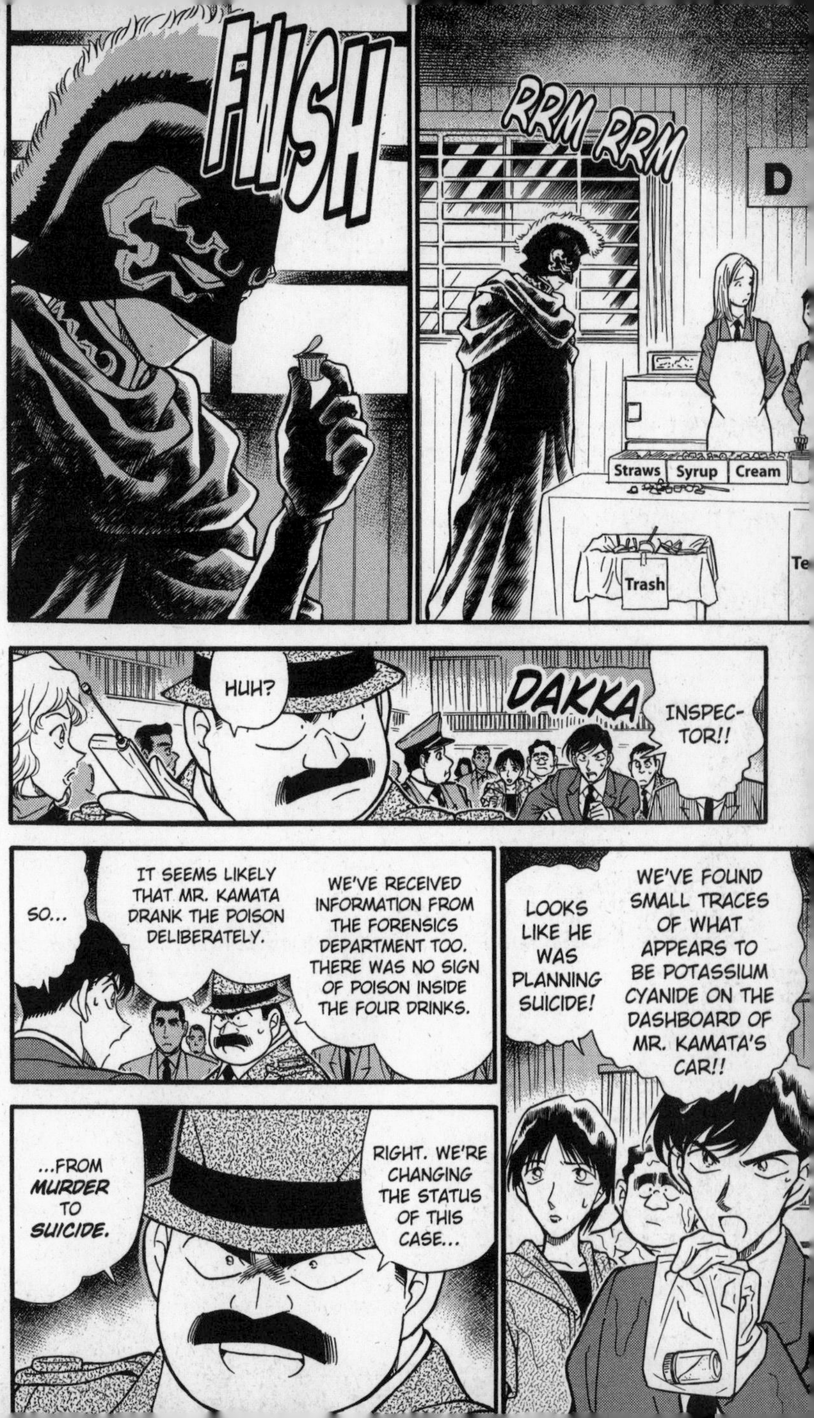
RRM RRM
D
Straws
Syrup
Cream
Trash
Te
FWSH
INSPECTOR!!
DAKKA
HUH?
WE'VE FOUND SMALL TRACES OF WHAT APPEARS TO BE POTASSIUM CYANIDE ON THE DASHBOARD OF MR. KAMATA'S CAR!!
LOOKS LIKE HE WAS PLANNING SUICIDE!
WE'VE RECEIVED INFORMATION FROM THE FORENSICS DEPARTMENT TOO. THERE WAS NO SIGN OF POISON INSIDE THE FOUR DRINKS.
IT SEEMS LIKELY THAT MR. KAMATA DRANK THE POISON DELIBERATELY.
SO...
RIGHT. WE'RE CHANGING THE STATUS OF THIS CASE...
...FROM MURDER TO SUICIDE.

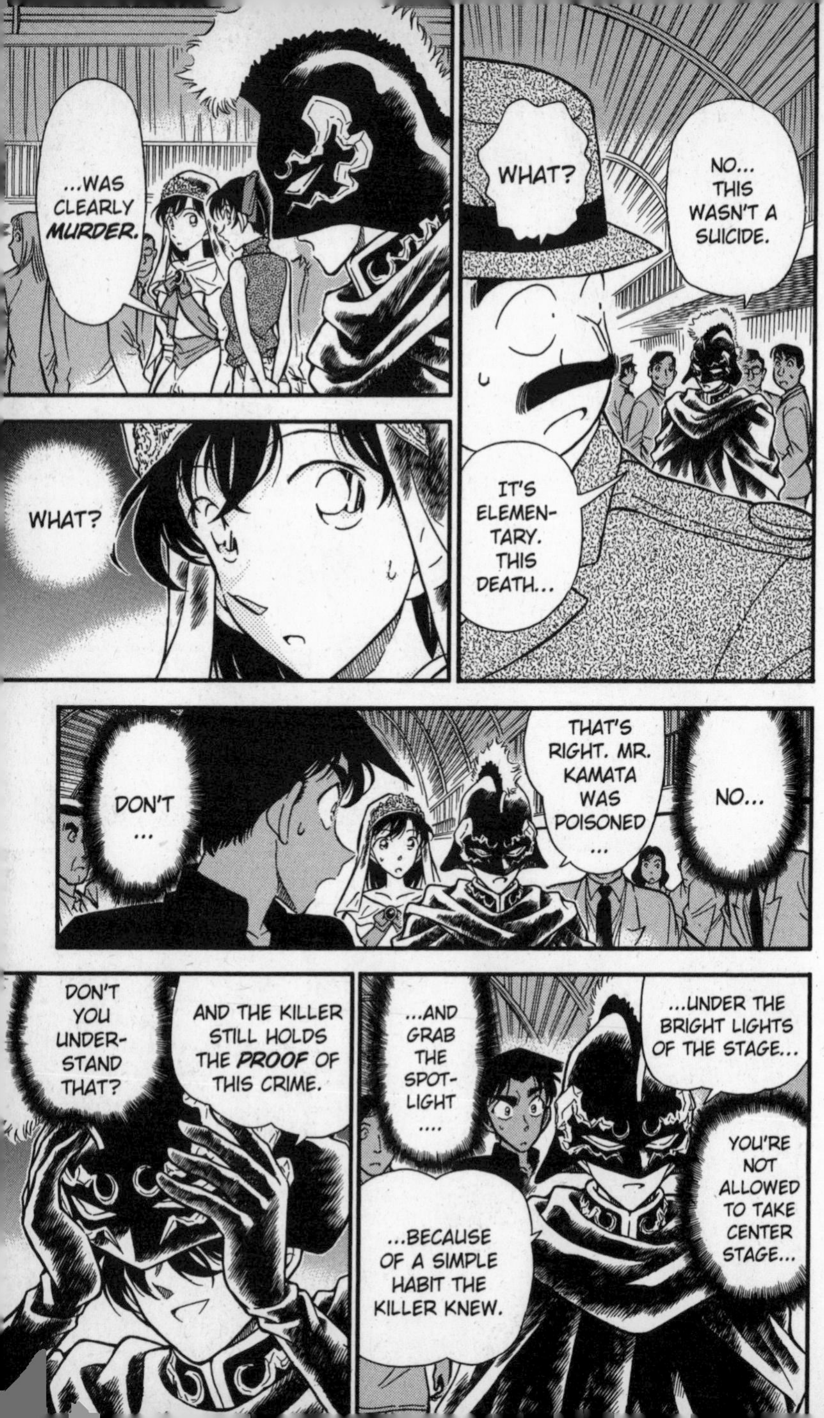
NO... THIS WASN'T A SUICIDE.
WHAT?
IT'S ELEMENTARY. THIS DEATH...
...WAS CLEARLY *MURDER.*
WHAT?
NO...
THAT'S RIGHT. MR. KAMATA WAS POISONED...
DON'T ...
...UNDER THE BRIGHT LIGHTS OF THE STAGE...
YOU'RE NOT ALLOWED TO TAKE CENTER STAGE...
...AND GRAB THE SPOTLIGHT....
...BECAUSE OF A SIMPLE HABIT THE KILLER KNEW.
AND THE KILLER STILL HOLDS THE *PROOF* OF THIS CRIME.
DON'T YOU UNDERSTAND THAT?

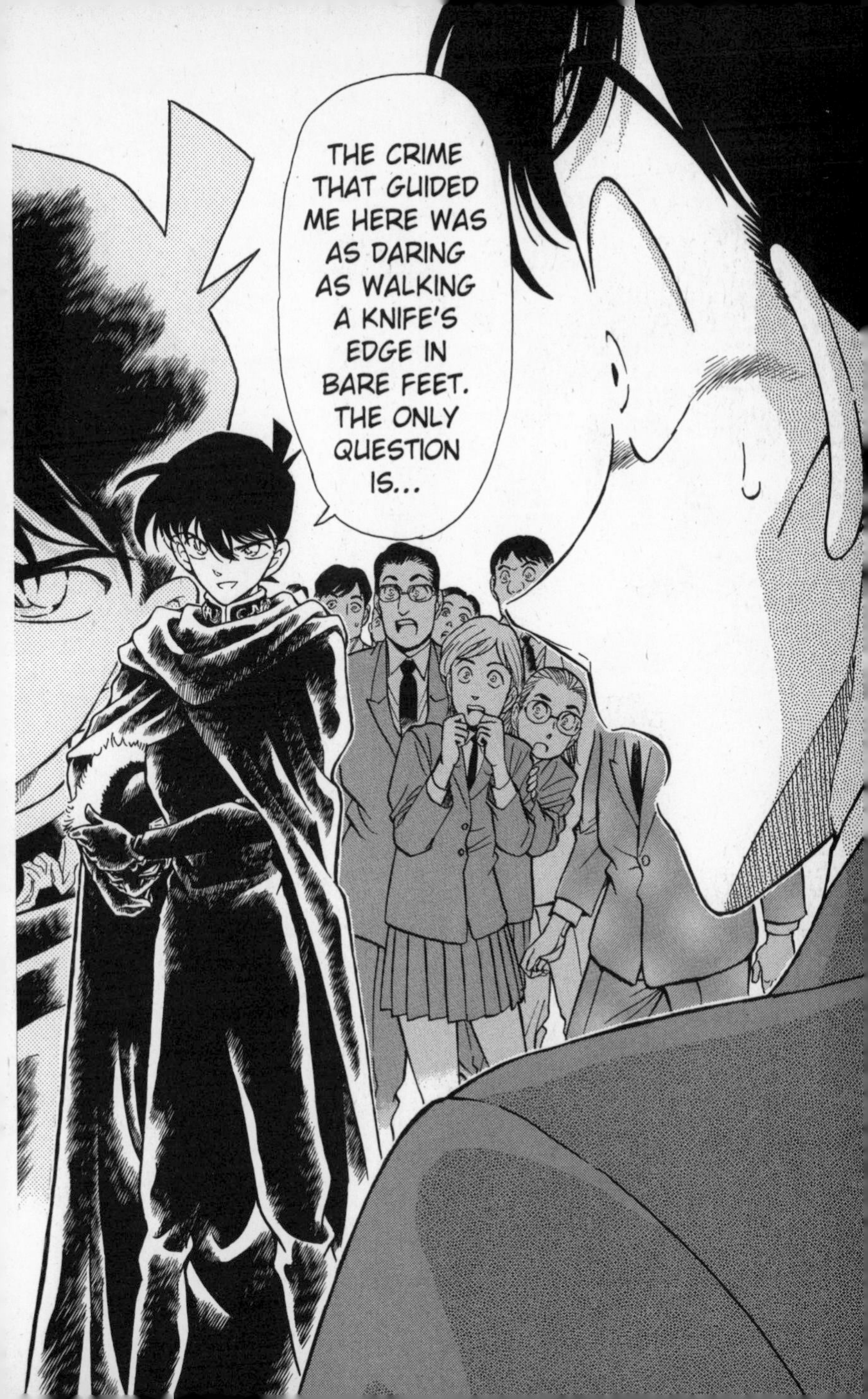
THE CRIME THAT GUIDED ME HERE WAS AS DARING AS WALKING A KNIFE'S EDGE IN BARE FEET. THE ONLY QUESTION IS...

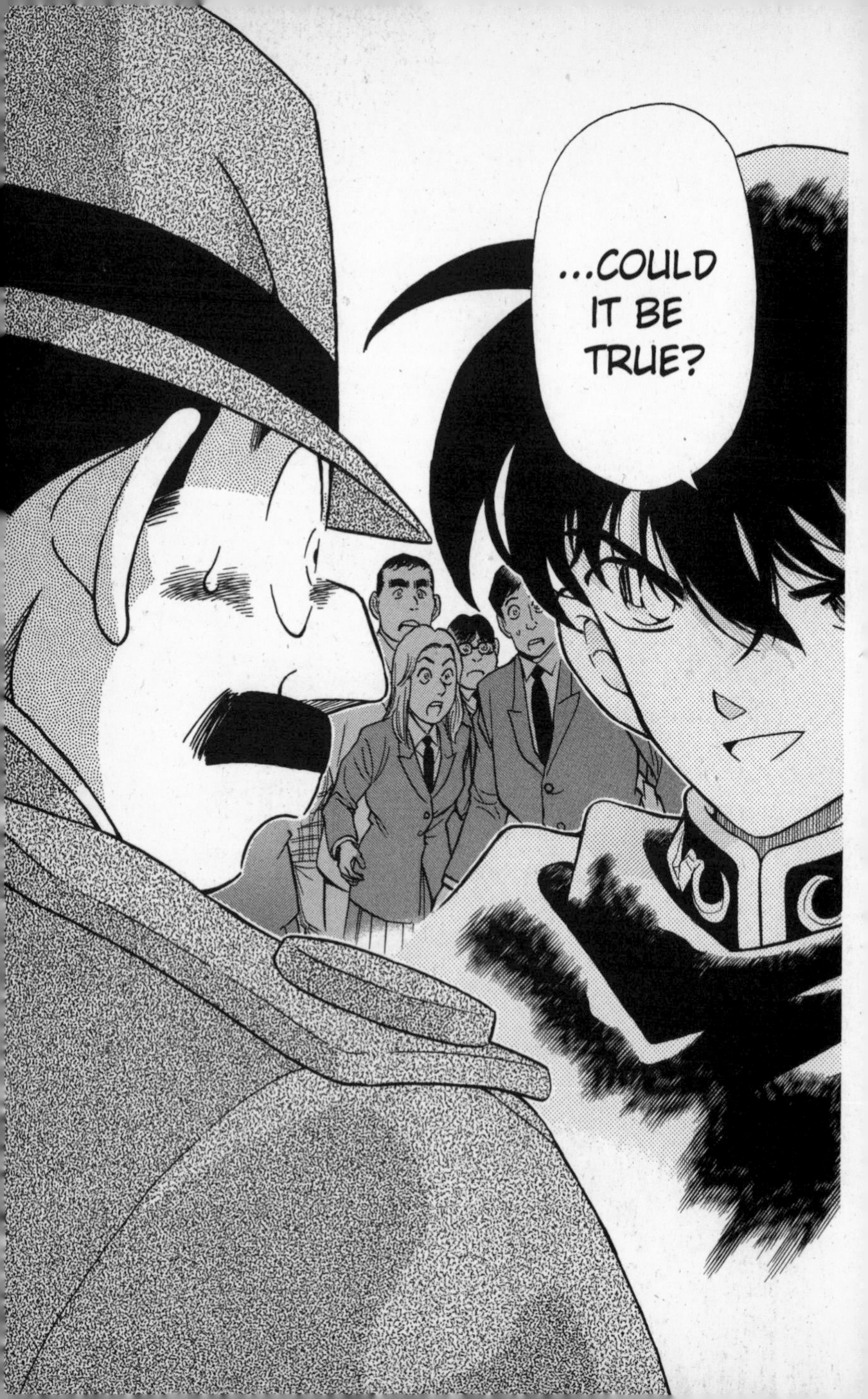
...COULD IT BE TRUE?

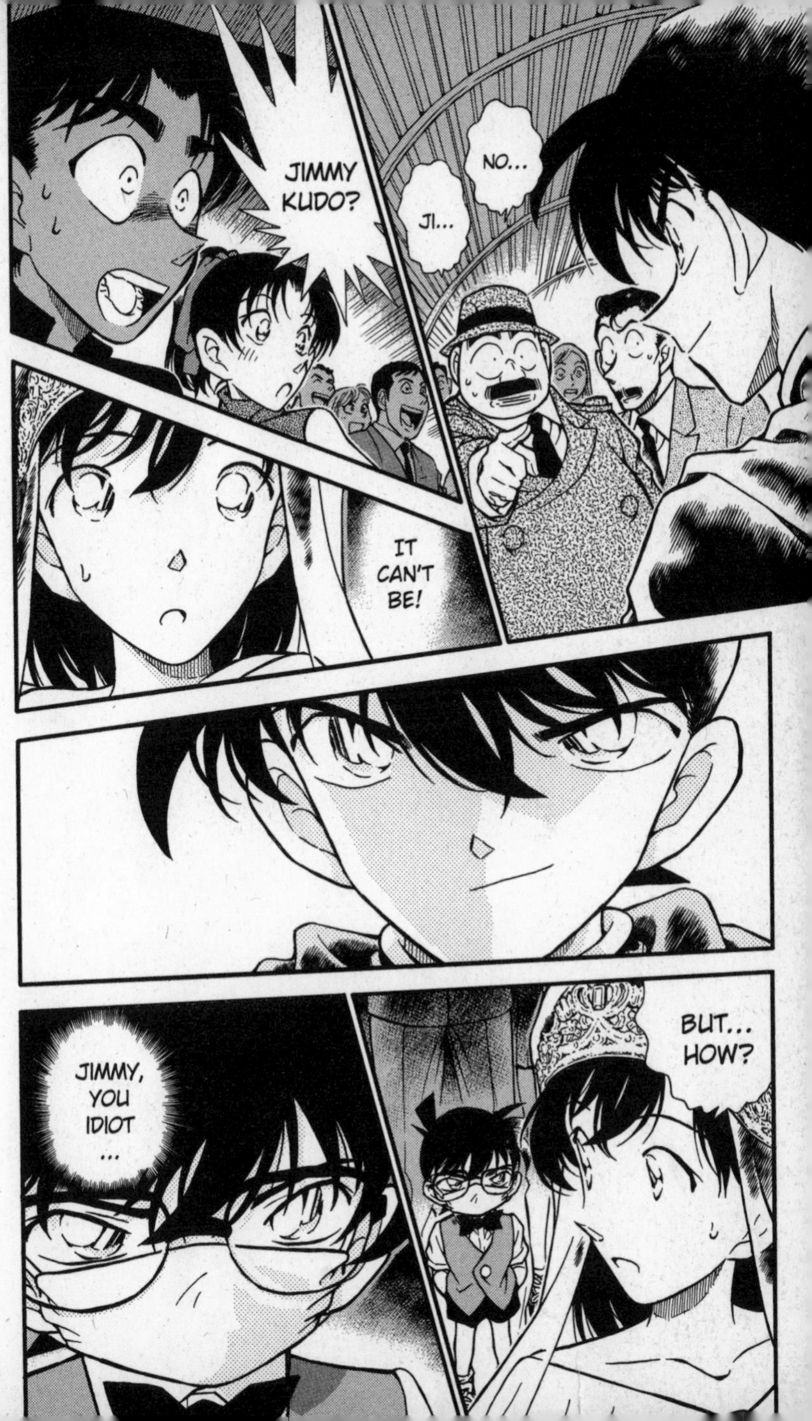
NO...
JI...
JIMMY KUDO?
IT CAN'T BE!
BUT... HOW?
JIMMY, YOU IDIOT ...

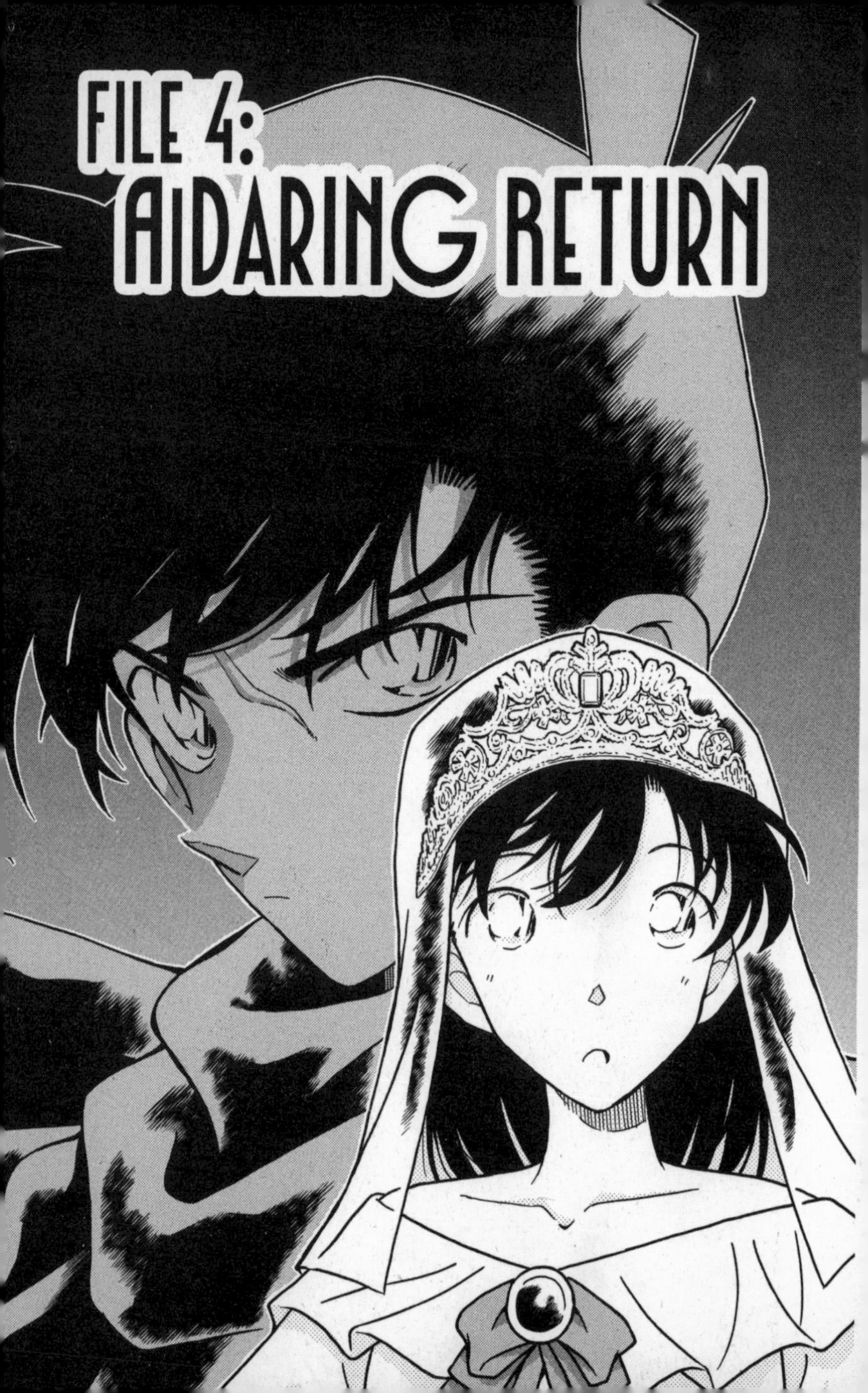
FILE 4:
A DARING RETURN

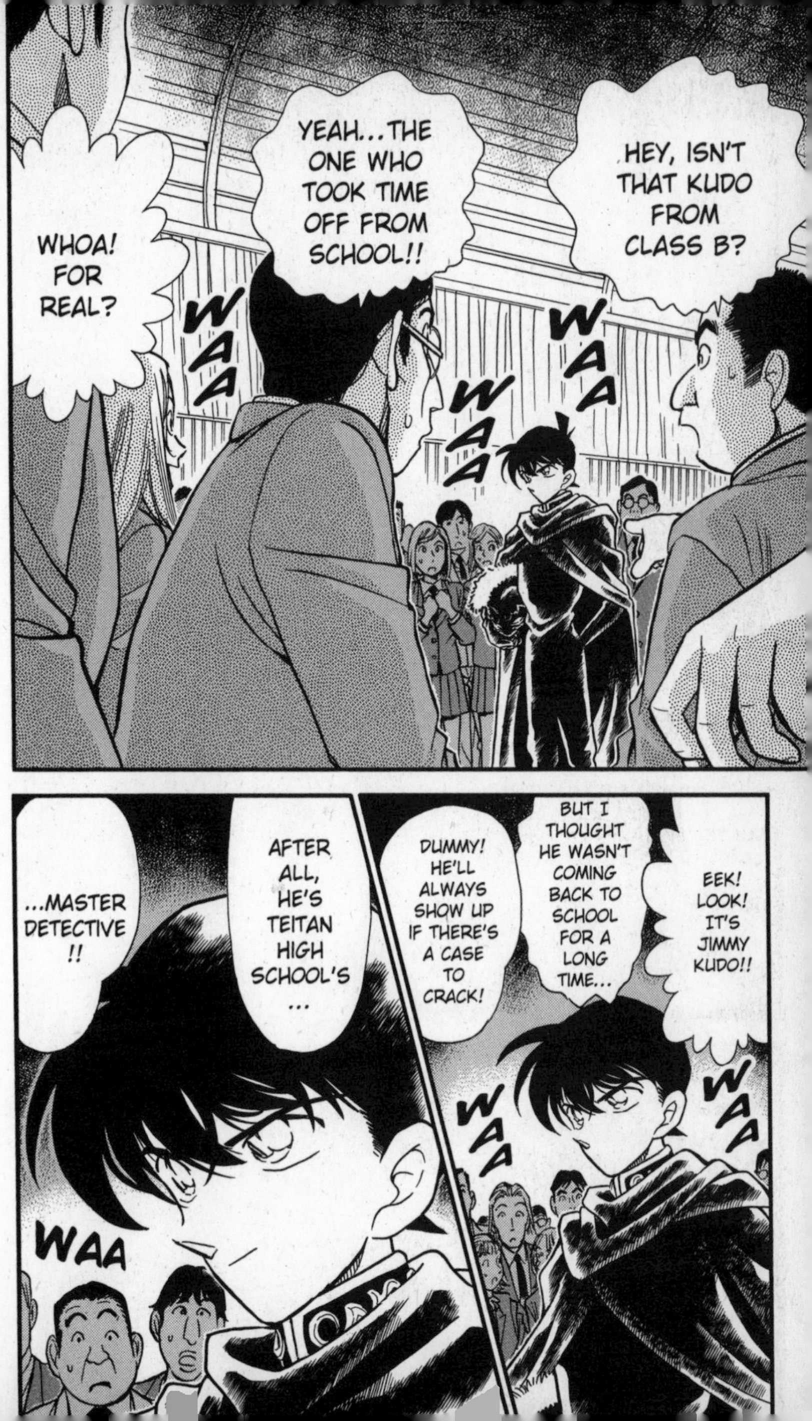
HEY, ISN'T THAT KUDO FROM CLASS B?
YEAH...THE ONE WHO TOOK TIME OFF FROM SCHOOL!!
WHOA! FOR REAL?
WAAA
WAAA
WAAA
EEK! LOOK! IT'S JIMMY KUDO!!
BUT I THOUGHT HE WASN'T COMING BACK TO SCHOOL FOR A LONG TIME...
DUMMY! HE'LL ALWAYS SHOW UP IF THERE'S A CASE TO CRACK!
WAA
WAA
AFTER ALL, HE'S TEITAN HIGH SCHOOL'S...
...MASTER DETECTIVE!!
WAA

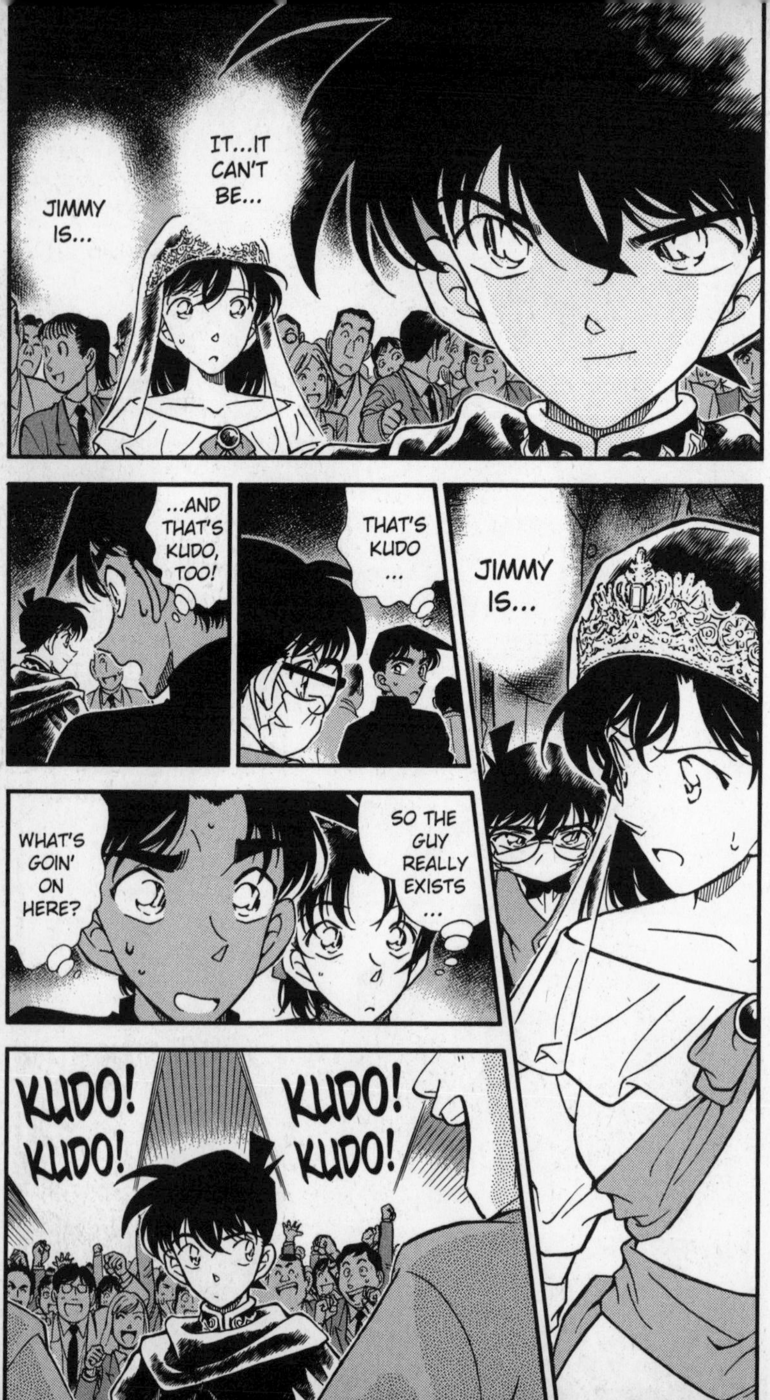
IT...IT CAN'T BE...
JIMMY IS...
JIMMY IS...
THAT'S KUDO ...
...AND THAT'S KUDO, TOO!
SO THE GUY REALLY EXISTS ...
WHAT'S GOIN' ON HERE?
KUDO! KUDO!
KUDO! KUDO!

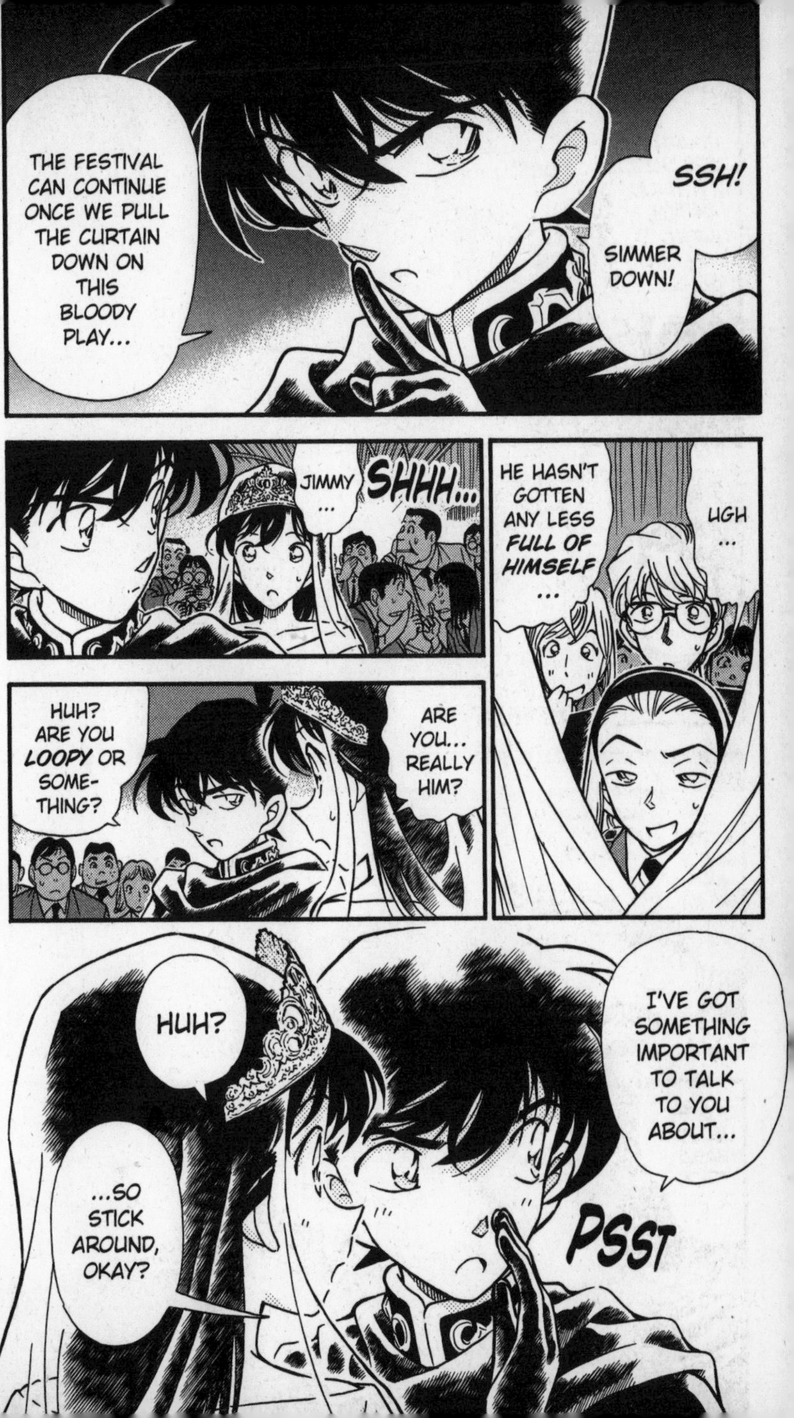
SSH!
SIMMER DOWN!
THE FESTIVAL CAN CONTINUE ONCE WE PULL THE CURTAIN DOWN ON THIS BLOODY PLAY...
UGH ...
HE HASN'T GOTTEN ANY LESS FULL OF HIMSELF ...
SHHH...
JIMMY ...
ARE YOU... REALLY HIM?
HUH? ARE YOU LOOPY OR SOME-THING?
I'VE GOT SOMETHING IMPORTANT TO TALK TO YOU ABOUT...
PSST
HUH?
...SO STICK AROUND, OKAY?

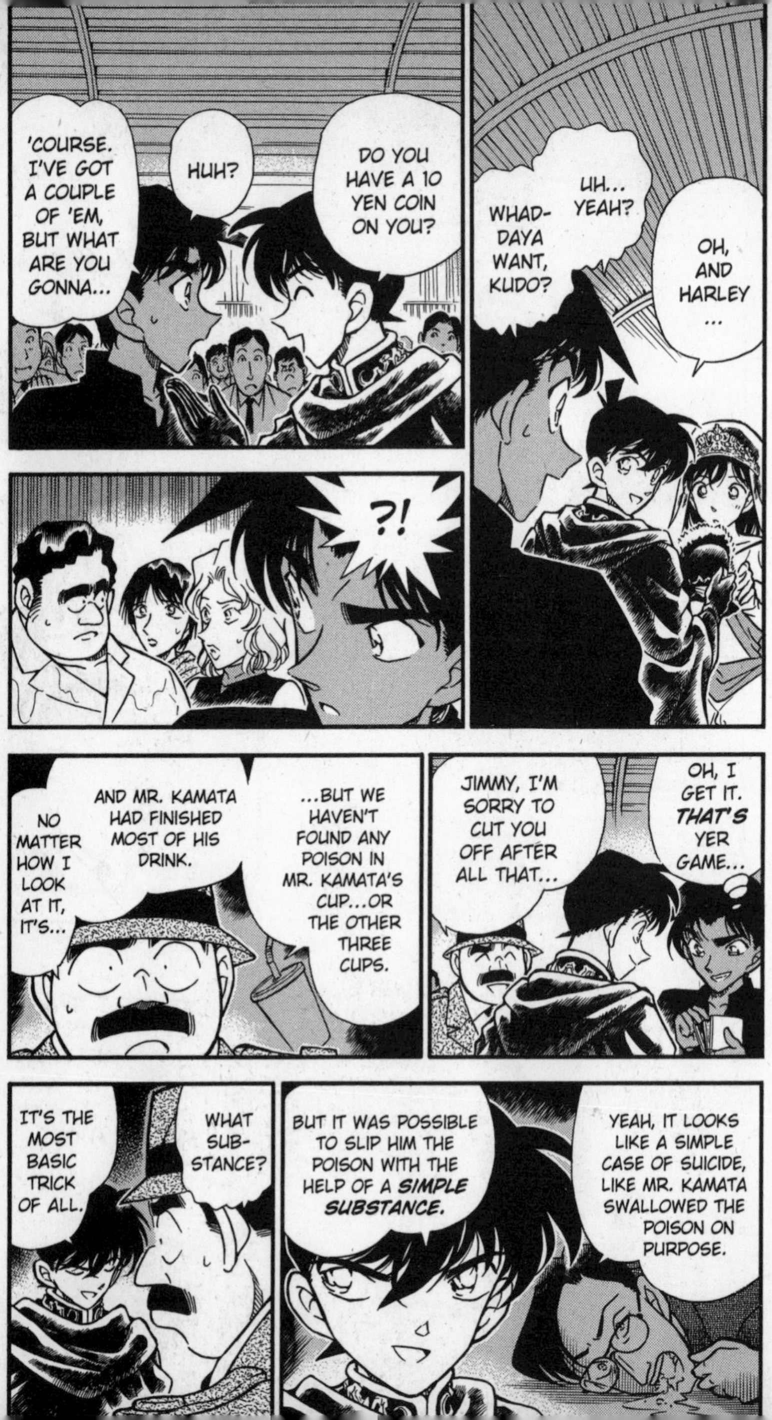
OH, AND HARLEY...
UH... YEAH?
WHAD-DAYA WANT, KUDO?
DO YOU HAVE A 10 YEN COIN ON YOU?
HUH?
'COURSE. I'VE GOT A COUPLE OF 'EM, BUT WHAT ARE YOU GONNA...
?!
OH, I GET IT. *THAT'S* YER GAME...
JIMMY, I'M SORRY TO CUT YOU OFF AFTER ALL THAT...
...BUT WE HAVEN'T FOUND ANY POISON IN MR. KAMATA'S CUP...OR THE OTHER THREE CUPS.
AND MR. KAMATA HAD FINISHED MOST OF HIS DRINK.
NO MATTER HOW I LOOK AT IT, IT'S...
YEAH, IT LOOKS LIKE A SIMPLE CASE OF SUICIDE, LIKE MR. KAMATA SWALLOWED THE POISON ON PURPOSE.
BUT IT WAS POSSIBLE TO SLIP HIM THE POISON WITH THE HELP OF A *SIMPLE SUBSTANCE.*
WHAT SUB-STANCE?
IT'S THE MOST BASIC TRICK OF ALL.

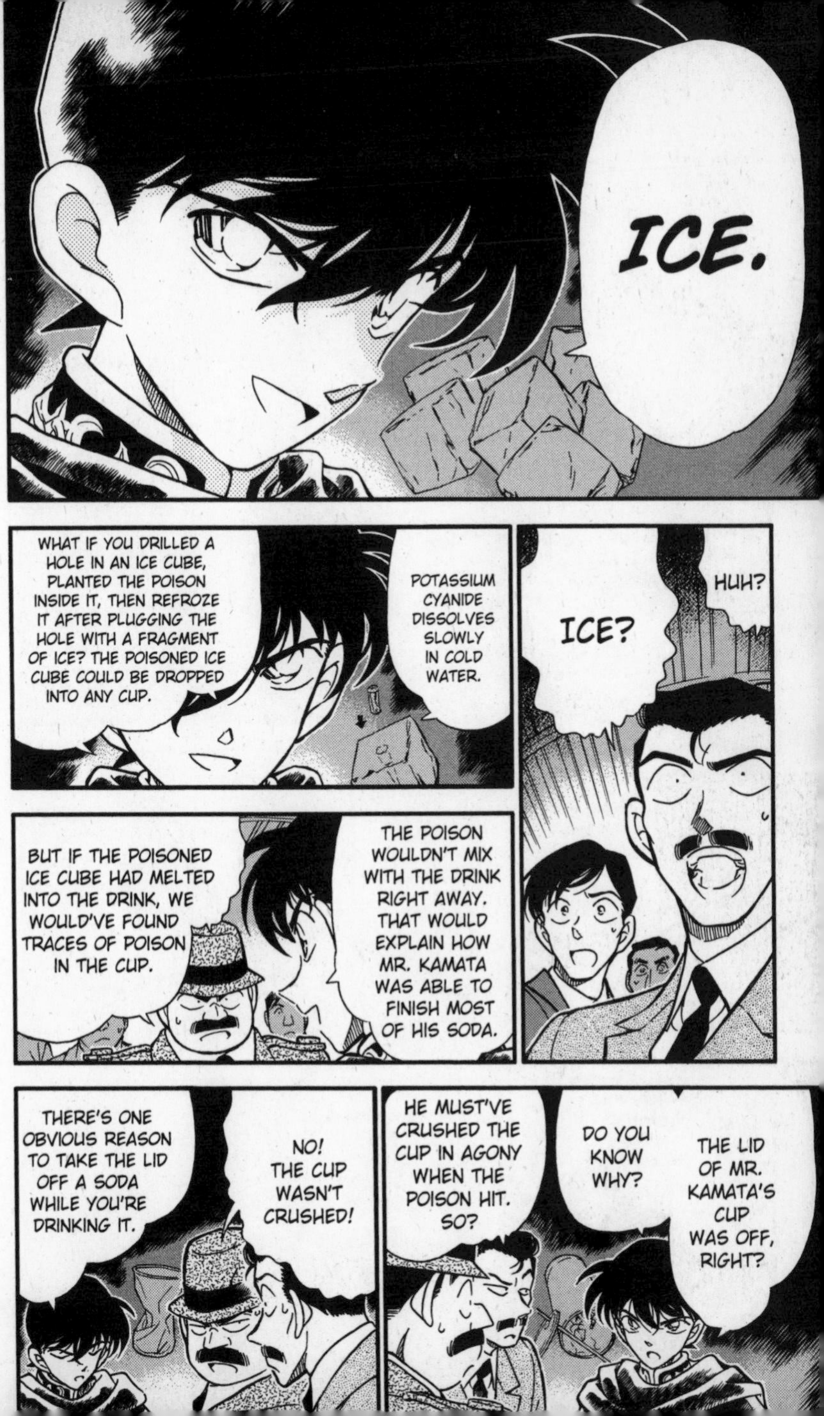
ICE.
HUH?
ICE?
POTASSIUM CYANIDE DISSOLVES SLOWLY IN COLD WATER.
WHAT IF YOU DRILLED A HOLE IN AN ICE CUBE, PLANTED THE POISON INSIDE IT, THEN REFROZE IT AFTER PLUGGING THE HOLE WITH A FRAGMENT OF ICE? THE POISONED ICE CUBE COULD BE DROPPED INTO ANY CUP.
THE POISON WOULDN'T MIX WITH THE DRINK RIGHT AWAY. THAT WOULD EXPLAIN HOW MR. KAMATA WAS ABLE TO FINISH MOST OF HIS SODA.
BUT IF THE POISONED ICE CUBE HAD MELTED INTO THE DRINK, WE WOULD'VE FOUND TRACES OF POISON IN THE CUP.
THE LID OF MR. KAMATA'S CUP WAS OFF, RIGHT?
DO YOU KNOW WHY?
HE MUST'VE CRUSHED THE CUP IN AGONY WHEN THE POISON HIT. SO?
NO! THE CUP WASN'T CRUSHED!
THERE'S ONE OBVIOUS REASON TO TAKE THE LID OFF A SODA WHILE YOU'RE DRINKING IT.

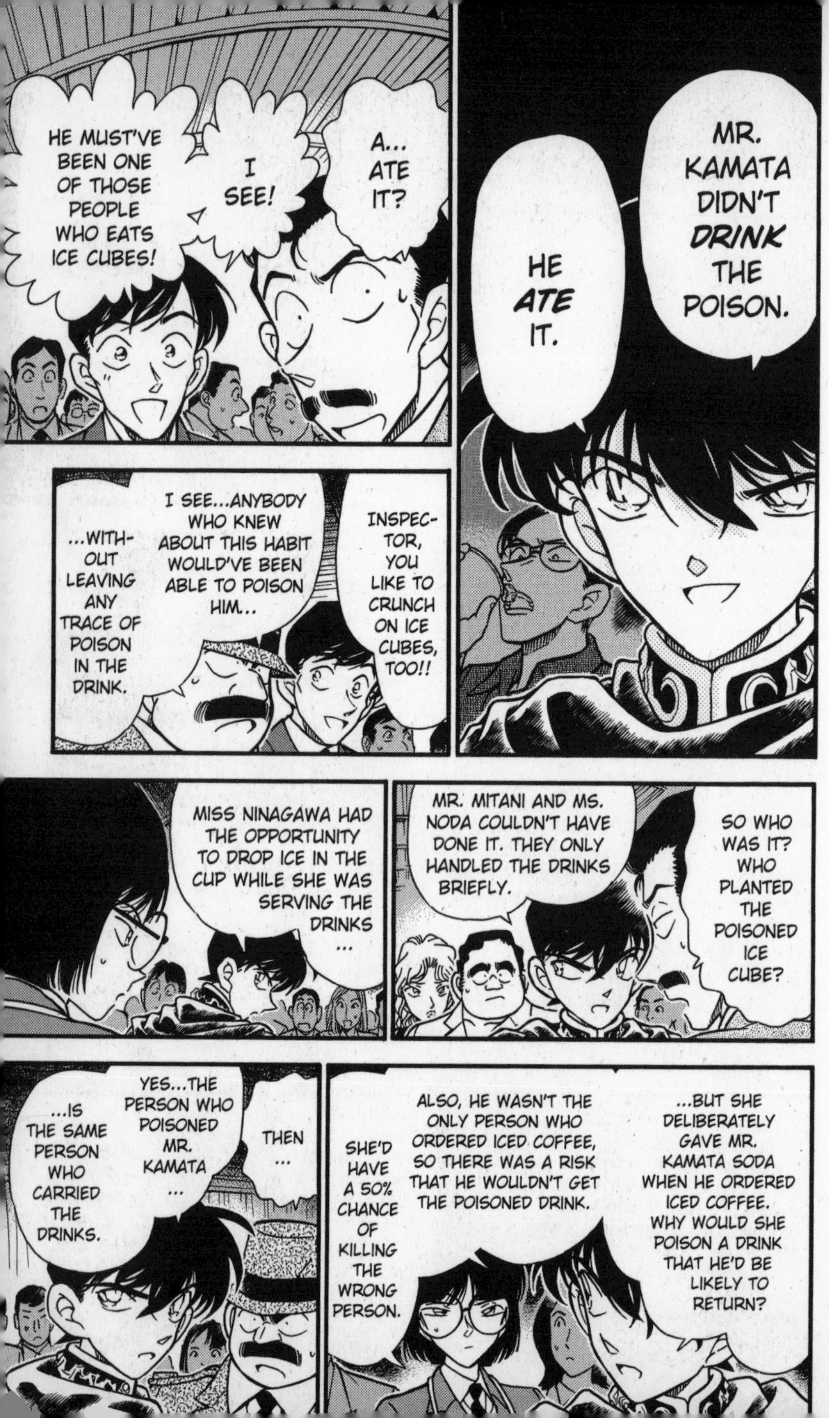
MR. KAMATA DIDN'T *DRINK* THE POISON.
HE *ATE* IT.
A... ATE IT?
I SEE!
HE MUST'VE BEEN ONE OF THOSE PEOPLE WHO EATS ICE CUBES!
INSPECTOR, YOU LIKE TO CRUNCH ON ICE CUBES, TOO!!
I SEE...ANYBODY WHO KNEW ABOUT THIS HABIT WOULD'VE BEEN ABLE TO POISON HIM...
...WITHOUT LEAVING ANY TRACE OF POISON IN THE DRINK.
SO WHO WAS IT? WHO PLANTED THE POISONED ICE CUBE?
MR. MITANI AND MS. NODA COULDN'T HAVE DONE IT. THEY ONLY HANDLED THE DRINKS BRIEFLY.
MISS NINAGAWA HAD THE OPPORTUNITY TO DROP ICE IN THE CUP WHILE SHE WAS SERVING THE DRINKS...
...BUT SHE DELIBERATELY GAVE MR. KAMATA SODA WHEN HE ORDERED ICED COFFEE. WHY WOULD SHE POISON A DRINK THAT HE'D BE LIKELY TO RETURN?
ALSO, HE WASN'T THE ONLY PERSON WHO ORDERED ICED COFFEE, SO THERE WAS A RISK THAT HE WOULDN'T GET THE POISONED DRINK.
SHE'D HAVE A 50% CHANCE OF KILLING THE WRONG PERSON.
THEN...
YES...THE PERSON WHO POISONED MR. KAMATA...
...IS THE SAME PERSON WHO CARRIED THE DRINKS.

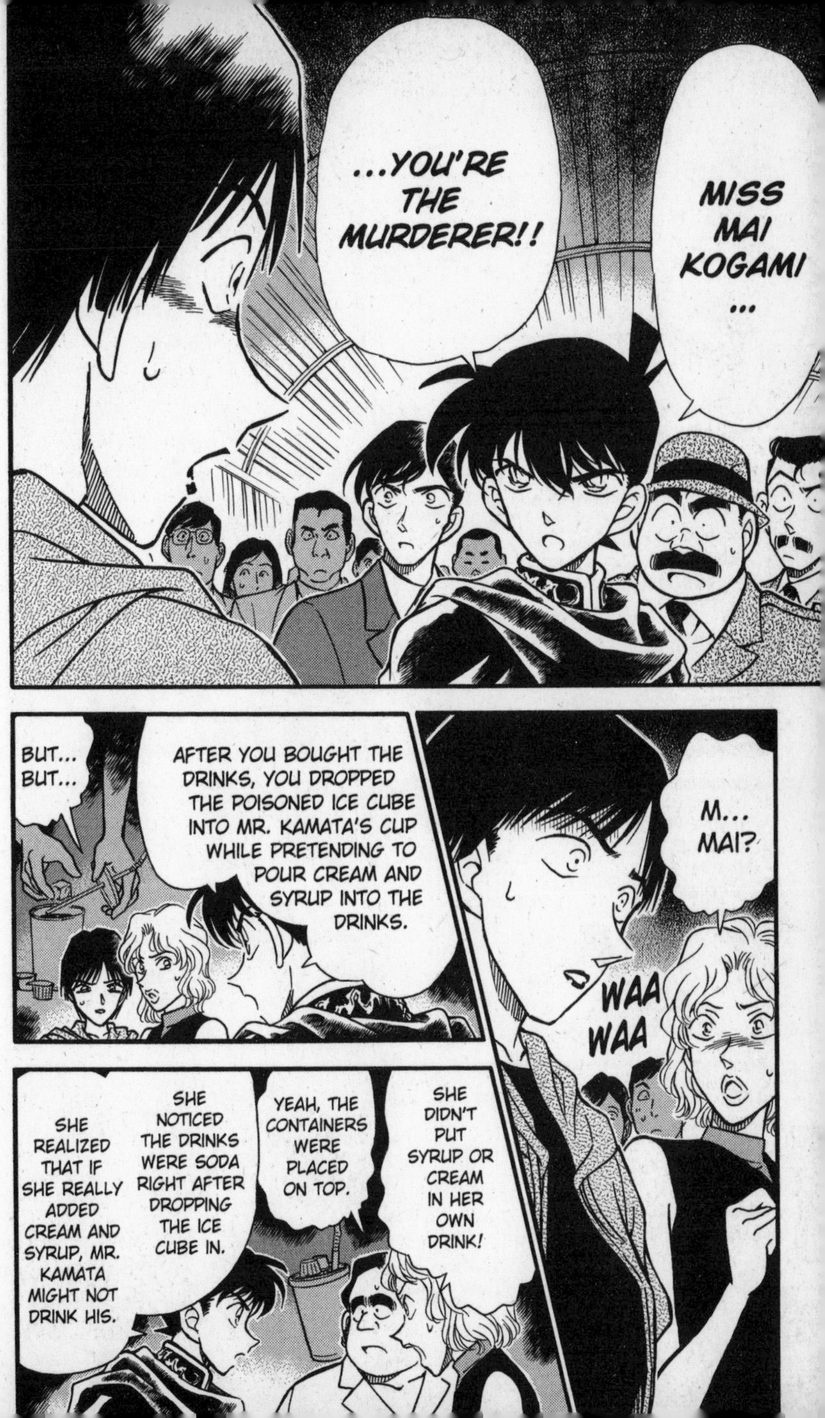
MISS MAI KOGAMI ...
...YOU'RE THE MURDERER!!
M... MAI?
WAA WAA
AFTER YOU BOUGHT THE DRINKS, YOU DROPPED THE POISONED ICE CUBE INTO MR. KAMATA'S CUP WHILE PRETENDING TO POUR CREAM AND SYRUP INTO THE DRINKS.
BUT... BUT...
SHE DIDN'T PUT SYRUP OR CREAM IN HER OWN DRINK!
YEAH, THE CONTAINERS WERE PLACED ON TOP.
SHE NOTICED THE DRINKS WERE SODA RIGHT AFTER DROPPING THE ICE CUBE IN.
SHE REALIZED THAT IF SHE REALLY ADDED CREAM AND SYRUP, MR. KAMATA MIGHT NOT DRINK HIS.

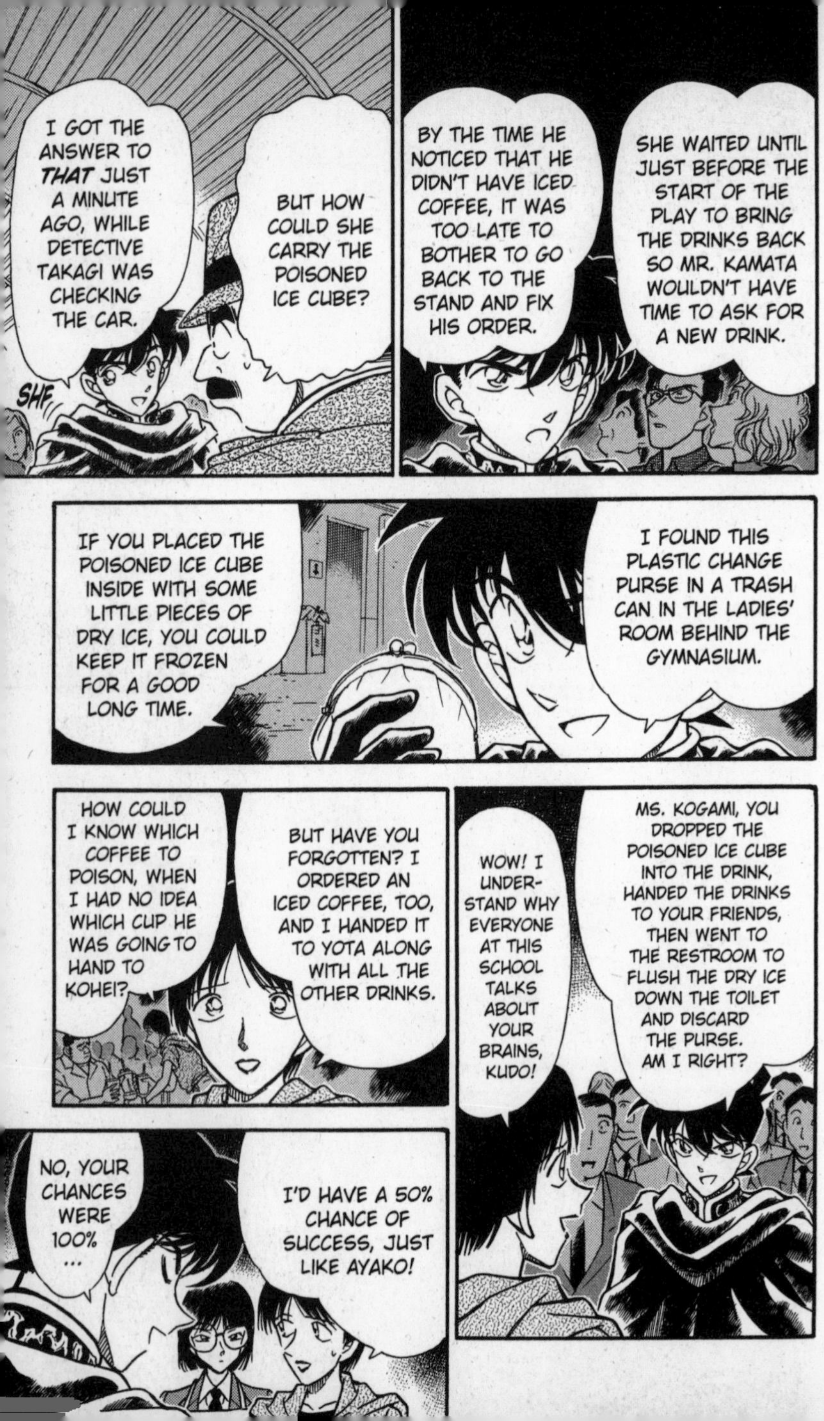
SHE WAITED UNTIL JUST BEFORE THE START OF THE PLAY TO BRING THE DRINKS BACK SO MR. KAMATA WOULDN'T HAVE TIME TO ASK FOR A NEW DRINK.
BY THE TIME HE NOTICED THAT HE DIDN'T HAVE ICED COFFEE, IT WAS TOO LATE TO BOTHER TO GO BACK TO THE STAND AND FIX HIS ORDER.
BUT HOW COULD SHE CARRY THE POISONED ICE CUBE?
I GOT THE ANSWER TO ***THAT*** JUST A MINUTE AGO, WHILE DETECTIVE TAKAGI WAS CHECKING THE CAR.
SHF
I FOUND THIS PLASTIC CHANGE PURSE IN A TRASH CAN IN THE LADIES' ROOM BEHIND THE GYMNASIUM.
IF YOU PLACED THE POISONED ICE CUBE INSIDE WITH SOME LITTLE PIECES OF DRY ICE, YOU COULD KEEP IT FROZEN FOR A GOOD LONG TIME.
MS. KOGAMI, YOU DROPPED THE POISONED ICE CUBE INTO THE DRINK, HANDED THE DRINKS TO YOUR FRIENDS, THEN WENT TO THE RESTROOM TO FLUSH THE DRY ICE DOWN THE TOILET AND DISCARD THE PURSE. AM I RIGHT?
WOW! I UNDER-STAND WHY EVERYONE AT THIS SCHOOL TALKS ABOUT YOUR BRAINS, KUDO!
BUT HAVE YOU FORGOTTEN? I ORDERED AN ICED COFFEE, TOO, AND I HANDED IT TO YOTA ALONG WITH ALL THE OTHER DRINKS.
HOW COULD I KNOW WHICH COFFEE TO POISON, WHEN I HAD NO IDEA WHICH CUP HE WAS GOING TO HAND TO KOHEI?
I'D HAVE A 50% CHANCE OF SUCCESS, JUST LIKE AYAKO!
NO, YOUR CHANCES WERE 100% ...

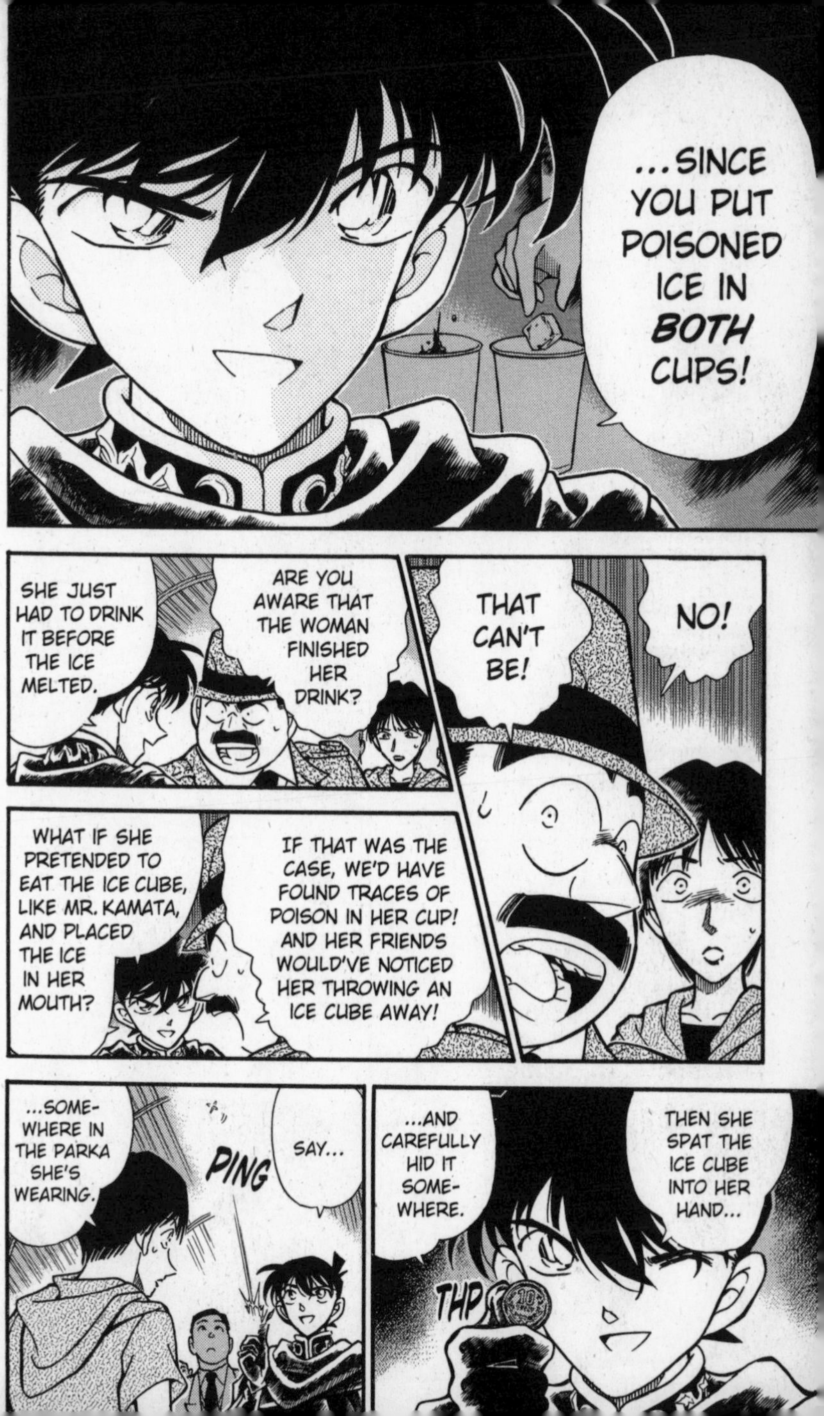
...SINCE YOU PUT POISONED ICE IN *BOTH* CUPS!
NO!
THAT CAN'T BE!
ARE YOU AWARE THAT THE WOMAN FINISHED HER DRINK?
SHE JUST HAD TO DRINK IT BEFORE THE ICE MELTED.
WHAT IF SHE PRETENDED TO EAT THE ICE CUBE, LIKE MR. KAMATA, AND PLACED THE ICE IN HER MOUTH?
IF THAT WAS THE CASE, WE'D HAVE FOUND TRACES OF POISON IN HER CUP! AND HER FRIENDS WOULD'VE NOTICED HER THROWING AN ICE CUBE AWAY!
THEN SHE SPAT THE ICE CUBE INTO HER HAND...
...AND CAREFULLY HID IT SOME-WHERE.
THP
SAY...
PING
...SOME-WHERE IN THE PARKA SHE'S WEARING.

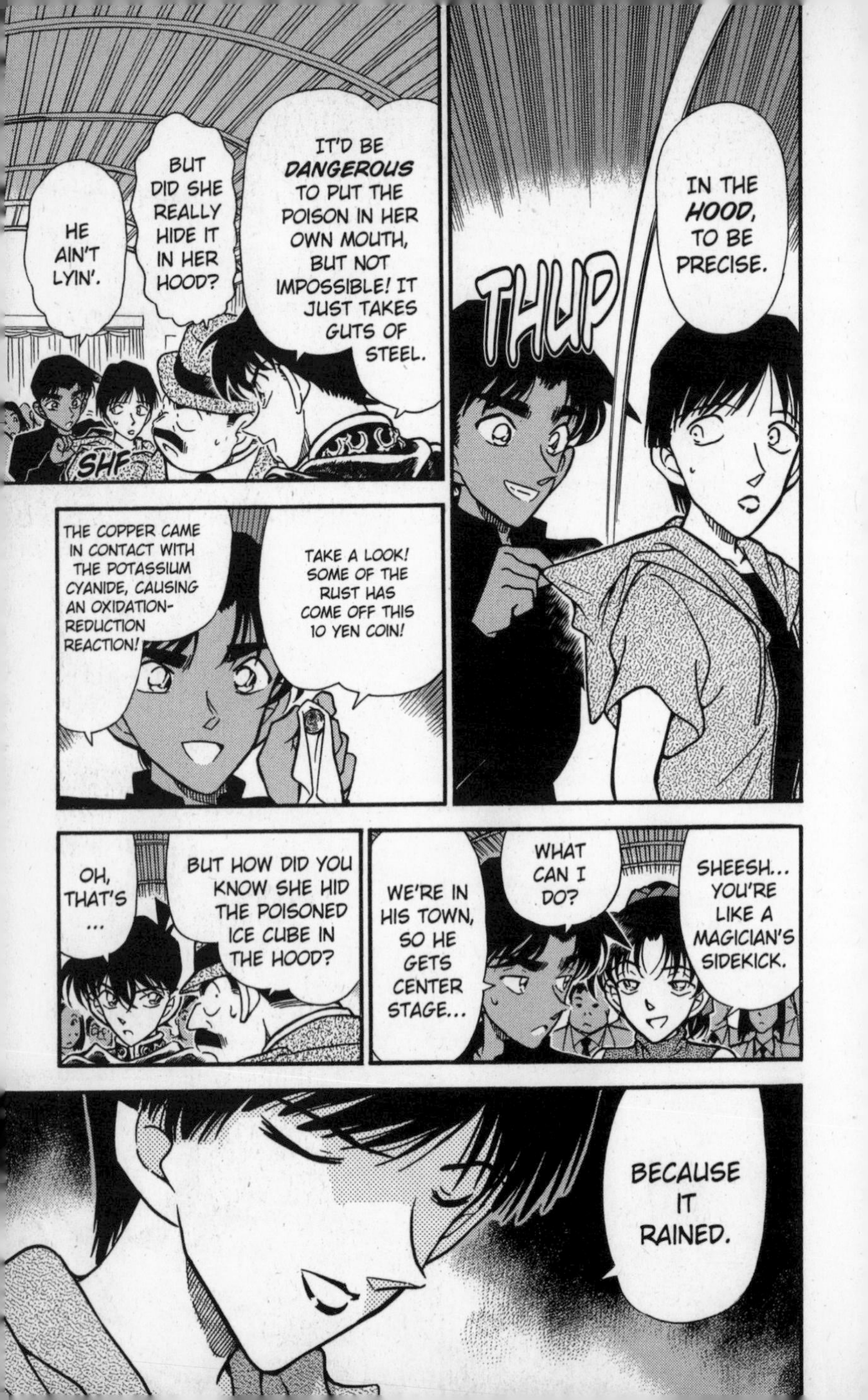
IN THE *HOOD*, TO BE PRECISE.
THUP
IT'D BE *DANGEROUS* TO PUT THE POISON IN HER OWN MOUTH, BUT NOT IMPOSSIBLE! IT JUST TAKES GUTS OF STEEL.
BUT DID SHE REALLY HIDE IT IN HER HOOD?
HE AIN'T LYIN'.
SHF
TAKE A LOOK! SOME OF THE RUST HAS COME OFF THIS 10 YEN COIN!
THE COPPER CAME IN CONTACT WITH THE POTASSIUM CYANIDE, CAUSING AN OXIDATION-REDUCTION REACTION!
SHEESH... YOU'RE LIKE A MAGICIAN'S SIDEKICK.
WHAT CAN I DO?
WE'RE IN HIS TOWN, SO HE GETS CENTER STAGE...
BUT HOW DID YOU KNOW SHE HID THE POISONED ICE CUBE IN THE HOOD?
OH, THAT'S ...
BECAUSE IT RAINED.

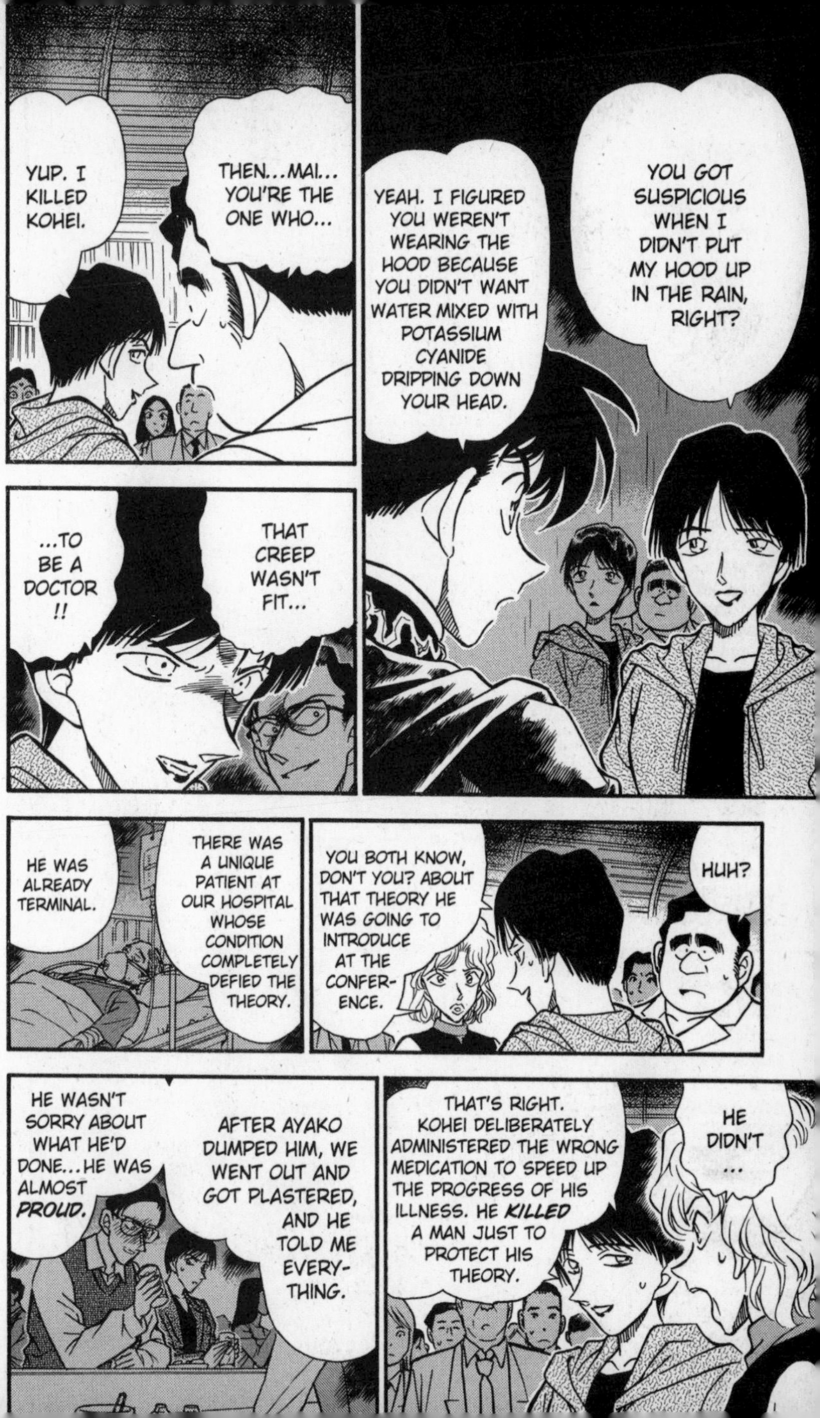
YOU GOT SUSPICIOUS WHEN I DIDN'T PUT MY HOOD UP IN THE RAIN, RIGHT?
YEAH. I FIGURED YOU WEREN'T WEARING THE HOOD BECAUSE YOU DIDN'T WANT WATER MIXED WITH POTASSIUM CYANIDE DRIPPING DOWN YOUR HEAD.
THEN...MAI... YOU'RE THE ONE WHO...
YUP. I KILLED KOHEI.
THAT CREEP WASN'T FIT...
...TO BE A DOCTOR !!
HUH?
YOU BOTH KNOW, DON'T YOU? ABOUT THAT THEORY HE WAS GOING TO INTRODUCE AT THE CONFER-ENCE.
THERE WAS A UNIQUE PATIENT AT OUR HOSPITAL WHOSE CONDITION COMPLETELY DEFIED THE THEORY.
HE WAS ALREADY TERMINAL.
HE DIDN'T ...
THAT'S RIGHT. KOHEI DELIBERATELY ADMINISTERED THE WRONG MEDICATION TO SPEED UP THE PROGRESS OF HIS ILLNESS. HE ***KILLED*** A MAN JUST TO PROTECT HIS THEORY.
AFTER AYAKO DUMPED HIM, WE WENT OUT AND GOT PLASTERED, AND HE TOLD ME EVERY-THING.
HE WASN'T SORRY ABOUT WHAT HE'D DONE...HE WAS ALMOST ***PROUD.***

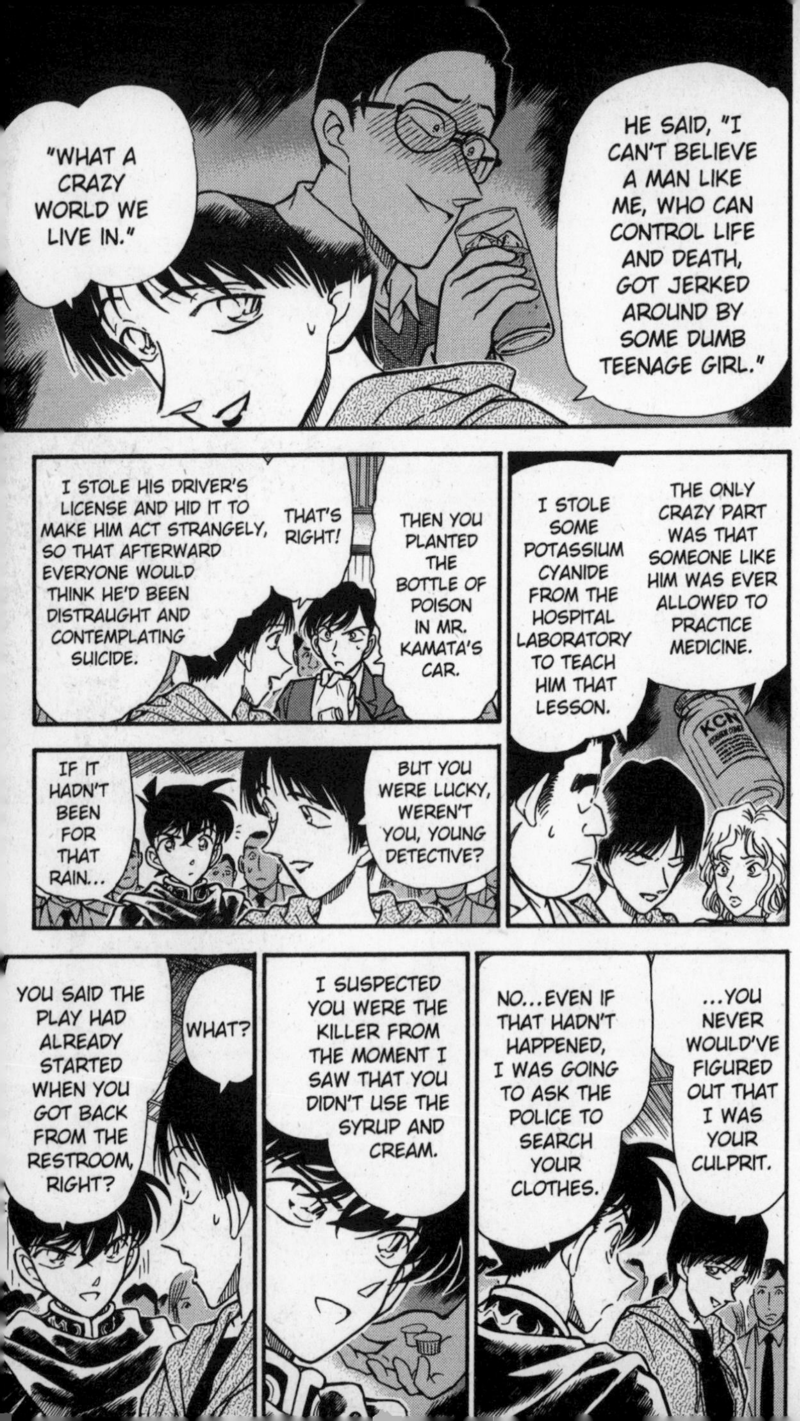
HE SAID, "I CAN'T BELIEVE A MAN LIKE ME, WHO CAN CONTROL LIFE AND DEATH, GOT JERKED AROUND BY SOME DUMB TEENAGE GIRL."
"WHAT A CRAZY WORLD WE LIVE IN."
THE ONLY CRAZY PART WAS THAT SOMEONE LIKE HIM WAS EVER ALLOWED TO PRACTICE MEDICINE.
I STOLE SOME POTASSIUM CYANIDE FROM THE HOSPITAL LABORATORY TO TEACH HIM THAT LESSON.
KCN
THEN YOU PLANTED THE BOTTLE OF POISON IN MR. KAMATA'S CAR.
THAT'S RIGHT!
I STOLE HIS DRIVER'S LICENSE AND HID IT TO MAKE HIM ACT STRANGELY, SO THAT AFTERWARD EVERYONE WOULD THINK HE'D BEEN DISTRAUGHT AND CONTEMPLATING SUICIDE.
BUT YOU WERE LUCKY, WEREN'T YOU, YOUNG DETECTIVE?
IF IT HADN'T BEEN FOR THAT RAIN...
...YOU NEVER WOULD'VE FIGURED OUT THAT I WAS YOUR CULPRIT.
NO...EVEN IF THAT HADN'T HAPPENED, I WAS GOING TO ASK THE POLICE TO SEARCH YOUR CLOTHES.
I SUSPECTED YOU WERE THE KILLER FROM THE MOMENT I SAW THAT YOU DIDN'T USE THE SYRUP AND CREAM.
WHAT?
YOU SAID THE PLAY HAD ALREADY STARTED WHEN YOU GOT BACK FROM THE RESTROOM, RIGHT?

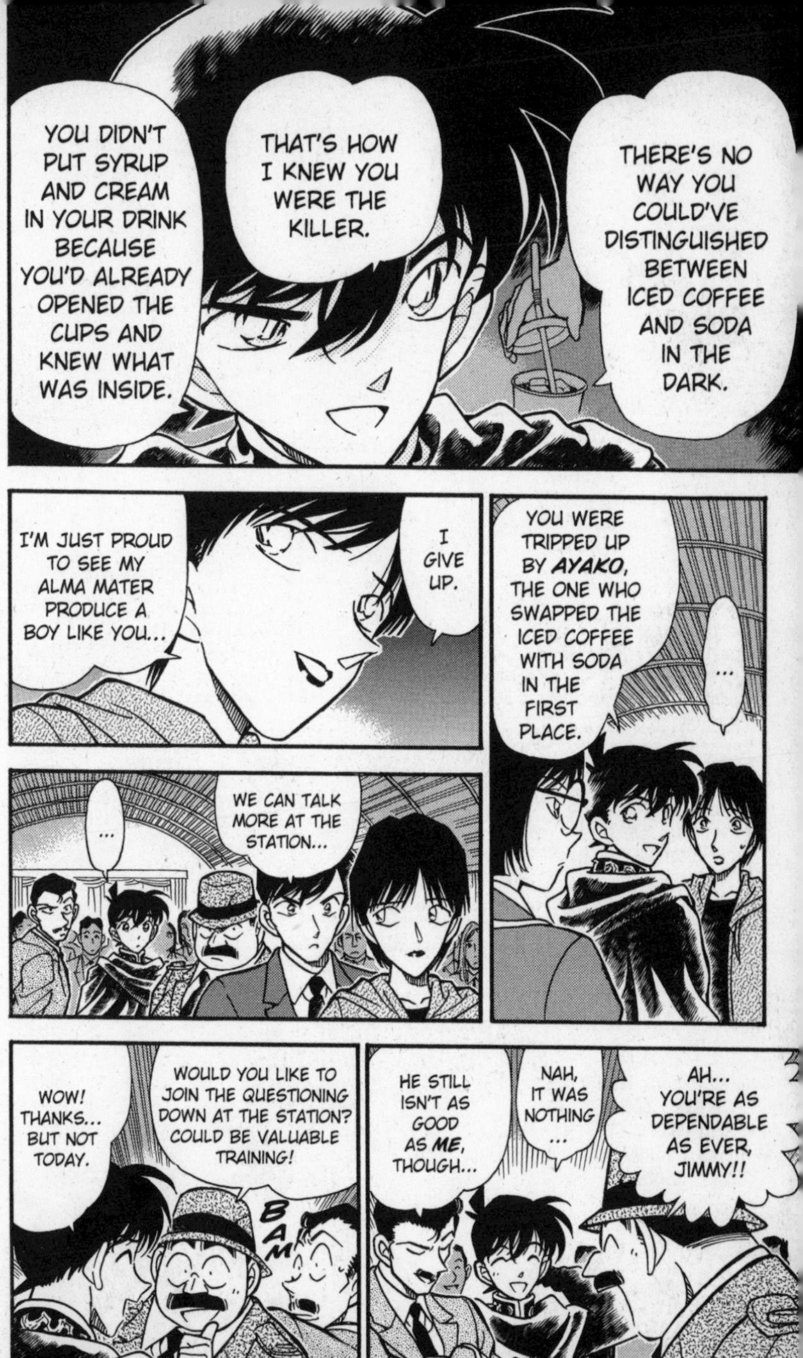
THERE'S NO WAY YOU COULD'VE DISTINGUISHED BETWEEN ICED COFFEE AND SODA IN THE DARK.
THAT'S HOW I KNEW YOU WERE THE KILLER.
YOU DIDN'T PUT SYRUP AND CREAM IN YOUR DRINK BECAUSE YOU'D ALREADY OPENED THE CUPS AND KNEW WHAT WAS INSIDE.
YOU WERE TRIPPED UP BY **AYAKO**, THE ONE WHO SWAPPED THE ICED COFFEE WITH SODA IN THE FIRST PLACE.
...
I GIVE UP.
I'M JUST PROUD TO SEE MY ALMA MATER PRODUCE A BOY LIKE YOU...
WE CAN TALK MORE AT THE STATION...
...
AH... YOU'RE AS DEPENDABLE AS EVER, JIMMY!!
NAH, IT WAS NOTHING...
HE STILL ISN'T AS GOOD AS **ME**, THOUGH...
WOULD YOU LIKE TO JOIN THE QUESTIONING DOWN AT THE STATION? COULD BE VALUABLE TRAINING!
BAM
WOW! THANKS... BUT NOT TODAY.

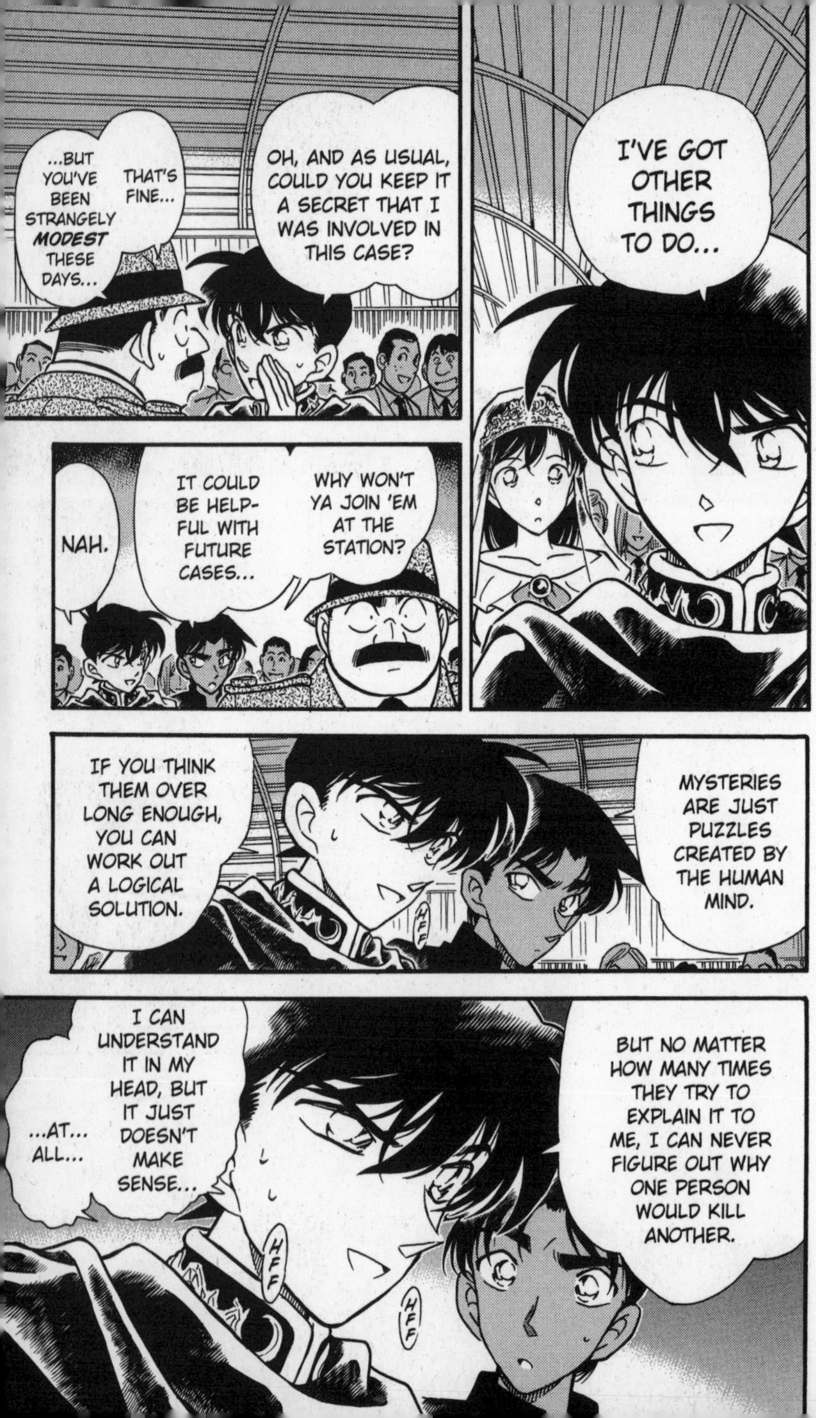
I'VE GOT OTHER THINGS TO DO...
OH, AND AS USUAL, COULD YOU KEEP IT A SECRET THAT I WAS INVOLVED IN THIS CASE?
THAT'S FINE...
...BUT YOU'VE BEEN STRANGELY *MODEST* THESE DAYS...
WHY WON'T YA JOIN 'EM AT THE STATION?
IT COULD BE HELPFUL WITH FUTURE CASES...
NAH.
MYSTERIES ARE JUST PUZZLES CREATED BY THE HUMAN MIND.
HFF
IF YOU THINK THEM OVER LONG ENOUGH, YOU CAN WORK OUT A LOGICAL SOLUTION.
BUT NO MATTER HOW MANY TIMES THEY TRY TO EXPLAIN IT TO ME, I CAN NEVER FIGURE OUT WHY ONE PERSON WOULD KILL ANOTHER.
HFF
HFF
I CAN UNDERSTAND IT IN MY HEAD, BUT IT JUST DOESN'T MAKE SENSE...
...AT... ALL...

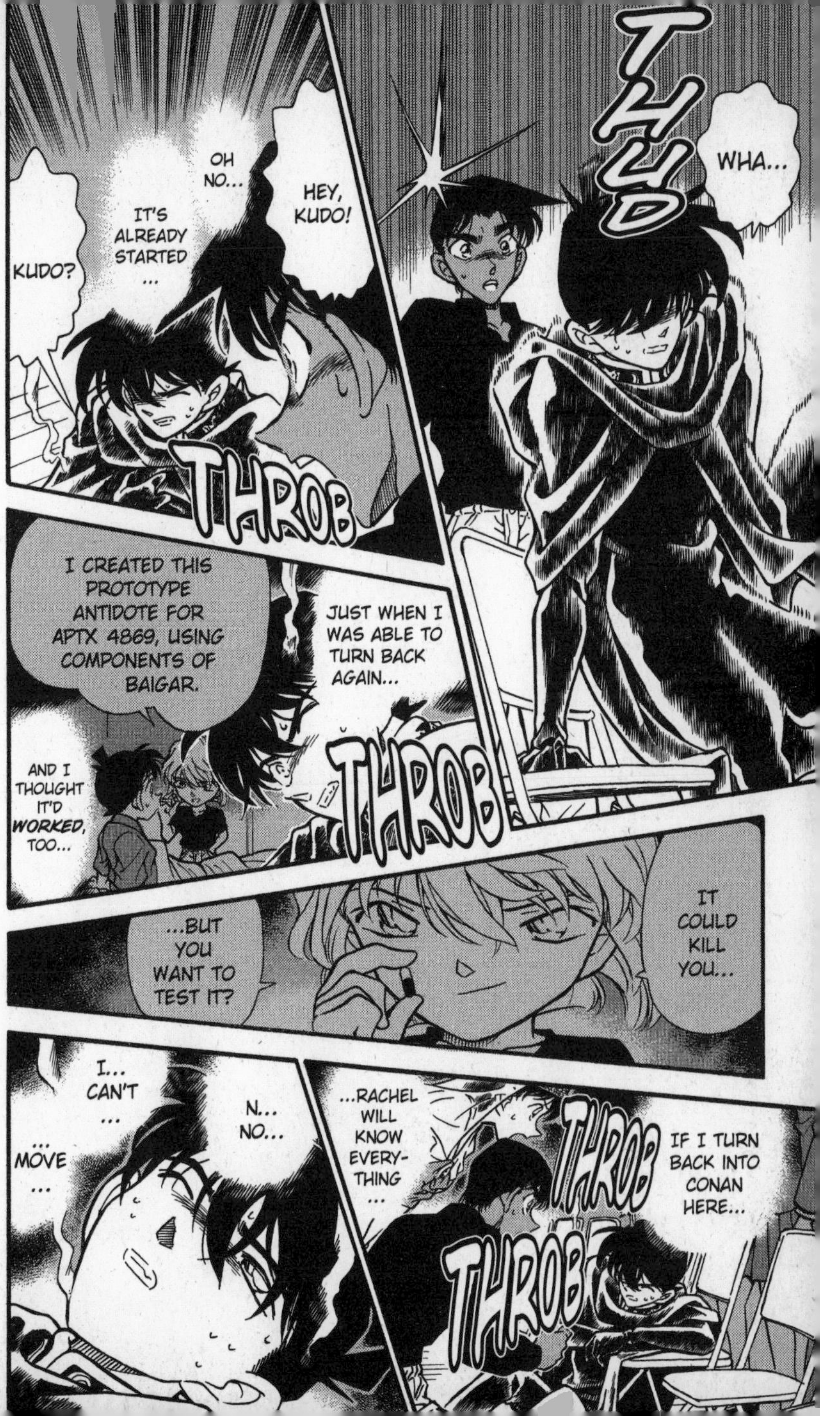
THUD
WHA...
HEY, KUDO!
OH NO...
IT'S ALREADY STARTED ...
KUDO?
THROB
JUST WHEN I WAS ABLE TO TURN BACK AGAIN...
I CREATED THIS PROTOTYPE ANTIDOTE FOR APTX 4869, USING COMPONENTS OF BAIGAR.
THROB
AND I THOUGHT IT'D *WORKED*, TOO...
IT COULD KILL YOU...
...BUT YOU WANT TO TEST IT?
IF I TURN BACK INTO CONAN HERE...
THROB
...RACHEL WILL KNOW EVERYTHING ...
THROB
N... NO...
I... CAN'T ...
... MOVE ...

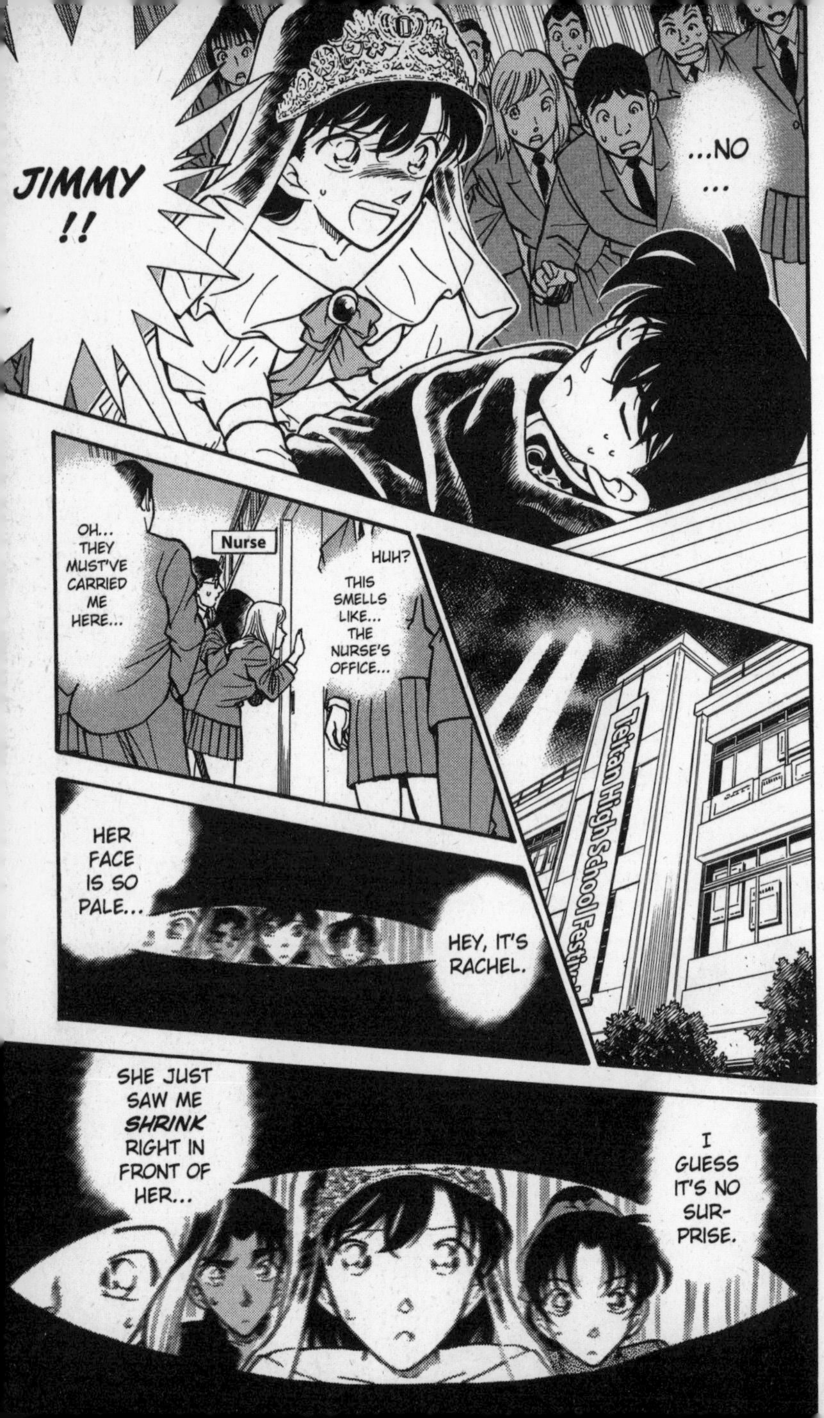

...NO ...
JIMMY !!
Teitan High School Festi
HUH? THIS SMELLS LIKE... THE NURSE'S OFFICE...
Nurse
OH... THEY MUST'VE CARRIED ME HERE...
HEY, IT'S RACHEL.
HER FACE IS SO PALE...
I GUESS IT'S NO SUR-PRISE.
SHE JUST SAW ME *SHRINK* RIGHT IN FRONT OF HER...

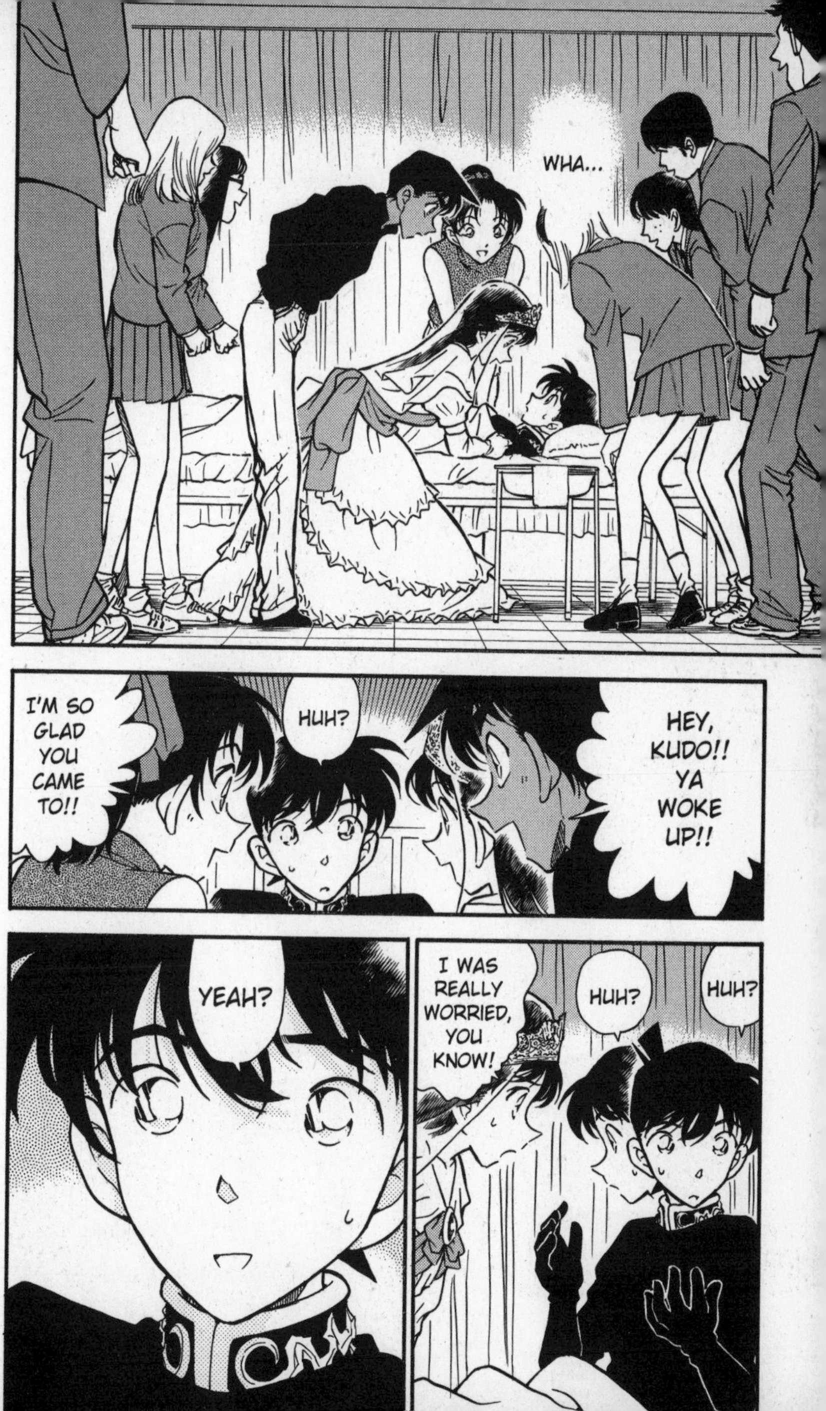
WHA...
HEY, KUDO!! YA WOKE UP!!
HUH?
I'M SO GLAD YOU CAME TO!!
HUH?
HUH?
I WAS REALLY WORRIED, YOU KNOW!
YEAH?

FILE 5: A QUICK BREAK

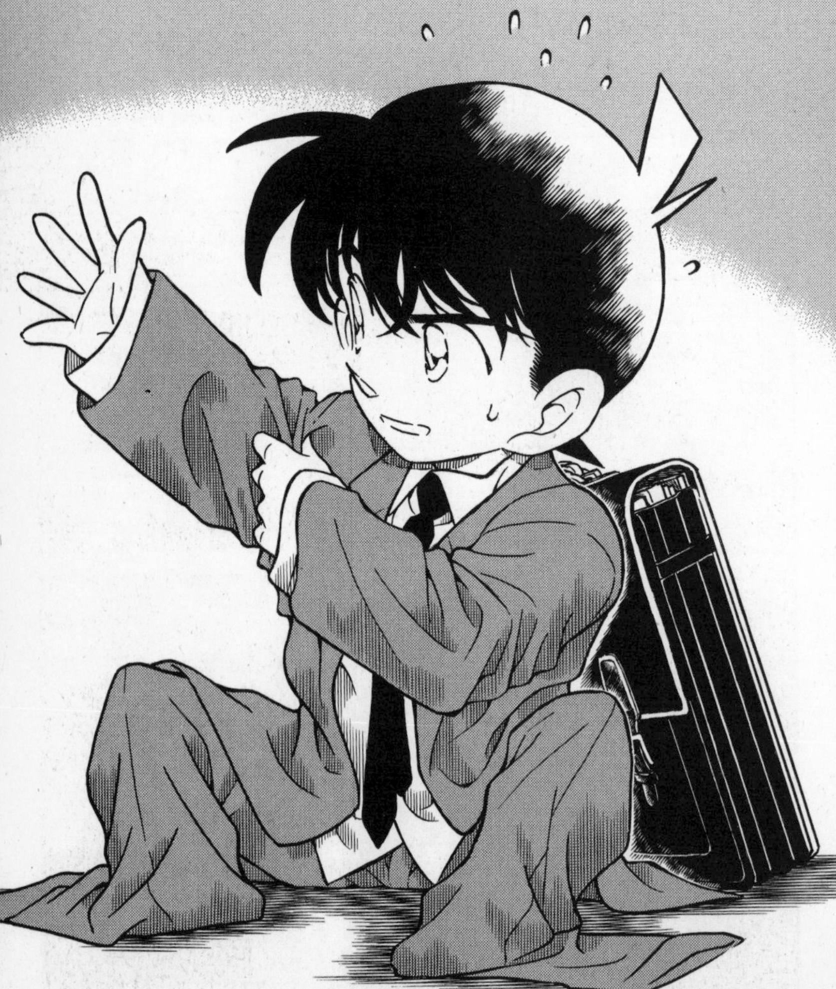

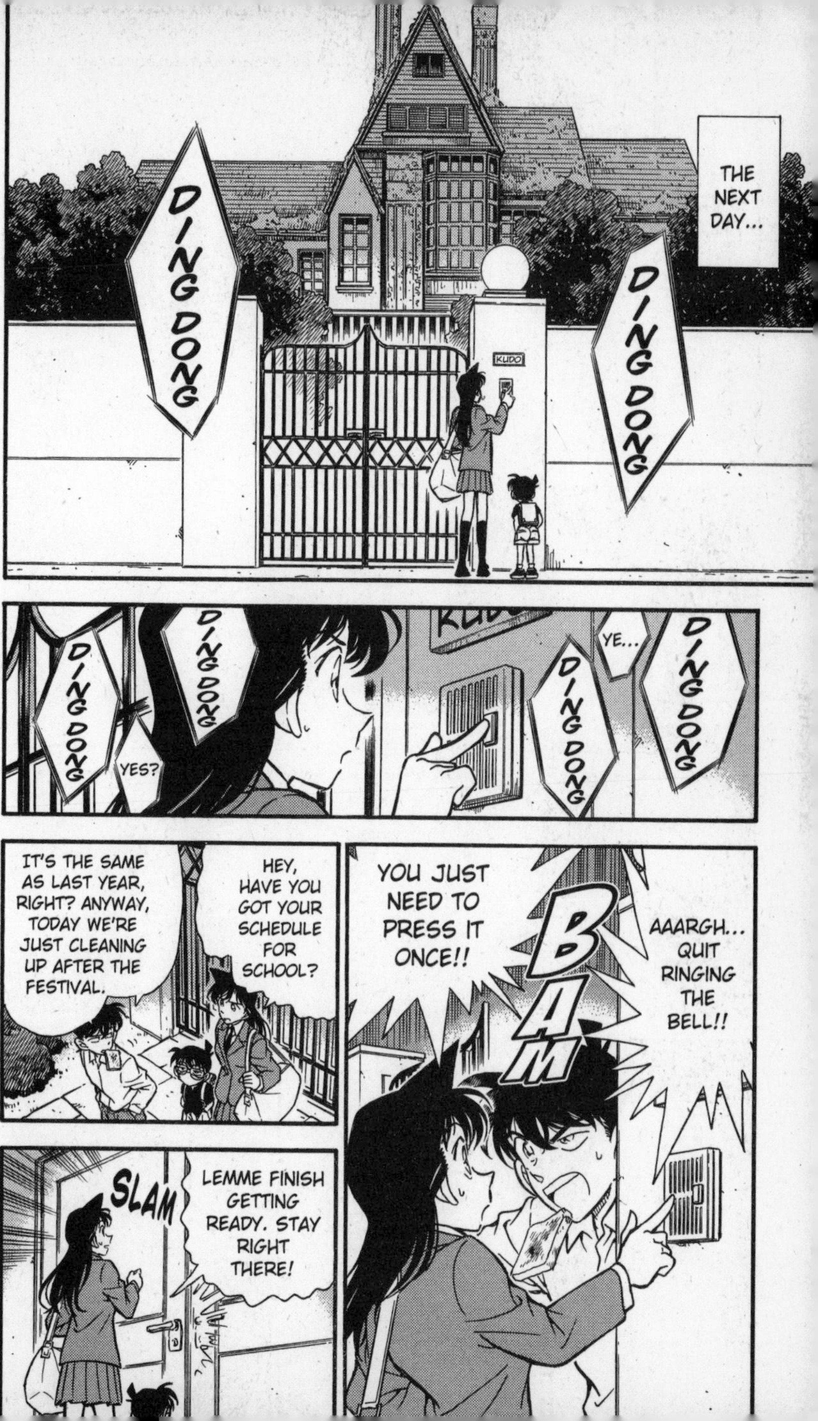

THE NEXT DAY...
DING DONG
DING DONG
KUDO
DING DONG
YE...
DING DONG
DING DONG
DING DONG
YES?
AAARGH... QUIT RINGING THE BELL!!
BAM
YOU JUST NEED TO PRESS IT ONCE!!
HEY, HAVE YOU GOT YOUR SCHEDULE FOR SCHOOL?
IT'S THE SAME AS LAST YEAR, RIGHT? ANYWAY, TODAY WE'RE JUST CLEANING UP AFTER THE FESTIVAL.
LEMME FINISH GETTING READY. STAY RIGHT THERE!
SLAM

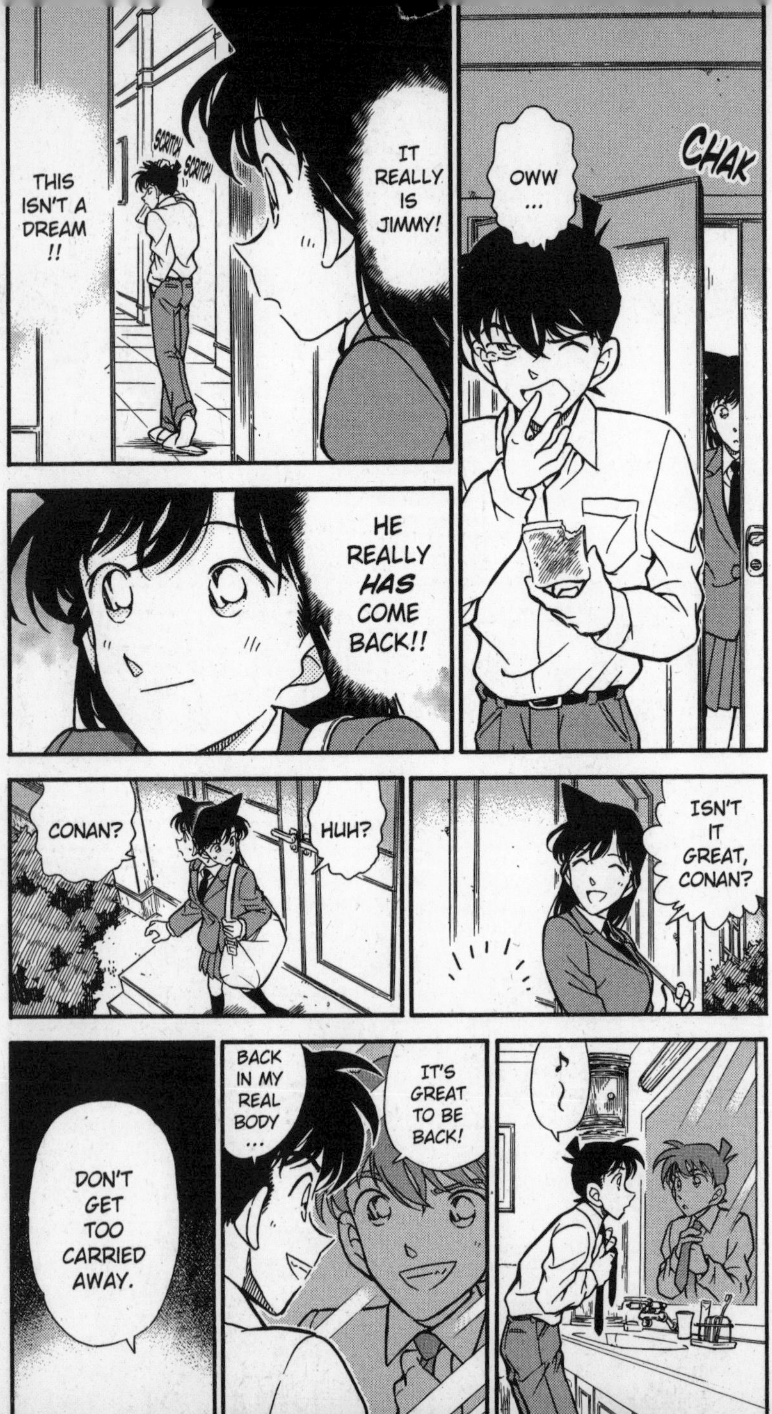
CHAK
OWW ...
IT REALLY IS JIMMY!
SCRITCH SCRITCH
THIS ISN'T A DREAM !!
HE REALLY HAS COME BACK!!
ISN'T IT GREAT, CONAN?
HUH?
CONAN?
♪ ~
IT'S GREAT TO BE BACK!
BACK IN MY REAL BODY ...
DON'T GET TOO CARRIED AWAY.

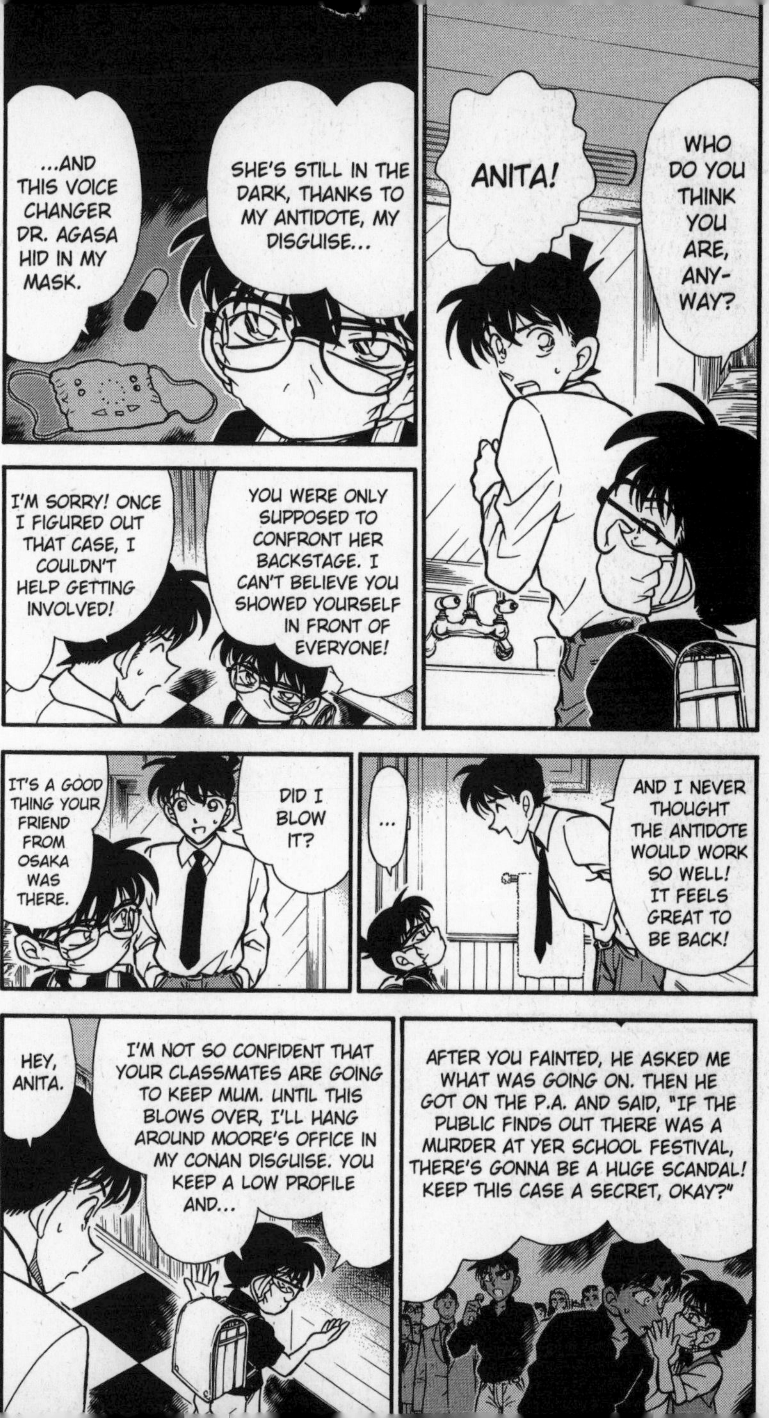

WHO DO YOU THINK YOU ARE, ANY-WAY?
ANITA!
SHE'S STILL IN THE DARK, THANKS TO MY ANTIDOTE, MY DISGUISE...
...AND THIS VOICE CHANGER DR. AGASA HID IN MY MASK.
YOU WERE ONLY SUPPOSED TO CONFRONT HER BACKSTAGE. I CAN'T BELIEVE YOU SHOWED YOURSELF IN FRONT OF EVERYONE!
I'M SORRY! ONCE I FIGURED OUT THAT CASE, I COULDN'T HELP GETTING INVOLVED!
AND I NEVER THOUGHT THE ANTIDOTE WOULD WORK SO WELL! IT FEELS GREAT TO BE BACK!
...
DID I BLOW IT?
IT'S A GOOD THING YOUR FRIEND FROM OSAKA WAS THERE.
AFTER YOU FAINTED, HE ASKED ME WHAT WAS GOING ON. THEN HE GOT ON THE P.A. AND SAID, "IF THE PUBLIC FINDS OUT THERE WAS A MURDER AT YER SCHOOL FESTIVAL, THERE'S GONNA BE A HUGE SCANDAL! KEEP THIS CASE A SECRET, OKAY?"
I'M NOT SO CONFIDENT THAT YOUR CLASSMATES ARE GOING TO KEEP MUM. UNTIL THIS BLOWS OVER, I'LL HANG AROUND MOORE'S OFFICE IN MY CONAN DISGUISE. YOU KEEP A LOW PROFILE AND...
HEY, ANITA.

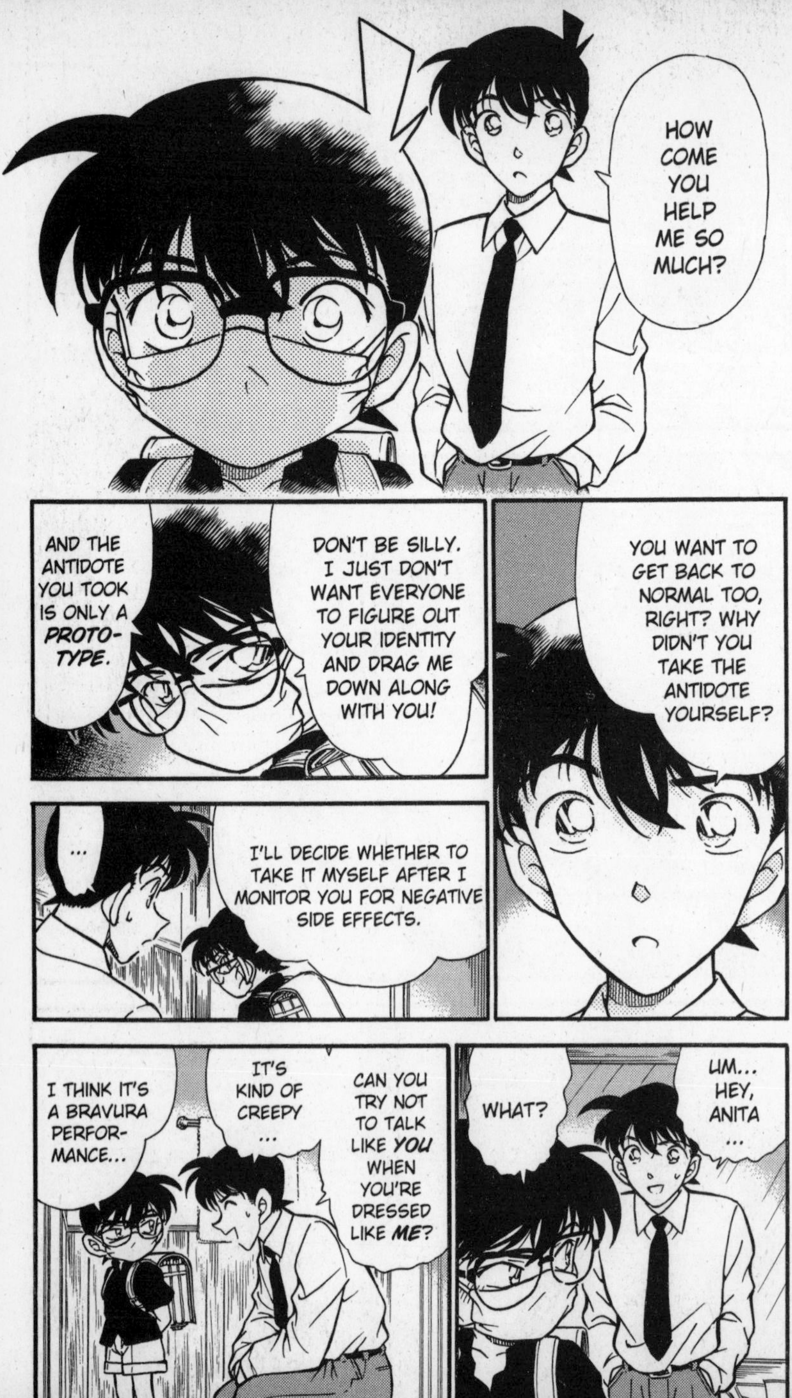
HOW COME YOU HELP ME SO MUCH?
YOU WANT TO GET BACK TO NORMAL TOO, RIGHT? WHY DIDN'T YOU TAKE THE ANTIDOTE YOURSELF?
DON'T BE SILLY. I JUST DON'T WANT EVERYONE TO FIGURE OUT YOUR IDENTITY AND DRAG ME DOWN ALONG WITH YOU!
AND THE ANTIDOTE YOU TOOK IS ONLY A *PROTOTYPE*.
I'LL DECIDE WHETHER TO TAKE IT MYSELF AFTER I MONITOR YOU FOR NEGATIVE SIDE EFFECTS.
...
UM... HEY, ANITA...
WHAT?
CAN YOU TRY NOT TO TALK LIKE *YOU* WHEN YOU'RE DRESSED LIKE *ME*?
IT'S KIND OF CREEPY...
I THINK IT'S A BRAVURA PERFORMANCE...

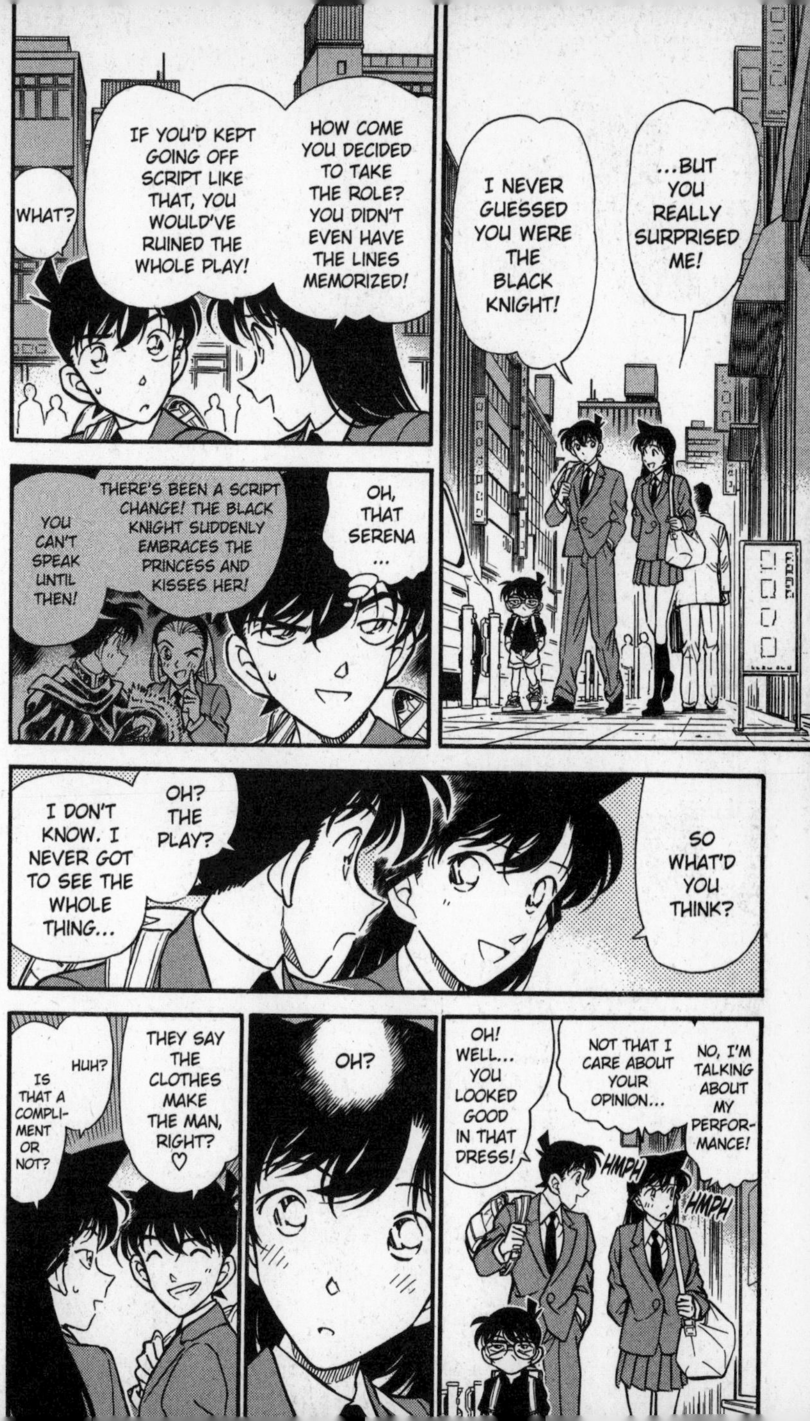
...BUT YOU REALLY SURPRISED ME!
I NEVER GUESSED YOU WERE THE BLACK KNIGHT!
HOW COME YOU DECIDED TO TAKE THE ROLE? YOU DIDN'T EVEN HAVE THE LINES MEMORIZED!
IF YOU'D KEPT GOING OFF SCRIPT LIKE THAT, YOU WOULD'VE RUINED THE WHOLE PLAY!
WHAT?
OH, THAT SERENA ...
THERE'S BEEN A SCRIPT CHANGE! THE BLACK KNIGHT SUDDENLY EMBRACES THE PRINCESS AND KISSES HER!
YOU CAN'T SPEAK UNTIL THEN!
SO WHAT'D YOU THINK?
OH? THE PLAY?
I DON'T KNOW. I NEVER GOT TO SEE THE WHOLE THING...
NO, I'M TALKING ABOUT MY PERFORMANCE!
NOT THAT I CARE ABOUT YOUR OPINION...
HMPH
HMPH
OH! WELL... YOU LOOKED GOOD IN THAT DRESS!
OH?
THEY SAY THE CLOTHES MAKE THE MAN, RIGHT? ♡
HUH?
IS THAT A COMPLIMENT OR NOT?

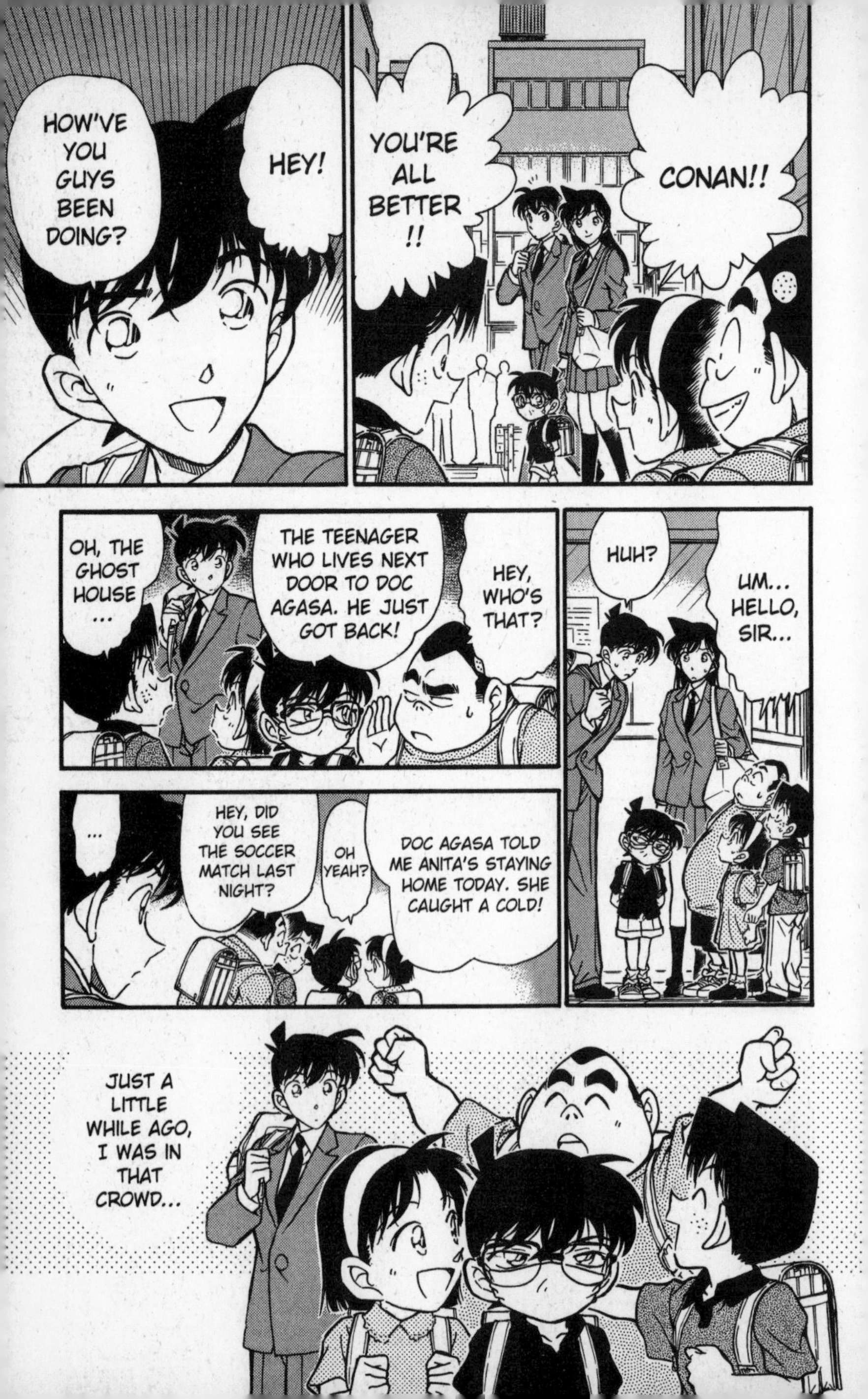
CONAN!!
YOU'RE ALL BETTER!!
HEY!
HOW'VE YOU GUYS BEEN DOING?
UM... HELLO, SIR...
HUH?
HEY, WHO'S THAT?
THE TEENAGER WHO LIVES NEXT DOOR TO DOC AGASA. HE JUST GOT BACK!
OH, THE GHOST HOUSE...
DOC AGASA TOLD ME ANITA'S STAYING HOME TODAY. SHE CAUGHT A COLD!
OH YEAH?
HEY, DID YOU SEE THE SOCCER MATCH LAST NIGHT?
...
JUST A LITTLE WHILE AGO, I WAS IN THAT CROWD...

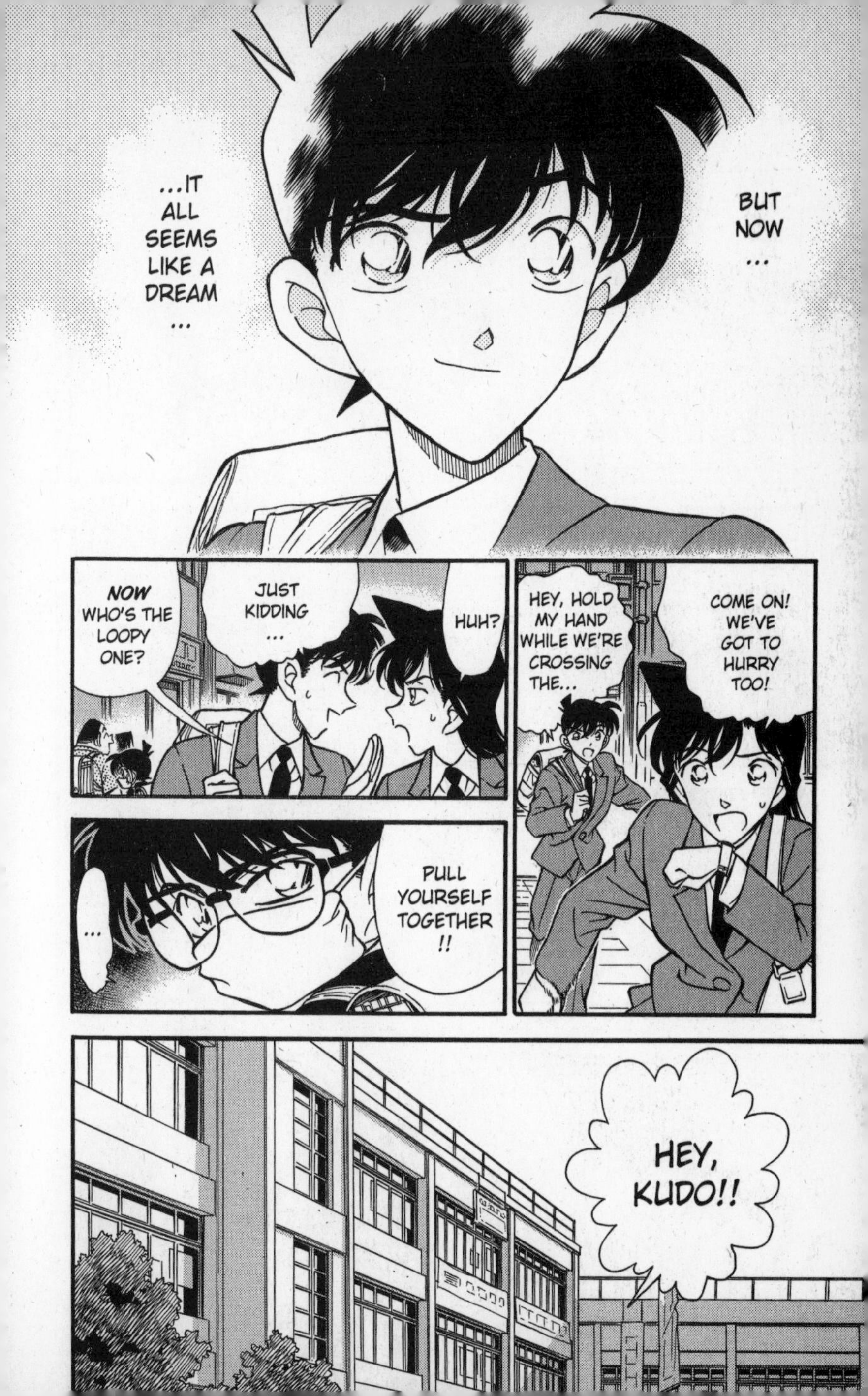
BUT NOW ...
...IT ALL SEEMS LIKE A DREAM ...
COME ON! WE'VE GOT TO HURRY TOO!
HEY, HOLD MY HAND WHILE WE'RE CROSSING THE...
HUH?
JUST KIDDING ...
NOW WHO'S THE LOOPY ONE?
PULL YOURSELF TOGETHER !!
...
HEY, KUDO!!

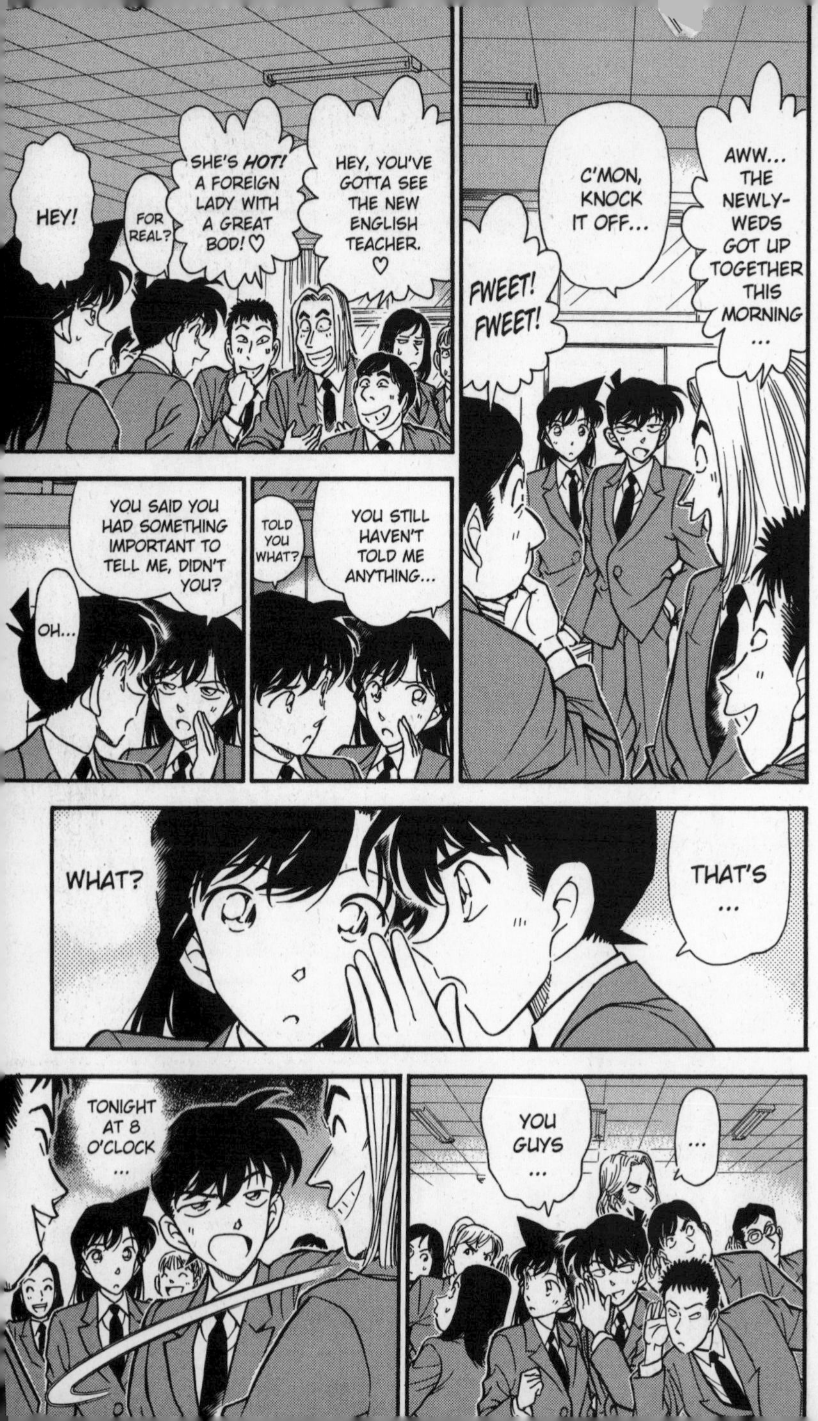
AWW... THE NEWLY-WEDS GOT UP TOGETHER THIS MORNING ...
C'MON, KNOCK IT OFF...
FWEET! FWEET!
HEY, YOU'VE GOTTA SEE THE NEW ENGLISH TEACHER. ♡
SHE'S ***HOT!*** A FOREIGN LADY WITH A GREAT BOD! ♡
FOR REAL?
HEY!
YOU STILL HAVEN'T TOLD ME ANYTHING...
TOLD YOU WHAT?
YOU SAID YOU HAD SOMETHING IMPORTANT TO TELL ME, DIDN'T YOU?
OH...
THAT'S ...
WHAT?
...
YOU GUYS ...
TONIGHT AT 8 O'CLOCK ...

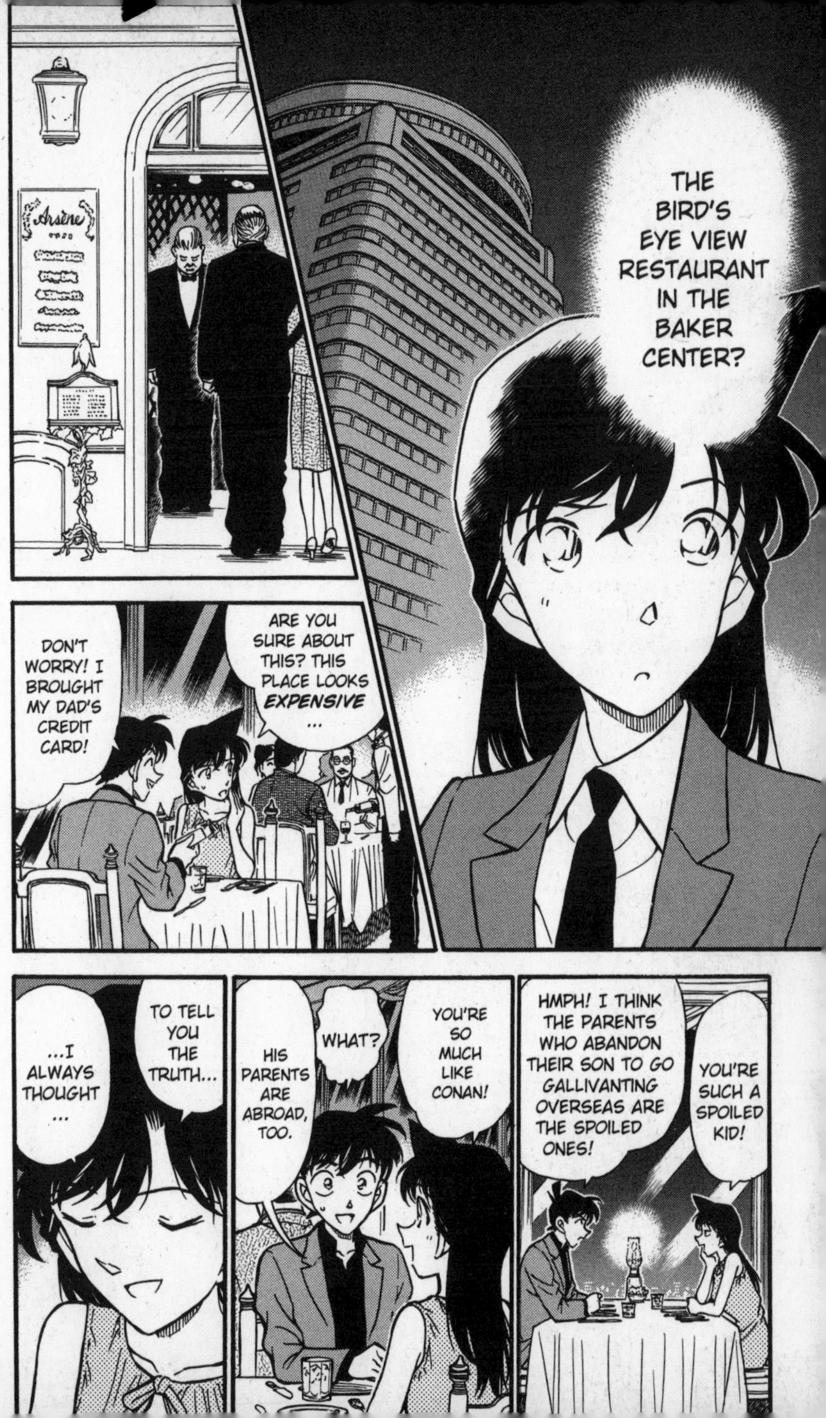

THE BIRD'S EYE VIEW RESTAURANT IN THE BAKER CENTER?
Arsène
ARE YOU SURE ABOUT THIS? THIS PLACE LOOKS *EXPENSIVE* ...
DON'T WORRY! I BROUGHT MY DAD'S CREDIT CARD!
YOU'RE SUCH A SPOILED KID!
HMPH! I THINK THE PARENTS WHO ABANDON THEIR SON TO GO GALLIVANTING OVERSEAS ARE THE SPOILED ONES!
YOU'RE SO MUCH LIKE CONAN!
WHAT?
HIS PARENTS ARE ABROAD, TOO.
TO TELL YOU THE TRUTH...
...I ALWAYS THOUGHT ...

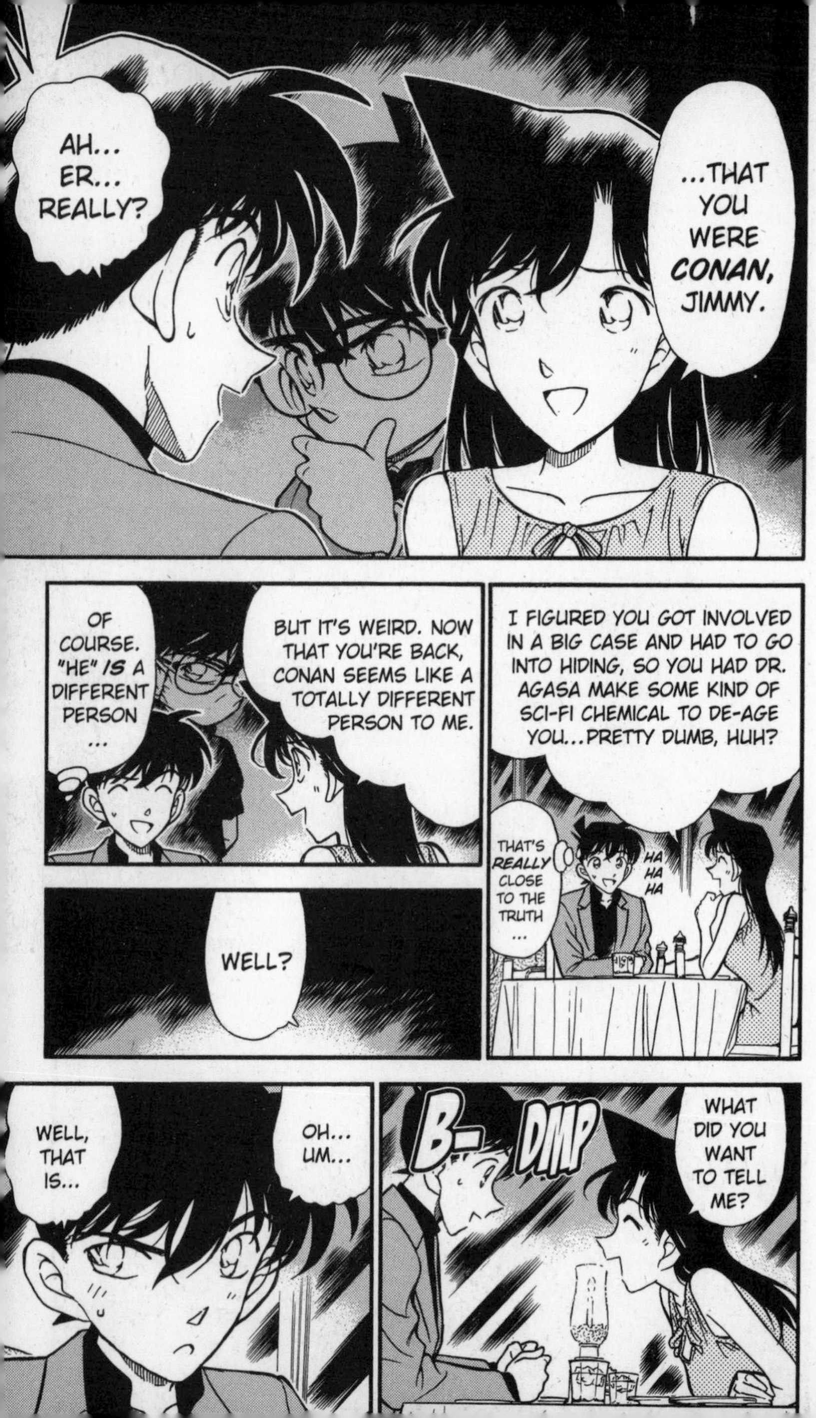
...THAT YOU WERE CONAN, JIMMY.
AH... ER... REALLY?
I FIGURED YOU GOT INVOLVED IN A BIG CASE AND HAD TO GO INTO HIDING, SO YOU HAD DR. AGASA MAKE SOME KIND OF SCI-FI CHEMICAL TO DE-AGE YOU...PRETTY DUMB, HUH?
HA HA HA
THAT'S REALLY CLOSE TO THE TRUTH...
BUT IT'S WEIRD. NOW THAT YOU'RE BACK, CONAN SEEMS LIKE A TOTALLY DIFFERENT PERSON TO ME.
OF COURSE. "HE" IS A DIFFERENT PERSON...
WELL?
WHAT DID YOU WANT TO TELL ME?
B-DMP
OH... UM...
WELL, THAT IS...

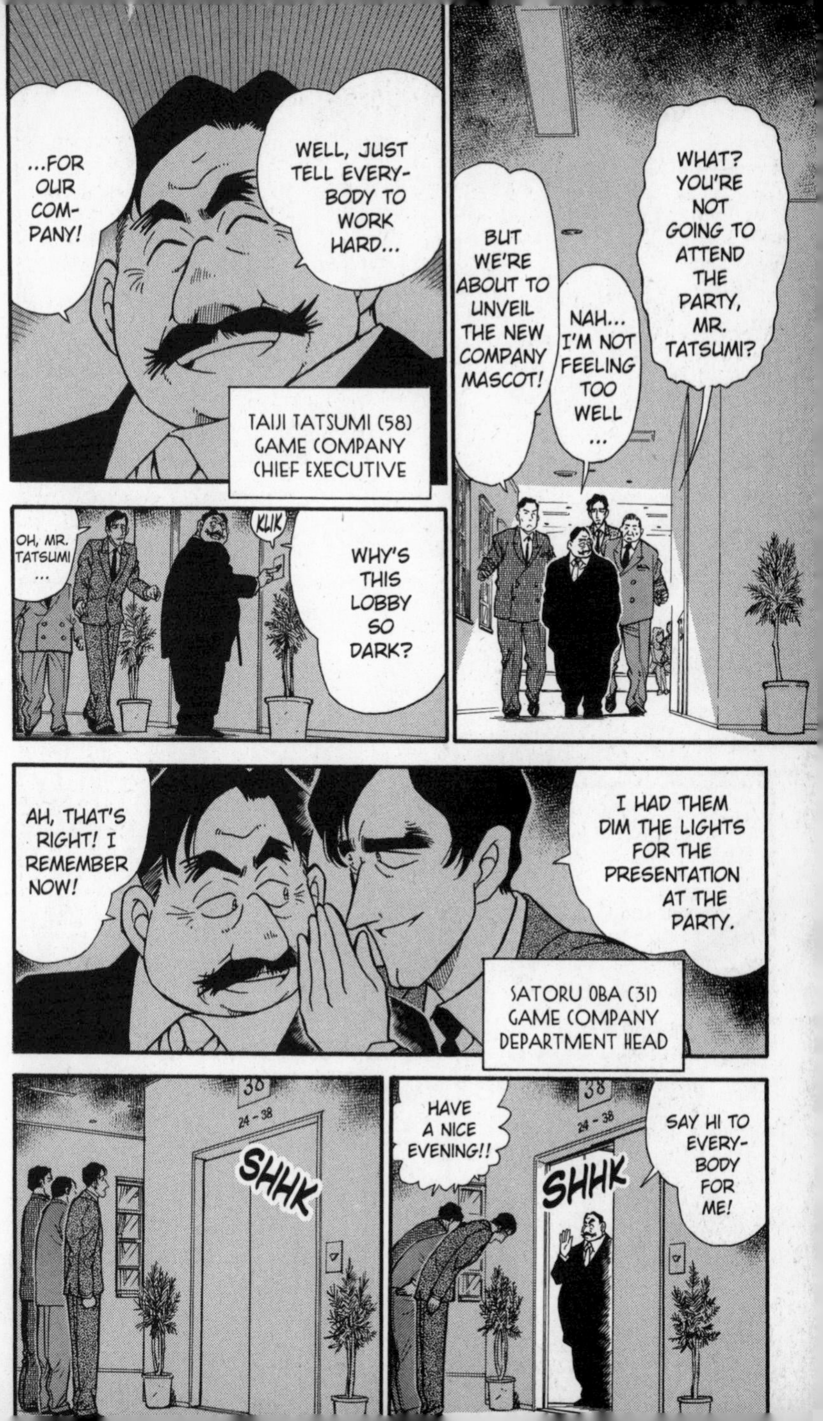
WHAT? YOU'RE NOT GOING TO ATTEND THE PARTY, MR. TATSUMI?
NAH... I'M NOT FEELING TOO WELL...
BUT WE'RE ABOUT TO UNVEIL THE NEW COMPANY MASCOT!
WELL, JUST TELL EVERY-BODY TO WORK HARD...
...FOR OUR COM-PANY!
TAIJI TATSUMI (58) GAME COMPANY CHIEF EXECUTIVE
KLIK
WHY'S THIS LOBBY SO DARK?
OH, MR. TATSUMI...
I HAD THEM DIM THE LIGHTS FOR THE PRESENTATION AT THE PARTY.
AH, THAT'S RIGHT! I REMEMBER NOW!
SATORU OBA (31) GAME COMPANY DEPARTMENT HEAD
38
24 - 38
SAY HI TO EVERY-BODY FOR ME!
SHHK
HAVE A NICE EVENING!!
38
24 - 38
SHHK

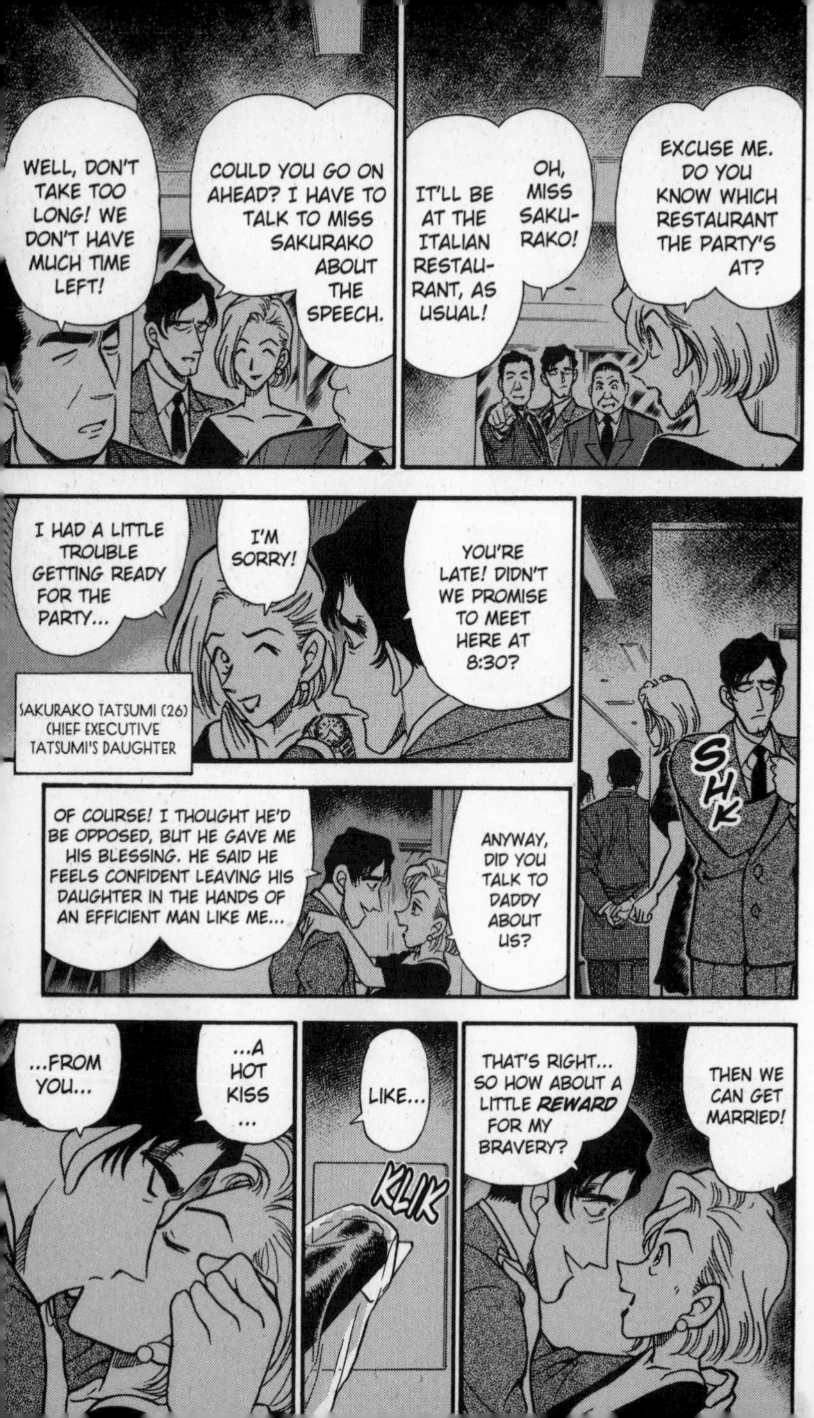
EXCUSE ME. DO YOU KNOW WHICH RESTAURANT THE PARTY'S AT?
OH, MISS SAKU-RAKO!
IT'LL BE AT THE ITALIAN RESTAU-RANT, AS USUAL!
COULD YOU GO ON AHEAD? I HAVE TO TALK TO MISS SAKURAKO ABOUT THE SPEECH.
WELL, DON'T TAKE TOO LONG! WE DON'T HAVE MUCH TIME LEFT!
SHK
YOU'RE LATE! DIDN'T WE PROMISE TO MEET HERE AT 8:30?
I'M SORRY!
I HAD A LITTLE TROUBLE GETTING READY FOR THE PARTY...
SAKURAKO TATSUMI (26) CHIEF EXECUTIVE TATSUMI'S DAUGHTER
ANYWAY, DID YOU TALK TO DADDY ABOUT US?
OF COURSE! I THOUGHT HE'D BE OPPOSED, BUT HE GAVE ME HIS BLESSING. HE SAID HE FEELS CONFIDENT LEAVING HIS DAUGHTER IN THE HANDS OF AN EFFICIENT MAN LIKE ME...
THEN WE CAN GET MARRIED!
THAT'S RIGHT... SO HOW ABOUT A LITTLE **REWARD** FOR MY BRAVERY?
LIKE...
KLIK
...A HOT KISS ...
...FROM YOU...

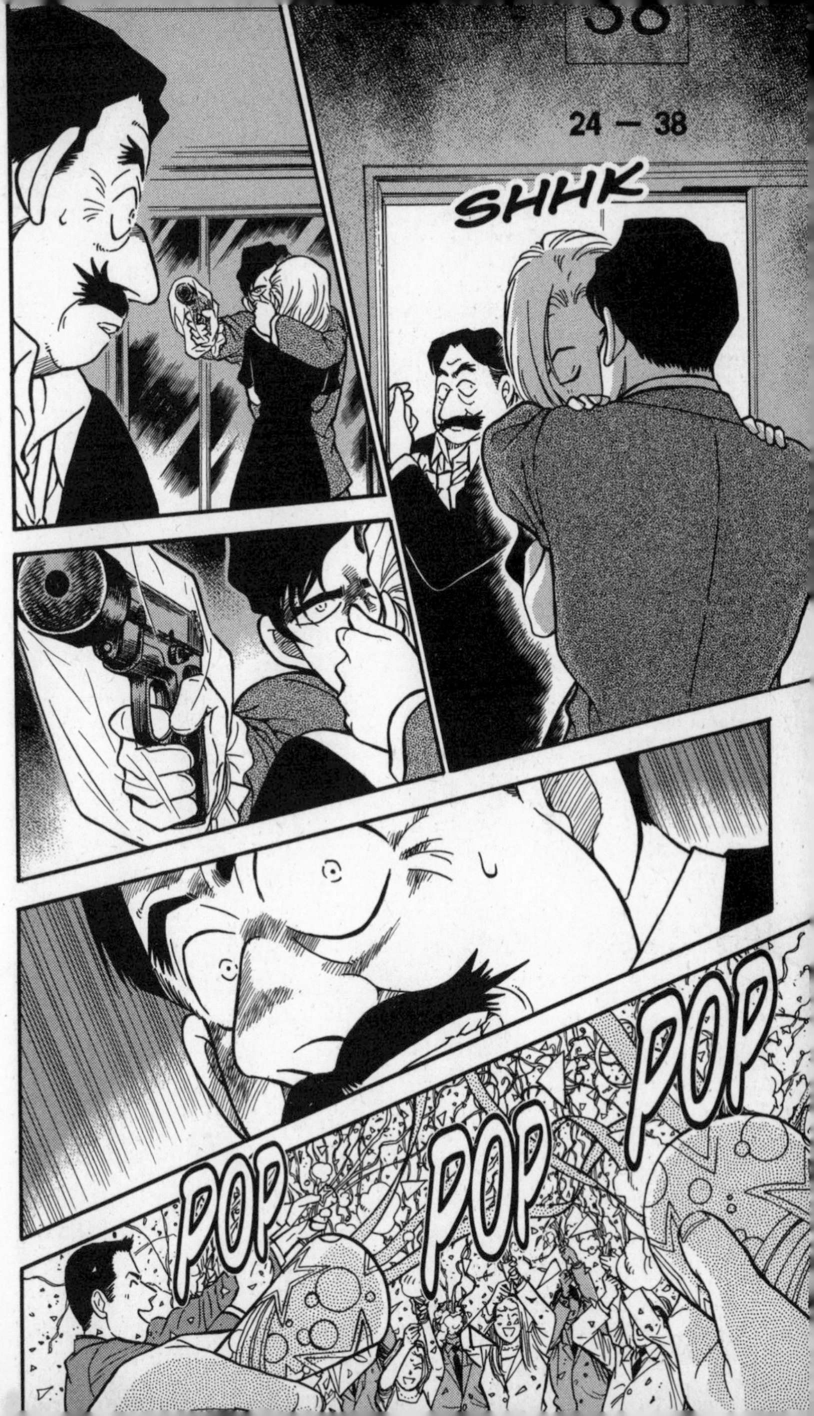
38
24 — 38
SHHK
POP
POP
POP

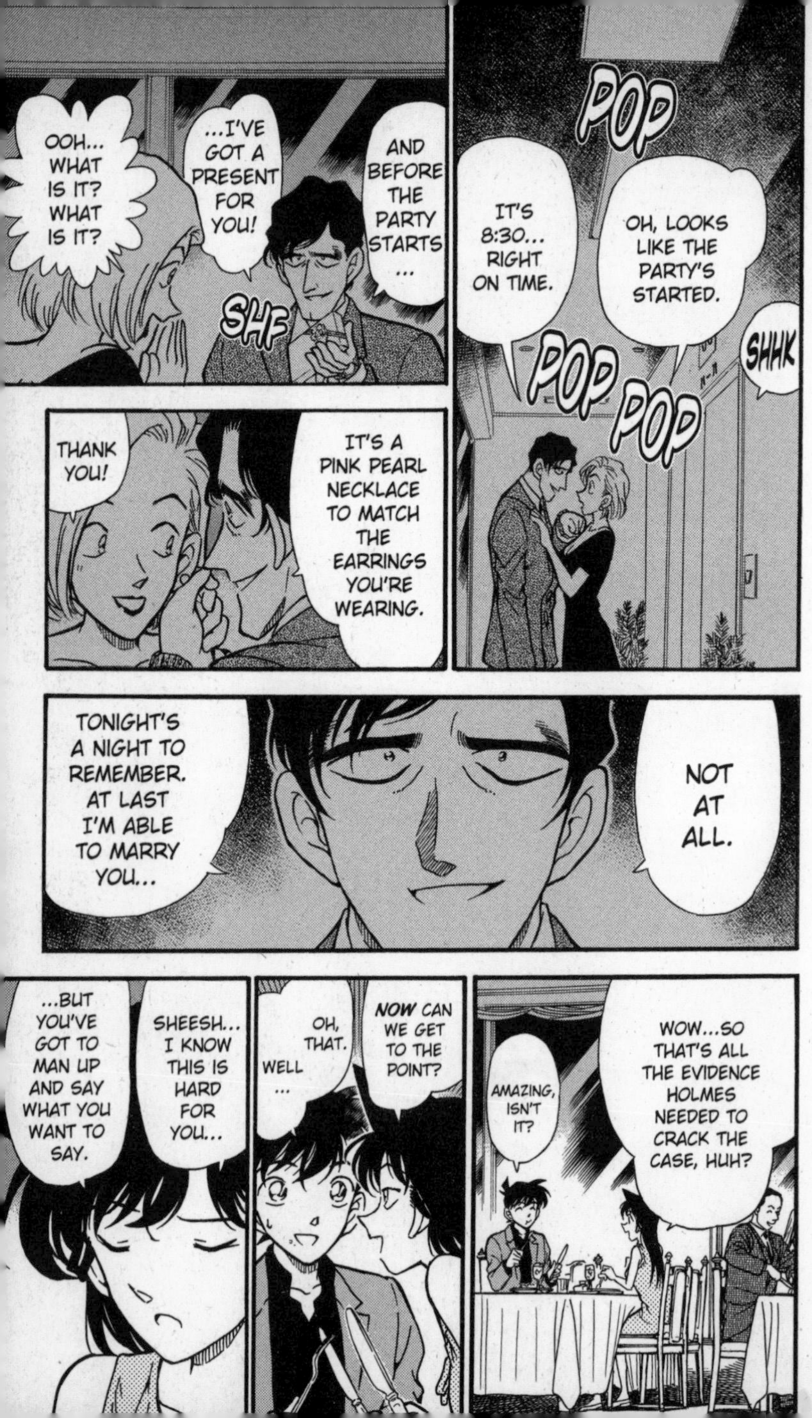
POP
OH, LOOKS LIKE THE PARTY'S STARTED.
IT'S 8:30... RIGHT ON TIME.
SHHK
POP POP
AND BEFORE THE PARTY STARTS...
...I'VE GOT A PRESENT FOR YOU!
OOH... WHAT IS IT? WHAT IS IT?
SHF
IT'S A PINK PEARL NECKLACE TO MATCH THE EARRINGS YOU'RE WEARING.
THANK YOU!
NOT AT ALL.
TONIGHT'S A NIGHT TO REMEMBER. AT LAST I'M ABLE TO MARRY YOU...
WOW...SO THAT'S ALL THE EVIDENCE HOLMES NEEDED TO CRACK THE CASE, HUH?
AMAZING, ISN'T IT?
NOW CAN WE GET TO THE POINT?
OH, THAT.
WELL...
SHEESH... I KNOW THIS IS HARD FOR YOU...
...BUT YOU'VE GOT TO MAN UP AND SAY WHAT YOU WANT TO SAY.

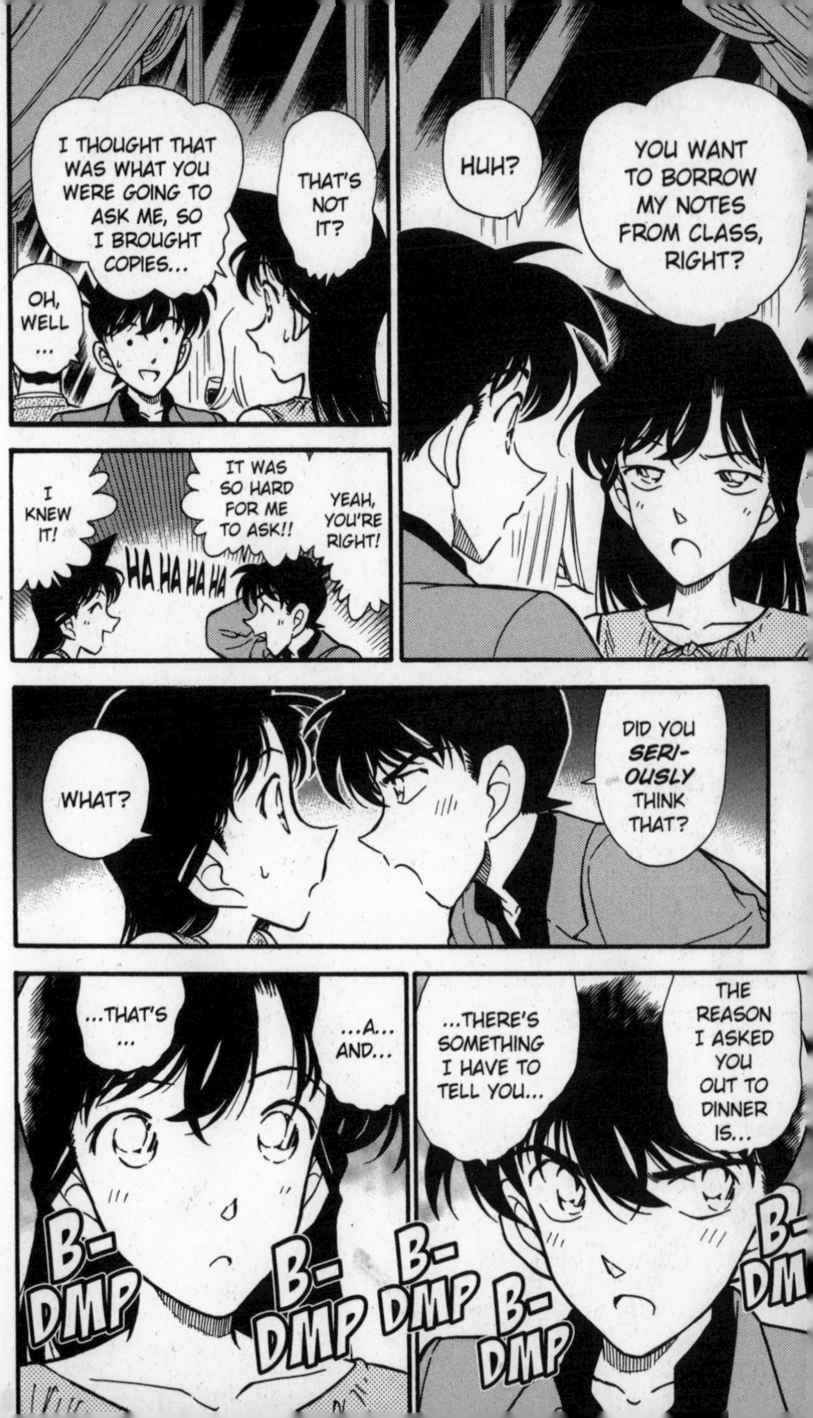
YOU WANT TO BORROW MY NOTES FROM CLASS, RIGHT?
HUH?
THAT'S NOT IT?
I THOUGHT THAT WAS WHAT YOU WERE GOING TO ASK ME, SO I BROUGHT COPIES...
OH, WELL...
YEAH, YOU'RE RIGHT!
IT WAS SO HARD FOR ME TO ASK!!
HA HA HA HA
I KNEW IT!
DID YOU *SERIOUSLY* THINK THAT?
WHAT?
THE REASON I ASKED YOU OUT TO DINNER IS...
...THERE'S SOMETHING I HAVE TO TELL YOU...
B-DMP
B-DMP
B-DMP
...A... AND...
...THAT'S...
B-DMP
B-DMP

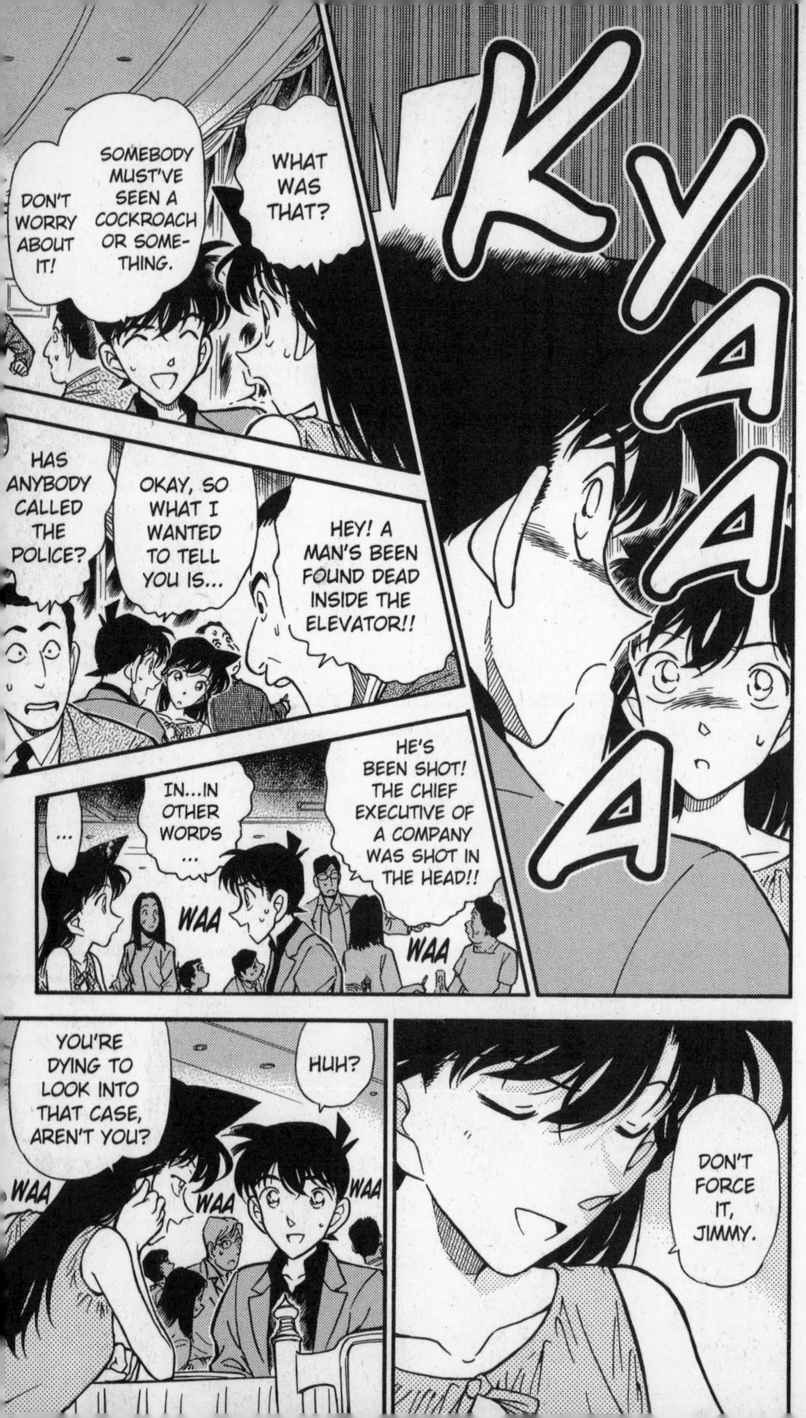
KYAAAA
WHAT WAS THAT?
SOMEBODY MUST'VE SEEN A COCKROACH OR SOME-THING.
DON'T WORRY ABOUT IT!
HEY! A MAN'S BEEN FOUND DEAD INSIDE THE ELEVATOR!!
OKAY, SO WHAT I WANTED TO TELL YOU IS...
HAS ANYBODY CALLED THE POLICE?
HE'S BEEN SHOT! THE CHIEF EXECUTIVE OF A COMPANY WAS SHOT IN THE HEAD!!
WAA
WAA
IN...IN OTHER WORDS ...
...
DON'T FORCE IT, JIMMY.
HUH?
YOU'RE DYING TO LOOK INTO THAT CASE, AREN'T YOU?
WAA
WAA
WAA

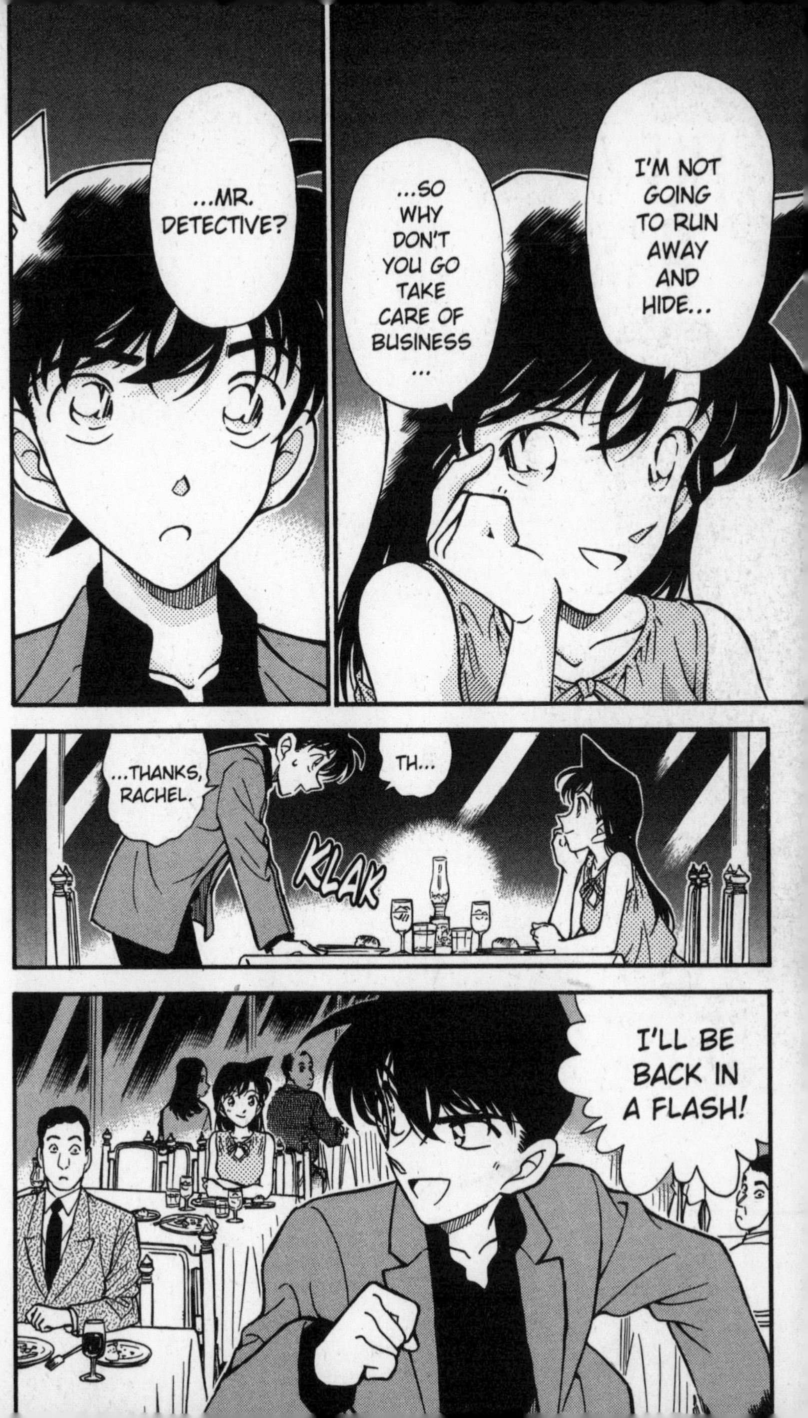
I'M NOT GOING TO RUN AWAY AND HIDE...
...SO WHY DON'T YOU GO TAKE CARE OF BUSINESS...
...MR. DETECTIVE?
TH...
...THANKS, RACHEL.
KLAK
I'LL BE BACK IN A FLASH!

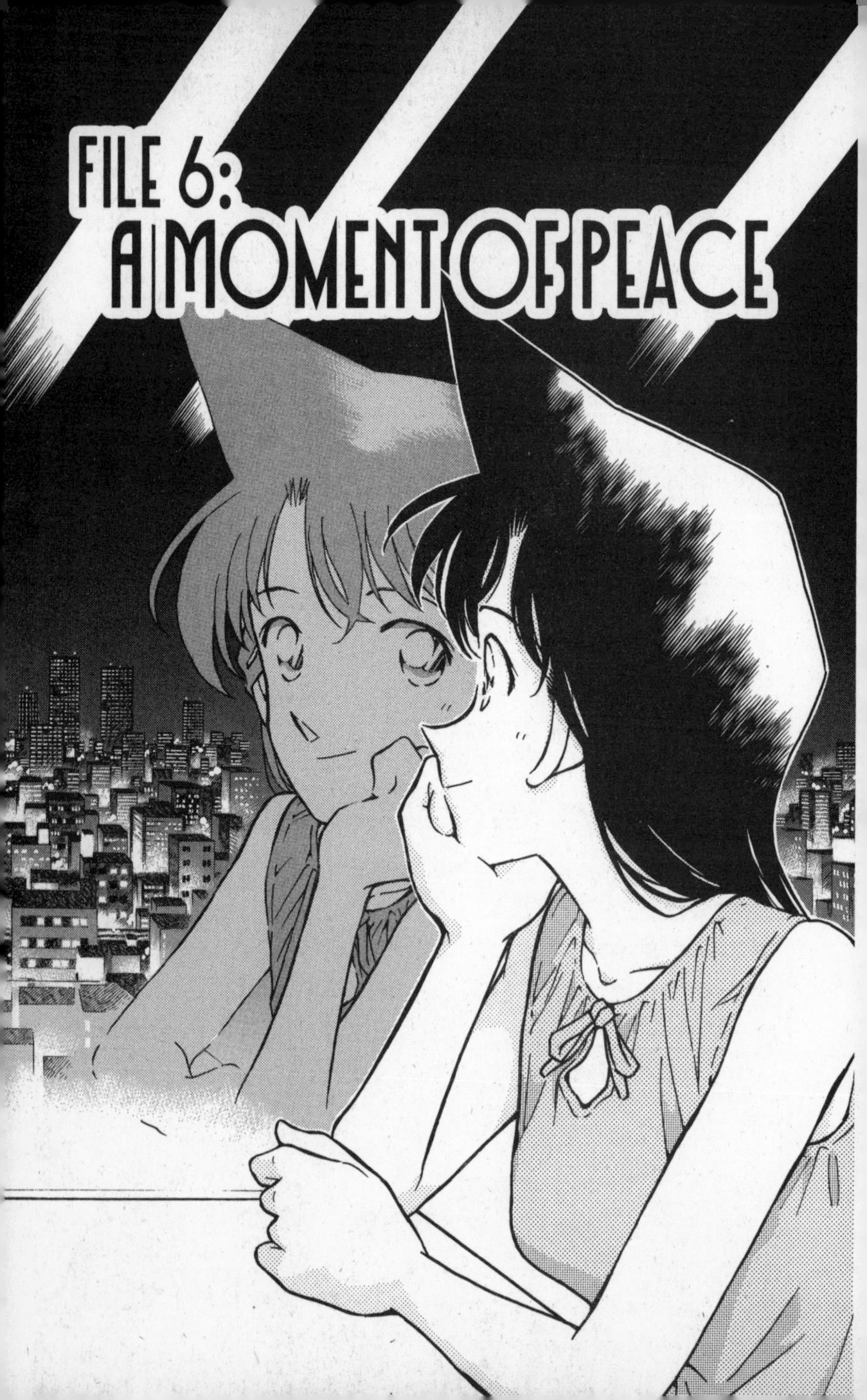
FILE 6:
A MOMENT OF PEACE

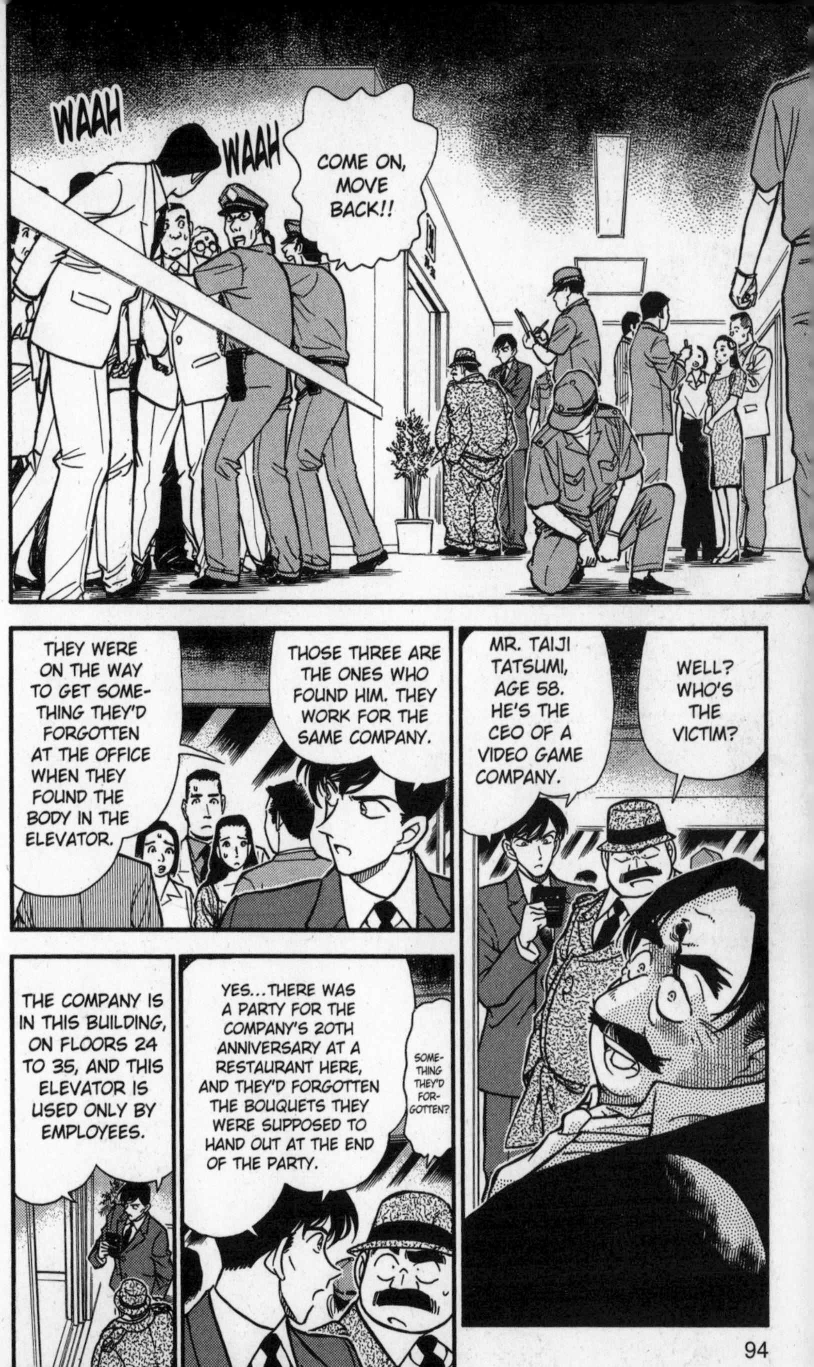
COME ON, MOVE BACK!!
WAAH
WAAH
WELL? WHO'S THE VICTIM?
MR. TAIJI TATSUMI, AGE 58. HE'S THE CEO OF A VIDEO GAME COMPANY.
THOSE THREE ARE THE ONES WHO FOUND HIM. THEY WORK FOR THE SAME COMPANY.
THEY WERE ON THE WAY TO GET SOME-THING THEY'D FORGOTTEN AT THE OFFICE WHEN THEY FOUND THE BODY IN THE ELEVATOR.
SOME-THING THEY'D FOR-GOTTEN?
YES...THERE WAS A PARTY FOR THE COMPANY'S 20TH ANNIVERSARY AT A RESTAURANT HERE, AND THEY'D FORGOTTEN THE BOUQUETS THEY WERE SUPPOSED TO HAND OUT AT THE END OF THE PARTY.
THE COMPANY IS IN THIS BUILDING, ON FLOORS 24 TO 35, AND THIS ELEVATOR IS USED ONLY BY EMPLOYEES.

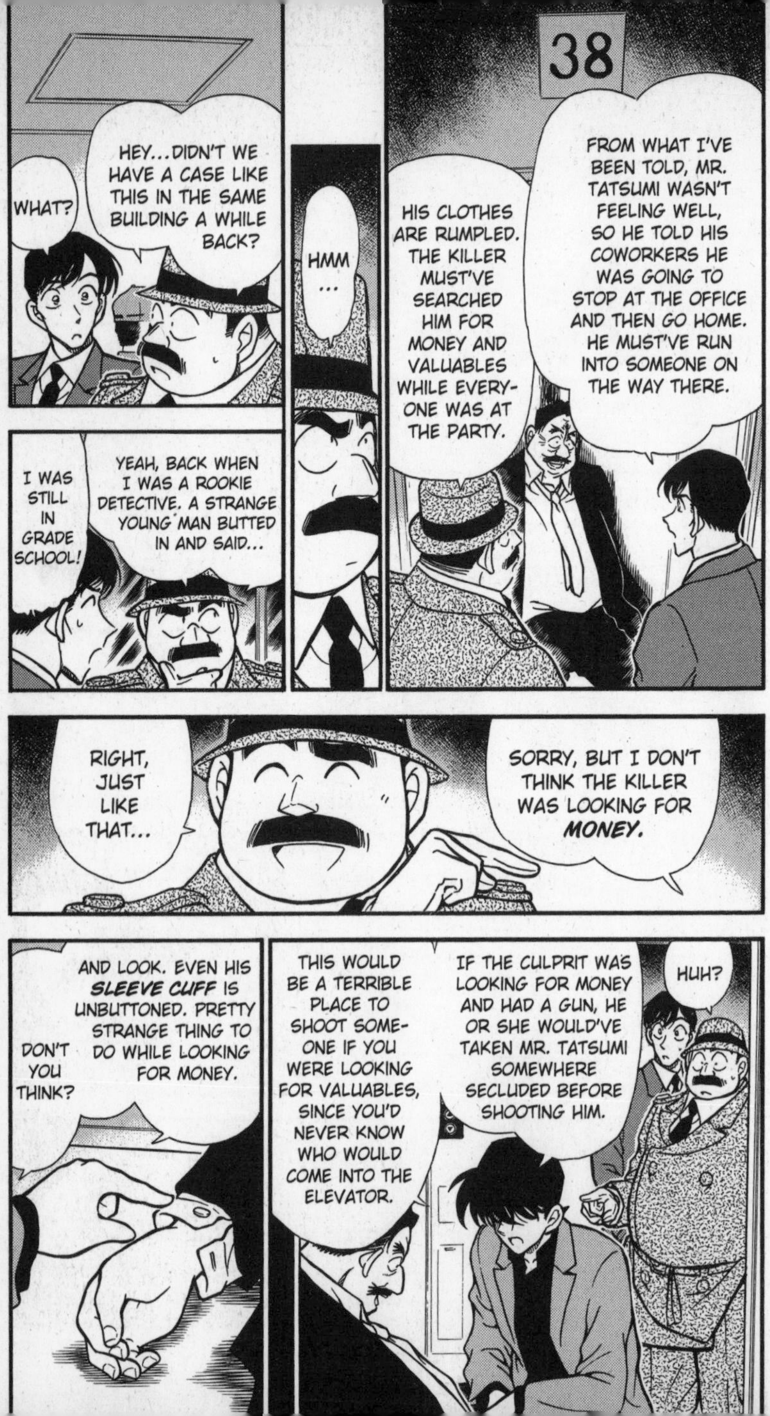
38
FROM WHAT I'VE BEEN TOLD, MR. TATSUMI WASN'T FEELING WELL, SO HE TOLD HIS COWORKERS HE WAS GOING TO STOP AT THE OFFICE AND THEN GO HOME. HE MUST'VE RUN INTO SOMEONE ON THE WAY THERE.
HIS CLOTHES ARE RUMPLED. THE KILLER MUST'VE SEARCHED HIM FOR MONEY AND VALUABLES WHILE EVERY-ONE WAS AT THE PARTY.
HMM ...
HEY...DIDN'T WE HAVE A CASE LIKE THIS IN THE SAME BUILDING A WHILE BACK?
WHAT?
YEAH, BACK WHEN I WAS A ROOKIE DETECTIVE. A STRANGE YOUNG MAN BUTTED IN AND SAID...
I WAS STILL IN GRADE SCHOOL!
SORRY, BUT I DON'T THINK THE KILLER WAS LOOKING FOR ***MONEY.***
RIGHT, JUST LIKE THAT...
HUH?
IF THE CULPRIT WAS LOOKING FOR MONEY AND HAD A GUN, HE OR SHE WOULD'VE TAKEN MR. TATSUMI SOMEWHERE SECLUDED BEFORE SHOOTING HIM.
THIS WOULD BE A TERRIBLE PLACE TO SHOOT SOME-ONE IF YOU WERE LOOKING FOR VALUABLES, SINCE YOU'D NEVER KNOW WHO WOULD COME INTO THE ELEVATOR.
AND LOOK. EVEN HIS ***SLEEVE CUFF*** IS UNBUTTONED. PRETTY STRANGE THING TO DO WHILE LOOKING FOR MONEY.
DON'T YOU THINK?

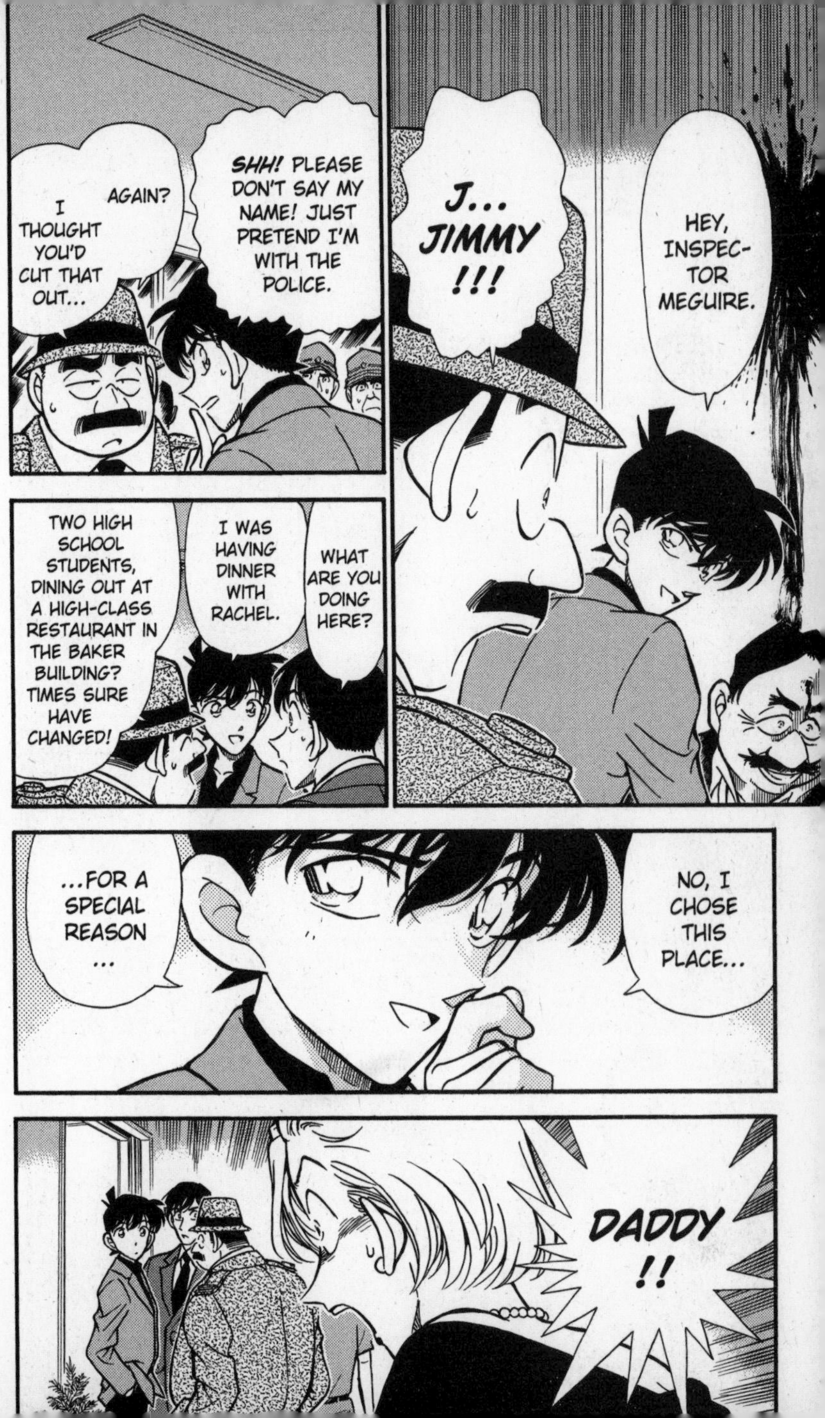
HEY, INSPECTOR MEGUIRE.
J... JIMMY!!!
SHH! PLEASE DON'T SAY MY NAME! JUST PRETEND I'M WITH THE POLICE.
AGAIN? I THOUGHT YOU'D CUT THAT OUT...
WHAT ARE YOU DOING HERE?
I WAS HAVING DINNER WITH RACHEL.
TWO HIGH SCHOOL STUDENTS, DINING OUT AT A HIGH-CLASS RESTAURANT IN THE BAKER BUILDING? TIMES SURE HAVE CHANGED!
NO, I CHOSE THIS PLACE...
...FOR A SPECIAL REASON ...
DADDY!!

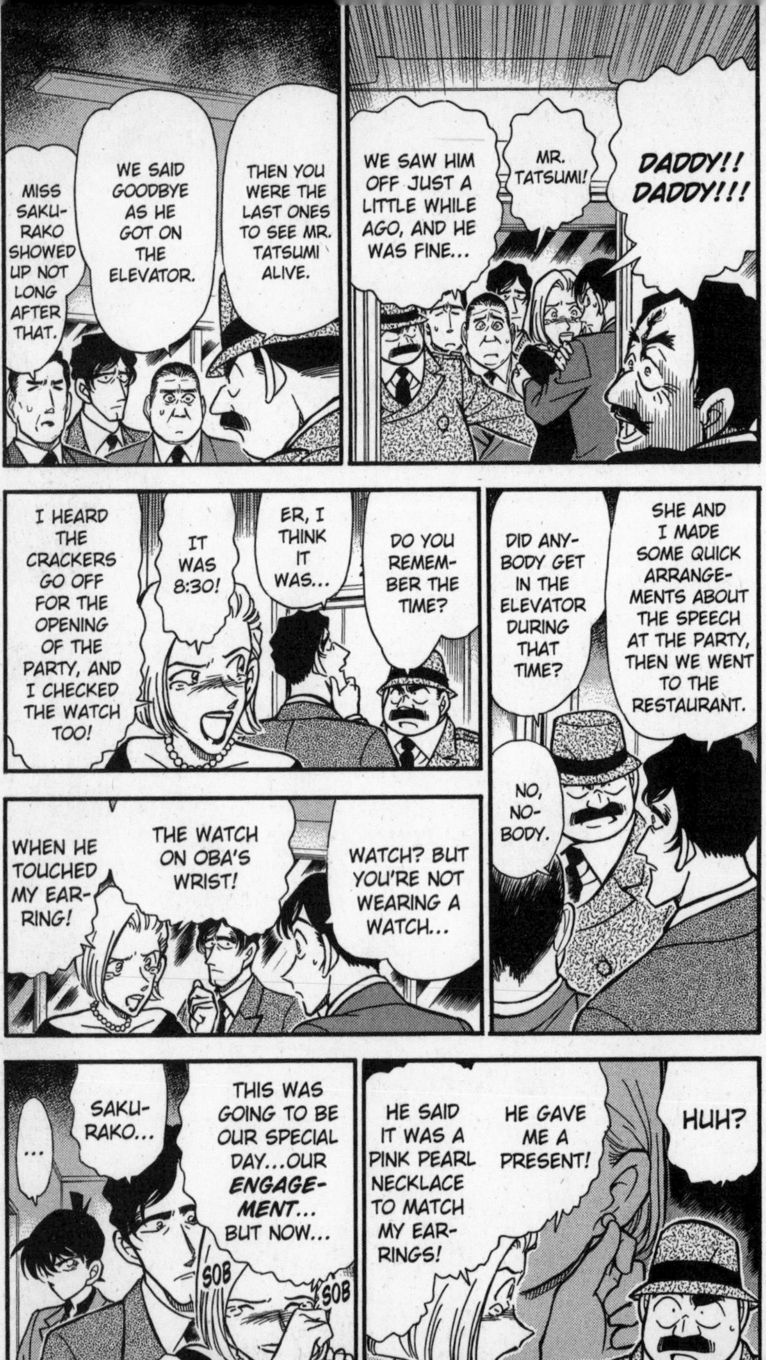

DADDY!! DADDY!!!
MR. TATSUMI!
WE SAW HIM OFF JUST A LITTLE WHILE AGO, AND HE WAS FINE...
THEN YOU WERE THE LAST ONES TO SEE MR. TATSUMI ALIVE.
WE SAID GOODBYE AS HE GOT ON THE ELEVATOR.
MISS SAKURAKO SHOWED UP NOT LONG AFTER THAT.
SHE AND I MADE SOME QUICK ARRANGEMENTS ABOUT THE SPEECH AT THE PARTY, THEN WE WENT TO THE RESTAURANT.
DID ANYBODY GET IN THE ELEVATOR DURING THAT TIME?
NO, NOBODY.
DO YOU REMEMBER THE TIME?
ER, I THINK IT WAS...
IT WAS 8:30!
I HEARD THE CRACKERS GO OFF FOR THE OPENING OF THE PARTY, AND I CHECKED THE WATCH TOO!
WATCH? BUT YOU'RE NOT WEARING A WATCH...
THE WATCH ON OBA'S WRIST!
WHEN HE TOUCHED MY EARRING!
HUH?
HE GAVE ME A PRESENT!
HE SAID IT WAS A PINK PEARL NECKLACE TO MATCH MY EARRINGS!
THIS WAS GOING TO BE OUR SPECIAL DAY...OUR ***ENGAGEMENT***... BUT NOW...
SOB
SOB
SAKURAKO...
...

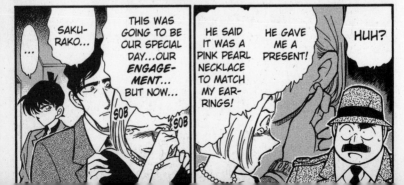

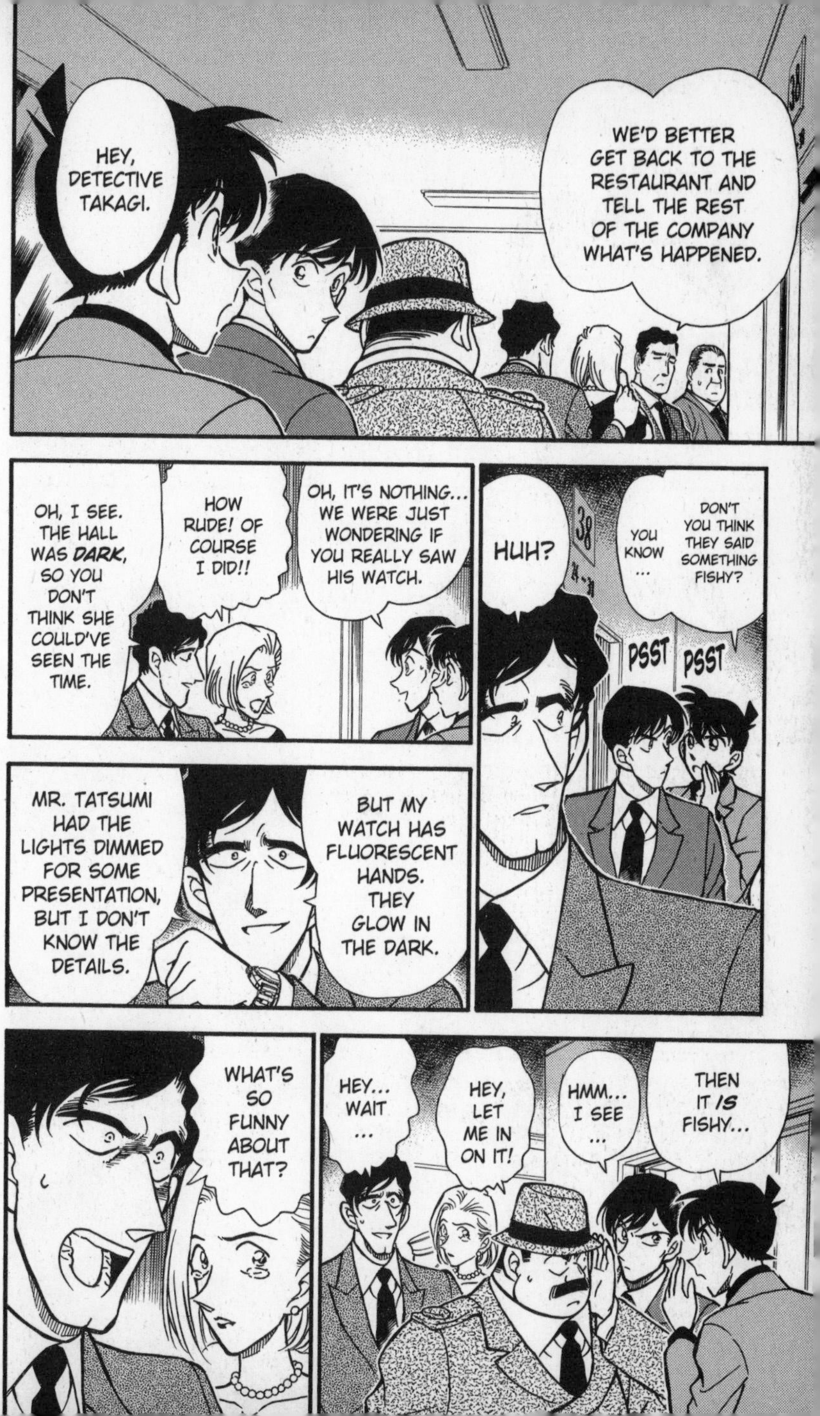
WE'D BETTER GET BACK TO THE RESTAURANT AND TELL THE REST OF THE COMPANY WHAT'S HAPPENED.
HEY, DETECTIVE TAKAGI.
DON'T YOU THINK THEY SAID SOMETHING FISHY?
YOU KNOW ...
HUH?
PSST
PSST
OH, IT'S NOTHING... WE WERE JUST WONDERING IF YOU REALLY SAW HIS WATCH.
HOW RUDE! OF COURSE I DID!!
OH, I SEE. THE HALL WAS *DARK*, SO YOU DON'T THINK SHE COULD'VE SEEN THE TIME.
BUT MY WATCH HAS FLUORESCENT HANDS. THEY GLOW IN THE DARK.
MR. TATSUMI HAD THE LIGHTS DIMMED FOR SOME PRESENTATION, BUT I DON'T KNOW THE DETAILS.
THEN IT *IS* FISHY...
HMM... I SEE ...
HEY, LET ME IN ON IT!
HEY... WAIT ...
WHAT'S SO FUNNY ABOUT THAT?

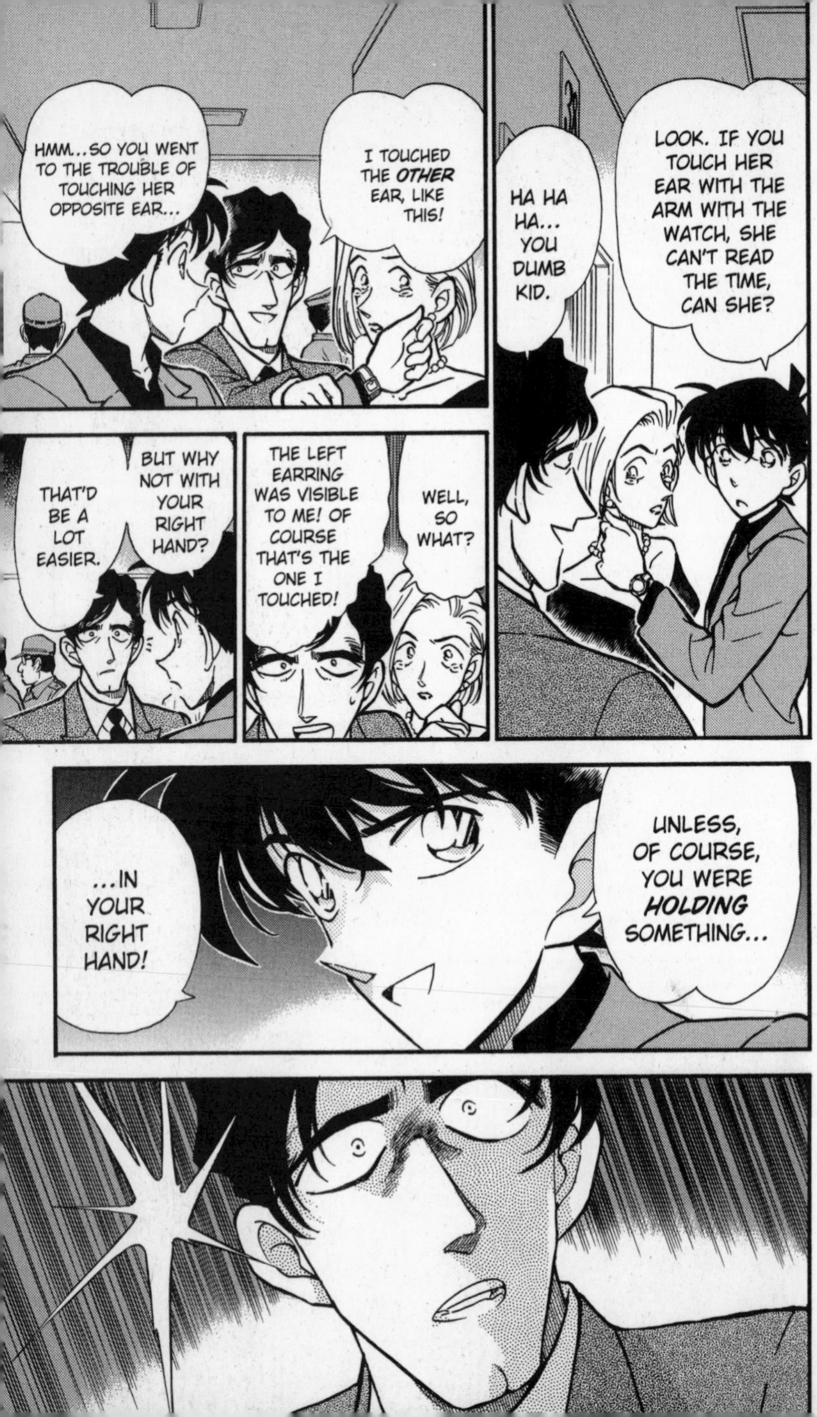
LOOK. IF YOU TOUCH HER EAR WITH THE ARM WITH THE WATCH, SHE CAN'T READ THE TIME, CAN SHE?
HA HA HA... YOU DUMB KID.
I TOUCHED THE ***OTHER*** EAR, LIKE THIS!
HMM...SO YOU WENT TO THE TROUBLE OF TOUCHING HER OPPOSITE EAR...
WELL, SO WHAT?
THE LEFT EARRING WAS VISIBLE TO ME! OF COURSE THAT'S THE ONE I TOUCHED!
BUT WHY NOT WITH YOUR RIGHT HAND?
THAT'D BE A LOT EASIER.
UNLESS, OF COURSE, YOU WERE ***HOLDING*** SOMETHING...
...IN YOUR RIGHT HAND!

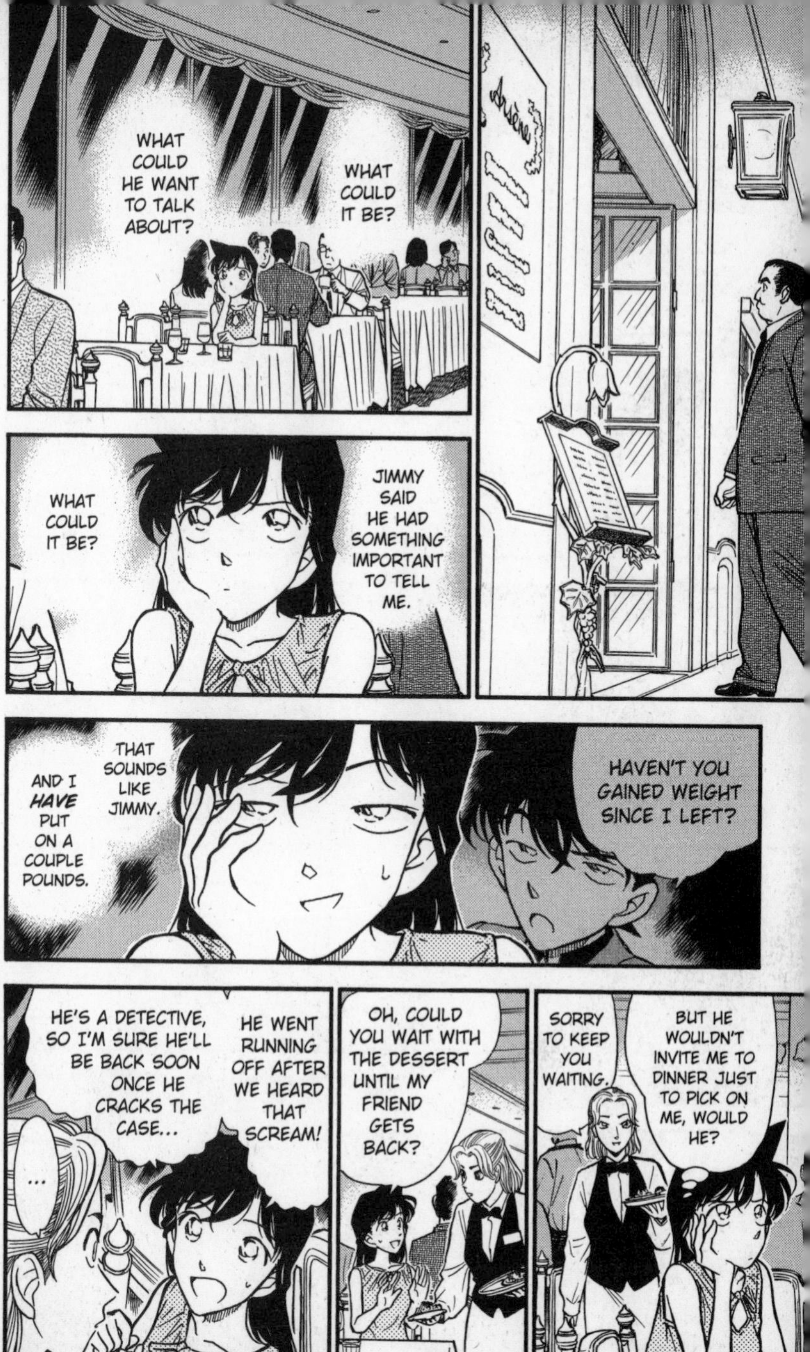
WHAT COULD IT BE?
WHAT COULD HE WANT TO TALK ABOUT?
JIMMY SAID HE HAD SOMETHING IMPORTANT TO TELL ME.
WHAT COULD IT BE?
HAVEN'T YOU GAINED WEIGHT SINCE I LEFT?
THAT SOUNDS LIKE JIMMY.
AND I *HAVE* PUT ON A COUPLE POUNDS.
BUT HE WOULDN'T INVITE ME TO DINNER JUST TO PICK ON ME, WOULD HE?
SORRY TO KEEP YOU WAITING.
OH, COULD YOU WAIT WITH THE DESSERT UNTIL MY FRIEND GETS BACK?
HE WENT RUNNING OFF AFTER WE HEARD THAT SCREAM!
HE'S A DETECTIVE, SO I'M SURE HE'LL BE BACK SOON ONCE HE CRACKS THE CASE...
...

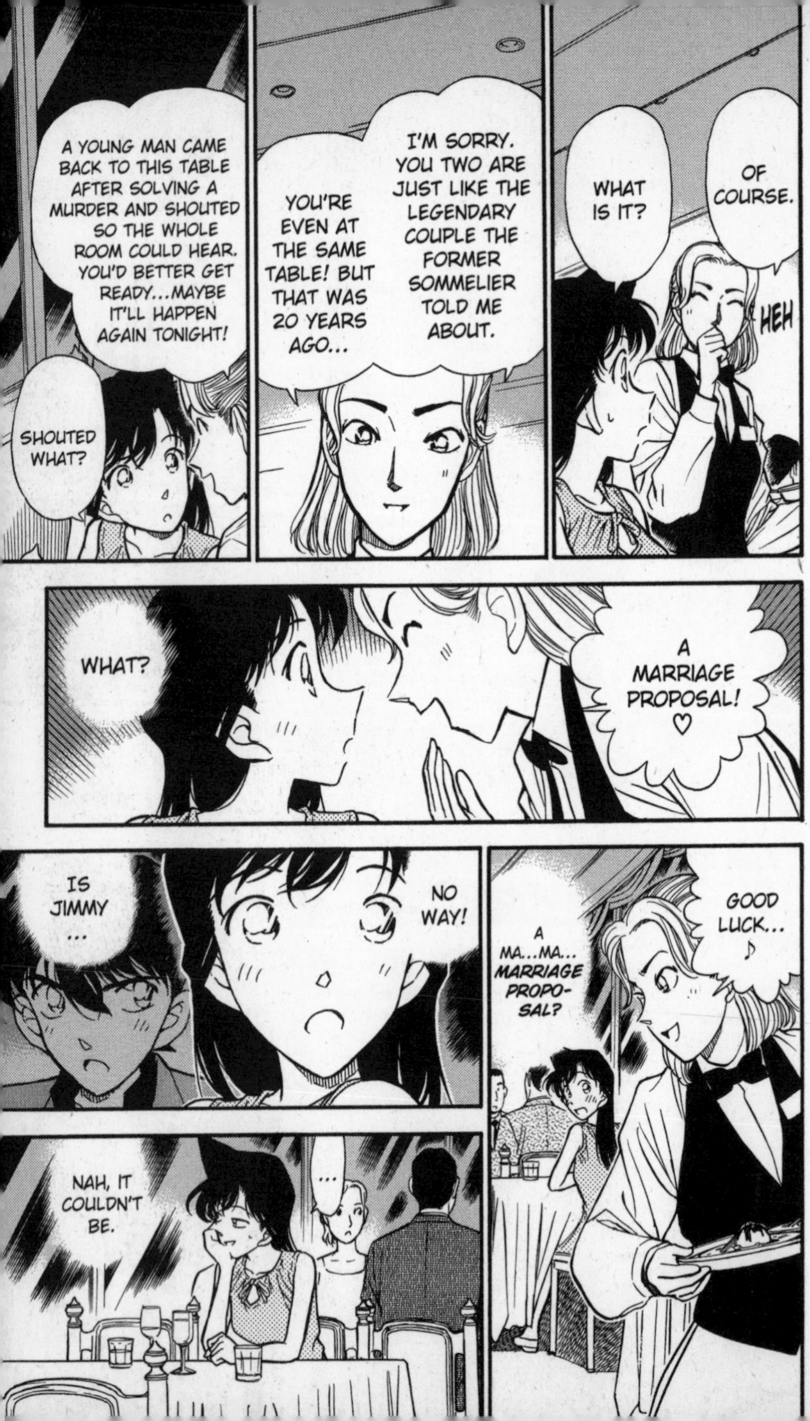
OF COURSE.
WHAT IS IT?
HEH
I'M SORRY. YOU TWO ARE JUST LIKE THE LEGENDARY COUPLE THE FORMER SOMMELIER TOLD ME ABOUT.
YOU'RE EVEN AT THE SAME TABLE! BUT THAT WAS 20 YEARS AGO...
A YOUNG MAN CAME BACK TO THIS TABLE AFTER SOLVING A MURDER AND SHOUTED SO THE WHOLE ROOM COULD HEAR. YOU'D BETTER GET READY...MAYBE IT'LL HAPPEN AGAIN TONIGHT!
SHOUTED WHAT?
A MARRIAGE PROPOSAL! ♡
WHAT?
GOOD LUCK... ♪
A MA...MA... **MARRIAGE PROPOSAL?**
NO WAY!
IS JIMMY ...
...
NAH, IT COULDN'T BE.

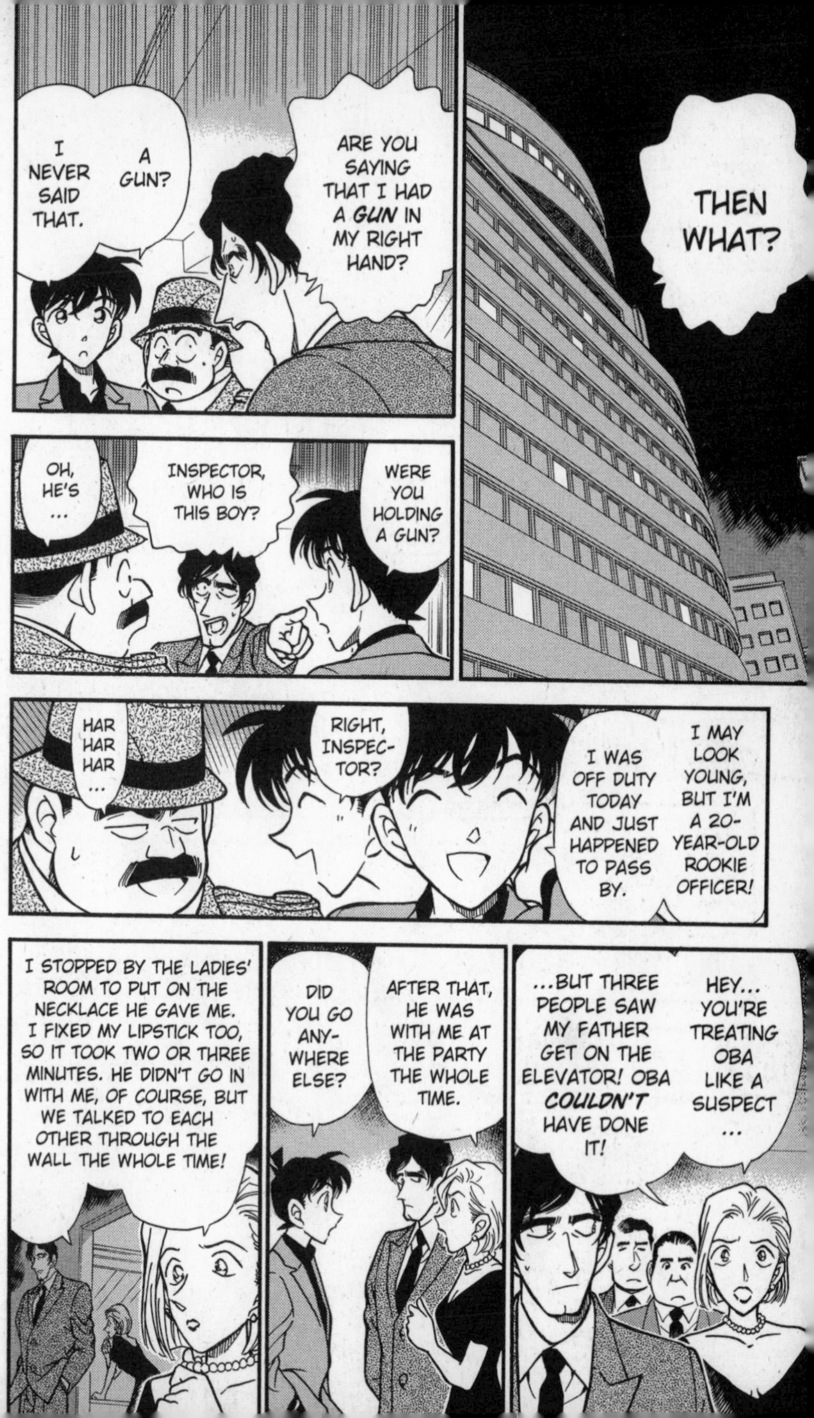
THEN WHAT?
ARE YOU SAYING THAT I HAD A ***GUN*** IN MY RIGHT HAND?
A GUN?
I NEVER SAID THAT.
WERE YOU HOLDING A GUN?
INSPECTOR, WHO IS THIS BOY?
OH, HE'S ...
I MAY LOOK YOUNG, BUT I'M A 20-YEAR-OLD ROOKIE OFFICER!
I WAS OFF DUTY TODAY AND JUST HAPPENED TO PASS BY.
RIGHT, INSPECTOR?
HAR HAR HAR ...
HEY... YOU'RE TREATING OBA LIKE A SUSPECT ...
...BUT THREE PEOPLE SAW MY FATHER GET ON THE ELEVATOR! OBA ***COULDN'T*** HAVE DONE IT!
AFTER THAT, HE WAS WITH ME AT THE PARTY THE WHOLE TIME.
DID YOU GO ANYWHERE ELSE?
I STOPPED BY THE LADIES' ROOM TO PUT ON THE NECKLACE HE GAVE ME. I FIXED MY LIPSTICK TOO, SO IT TOOK TWO OR THREE MINUTES. HE DIDN'T GO IN WITH ME, OF COURSE, BUT WE TALKED TO EACH OTHER THROUGH THE WALL THE WHOLE TIME!

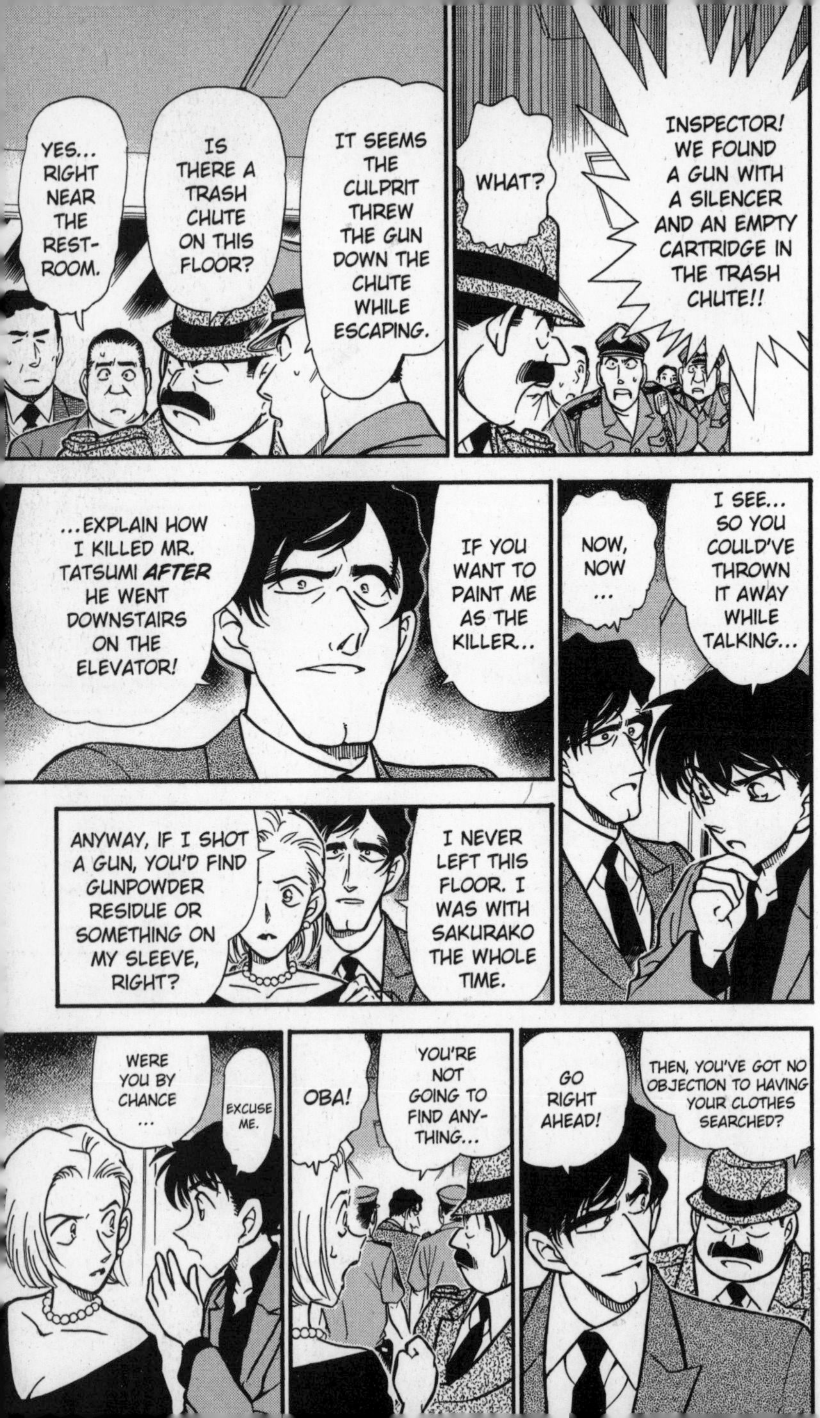
INSPECTOR! WE FOUND A GUN WITH A SILENCER AND AN EMPTY CARTRIDGE IN THE TRASH CHUTE!!
WHAT?
IT SEEMS THE CULPRIT THREW THE GUN DOWN THE CHUTE WHILE ESCAPING.
IS THERE A TRASH CHUTE ON THIS FLOOR?
YES... RIGHT NEAR THE REST-ROOM.
I SEE... SO YOU COULD'VE THROWN IT AWAY WHILE TALKING...
NOW, NOW ...
IF YOU WANT TO PAINT ME AS THE KILLER...
...EXPLAIN HOW I KILLED MR. TATSUMI *AFTER* HE WENT DOWNSTAIRS ON THE ELEVATOR!
I NEVER LEFT THIS FLOOR. I WAS WITH SAKURAKO THE WHOLE TIME.
ANYWAY, IF I SHOT A GUN, YOU'D FIND GUNPOWDER RESIDUE OR SOMETHING ON MY SLEEVE, RIGHT?
THEN, YOU'VE GOT NO OBJECTION TO HAVING YOUR CLOTHES SEARCHED?
GO RIGHT AHEAD!
YOU'RE NOT GOING TO FIND ANY-THING...
OBA!
EXCUSE ME.
WERE YOU BY CHANCE ...

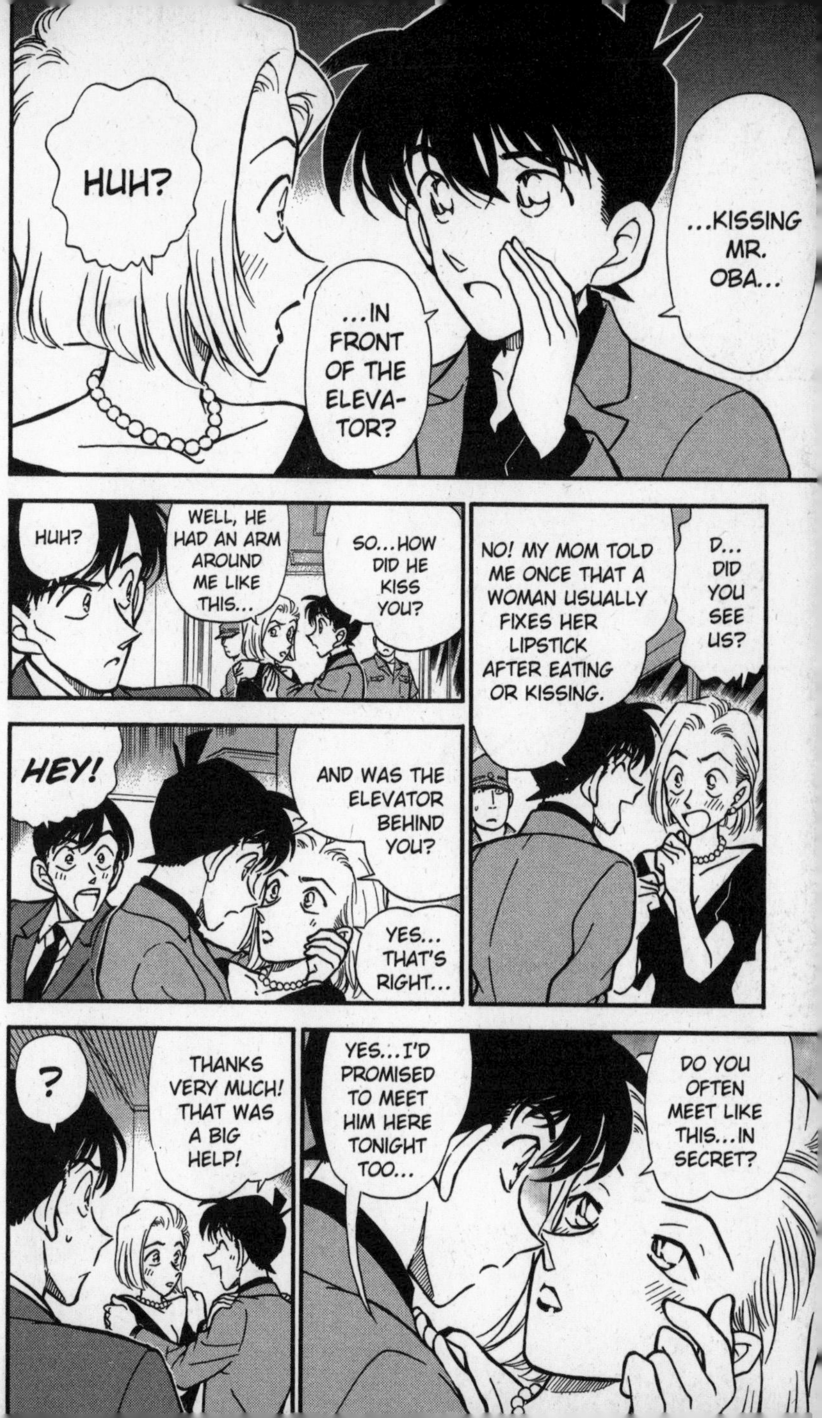
...KISSING MR. OBA...
...IN FRONT OF THE ELEVATOR?
HUH?
D... DID YOU SEE US?
NO! MY MOM TOLD ME ONCE THAT A WOMAN USUALLY FIXES HER LIPSTICK AFTER EATING OR KISSING.
SO...HOW DID HE KISS YOU?
WELL, HE HAD AN ARM AROUND ME LIKE THIS...
HUH?
AND WAS THE ELEVATOR BEHIND YOU?
YES... THAT'S RIGHT...
HEY!
DO YOU OFTEN MEET LIKE THIS...IN SECRET?
YES...I'D PROMISED TO MEET HIM HERE TONIGHT TOO...
THANKS VERY MUCH! THAT WAS A BIG HELP!
?

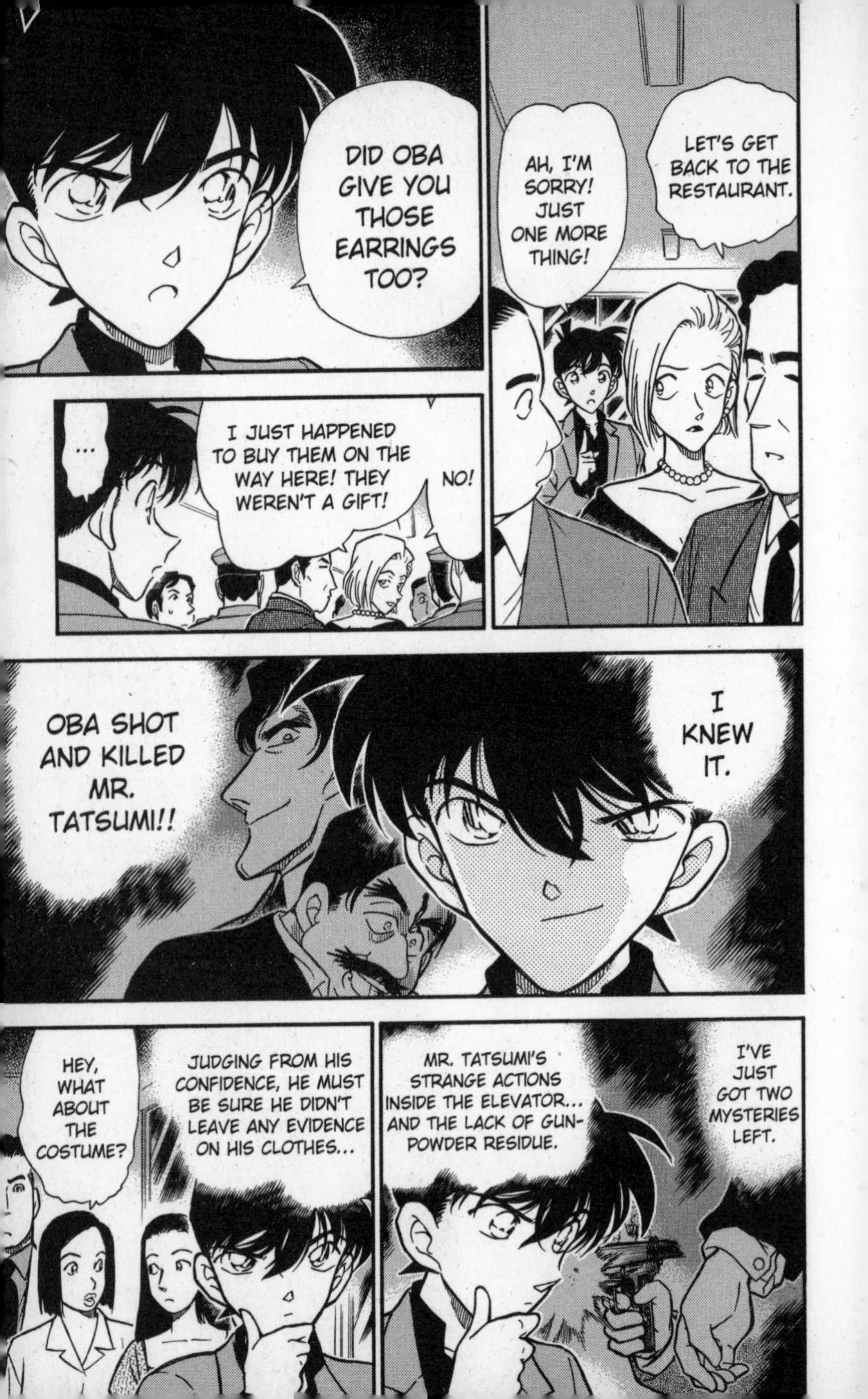
LET'S GET BACK TO THE RESTAURANT.
AH, I'M SORRY! JUST ONE MORE THING!
DID OBA GIVE YOU THOSE EARRINGS TOO?
NO!
I JUST HAPPENED TO BUY THEM ON THE WAY HERE! THEY WEREN'T A GIFT!
...
I KNEW IT.
OBA SHOT AND KILLED MR. TATSUMI!!
I'VE JUST GOT TWO MYSTERIES LEFT.
MR. TATSUMI'S STRANGE ACTIONS INSIDE THE ELEVATOR... AND THE LACK OF GUN-POWDER RESIDUE.
JUDGING FROM HIS CONFIDENCE, HE MUST BE SURE HE DIDN'T LEAVE ANY EVIDENCE ON HIS CLOTHES...
HEY, WHAT ABOUT THE COSTUME?

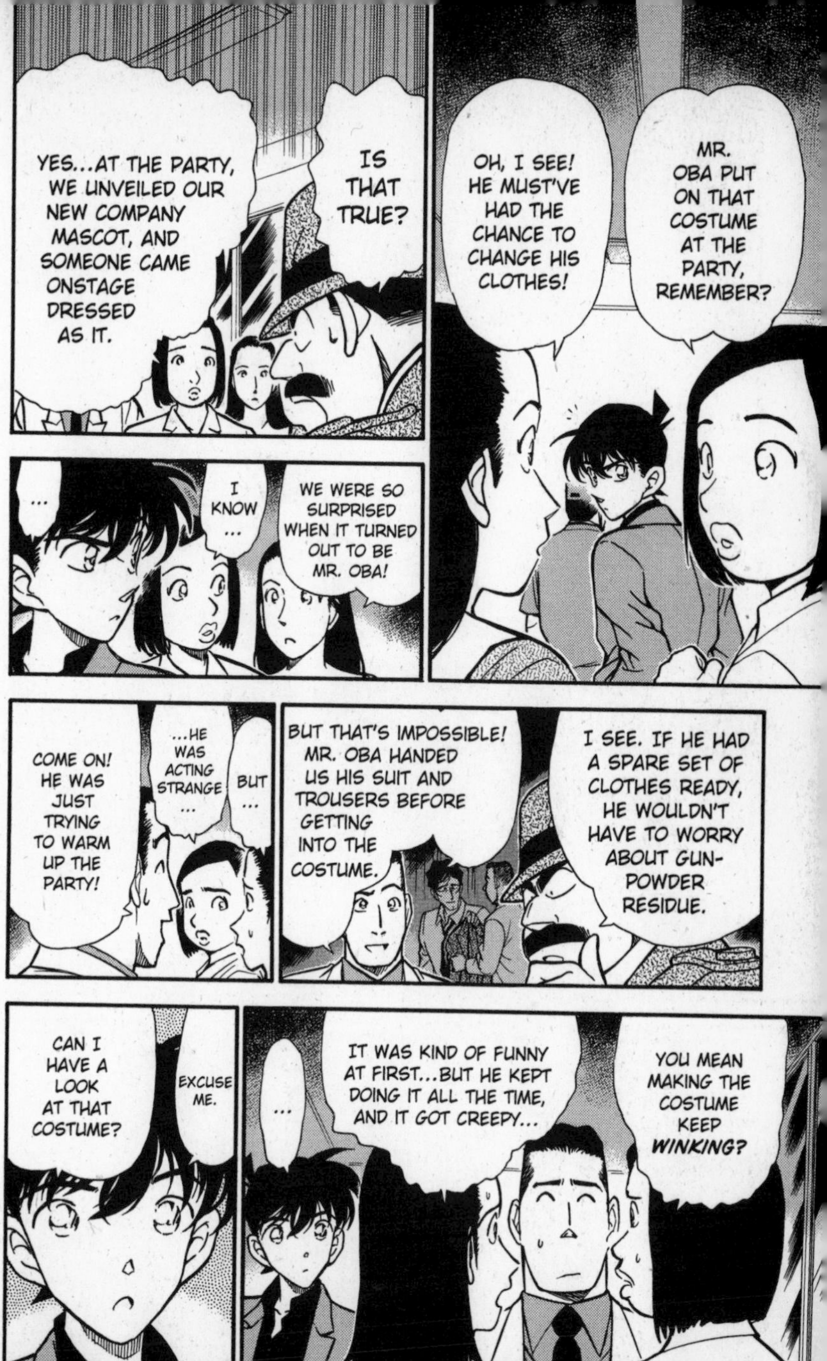
MR. OBA PUT ON THAT COSTUME AT THE PARTY, REMEMBER?
OH, I SEE! HE MUST'VE HAD THE CHANCE TO CHANGE HIS CLOTHES!
IS THAT TRUE?
YES...AT THE PARTY, WE UNVEILED OUR NEW COMPANY MASCOT, AND SOMEONE CAME ONSTAGE DRESSED AS IT.
WE WERE SO SURPRISED WHEN IT TURNED OUT TO BE MR. OBA!
I KNOW ...
...
I SEE. IF HE HAD A SPARE SET OF CLOTHES READY, HE WOULDN'T HAVE TO WORRY ABOUT GUN-POWDER RESIDUE.
BUT THAT'S IMPOSSIBLE! MR. OBA HANDED US HIS SUIT AND TROUSERS BEFORE GETTING INTO THE COSTUME.
BUT ...
...HE WAS ACTING STRANGE ...
COME ON! HE WAS JUST TRYING TO WARM UP THE PARTY!
YOU MEAN MAKING THE COSTUME KEEP *WINKING?*
IT WAS KIND OF FUNNY AT FIRST...BUT HE KEPT DOING IT ALL THE TIME, AND IT GOT CREEPY...
...
EXCUSE ME.
CAN I HAVE A LOOK AT THAT COSTUME?

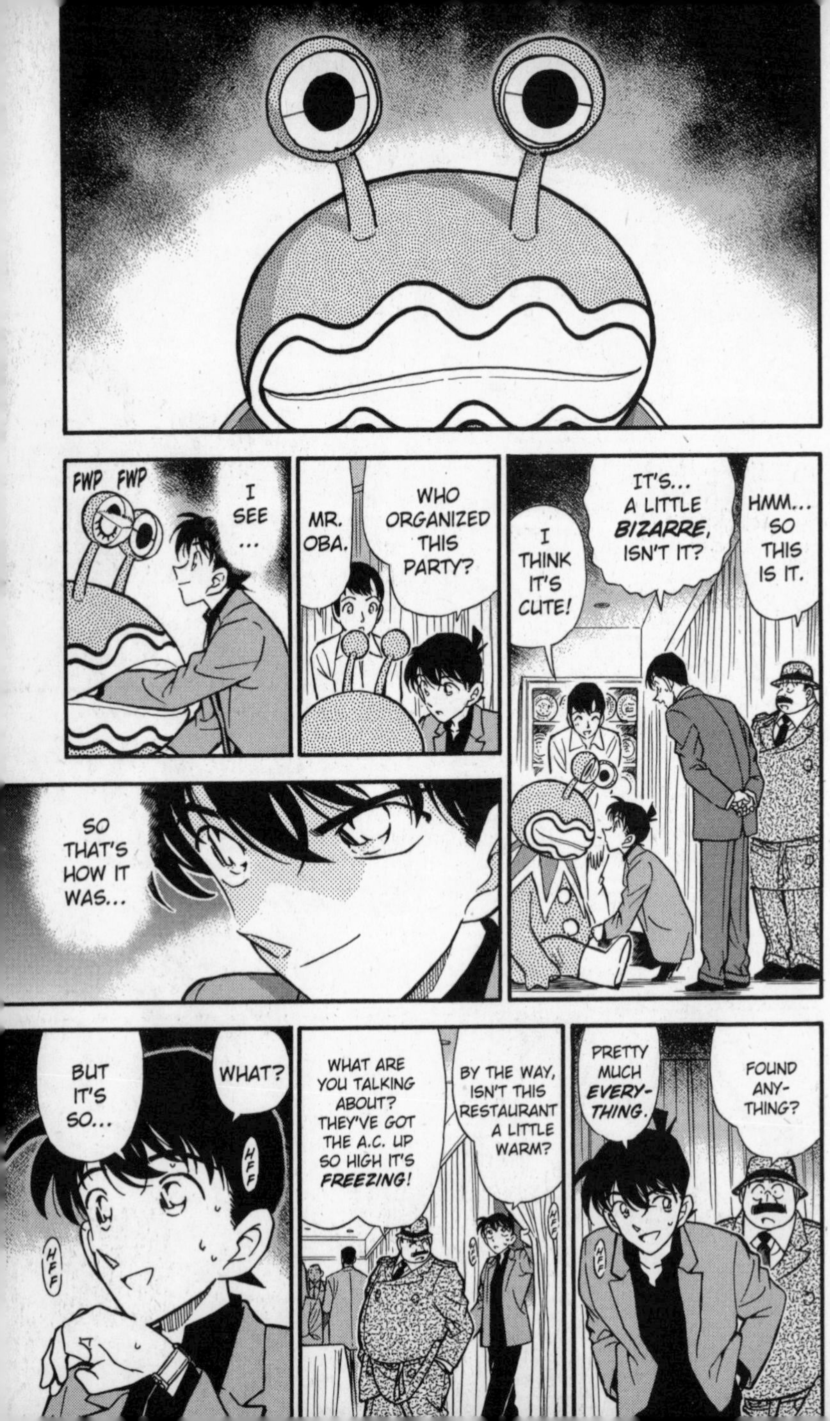
HMM... SO THIS IS IT.
IT'S... A LITTLE *BIZARRE*, ISN'T IT?
I THINK IT'S CUTE!
WHO ORGANIZED THIS PARTY?
MR. OBA.
FWP FWP
I SEE...
SO THAT'S HOW IT WAS...
FOUND ANYTHING?
PRETTY MUCH *EVERYTHING*.
HFF
BY THE WAY, ISN'T THIS RESTAURANT A LITTLE WARM?
HFF
WHAT ARE YOU TALKING ABOUT? THEY'VE GOT THE A.C. UP SO HIGH IT'S *FREEZING*!
WHAT?
HFF
BUT IT'S SO...
HFF

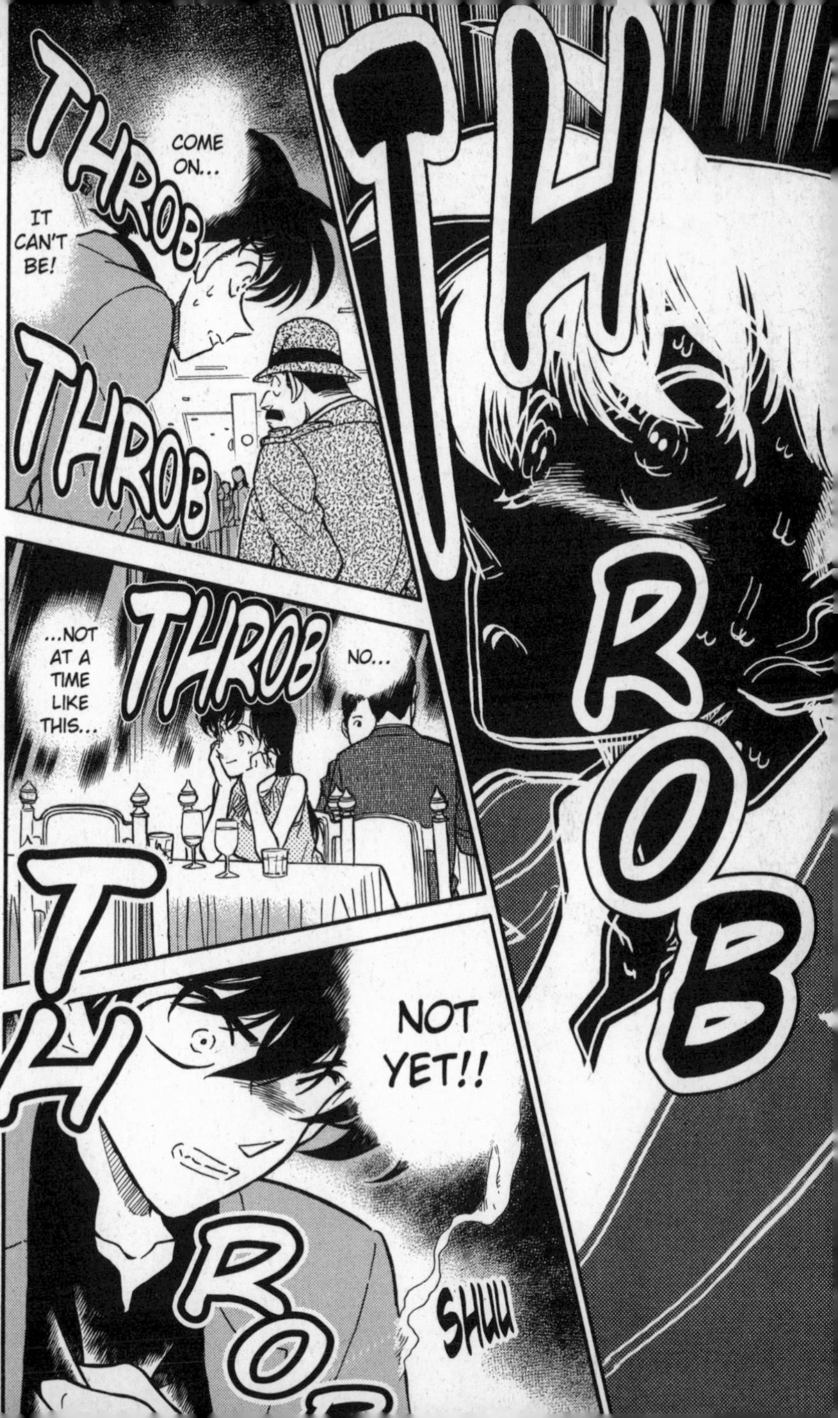
THROB
THROB
COME ON...
IT CAN'T BE!
THROB
NO...
THROB
...NOT AT A TIME LIKE THIS...
NOT YET!!
THRO
SHUU

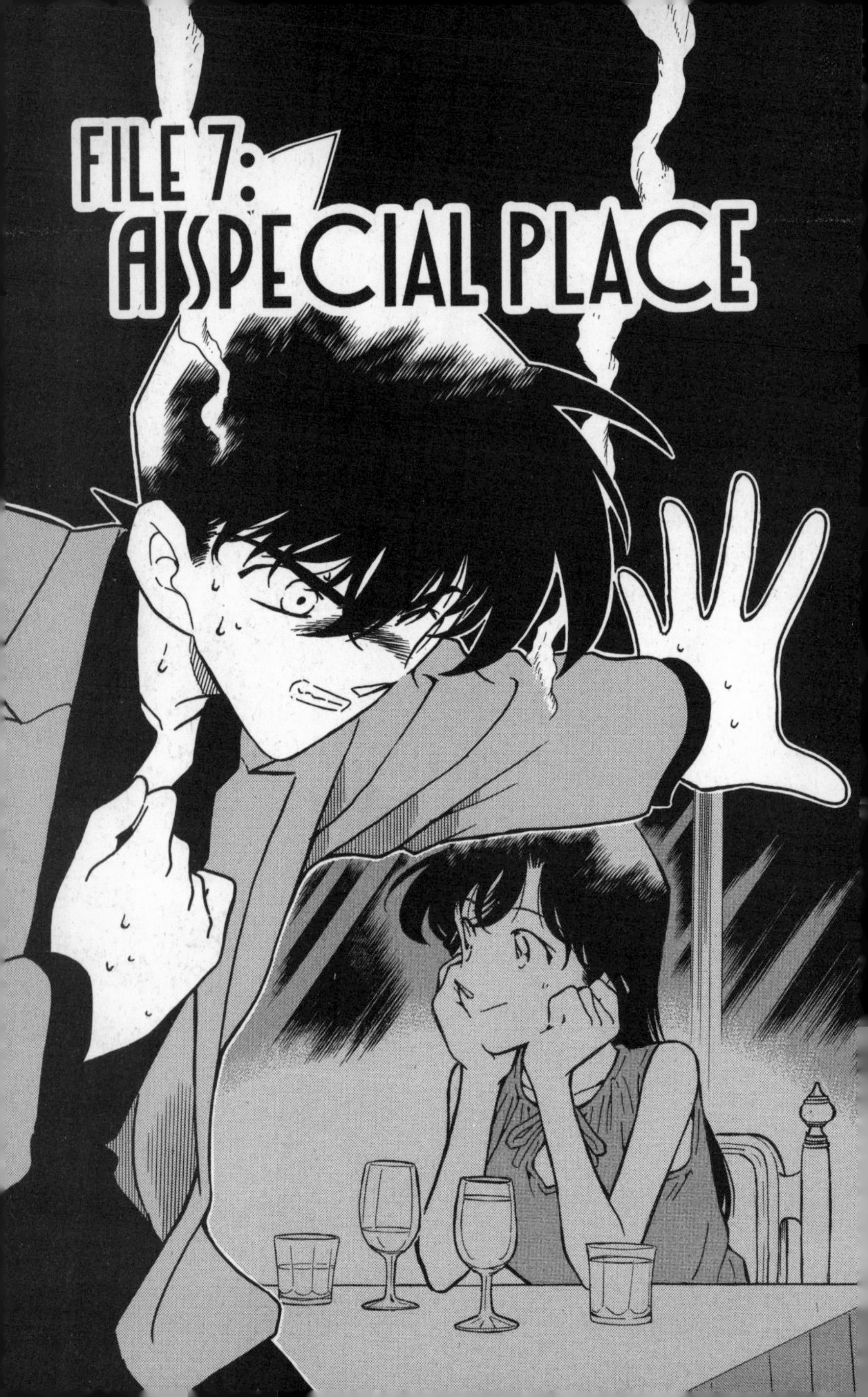
FILE 7:
A SPECIAL PLACE

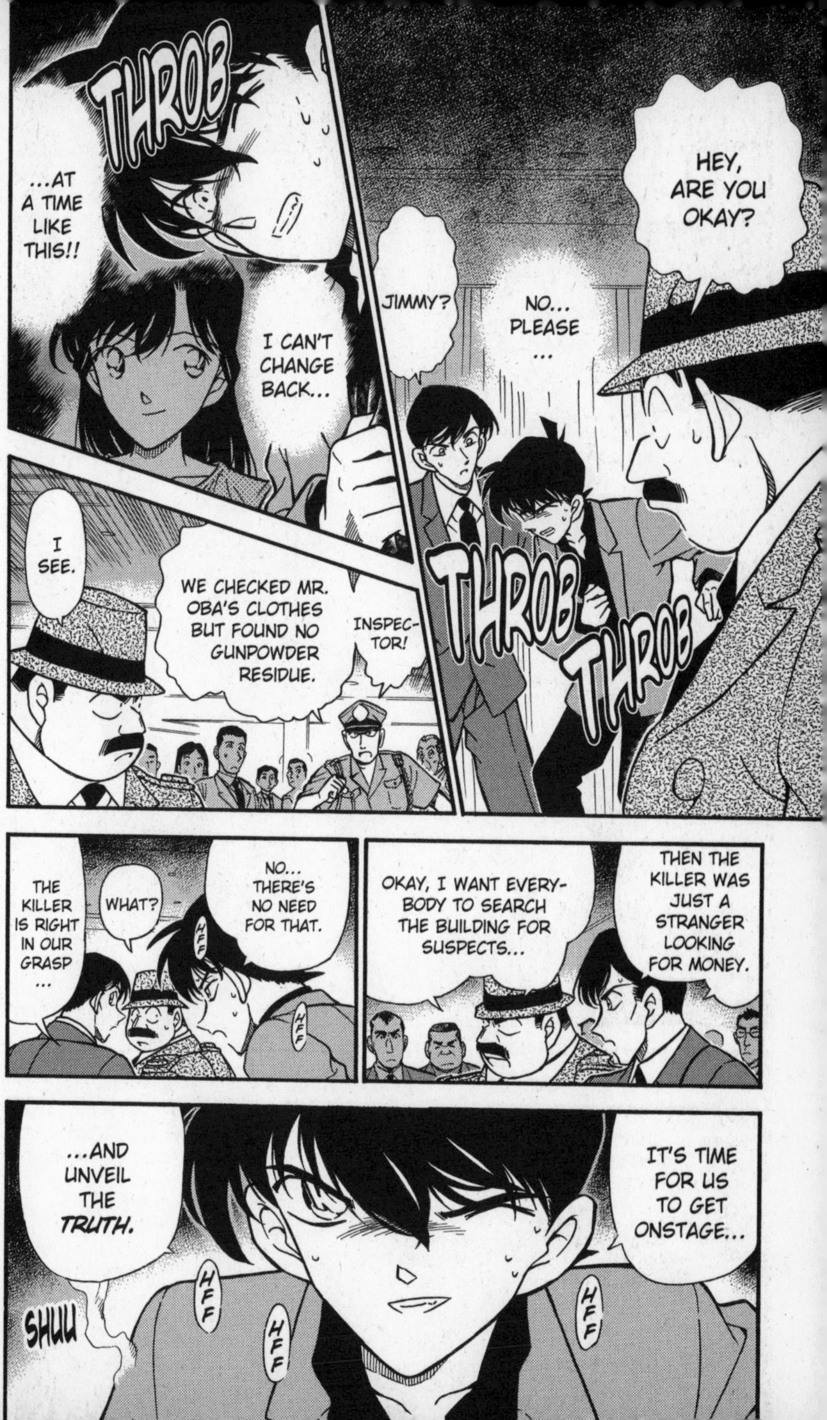
HEY, ARE YOU OKAY?
NO... PLEASE...
JIMMY?
THROB
THROB
THROB
I CAN'T CHANGE BACK...
...AT A TIME LIKE THIS!!
INSPECTOR!
WE CHECKED MR. OBA'S CLOTHES BUT FOUND NO GUNPOWDER RESIDUE.
I SEE.
THEN THE KILLER WAS JUST A STRANGER LOOKING FOR MONEY.
OKAY, I WANT EVERYBODY TO SEARCH THE BUILDING FOR SUSPECTS...
NO... THERE'S NO NEED FOR THAT.
HFF
HFF
WHAT?
THE KILLER IS RIGHT IN OUR GRASP...
IT'S TIME FOR US TO GET ONSTAGE...
...AND UNVEIL THE *TRUTH.*
HFF
HFF
HFF
SHUU

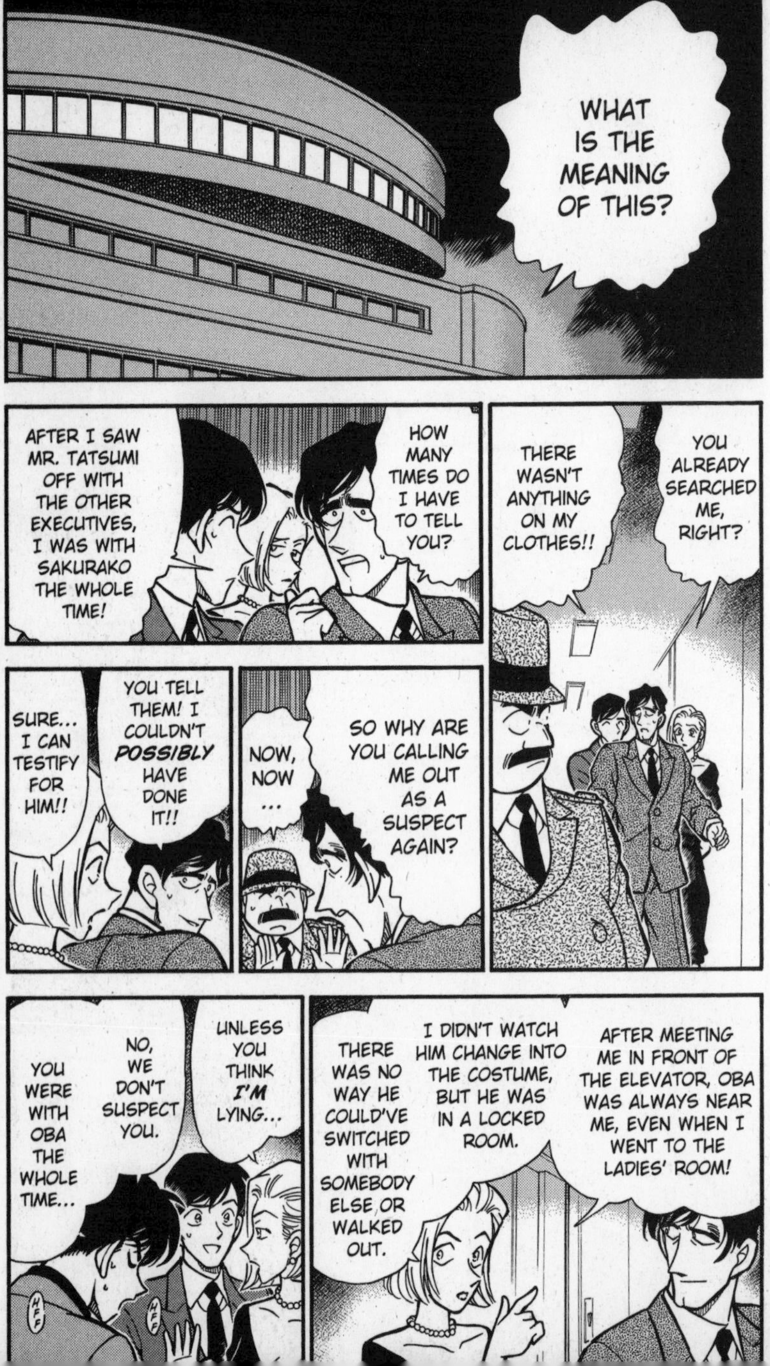
WHAT IS THE MEANING OF THIS?
YOU ALREADY SEARCHED ME, RIGHT?
THERE WASN'T ANYTHING ON MY CLOTHES!!
HOW MANY TIMES DO I HAVE TO TELL YOU?
AFTER I SAW MR. TATSUMI OFF WITH THE OTHER EXECUTIVES, I WAS WITH SAKURAKO THE WHOLE TIME!
SO WHY ARE YOU CALLING ME OUT AS A SUSPECT AGAIN?
NOW, NOW...
YOU TELL THEM! I COULDN'T *POSSIBLY* HAVE DONE IT!!
SURE... I CAN TESTIFY FOR HIM!!
AFTER MEETING ME IN FRONT OF THE ELEVATOR, OBA WAS ALWAYS NEAR ME, EVEN WHEN I WENT TO THE LADIES' ROOM!
I DIDN'T WATCH HIM CHANGE INTO THE COSTUME, BUT HE WAS IN A LOCKED ROOM.
THERE WAS NO WAY HE COULD'VE SWITCHED WITH SOMEBODY ELSE OR WALKED OUT.
UNLESS YOU THINK *I'M* LYING...
NO, WE DON'T SUSPECT YOU.
YOU WERE WITH OBA THE WHOLE TIME...
HFF
HFF

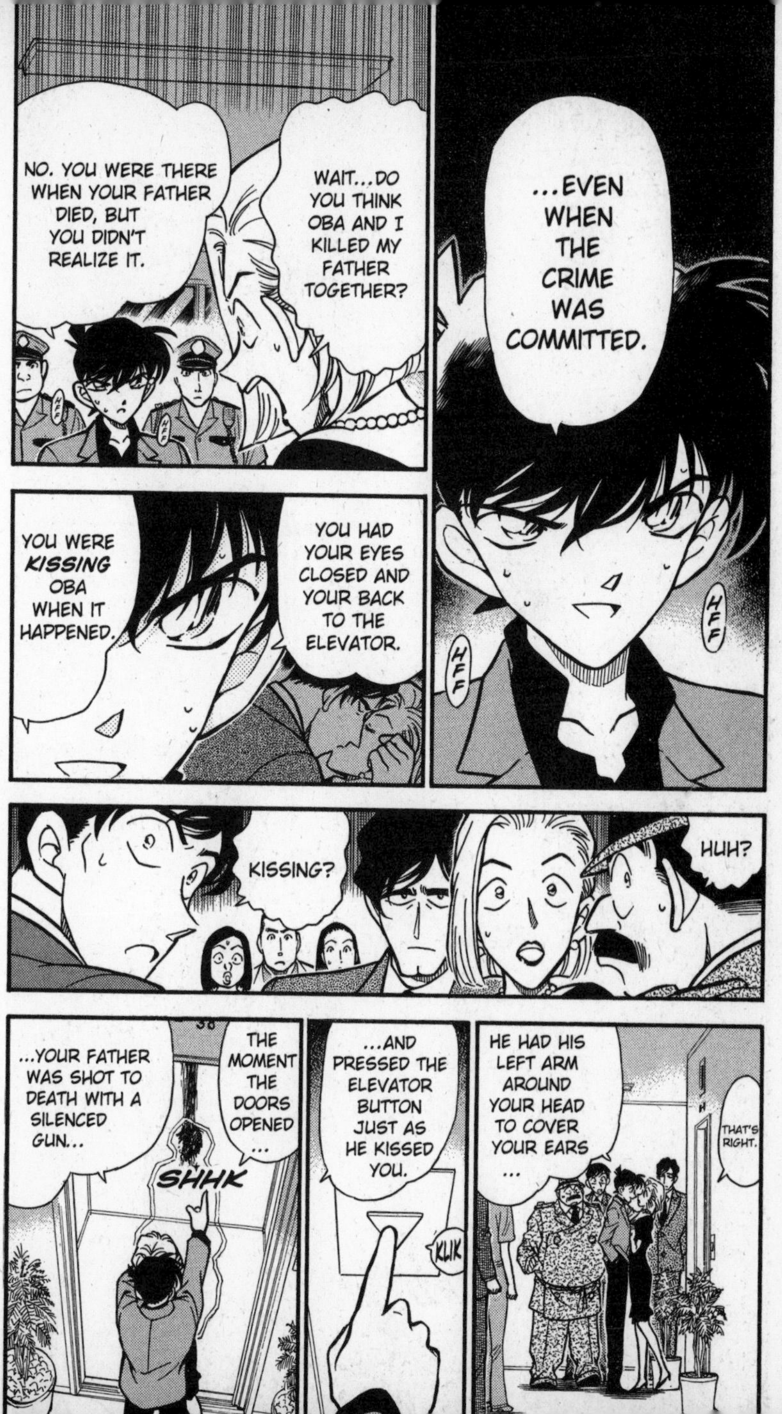
...EVEN WHEN THE CRIME WAS COMMITTED.
HFF
HFF
WAIT...DO YOU THINK OBA AND I KILLED MY FATHER TOGETHER?
NO. YOU WERE THERE WHEN YOUR FATHER DIED, BUT YOU DIDN'T REALIZE IT.
HFF
HFF
YOU HAD YOUR EYES CLOSED AND YOUR BACK TO THE ELEVATOR.
YOU WERE *KISSING* OBA WHEN IT HAPPENED.
HUH?
KISSING?
HE HAD HIS LEFT ARM AROUND YOUR HEAD TO COVER YOUR EARS ...
THAT'S RIGHT.
...AND PRESSED THE ELEVATOR BUTTON JUST AS HE KISSED YOU.
KLIK
THE MOMENT THE DOORS OPENED ...
...YOUR FATHER WAS SHOT TO DEATH WITH A SILENCED GUN...
SHHK

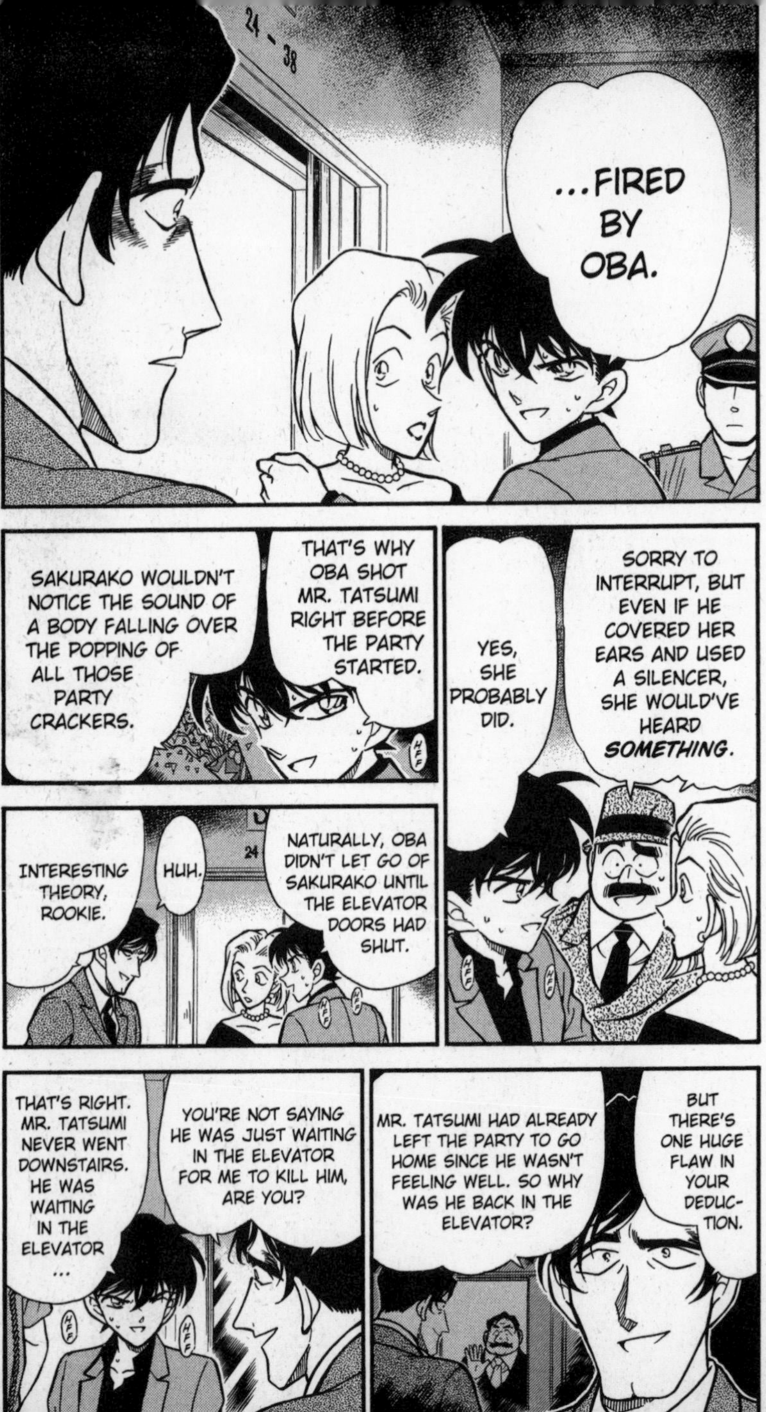
...FIRED BY OBA.
SORRY TO INTERRUPT, BUT EVEN IF HE COVERED HER EARS AND USED A SILENCER, SHE WOULD'VE HEARD *SOMETHING*.
YES, SHE PROBABLY DID.
THAT'S WHY OBA SHOT MR. TATSUMI RIGHT BEFORE THE PARTY STARTED.
SAKURAKO WOULDN'T NOTICE THE SOUND OF A BODY FALLING OVER THE POPPING OF ALL THOSE PARTY CRACKERS.
NATURALLY, OBA DIDN'T LET GO OF SAKURAKO UNTIL THE ELEVATOR DOORS HAD SHUT.
HUH.
INTERESTING THEORY, ROOKIE.
BUT THERE'S ONE HUGE FLAW IN YOUR DEDUCTION.
MR. TATSUMI HAD ALREADY LEFT THE PARTY TO GO HOME SINCE HE WASN'T FEELING WELL. SO WHY WAS HE BACK IN THE ELEVATOR?
YOU'RE NOT SAYING HE WAS JUST WAITING IN THE ELEVATOR FOR ME TO KILL HIM, ARE YOU?
THAT'S RIGHT. MR. TATSUMI NEVER WENT DOWNSTAIRS. HE WAS WAITING IN THE ELEVATOR...

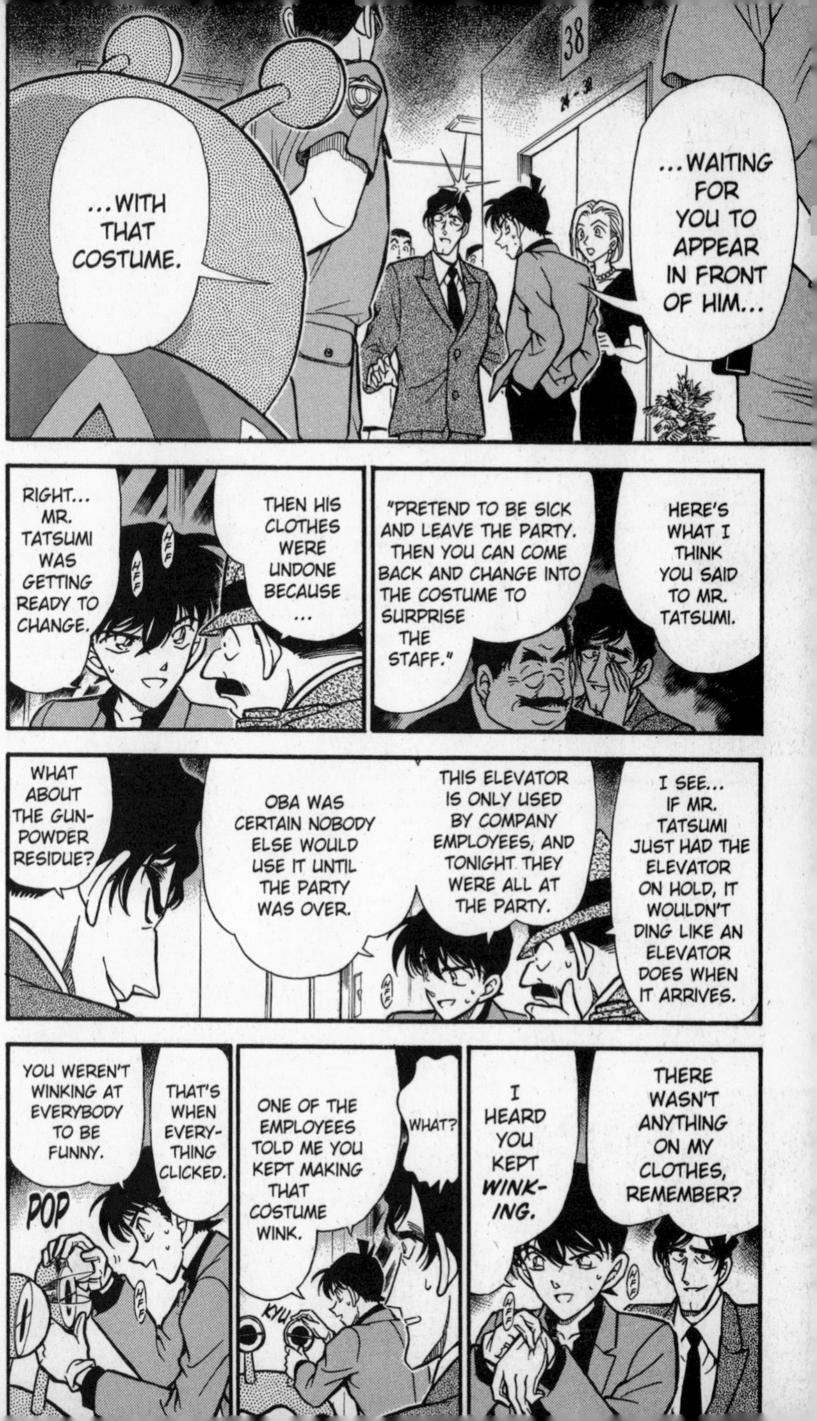
38
...WAITING FOR YOU TO APPEAR IN FRONT OF HIM...
...WITH THAT COSTUME.
HERE'S WHAT I THINK YOU SAID TO MR. TATSUMI.
"PRETEND TO BE SICK AND LEAVE THE PARTY. THEN YOU CAN COME BACK AND CHANGE INTO THE COSTUME TO SURPRISE THE STAFF."
THEN HIS CLOTHES WERE UNDONE BECAUSE...
HFF HFF
RIGHT... MR. TATSUMI WAS GETTING READY TO CHANGE.
I SEE... IF MR. TATSUMI JUST HAD THE ELEVATOR ON HOLD, IT WOULDN'T DING LIKE AN ELEVATOR DOES WHEN IT ARRIVES.
THIS ELEVATOR IS ONLY USED BY COMPANY EMPLOYEES, AND TONIGHT THEY WERE ALL AT THE PARTY.
OBA WAS CERTAIN NOBODY ELSE WOULD USE IT UNTIL THE PARTY WAS OVER.
HFF
WHAT ABOUT THE GUN-POWDER RESIDUE?
THERE WASN'T ANYTHING ON MY CLOTHES, REMEMBER?
I HEARD YOU KEPT *WINK-ING.*
HFF HFF
WHAT?
ONE OF THE EMPLOYEES TOLD ME YOU KEPT MAKING THAT COSTUME WINK.
KYU
THAT'S WHEN EVERY-THING CLICKED.
YOU WEREN'T WINKING AT EVERYBODY TO BE FUNNY.
POP
HFF

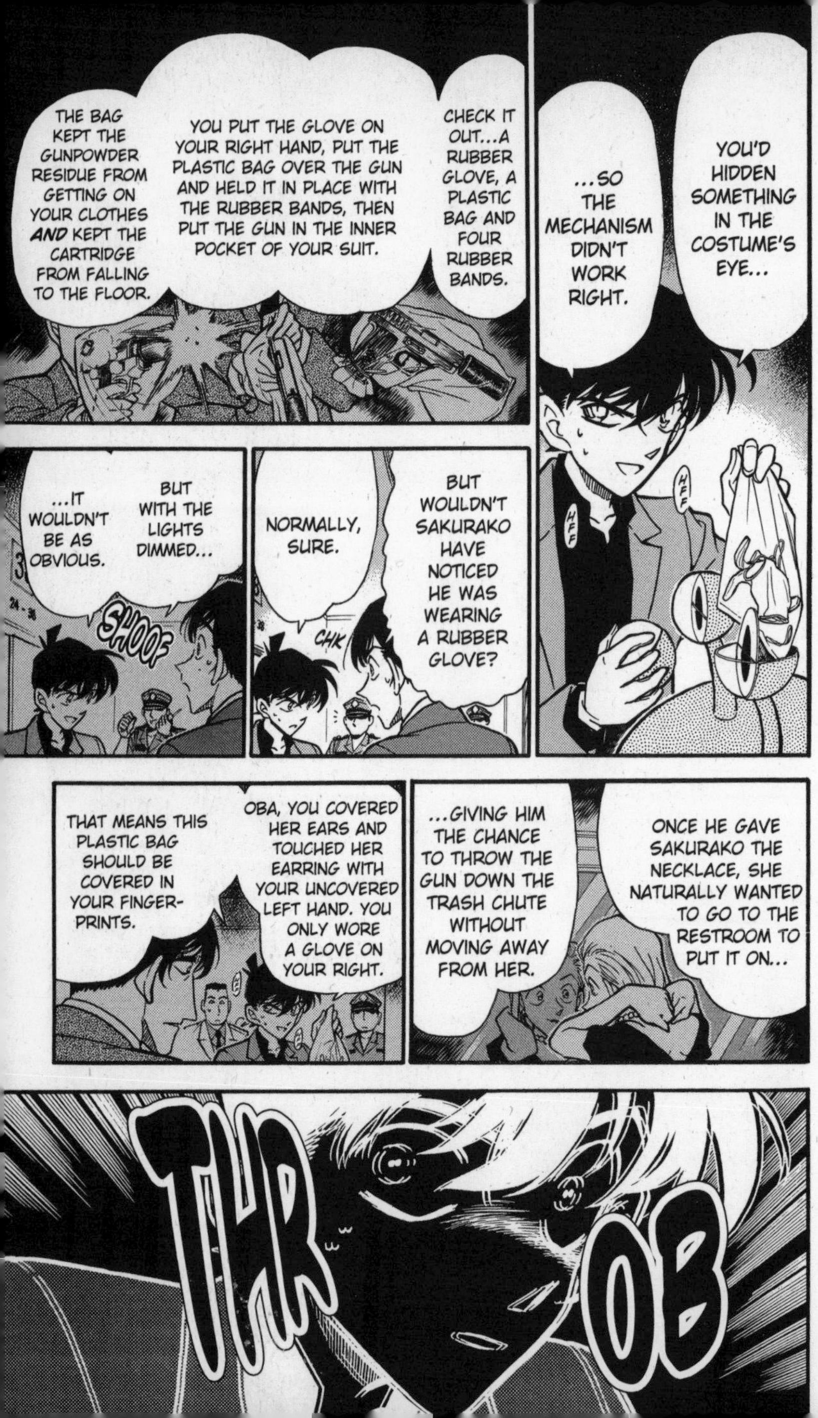
YOU'D HIDDEN SOMETHING IN THE COSTUME'S EYE...
...SO THE MECHANISM DIDN'T WORK RIGHT.
HFF
HFF
CHECK IT OUT...A RUBBER GLOVE, A PLASTIC BAG AND FOUR RUBBER BANDS.
YOU PUT THE GLOVE ON YOUR RIGHT HAND, PUT THE PLASTIC BAG OVER THE GUN AND HELD IT IN PLACE WITH THE RUBBER BANDS, THEN PUT THE GUN IN THE INNER POCKET OF YOUR SUIT.
THE BAG KEPT THE GUNPOWDER RESIDUE FROM GETTING ON YOUR CLOTHES *AND* KEPT THE CARTRIDGE FROM FALLING TO THE FLOOR.
BUT WOULDN'T SAKURAKO HAVE NOTICED HE WAS WEARING A RUBBER GLOVE?
NORMALLY, SURE.
CHK
BUT WITH THE LIGHTS DIMMED...
...IT WOULDN'T BE AS OBVIOUS.
SHOOF
ONCE HE GAVE SAKURAKO THE NECKLACE, SHE NATURALLY WANTED TO GO TO THE RESTROOM TO PUT IT ON...
...GIVING HIM THE CHANCE TO THROW THE GUN DOWN THE TRASH CHUTE WITHOUT MOVING AWAY FROM HER.
OBA, YOU COVERED HER EARS AND TOUCHED HER EARRING WITH YOUR UNCOVERED LEFT HAND. YOU ONLY WORE A GLOVE ON YOUR RIGHT.
THAT MEANS THIS PLASTIC BAG SHOULD BE COVERED IN YOUR FINGER-PRINTS.
THROB

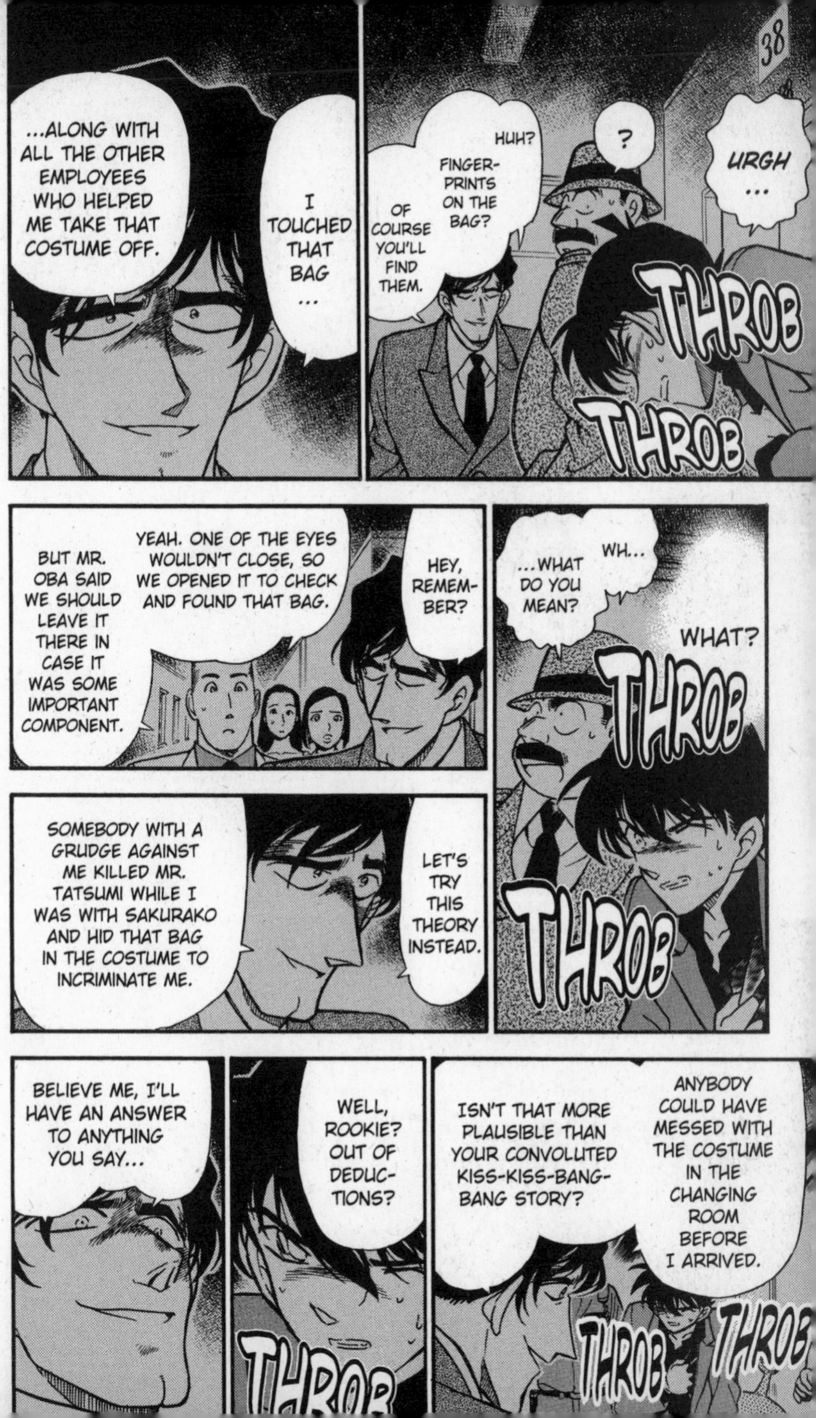
38
URGH…
?
HUH?
FINGER-PRINTS ON THE BAG?
OF COURSE YOU'LL FIND THEM.
THROB
THROB
I TOUCHED THAT BAG…
…ALONG WITH ALL THE OTHER EMPLOYEES WHO HELPED ME TAKE THAT COSTUME OFF.
WH…
…WHAT DO YOU MEAN?
WHAT?
THROB
THROB
HEY, REMEMBER?
YEAH. ONE OF THE EYES WOULDN'T CLOSE, SO WE OPENED IT TO CHECK AND FOUND THAT BAG.
BUT MR. OBA SAID WE SHOULD LEAVE IT THERE IN CASE IT WAS SOME IMPORTANT COMPONENT.
LET'S TRY THIS THEORY INSTEAD.
SOMEBODY WITH A GRUDGE AGAINST ME KILLED MR. TATSUMI WHILE I WAS WITH SAKURAKO AND HID THAT BAG IN THE COSTUME TO INCRIMINATE ME.
ANYBODY COULD HAVE MESSED WITH THE COSTUME IN THE CHANGING ROOM BEFORE I ARRIVED.
ISN'T THAT MORE PLAUSIBLE THAN YOUR CONVOLUTED KISS-KISS-BANG-BANG STORY?
THROB
THROB
WELL, ROOKIE? OUT OF DEDUCTIONS?
THROB
BELIEVE ME, I'LL HAVE AN ANSWER TO ANYTHING YOU SAY…

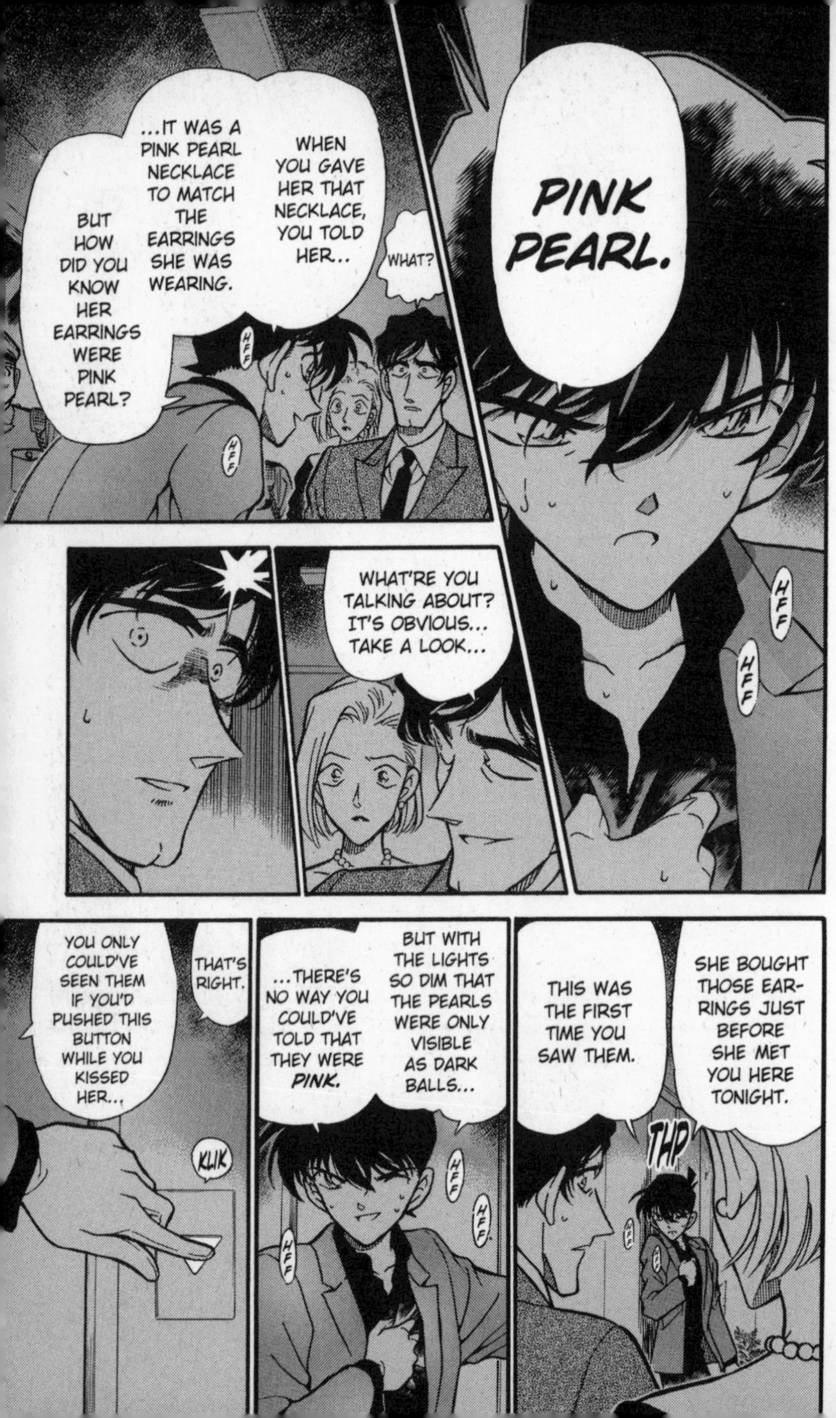
PINK PEARL.
HFF
HFF
WHAT?
WHEN YOU GAVE HER THAT NECKLACE, YOU TOLD HER...
...IT WAS A PINK PEARL NECKLACE TO MATCH THE EARRINGS SHE WAS WEARING.
BUT HOW DID YOU KNOW HER EARRINGS WERE PINK PEARL?
HFF
HFF
WHAT'RE YOU TALKING ABOUT? IT'S OBVIOUS... TAKE A LOOK...
SHE BOUGHT THOSE EAR-RINGS JUST BEFORE SHE MET YOU HERE TONIGHT.
THIS WAS THE FIRST TIME YOU SAW THEM.
THP
HFF
BUT WITH THE LIGHTS SO DIM THAT THE PEARLS WERE ONLY VISIBLE AS DARK BALLS...
...THERE'S NO WAY YOU COULD'VE TOLD THAT THEY WERE *PINK.*
HFF
HFF
HFF
THAT'S RIGHT.
YOU ONLY COULD'VE SEEN THEM IF YOU'D PUSHED THIS BUTTON WHILE YOU KISSED HER...
KLIK

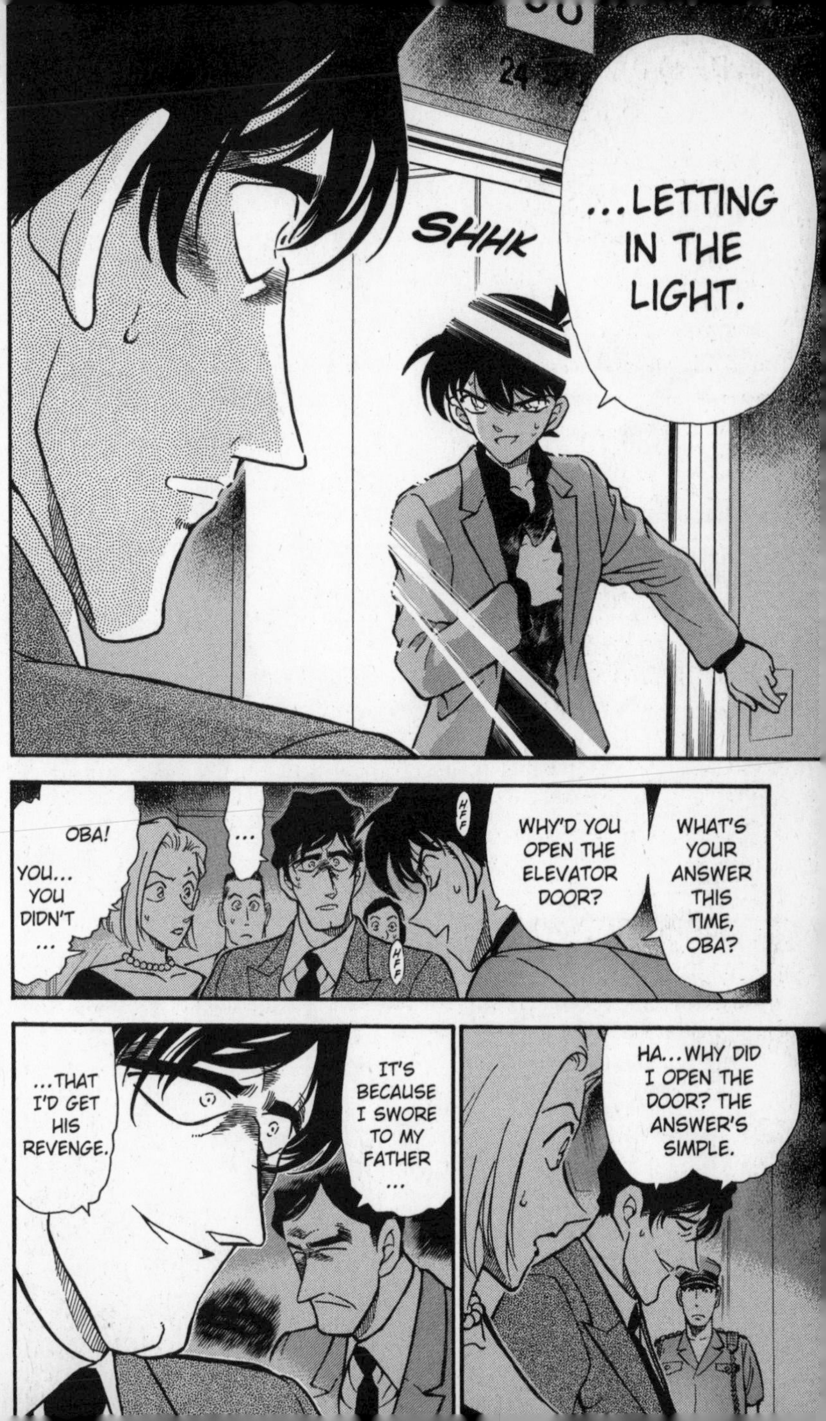
24
...LETTING IN THE LIGHT.
SHHK
WHAT'S YOUR ANSWER THIS TIME, OBA?
WHY'D YOU OPEN THE ELEVATOR DOOR?
HFF
HFF
...
OBA!
YOU... YOU DIDN'T ...
HA...WHY DID I OPEN THE DOOR? THE ANSWER'S SIMPLE.
IT'S BECAUSE I SWORE TO MY FATHER ...
...THAT I'D GET HIS REVENGE.

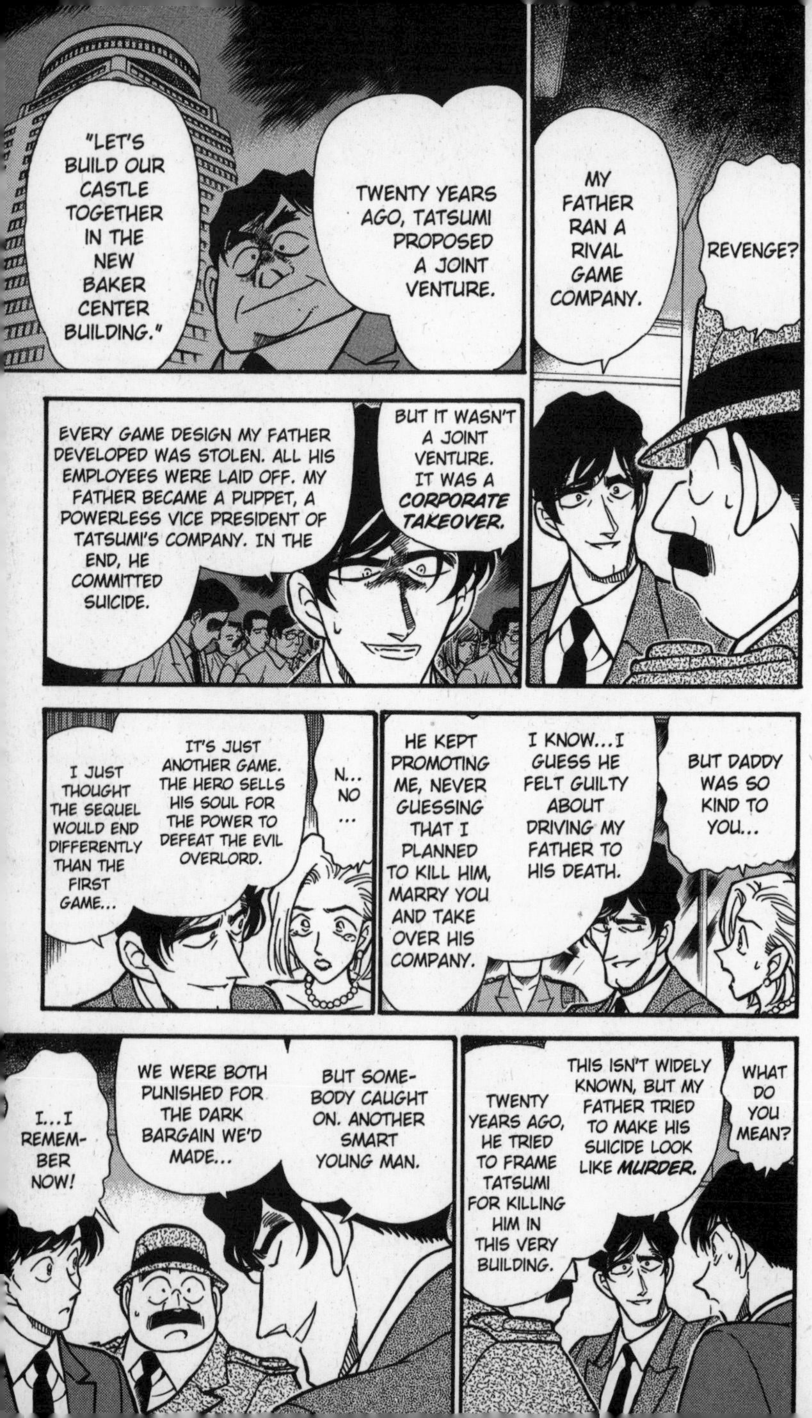
REVENGE?
MY FATHER RAN A RIVAL GAME COMPANY.
TWENTY YEARS AGO, TATSUMI PROPOSED A JOINT VENTURE.
"LET'S BUILD OUR CASTLE TOGETHER IN THE NEW BAKER CENTER BUILDING."
BUT IT WASN'T A JOINT VENTURE. IT WAS A *CORPORATE TAKEOVER.*
EVERY GAME DESIGN MY FATHER DEVELOPED WAS STOLEN. ALL HIS EMPLOYEES WERE LAID OFF. MY FATHER BECAME A PUPPET, A POWERLESS VICE PRESIDENT OF TATSUMI'S COMPANY. IN THE END, HE COMMITTED SUICIDE.
BUT DADDY WAS SO KIND TO YOU...
I KNOW...I GUESS HE FELT GUILTY ABOUT DRIVING MY FATHER TO HIS DEATH.
HE KEPT PROMOTING ME, NEVER GUESSING THAT I PLANNED TO KILL HIM, MARRY YOU AND TAKE OVER HIS COMPANY.
N... NO ...
IT'S JUST ANOTHER GAME. THE HERO SELLS HIS SOUL FOR THE POWER TO DEFEAT THE EVIL OVERLORD.
I JUST THOUGHT THE SEQUEL WOULD END DIFFERENTLY THAN THE FIRST GAME...
WHAT DO YOU MEAN?
THIS ISN'T WIDELY KNOWN, BUT MY FATHER TRIED TO MAKE HIS SUICIDE LOOK LIKE *MURDER.*
TWENTY YEARS AGO, HE TRIED TO FRAME TATSUMI FOR KILLING HIM IN THIS VERY BUILDING.
BUT SOMEBODY CAUGHT ON. ANOTHER SMART YOUNG MAN.
WE WERE BOTH PUNISHED FOR THE DARK BARGAIN WE'D MADE...
I...I REMEMBER NOW!

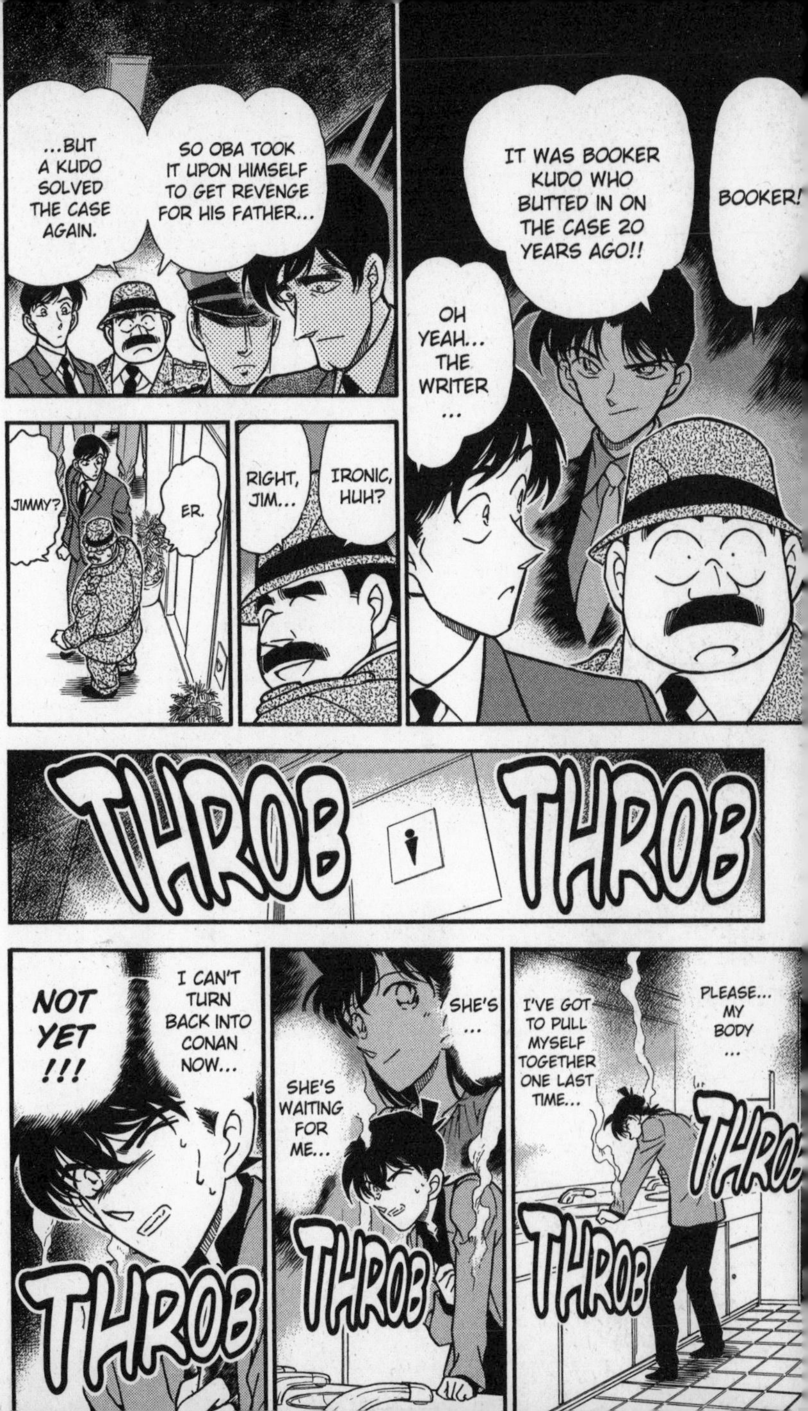
BOOKER!
IT WAS BOOKER KUDO WHO BUTTED IN ON THE CASE 20 YEARS AGO!!
OH YEAH... THE WRITER...
SO OBA TOOK IT UPON HIMSELF TO GET REVENGE FOR HIS FATHER...
...BUT A KUDO SOLVED THE CASE AGAIN.
IRONIC, HUH?
RIGHT, JIM...
ER.
JIMMY?
THROB
THROB
PLEASE... MY BODY...
I'VE GOT TO PULL MYSELF TOGETHER ONE LAST TIME...
THROB
THROB
SHE'S...
SHE'S WAITING FOR ME...
THROB
I CAN'T TURN BACK INTO CONAN NOW...
NOT YET!!!
THROB

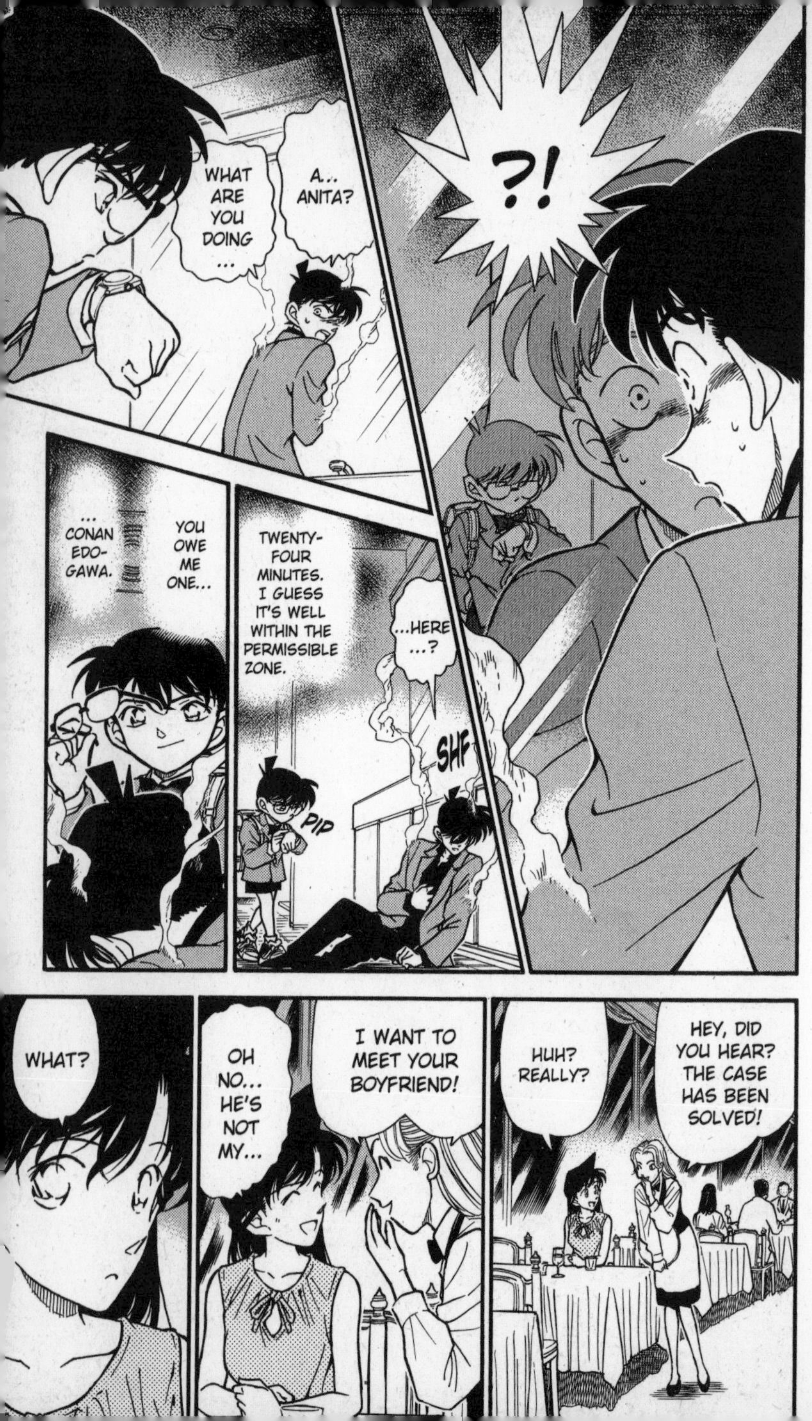
?!
A... ANITA?
WHAT ARE YOU DOING ...
TWENTY-FOUR MINUTES. I GUESS IT'S WELL WITHIN THE PERMISSIBLE ZONE.
...HERE ...?
SHF
PIP
YOU OWE ME ONE...
... CONAN EDOGAWA.
HEY, DID YOU HEAR? THE CASE HAS BEEN SOLVED!
HUH? REALLY?
I WANT TO MEET YOUR BOYFRIEND!
OH NO... HE'S NOT MY...
WHAT?

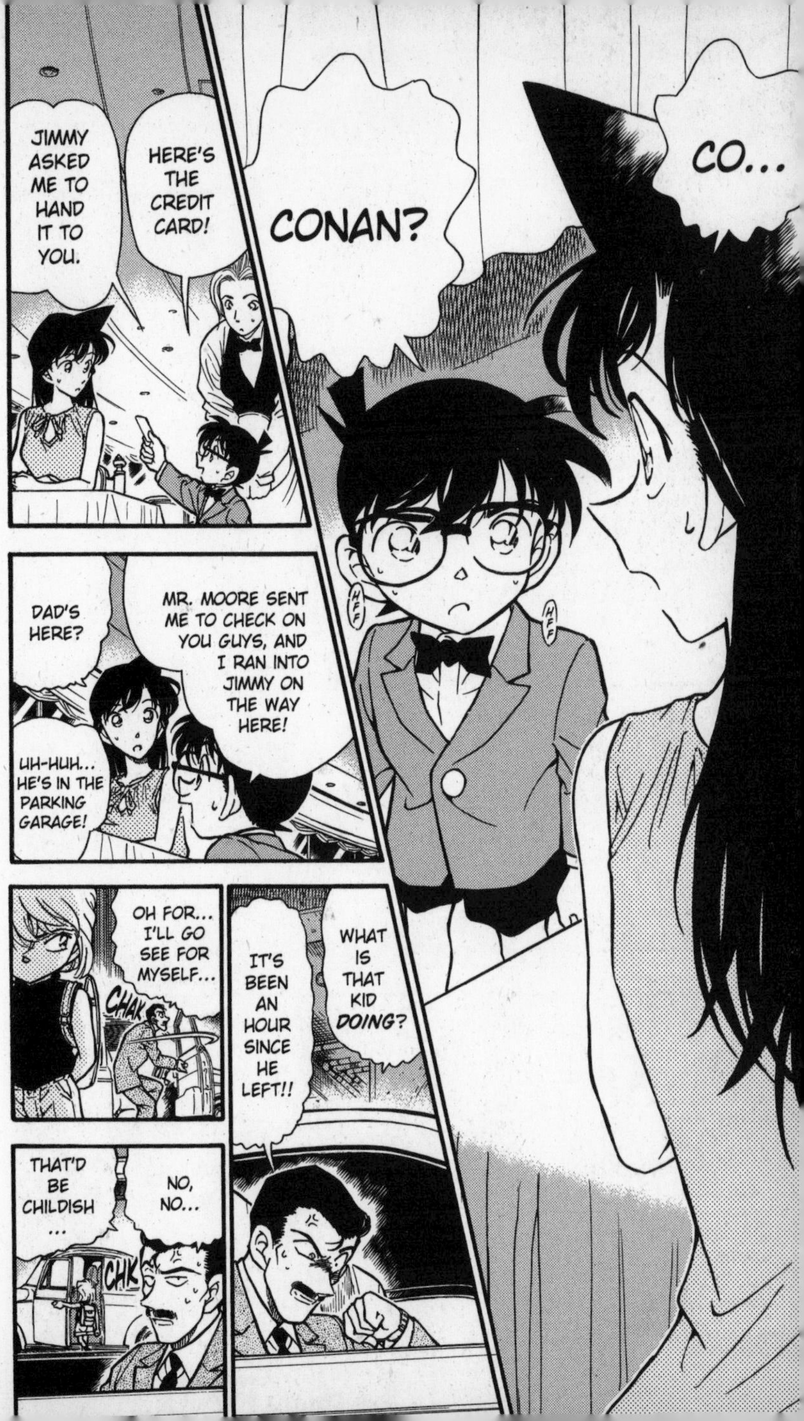
CO...
CONAN?
HFF
HFF
HERE'S THE CREDIT CARD!
JIMMY ASKED ME TO HAND IT TO YOU.
MR. MOORE SENT ME TO CHECK ON YOU GUYS, AND I RAN INTO JIMMY ON THE WAY HERE!
DAD'S HERE?
UH-HUH... HE'S IN THE PARKING GARAGE!
WHAT IS THAT KID DOING?
IT'S BEEN AN HOUR SINCE HE LEFT!!
OH FOR... I'LL GO SEE FOR MYSELF...
CHAK
NO, NO...
THAT'D BE CHILDISH ...
CHK

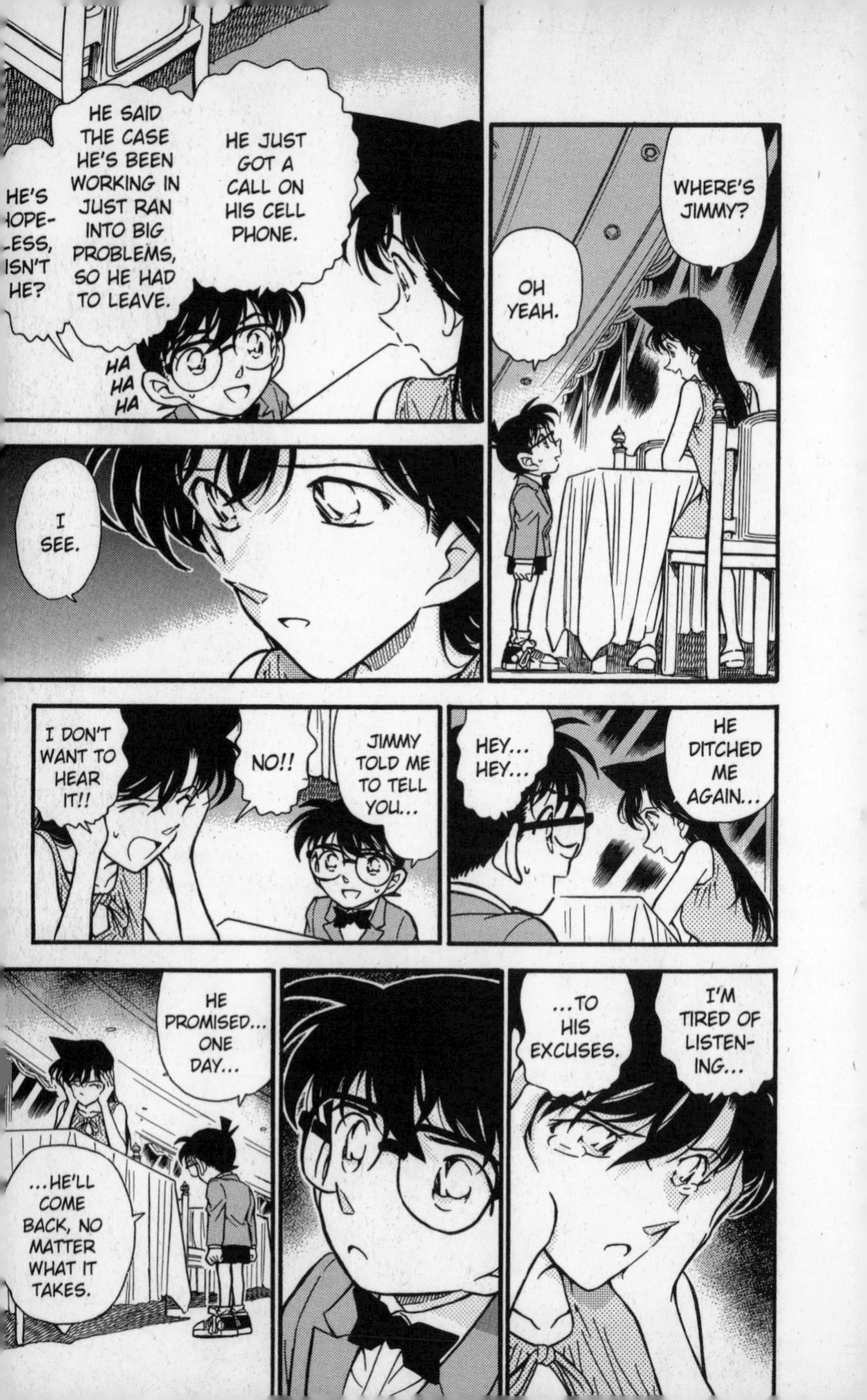
WHERE'S JIMMY?
OH YEAH.
HE JUST GOT A CALL ON HIS CELL PHONE.
HE SAID THE CASE HE'S BEEN WORKING IN JUST RAN INTO BIG PROBLEMS, SO HE HAD TO LEAVE.
HE'S HOPE-LESS, ISN'T HE?
HA HA HA
I SEE.
HE DITCHED ME AGAIN...
HEY... HEY...
JIMMY TOLD ME TO TELL YOU...
NO!!
I DON'T WANT TO HEAR IT!!
I'M TIRED OF LISTEN-ING...
...TO HIS EXCUSES.
HE PROMISED... ONE DAY...
...HE'LL COME BACK, NO MATTER WHAT IT TAKES.

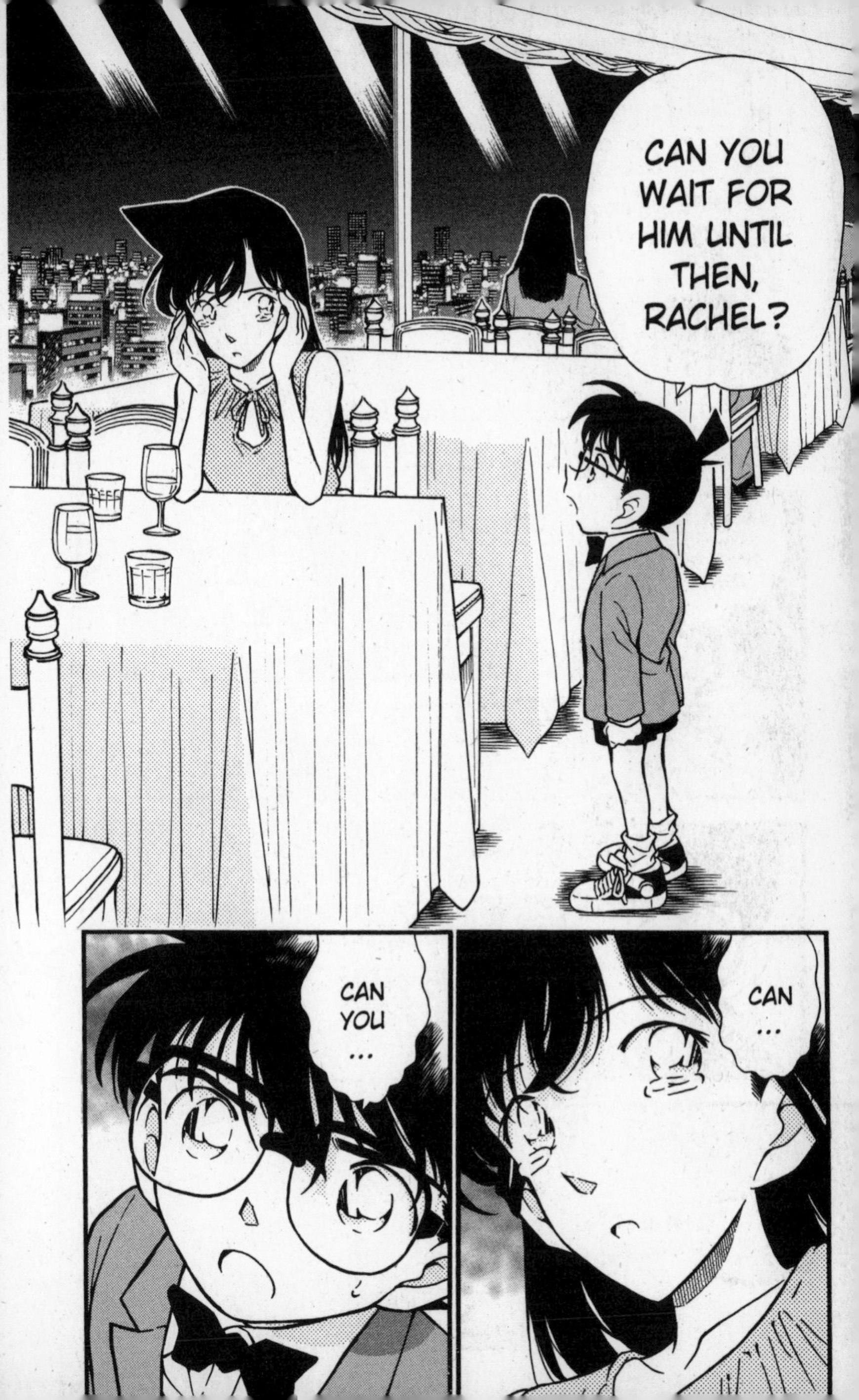
CAN YOU WAIT FOR HIM UNTIL THEN, RACHEL?
CAN ...
CAN YOU ...

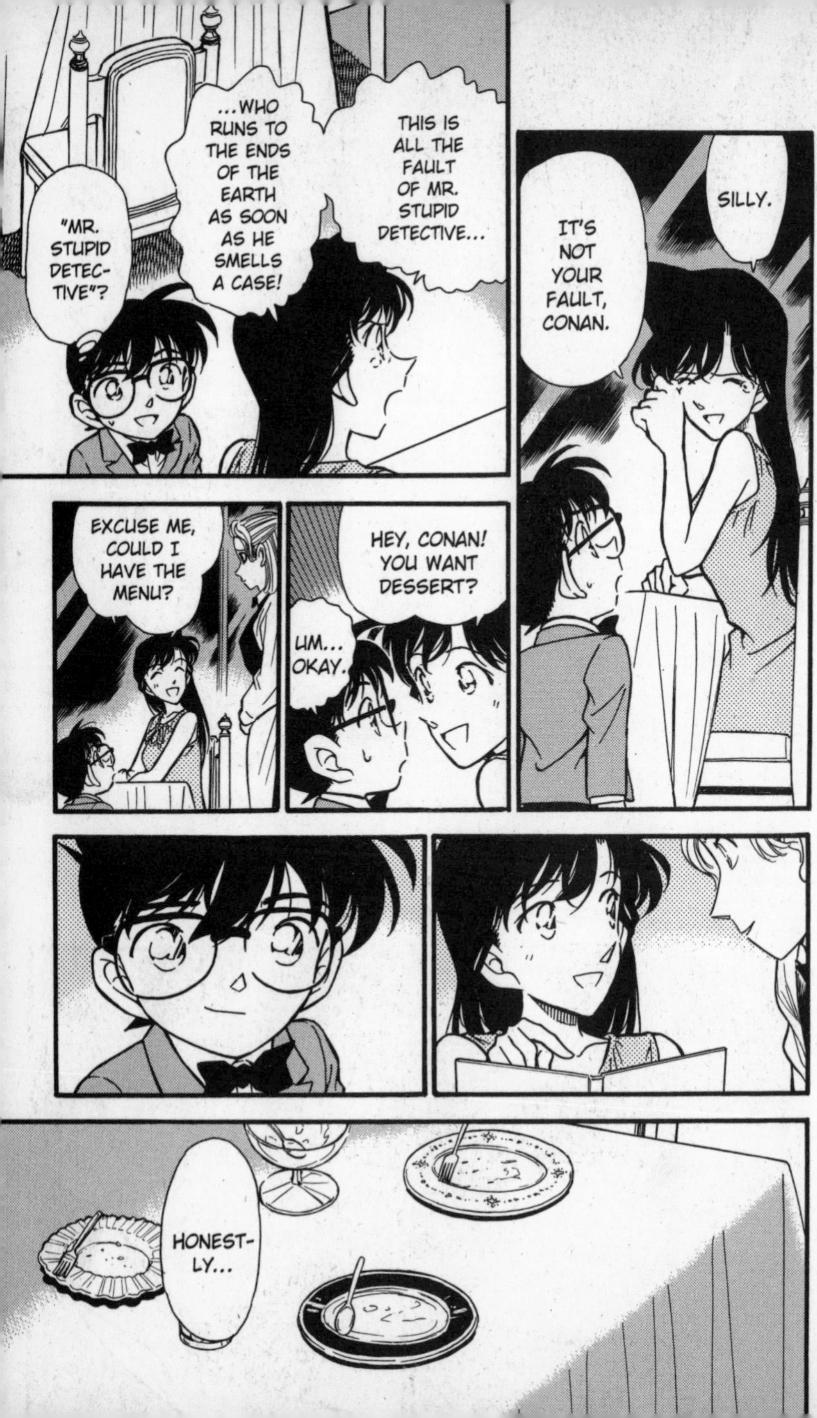
THIS IS ALL THE FAULT OF MR. STUPID DETECTIVE...
...WHO RUNS TO THE ENDS OF THE EARTH AS SOON AS HE SMELLS A CASE!
"MR. STUPID DETEC-TIVE"?
SILLY.
IT'S NOT YOUR FAULT, CONAN.
HEY, CONAN! YOU WANT DESSERT?
UM... OKAY.
EXCUSE ME, COULD I HAVE THE MENU?
HONEST-LY...

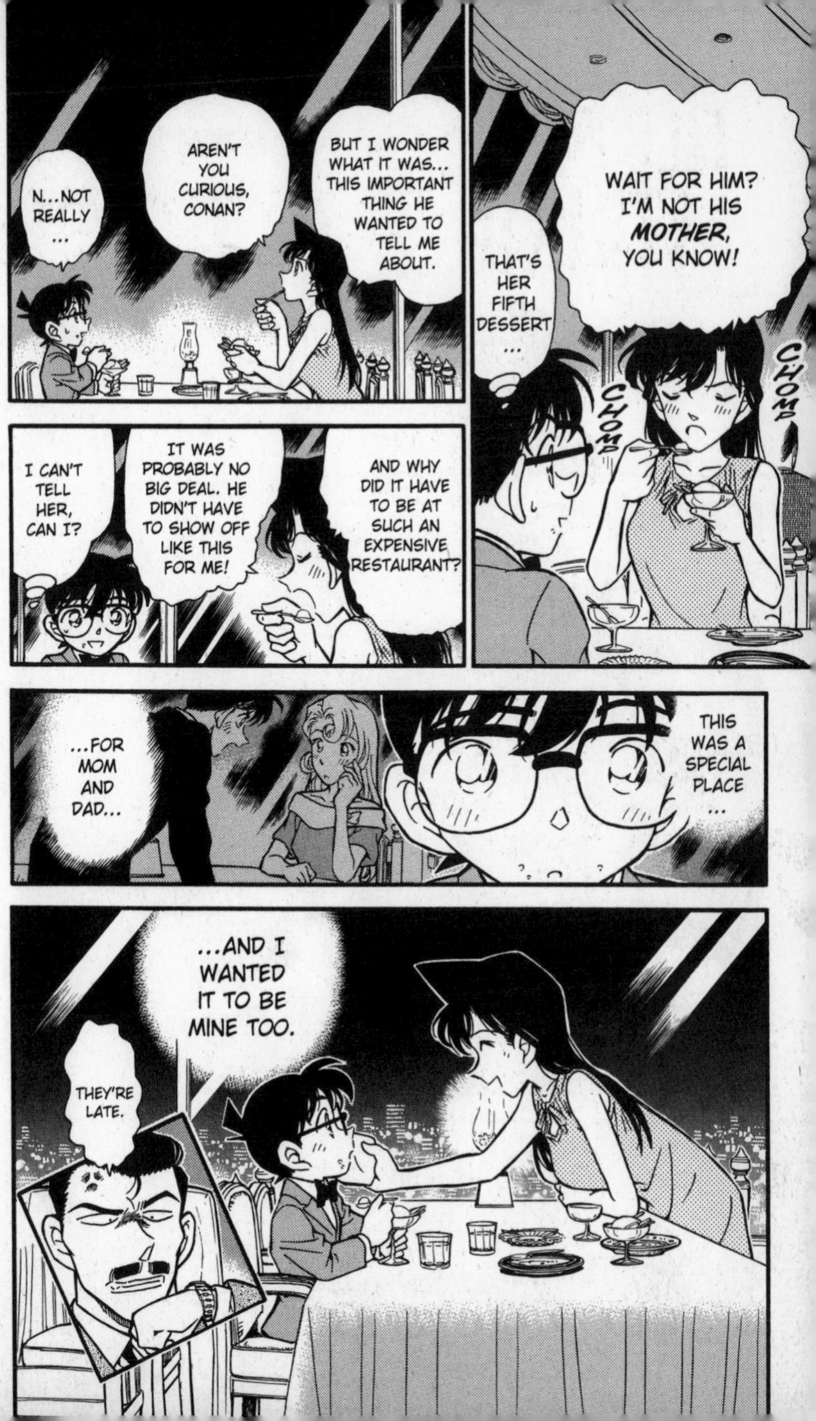
WAIT FOR HIM? I'M NOT HIS *MOTHER*, YOU KNOW!
CHOMP
THAT'S HER FIFTH DESSERT...
CHOMP
BUT I WONDER WHAT IT WAS... THIS IMPORTANT THING HE WANTED TO TELL ME ABOUT.
AREN'T YOU CURIOUS, CONAN?
N...NOT REALLY...
AND WHY DID IT HAVE TO BE AT SUCH AN EXPENSIVE RESTAURANT?
IT WAS PROBABLY NO BIG DEAL. HE DIDN'T HAVE TO SHOW OFF LIKE THIS FOR ME!
I CAN'T TELL HER, CAN I?
THIS WAS A SPECIAL PLACE...
...FOR MOM AND DAD...
...AND I WANTED IT TO BE MINE TOO.
THEY'RE LATE.

FILE 8: STRIKING A CHORD

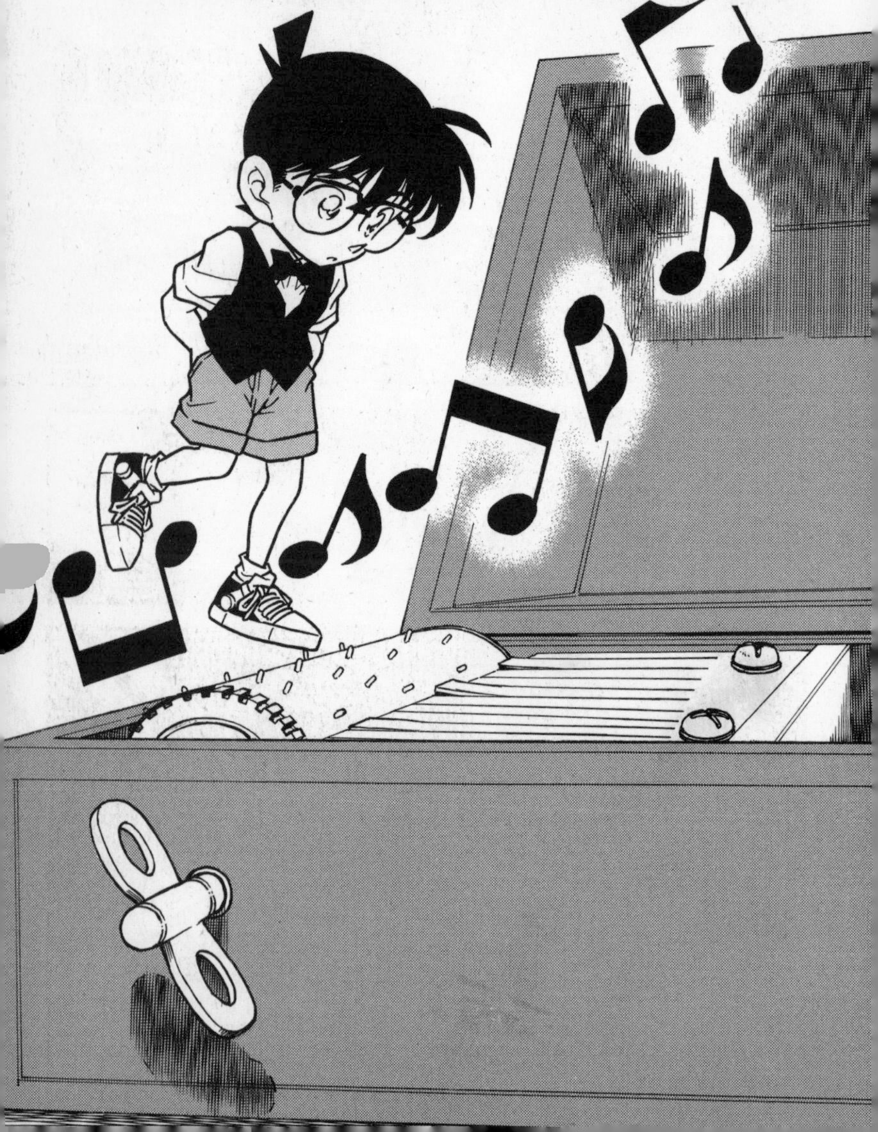

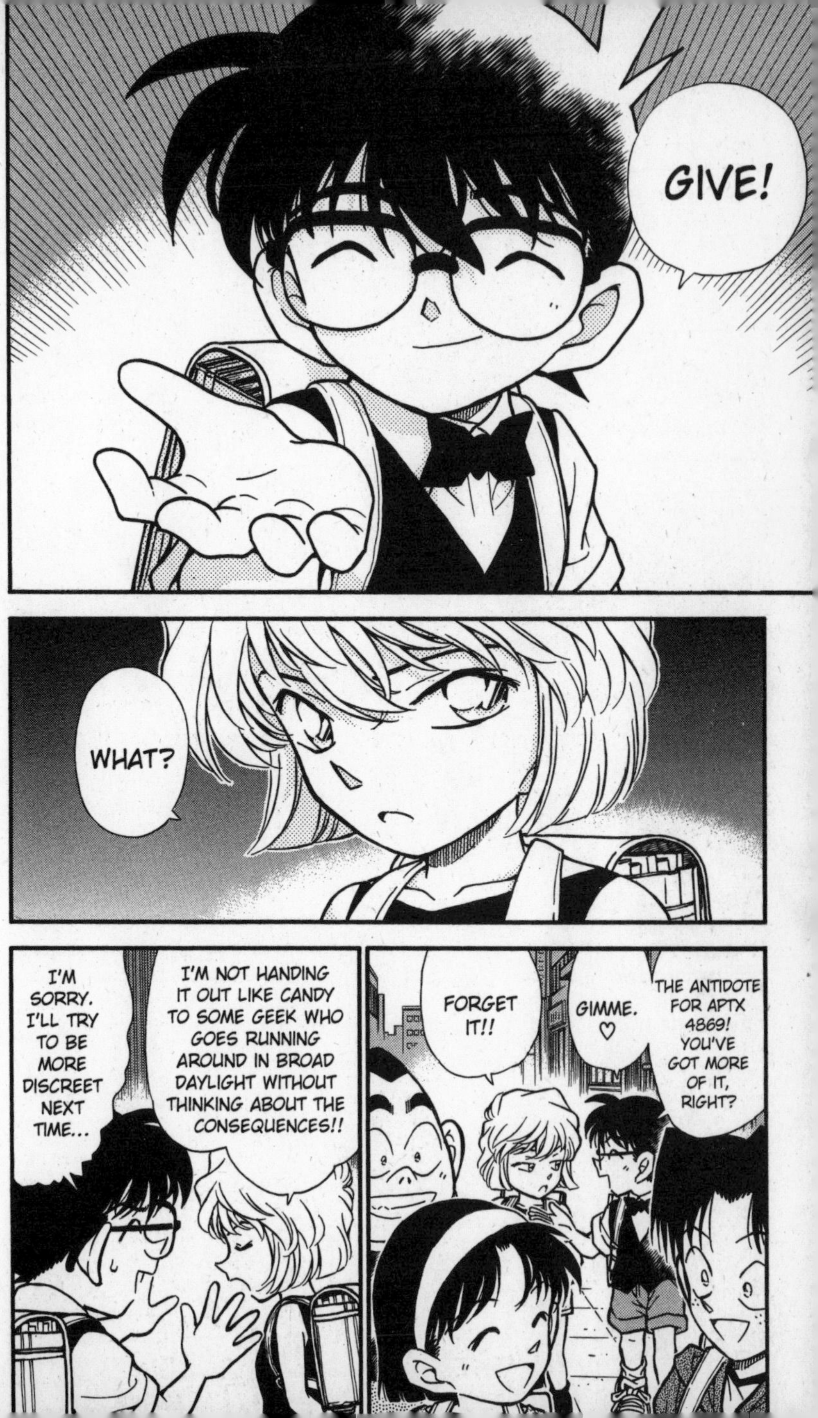
GIVE!
WHAT?
THE ANTIDOTE FOR APTX 4869! YOU'VE GOT MORE OF IT, RIGHT?
GIMME. ♡
FORGET IT!!
I'M NOT HANDING IT OUT LIKE CANDY TO SOME GEEK WHO GOES RUNNING AROUND IN BROAD DAYLIGHT WITHOUT THINKING ABOUT THE CONSEQUENCES!!
I'M SORRY. I'LL TRY TO BE MORE DISCREET NEXT TIME...

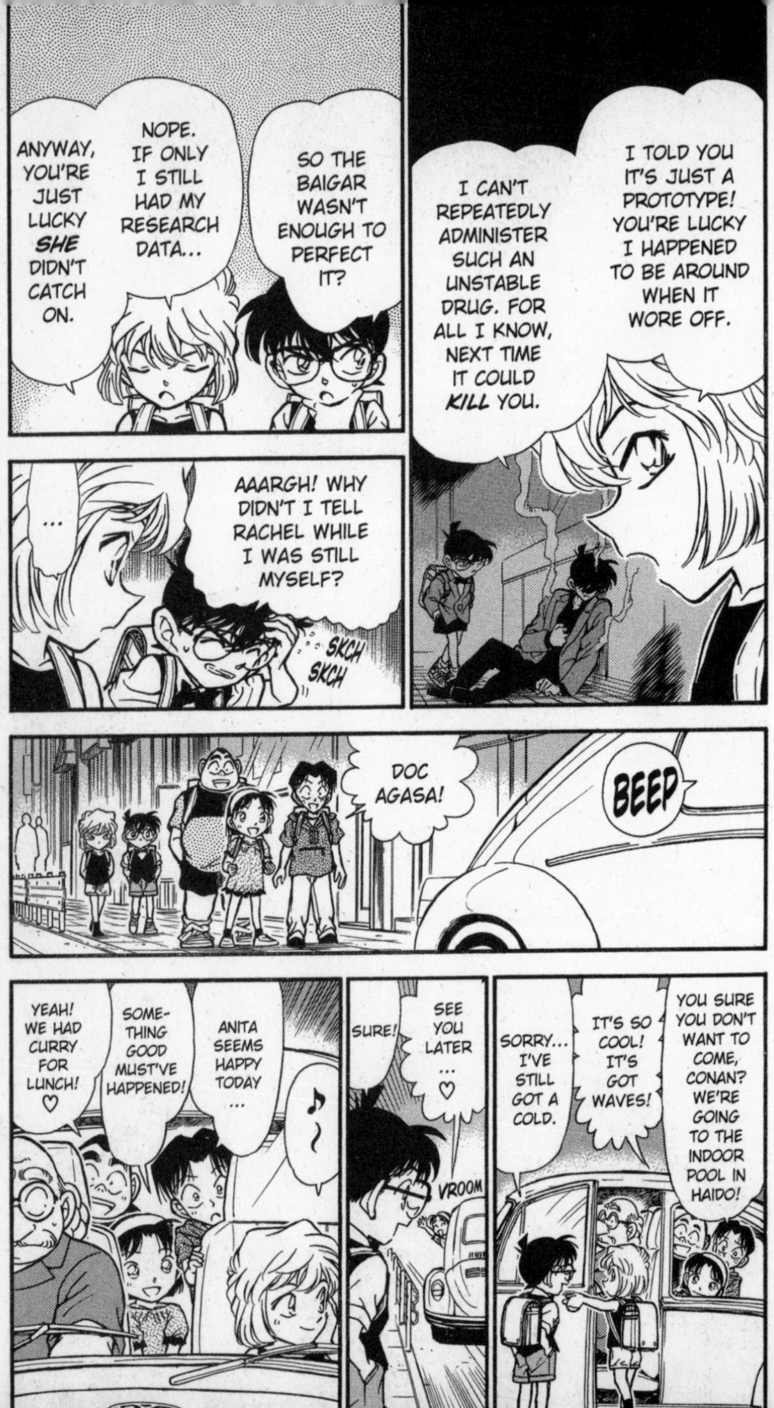
I TOLD YOU IT'S JUST A PROTOTYPE! YOU'RE LUCKY I HAPPENED TO BE AROUND WHEN IT WORE OFF.
I CAN'T REPEATEDLY ADMINISTER SUCH AN UNSTABLE DRUG. FOR ALL I KNOW, NEXT TIME IT COULD ***KILL*** YOU.
SO THE BAIGAR WASN'T ENOUGH TO PERFECT IT?
NOPE. IF ONLY I STILL HAD MY RESEARCH DATA...
ANYWAY, YOU'RE JUST LUCKY ***SHE*** DIDN'T CATCH ON.
AAARGH! WHY DIDN'T I TELL RACHEL WHILE I WAS STILL MYSELF?
...
SKCH SKCH
BEEP
DOC AGASA!
YOU SURE YOU DON'T WANT TO COME, CONAN? WE'RE GOING TO THE INDOOR POOL IN HAIDO!
IT'S SO COOL! IT'S GOT WAVES!
SORRY... I'VE STILL GOT A COLD.
SEE YOU LATER ...♡
SURE!
VROOM
♪~
ANITA SEEMS HAPPY TODAY...
SOME-THING GOOD MUST'VE HAPPENED!
YEAH! WE HAD CURRY FOR LUNCH! ♡

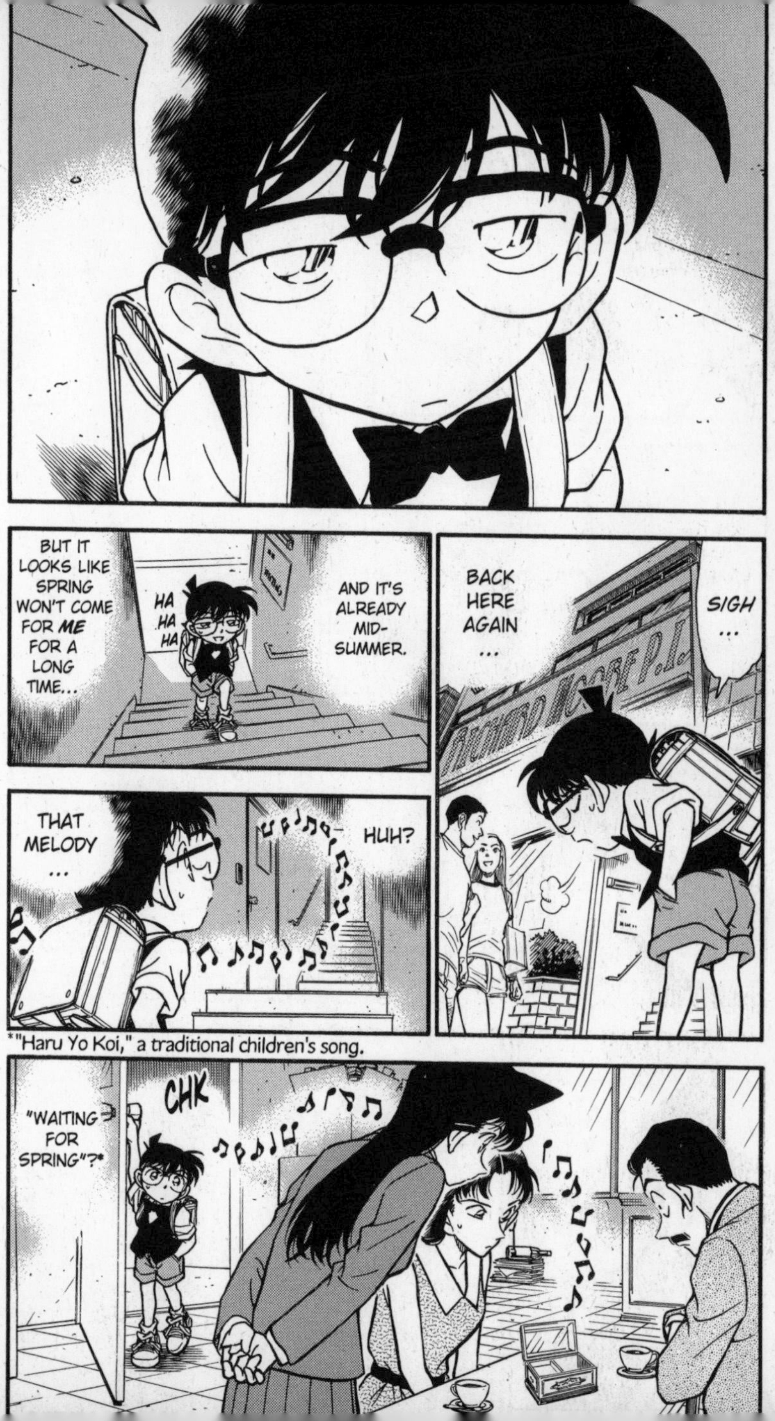
SIGH ...
BACK HERE AGAIN ...
AND IT'S ALREADY MID-SUMMER.
HA HA HA
BUT IT LOOKS LIKE SPRING WON'T COME FOR *ME* FOR A LONG TIME...
HUH?
THAT MELODY ...
CHK
"WAITING FOR SPRING"?*
*"Haru Yo Koi," a traditional children's song.

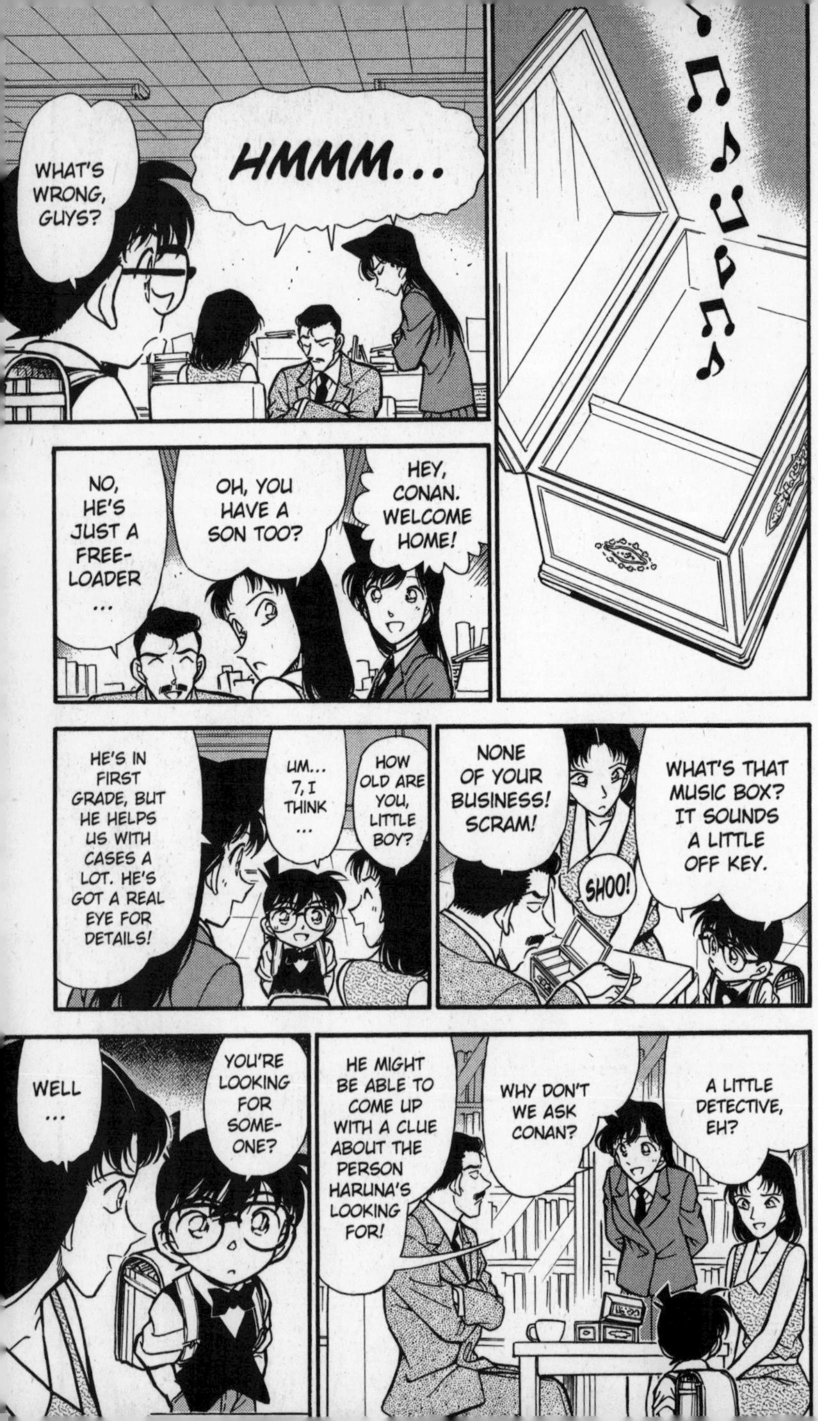
HMMM...
WHAT'S WRONG, GUYS?
HEY, CONAN. WELCOME HOME!
OH, YOU HAVE A SON TOO?
NO, HE'S JUST A FREE-LOADER...
WHAT'S THAT MUSIC BOX? IT SOUNDS A LITTLE OFF KEY.
NONE OF YOUR BUSINESS! SCRAM!
SHOO!
HOW OLD ARE YOU, LITTLE BOY?
UM... 7, I THINK...
HE'S IN FIRST GRADE, BUT HE HELPS US WITH CASES A LOT. HE'S GOT A REAL EYE FOR DETAILS!
A LITTLE DETECTIVE, EH?
WHY DON'T WE ASK CONAN?
HE MIGHT BE ABLE TO COME UP WITH A CLUE ABOUT THE PERSON HARUNA'S LOOKING FOR!
YOU'RE LOOKING FOR SOME-ONE?
WELL...

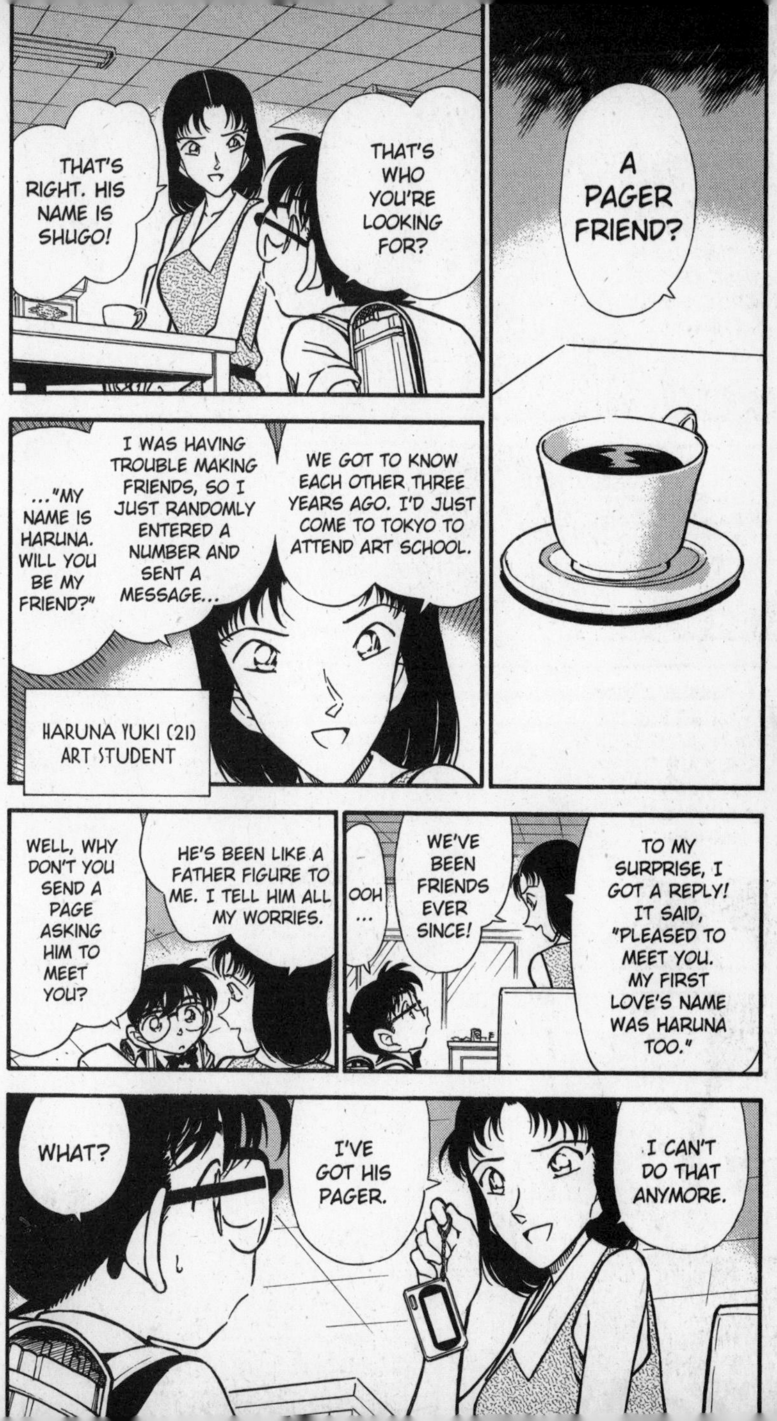
A PAGER FRIEND?
THAT'S WHO YOU'RE LOOKING FOR?
THAT'S RIGHT. HIS NAME IS SHUGO!
WE GOT TO KNOW EACH OTHER THREE YEARS AGO. I'D JUST COME TO TOKYO TO ATTEND ART SCHOOL.
I WAS HAVING TROUBLE MAKING FRIENDS, SO I JUST RANDOMLY ENTERED A NUMBER AND SENT A MESSAGE...
..."MY NAME IS HARUNA. WILL YOU BE MY FRIEND?"
HARUNA YUKI (21) ART STUDENT
TO MY SURPRISE, I GOT A REPLY! IT SAID, "PLEASED TO MEET YOU. MY FIRST LOVE'S NAME WAS HARUNA TOO."
WE'VE BEEN FRIENDS EVER SINCE!
OOH...
HE'S BEEN LIKE A FATHER FIGURE TO ME. I TELL HIM ALL MY WORRIES.
WELL, WHY DON'T YOU SEND A PAGE ASKING HIM TO MEET YOU?
I CAN'T DO THAT ANYMORE.
I'VE GOT HIS PAGER.
WHAT?

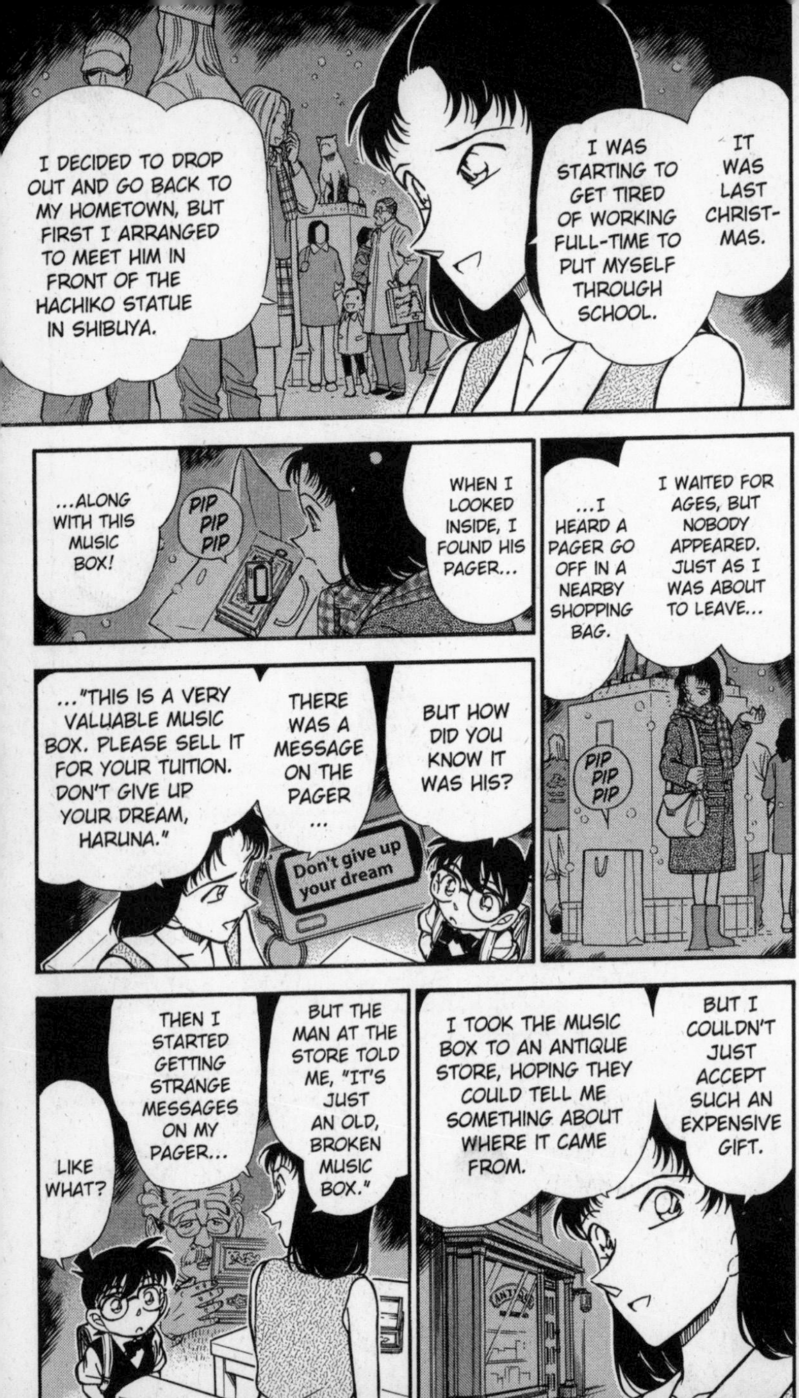
IT WAS LAST CHRISTMAS.
I WAS STARTING TO GET TIRED OF WORKING FULL-TIME TO PUT MYSELF THROUGH SCHOOL.
I DECIDED TO DROP OUT AND GO BACK TO MY HOMETOWN, BUT FIRST I ARRANGED TO MEET HIM IN FRONT OF THE HACHIKO STATUE IN SHIBUYA.
I WAITED FOR AGES, BUT NOBODY APPEARED. JUST AS I WAS ABOUT TO LEAVE...
...I HEARD A PAGER GO OFF IN A NEARBY SHOPPING BAG.
PIP PIP PIP
WHEN I LOOKED INSIDE, I FOUND HIS PAGER...
PIP PIP PIP
...ALONG WITH THIS MUSIC BOX!
BUT HOW DID YOU KNOW IT WAS HIS?
THERE WAS A MESSAGE ON THE PAGER ...
Don't give up your dream
..."THIS IS A VERY VALUABLE MUSIC BOX. PLEASE SELL IT FOR YOUR TUITION. DON'T GIVE UP YOUR DREAM, HARUNA."
BUT I COULDN'T JUST ACCEPT SUCH AN EXPENSIVE GIFT.
I TOOK THE MUSIC BOX TO AN ANTIQUE STORE, HOPING THEY COULD TELL ME SOMETHING ABOUT WHERE IT CAME FROM.
BUT THE MAN AT THE STORE TOLD ME, "IT'S JUST AN OLD, BROKEN MUSIC BOX."
THEN I STARTED GETTING STRANGE MESSAGES ON MY PAGER...
LIKE WHAT?

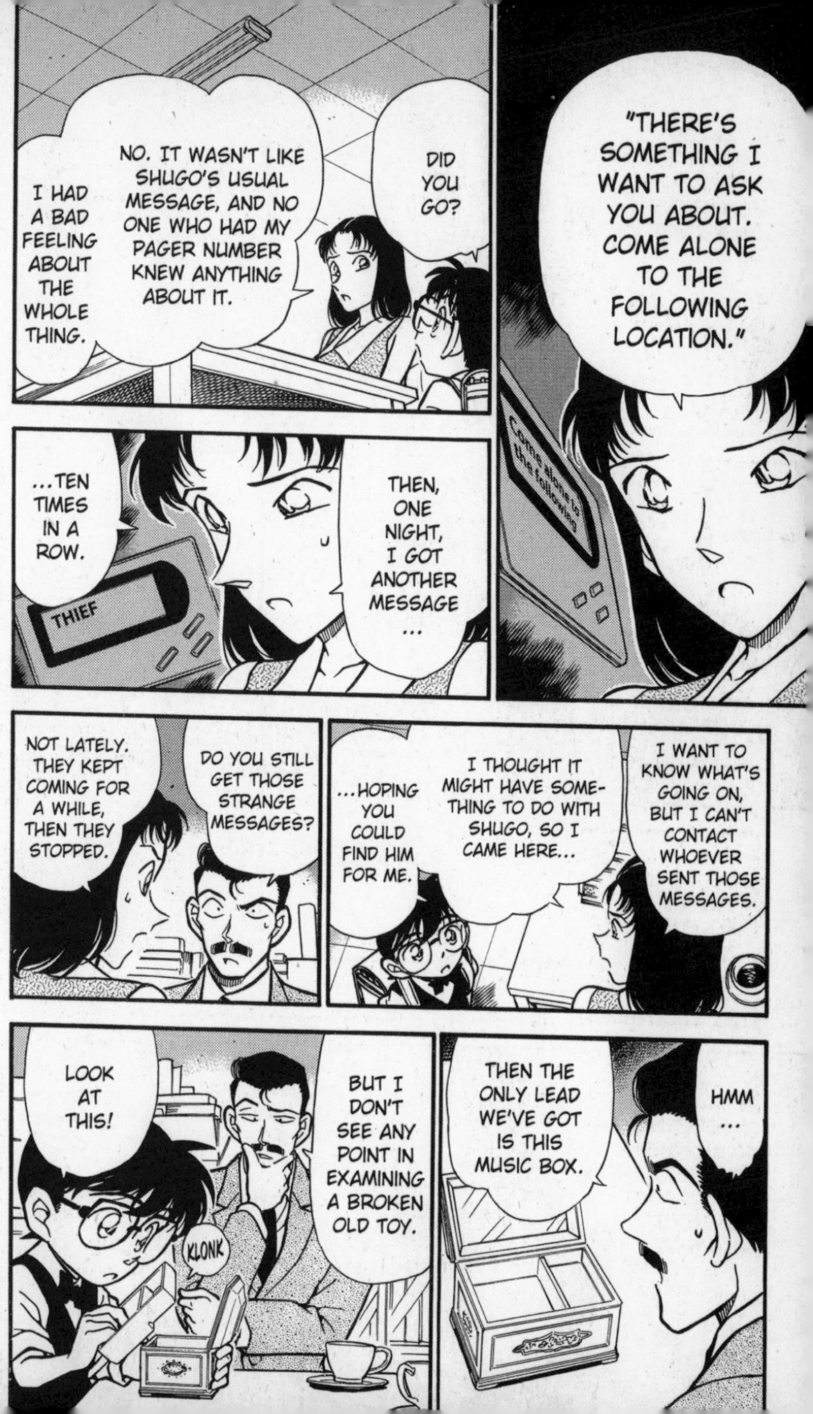
"THERE'S SOMETHING I WANT TO ASK YOU ABOUT. COME ALONE TO THE FOLLOWING LOCATION."
Come alone to the following
NO. IT WASN'T LIKE SHUGO'S USUAL MESSAGE, AND NO ONE WHO HAD MY PAGER NUMBER KNEW ANYTHING ABOUT IT.
I HAD A BAD FEELING ABOUT THE WHOLE THING.
DID YOU GO?
THEN, ONE NIGHT, I GOT ANOTHER MESSAGE...
THIEF
...TEN TIMES IN A ROW.
I WANT TO KNOW WHAT'S GOING ON, BUT I CAN'T CONTACT WHOEVER SENT THOSE MESSAGES.
I THOUGHT IT MIGHT HAVE SOME-THING TO DO WITH SHUGO, SO I CAME HERE...
...HOPING YOU COULD FIND HIM FOR ME.
DO YOU STILL GET THOSE STRANGE MESSAGES?
NOT LATELY. THEY KEPT COMING FOR A WHILE, THEN THEY STOPPED.
HMM...
THEN THE ONLY LEAD WE'VE GOT IS THIS MUSIC BOX.
BUT I DON'T SEE ANY POINT IN EXAMINING A BROKEN OLD TOY.
KLONK
LOOK AT THIS!

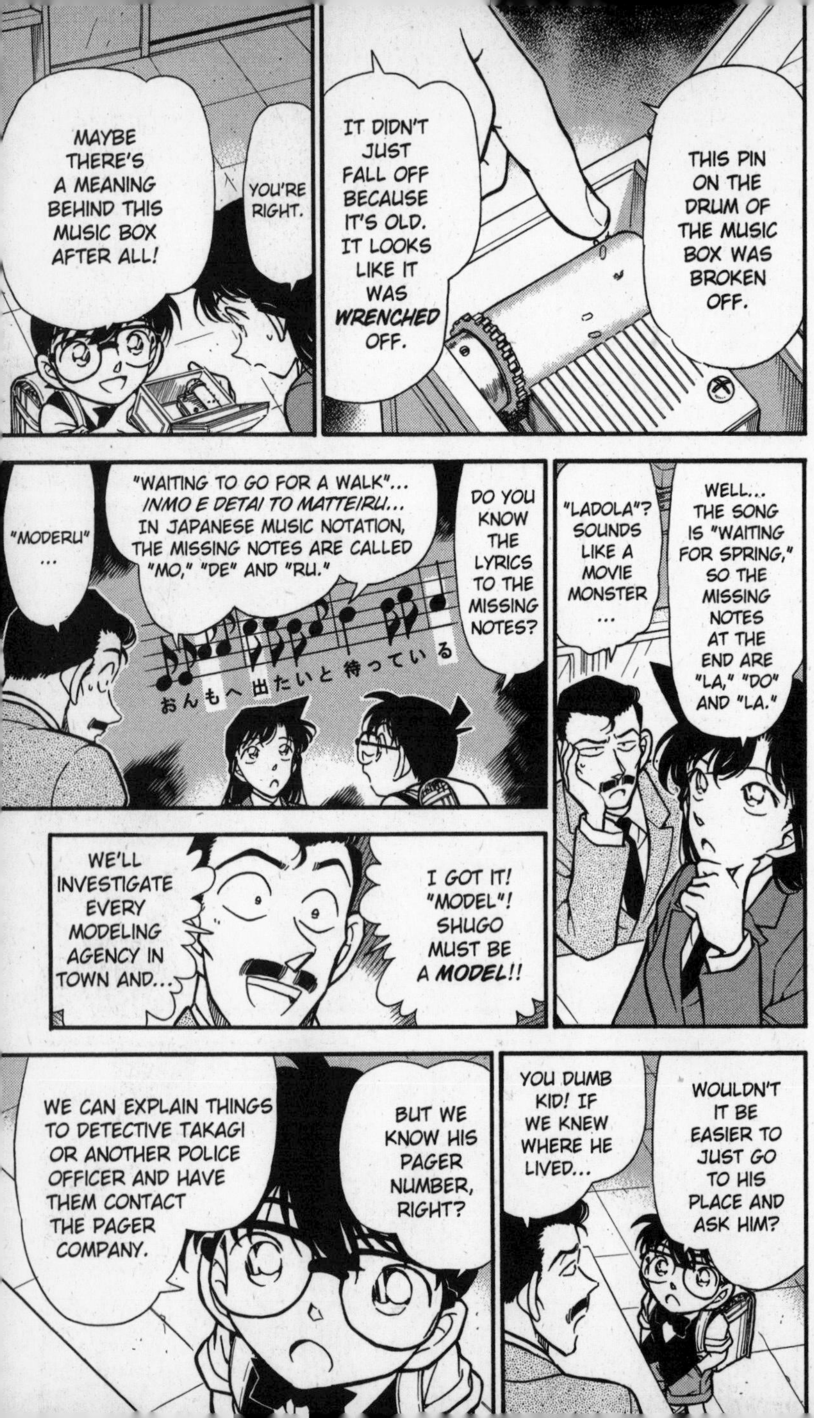
THIS PIN ON THE DRUM OF THE MUSIC BOX WAS BROKEN OFF.
IT DIDN'T JUST FALL OFF BECAUSE IT'S OLD. IT LOOKS LIKE IT WAS **WRENCHED** OFF.
MAYBE THERE'S A MEANING BEHIND THIS MUSIC BOX AFTER ALL!
YOU'RE RIGHT.
WELL... THE SONG IS "WAITING FOR SPRING," SO THE MISSING NOTES AT THE END ARE "LA," "DO" AND "LA."
"LADOLA"? SOUNDS LIKE A MOVIE MONSTER...
DO YOU KNOW THE LYRICS TO THE MISSING NOTES?
"WAITING TO GO FOR A WALK"... *INMO E DETAI TO MATTEIRU*... IN JAPANESE MUSIC NOTATION, THE MISSING NOTES ARE CALLED "MO," "DE" AND "RU."
おんもへ出たいと待っている
"MODERU"...
I GOT IT! "MODEL"! SHUGO MUST BE A **MODEL**!!
WE'LL INVESTIGATE EVERY MODELING AGENCY IN TOWN AND...
WOULDN'T IT BE EASIER TO JUST GO TO HIS PLACE AND ASK HIM?
YOU DUMB KID! IF WE KNEW WHERE HE LIVED...
BUT WE KNOW HIS PAGER NUMBER, RIGHT?
WE CAN EXPLAIN THINGS TO DETECTIVE TAKAGI OR ANOTHER POLICE OFFICER AND HAVE THEM CONTACT THE PAGER COMPANY.

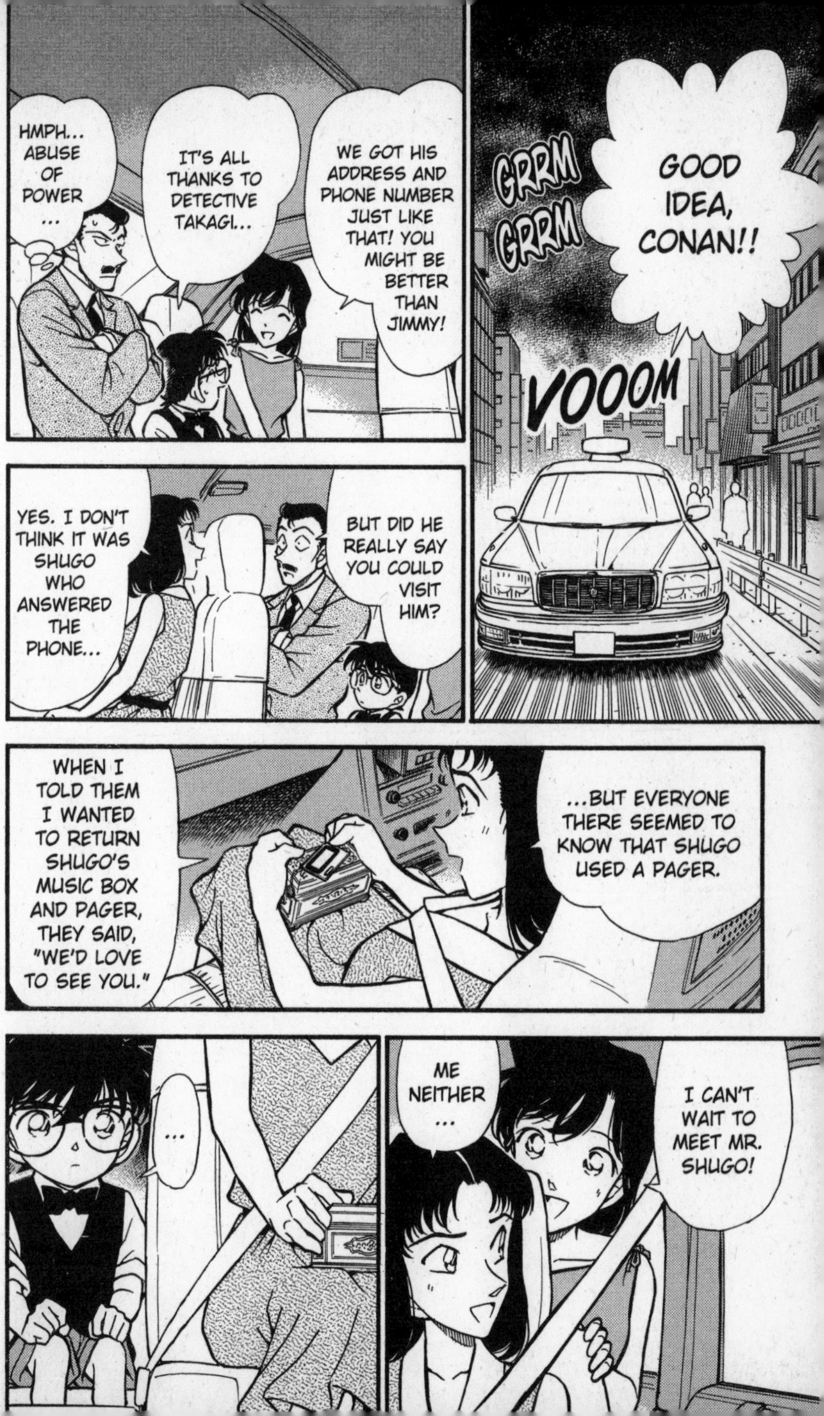
GRRM
GRRM
GOOD IDEA, CONAN!!
VOOOM
WE GOT HIS ADDRESS AND PHONE NUMBER JUST LIKE THAT! YOU MIGHT BE BETTER THAN JIMMY!
IT'S ALL THANKS TO DETECTIVE TAKAGI...
HMPH... ABUSE OF POWER...
BUT DID HE REALLY SAY YOU COULD VISIT HIM?
YES. I DON'T THINK IT WAS SHUGO WHO ANSWERED THE PHONE...
...BUT EVERYONE THERE SEEMED TO KNOW THAT SHUGO USED A PAGER.
WHEN I TOLD THEM I WANTED TO RETURN SHUGO'S MUSIC BOX AND PAGER, THEY SAID, "WE'D LOVE TO SEE YOU."
I CAN'T WAIT TO MEET MR. SHUGO!
ME NEITHER...
...

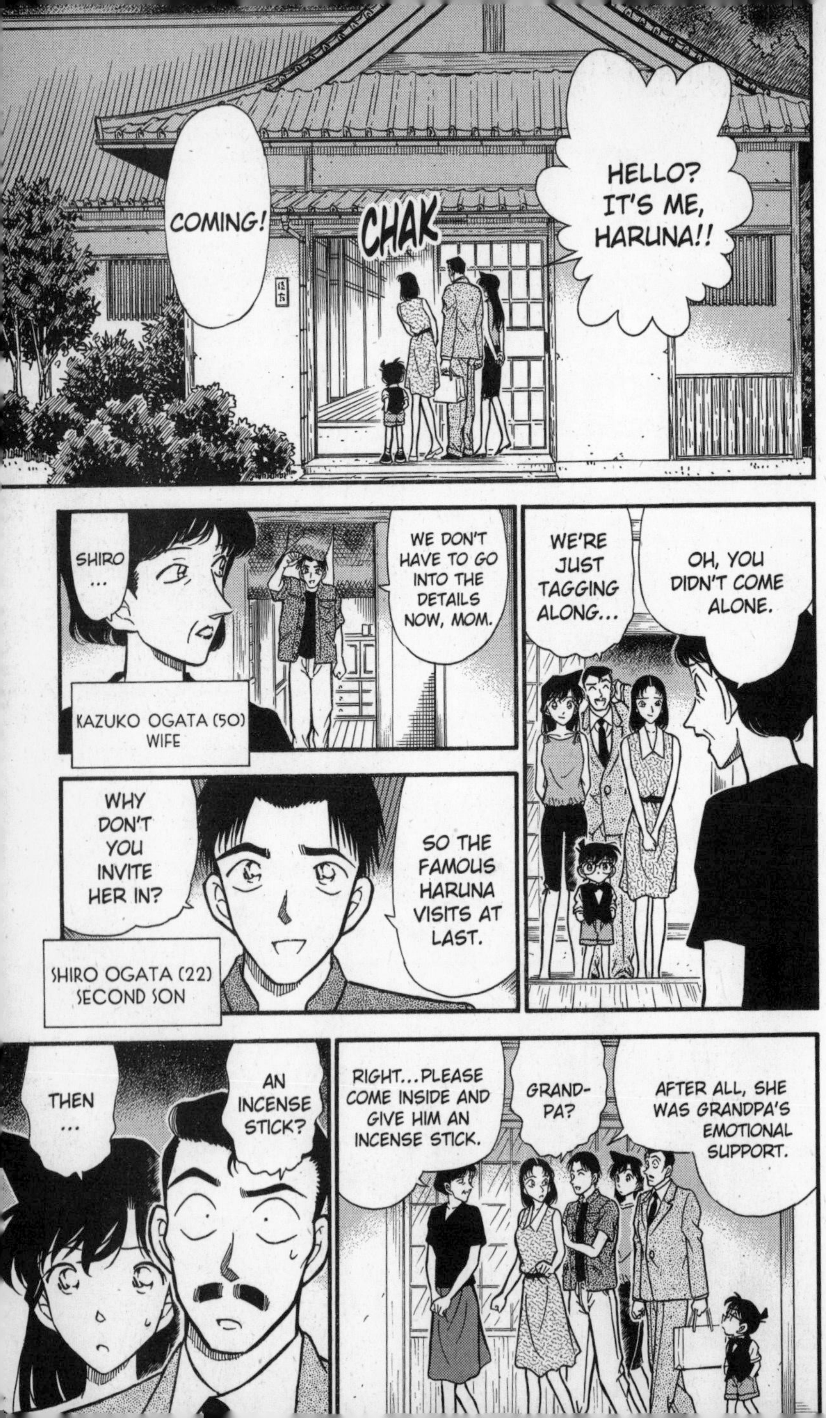
HELLO? IT'S ME, HARUNA!!
CHAK
COMING!
OH, YOU DIDN'T COME ALONE.
WE'RE JUST TAGGING ALONG...
WE DON'T HAVE TO GO INTO THE DETAILS NOW, MOM.
SHIRO ...
KAZUKO OGATA (50) WIFE
SO THE FAMOUS HARUNA VISITS AT LAST.
WHY DON'T YOU INVITE HER IN?
SHIRO OGATA (22) SECOND SON
AFTER ALL, SHE WAS GRANDPA'S EMOTIONAL SUPPORT.
GRAND-PA?
RIGHT...PLEASE COME INSIDE AND GIVE HIM AN INCENSE STICK.
AN INCENSE STICK?
THEN ...

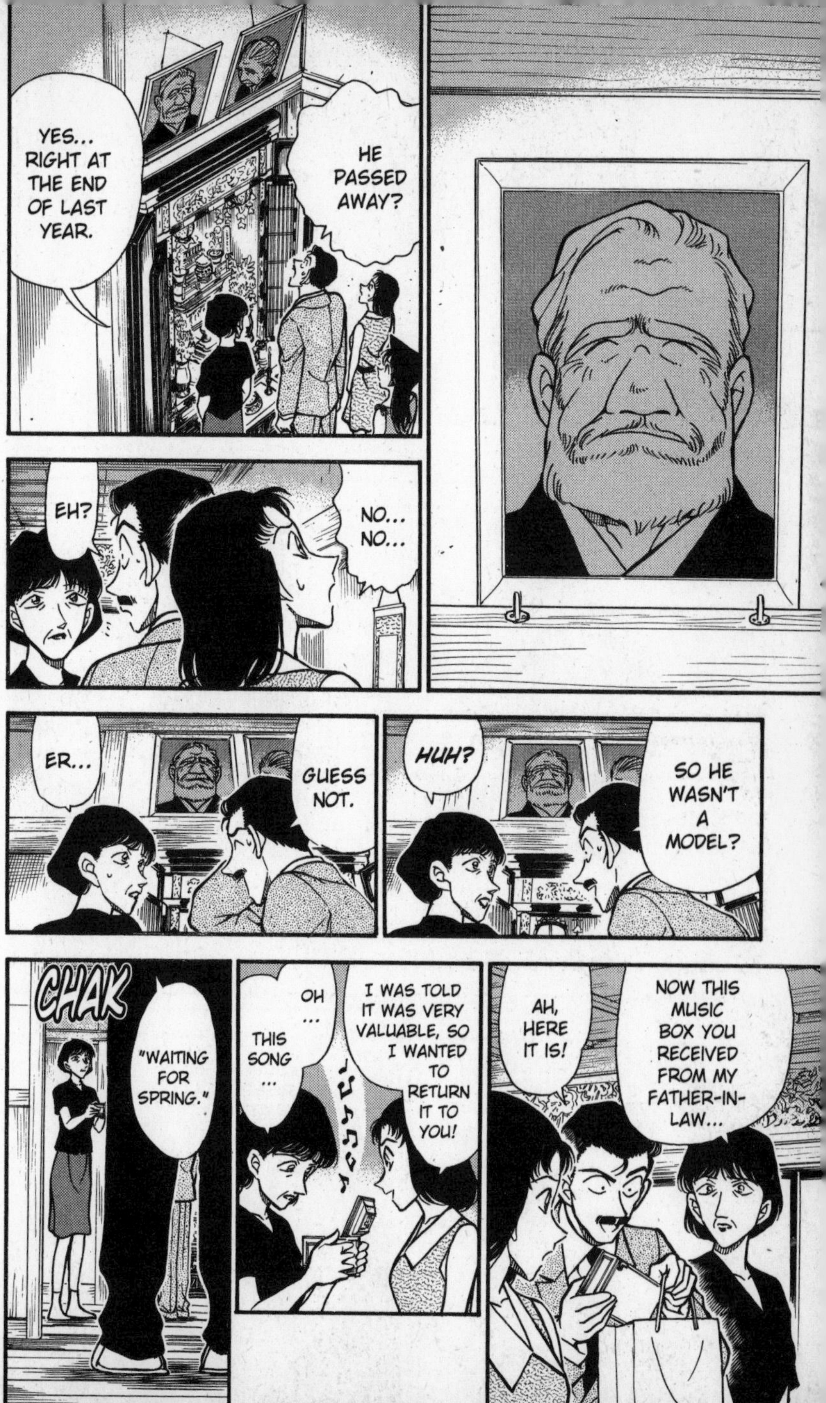
HE PASSED AWAY?
YES... RIGHT AT THE END OF LAST YEAR.
NO... NO...
EH?
SO HE WASN'T A MODEL?
HUH?
GUESS NOT.
ER...
NOW THIS MUSIC BOX YOU RECEIVED FROM MY FATHER-IN-LAW...
AH, HERE IT IS!
I WAS TOLD IT WAS VERY VALUABLE, SO I WANTED TO RETURN IT TO YOU!
OH ...
THIS SONG ...
CHAK
"WAITING FOR SPRING."

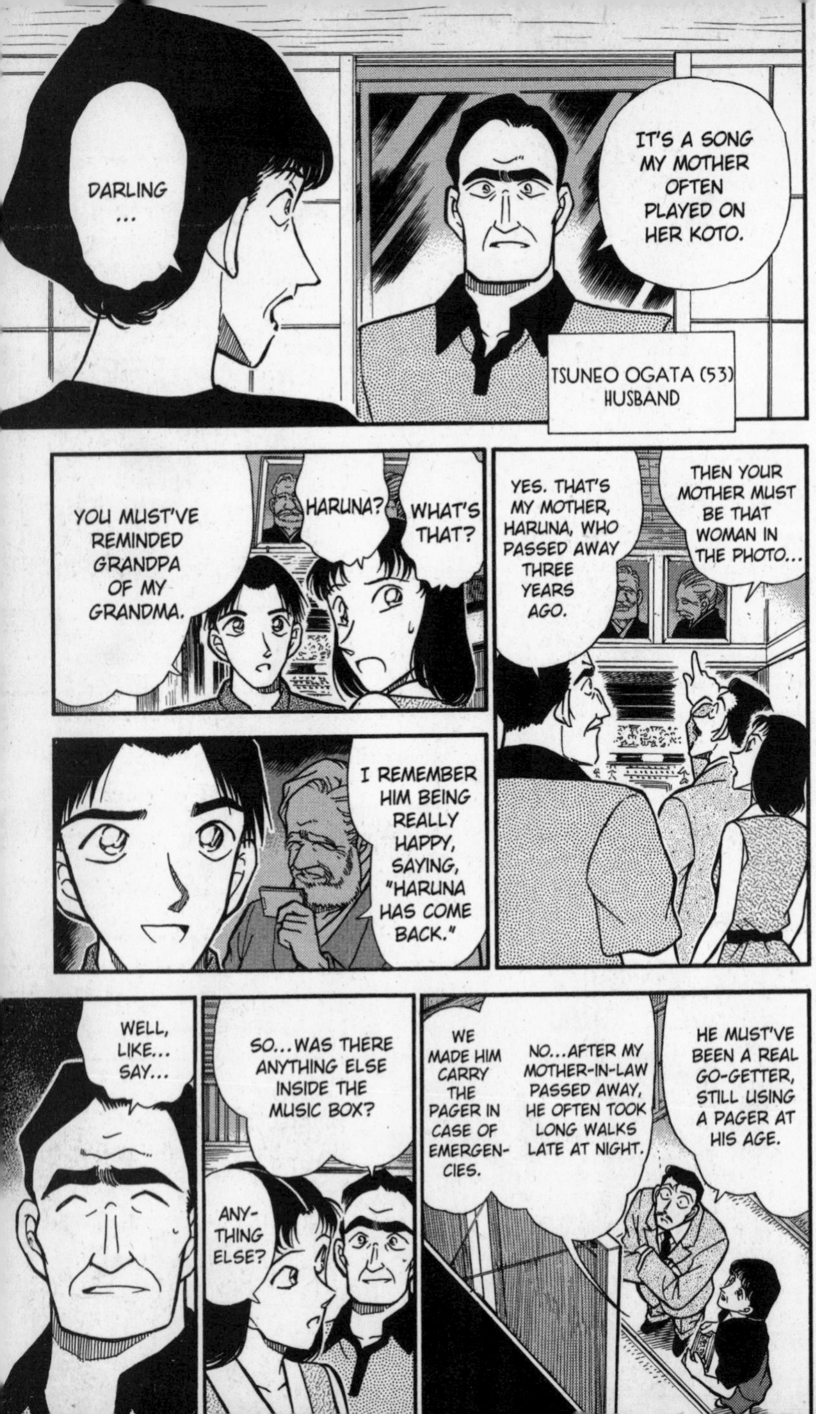
IT'S A SONG MY MOTHER OFTEN PLAYED ON HER KOTO.
TSUNEO OGATA (53) HUSBAND
DARLING ...
THEN YOUR MOTHER MUST BE THAT WOMAN IN THE PHOTO...
YES. THAT'S MY MOTHER, HARUNA, WHO PASSED AWAY THREE YEARS AGO.
WHAT'S THAT?
HARUNA?
YOU MUST'VE REMINDED GRANDPA OF MY GRANDMA.
I REMEMBER HIM BEING REALLY HAPPY, SAYING, "HARUNA HAS COME BACK."
HE MUST'VE BEEN A REAL GO-GETTER, STILL USING A PAGER AT HIS AGE.
NO...AFTER MY MOTHER-IN-LAW PASSED AWAY, HE OFTEN TOOK LONG WALKS LATE AT NIGHT.
WE MADE HIM CARRY THE PAGER IN CASE OF EMERGEN-CIES.
SO...WAS THERE ANYTHING ELSE INSIDE THE MUSIC BOX?
ANY-THING ELSE?
WELL, LIKE... SAY...

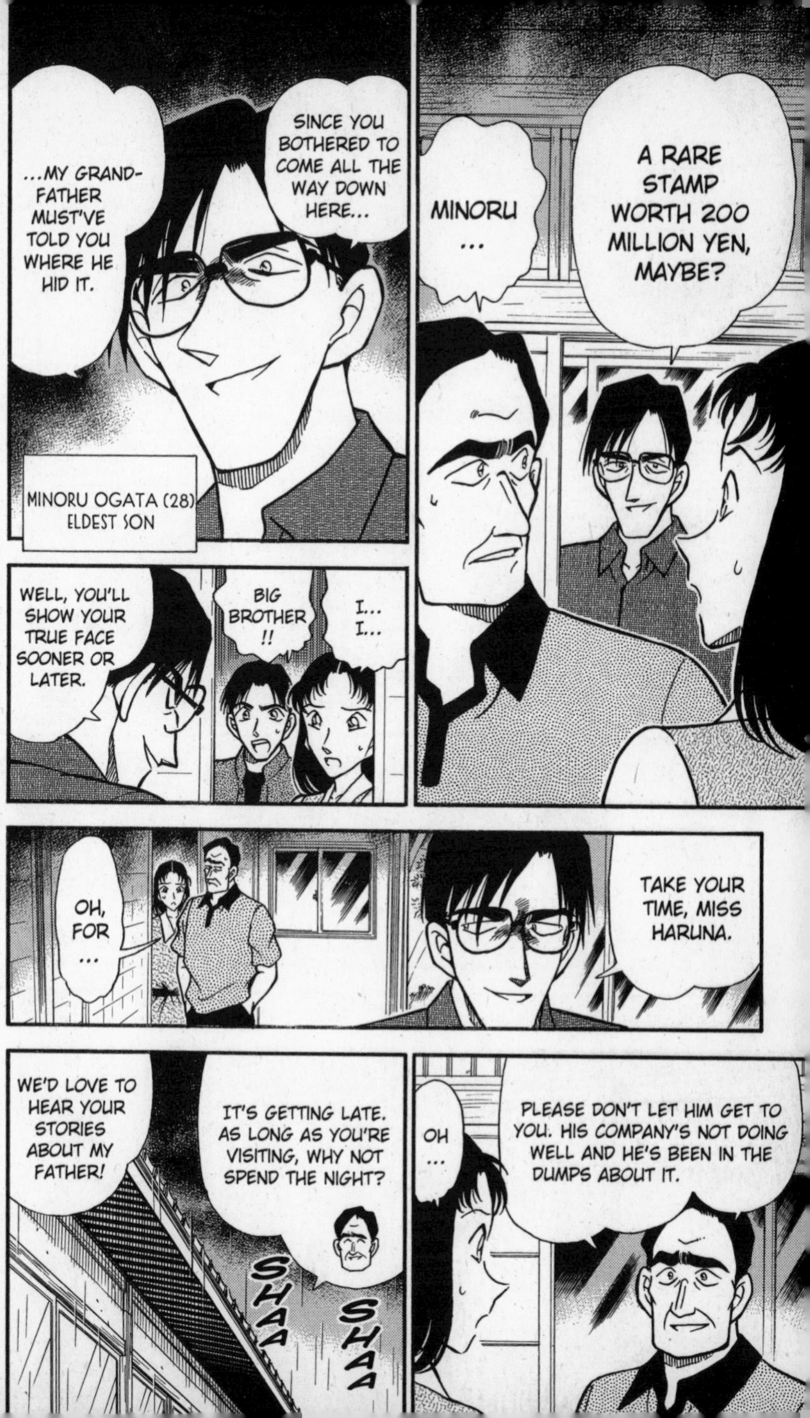
SINCE YOU BOTHERED TO COME ALL THE WAY DOWN HERE...
...MY GRAND-FATHER MUST'VE TOLD YOU WHERE HE HID IT.
MINORU OGATA (28) ELDEST SON
A RARE STAMP WORTH 200 MILLION YEN, MAYBE?
MINORU ...
I... I...
BIG BROTHER !!
WELL, YOU'LL SHOW YOUR TRUE FACE SOONER OR LATER.
TAKE YOUR TIME, MISS HARUNA.
OH, FOR ...
PLEASE DON'T LET HIM GET TO YOU. HIS COMPANY'S NOT DOING WELL AND HE'S BEEN IN THE DUMPS ABOUT IT.
OH ...
IT'S GETTING LATE. AS LONG AS YOU'RE VISITING, WHY NOT SPEND THE NIGHT?
WE'D LOVE TO HEAR YOUR STORIES ABOUT MY FATHER!
SHAA
SHAA

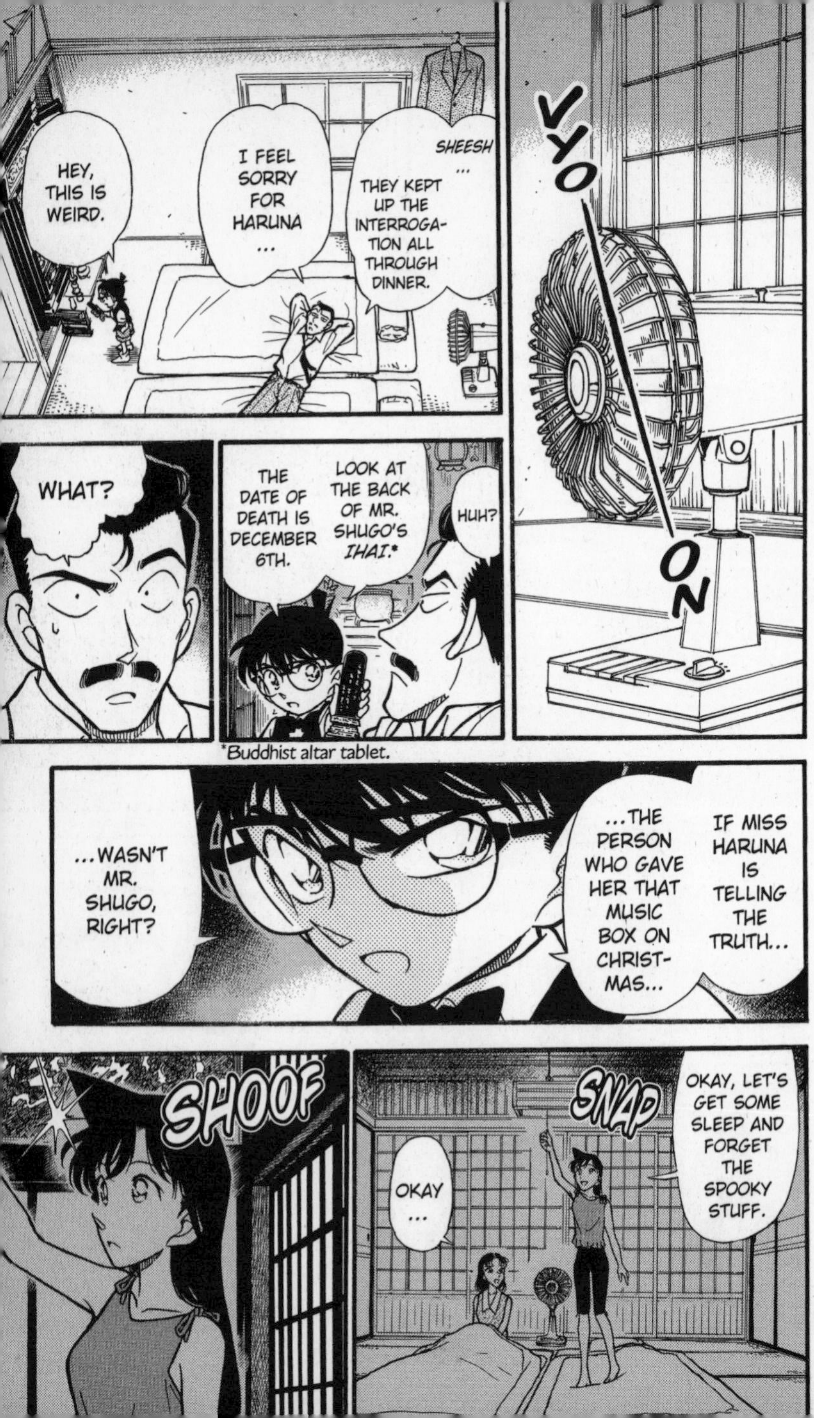
VYO
ON
SHEESH ...
THEY KEPT UP THE INTERROGATION ALL THROUGH DINNER.
I FEEL SORRY FOR HARUNA ...
HEY, THIS IS WEIRD.
HUH?
LOOK AT THE BACK OF MR. SHUGO'S *IHAI.**
THE DATE OF DEATH IS DECEMBER 6TH.
WHAT?
IF MISS HARUNA IS TELLING THE TRUTH...
...THE PERSON WHO GAVE HER THAT MUSIC BOX ON CHRISTMAS...
...WASN'T MR. SHUGO, RIGHT?
SNAP
OKAY, LET'S GET SOME SLEEP AND FORGET THE SPOOKY STUFF.
OKAY ...
SHOOF
*Buddhist altar tablet.

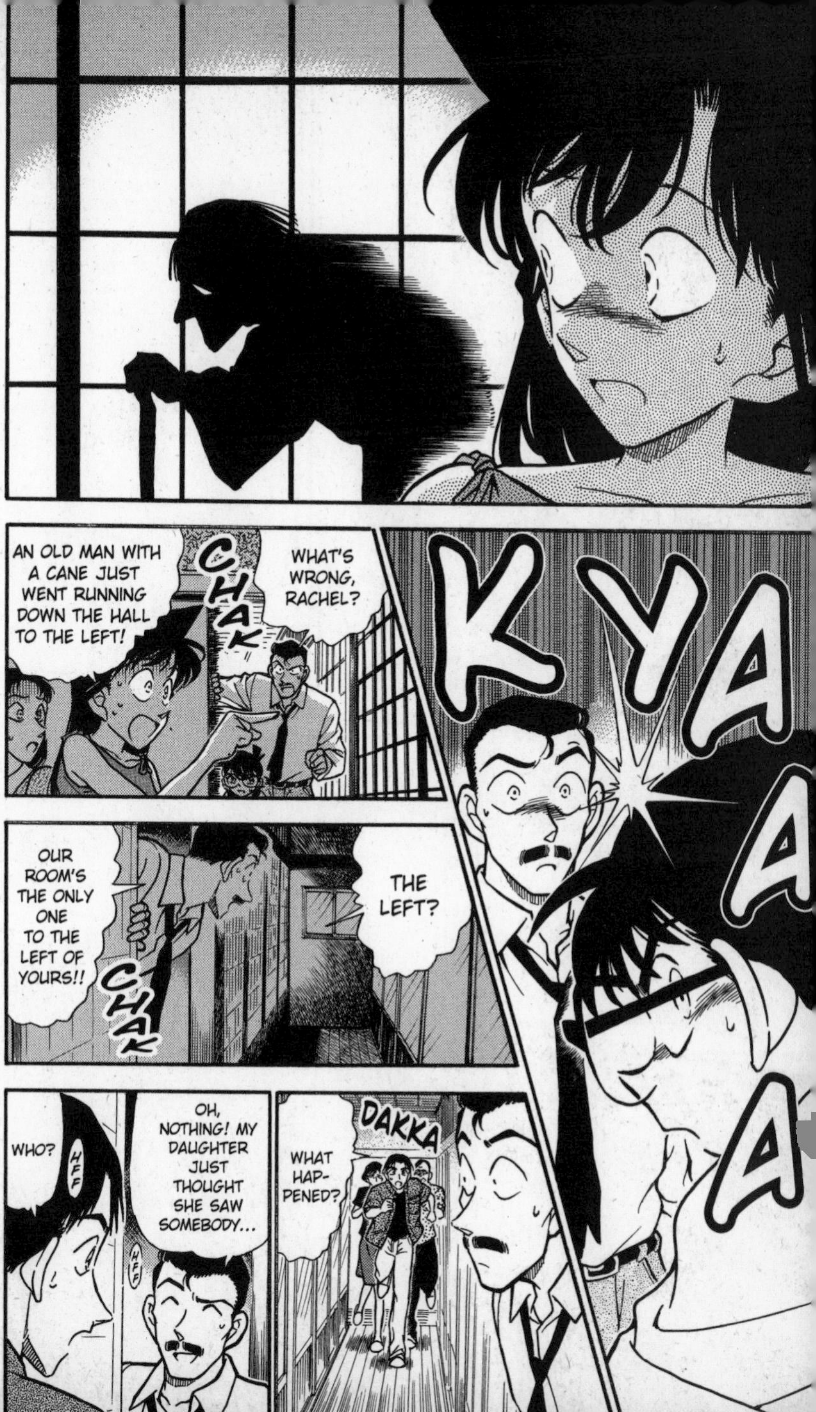
KYAAAA
WHAT'S WRONG, RACHEL?
CHAK
AN OLD MAN WITH A CANE JUST WENT RUNNING DOWN THE HALL TO THE LEFT!
THE LEFT?
OUR ROOM'S THE ONLY ONE TO THE LEFT OF YOURS!!
CHAK
DAKKA
WHAT HAPPENED?
OH, NOTHING! MY DAUGHTER JUST THOUGHT SHE SAW SOMEBODY...
HFF
WHO?
HFF

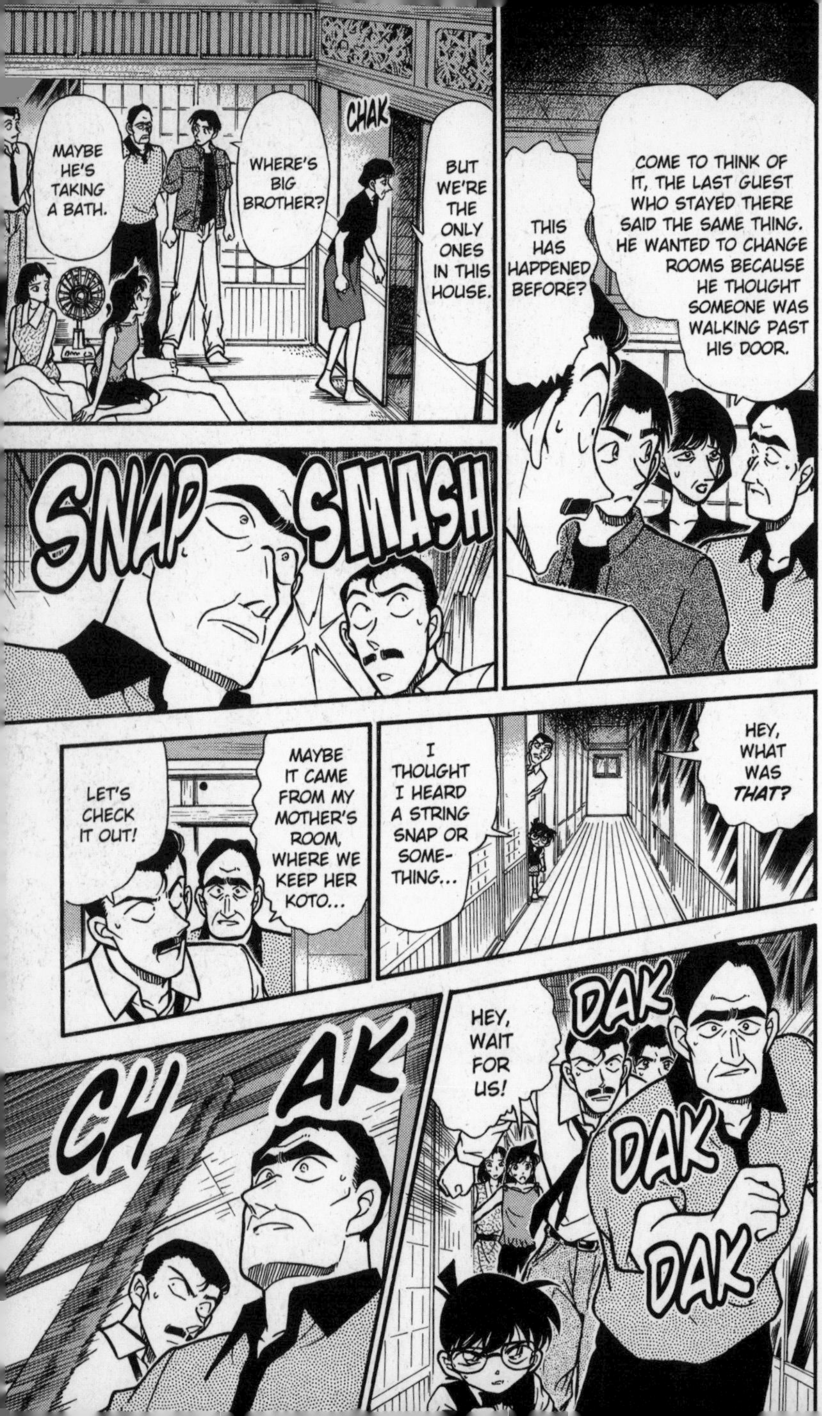

COME TO THINK OF IT, THE LAST GUEST WHO STAYED THERE SAID THE SAME THING. HE WANTED TO CHANGE ROOMS BECAUSE HE THOUGHT SOMEONE WAS WALKING PAST HIS DOOR.
THIS HAS HAPPENED BEFORE?
CHAK
BUT WE'RE THE ONLY ONES IN THIS HOUSE.
WHERE'S BIG BROTHER?
MAYBE HE'S TAKING A BATH.
SMASH
SNAP
HEY, WHAT WAS *THAT?*
I THOUGHT I HEARD A STRING SNAP OR SOME-THING...
MAYBE IT CAME FROM MY MOTHER'S ROOM, WHERE WE KEEP HER KOTO...
LET'S CHECK IT OUT!
DAK
HEY, WAIT FOR US!
DAK
DAK
AK
CH

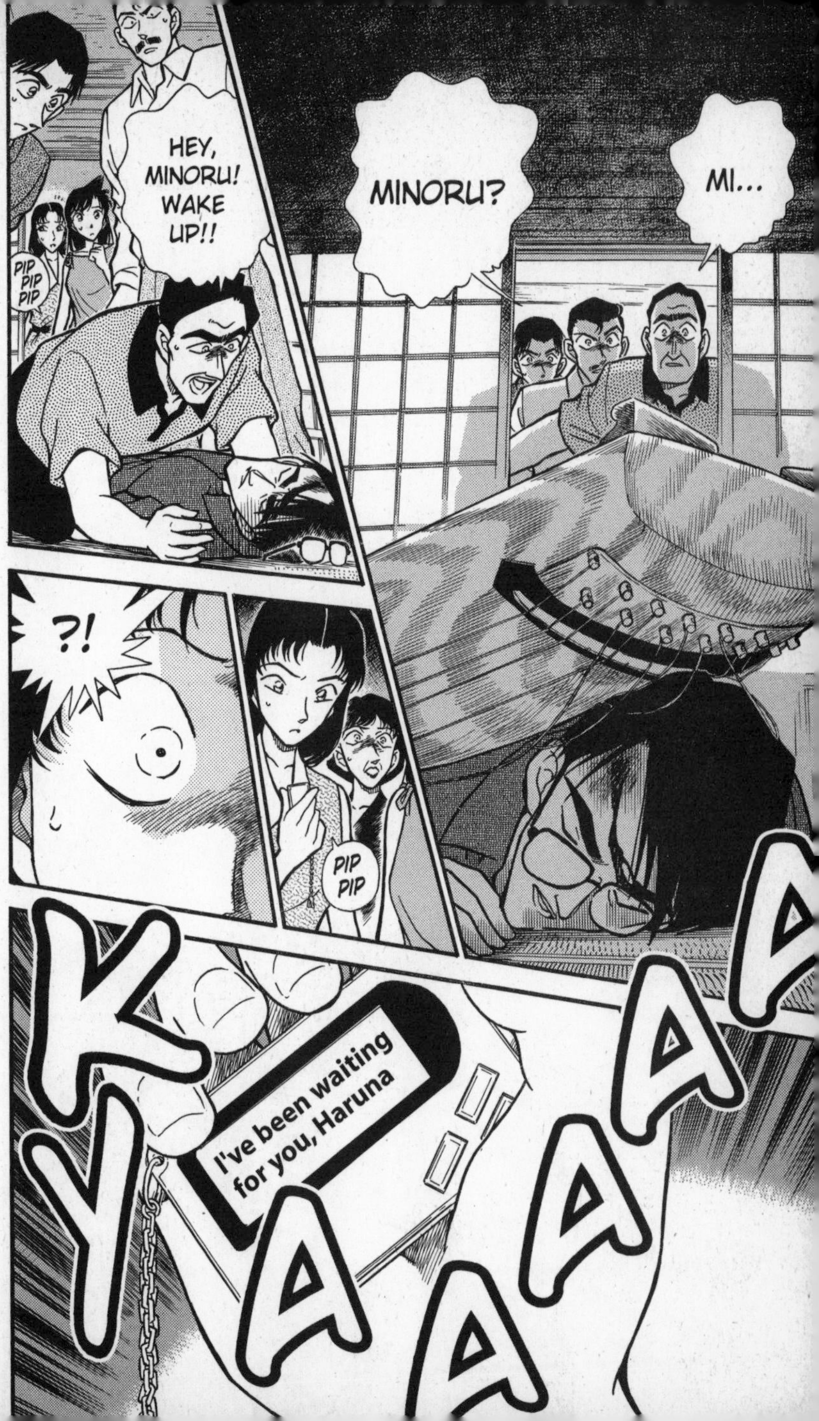
MI...
MINORU?
HEY, MINORU! WAKE UP!!
PIP PIP PIP
PIP PIP
?!
KYAAAAAAA
I've been waiting for you, Haruna

THE DISAPPEARING SOUND

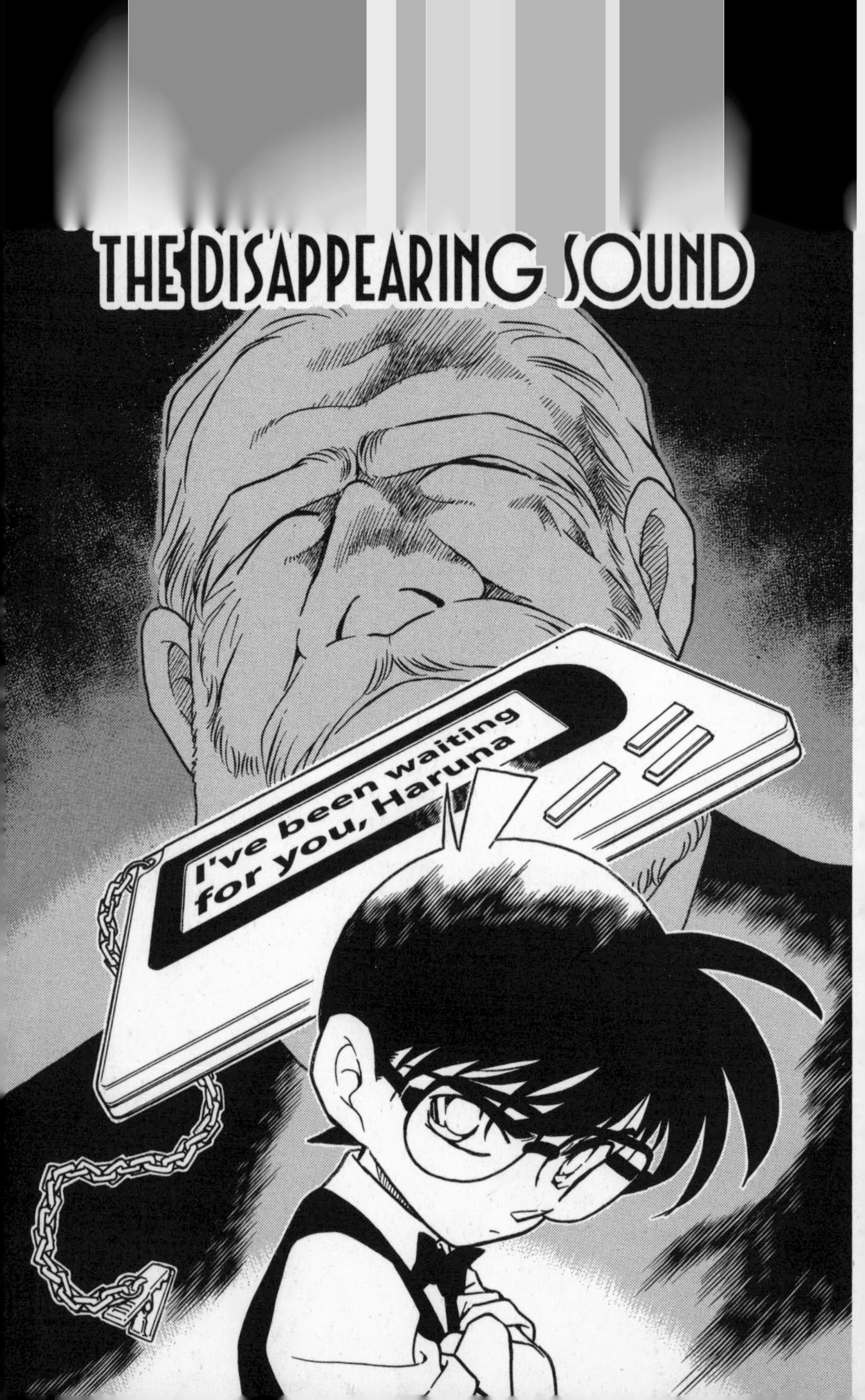

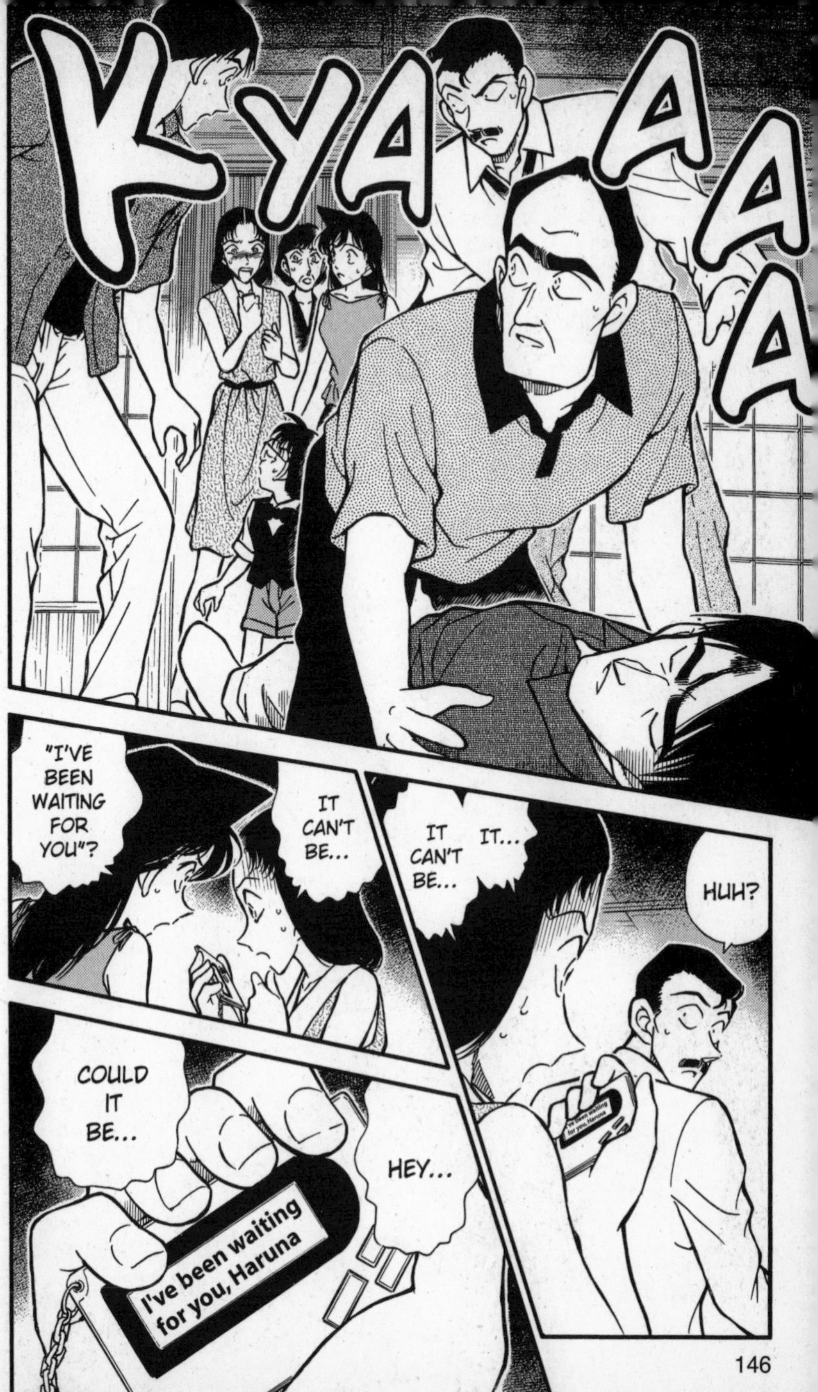
KYAAAAA
HUH?
IT... IT CAN'T BE...
IT CAN'T BE...
"I'VE BEEN WAITING FOR YOU"?
HEY...
COULD IT BE...
I've been waiting for you, Haruna

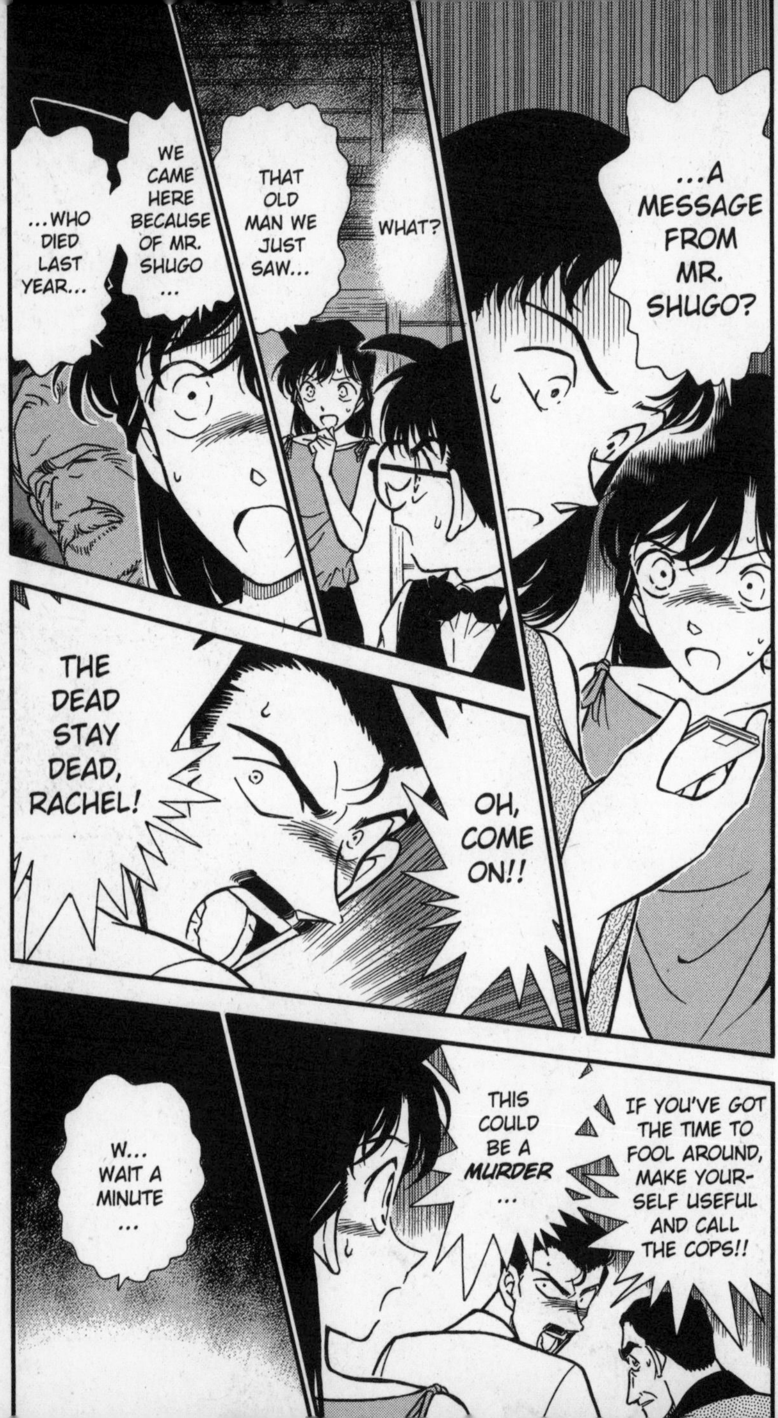
...A MESSAGE FROM MR. SHUGO?
WHAT?
THAT OLD MAN WE JUST SAW...
WE CAME HERE BECAUSE OF MR. SHUGO...
...WHO DIED LAST YEAR...
OH, COME ON!!
THE DEAD STAY DEAD, RACHEL!
IF YOU'VE GOT THE TIME TO FOOL AROUND, MAKE YOURSELF USEFUL AND CALL THE COPS!!
THIS COULD BE A *MURDER*...
W... WAIT A MINUTE...

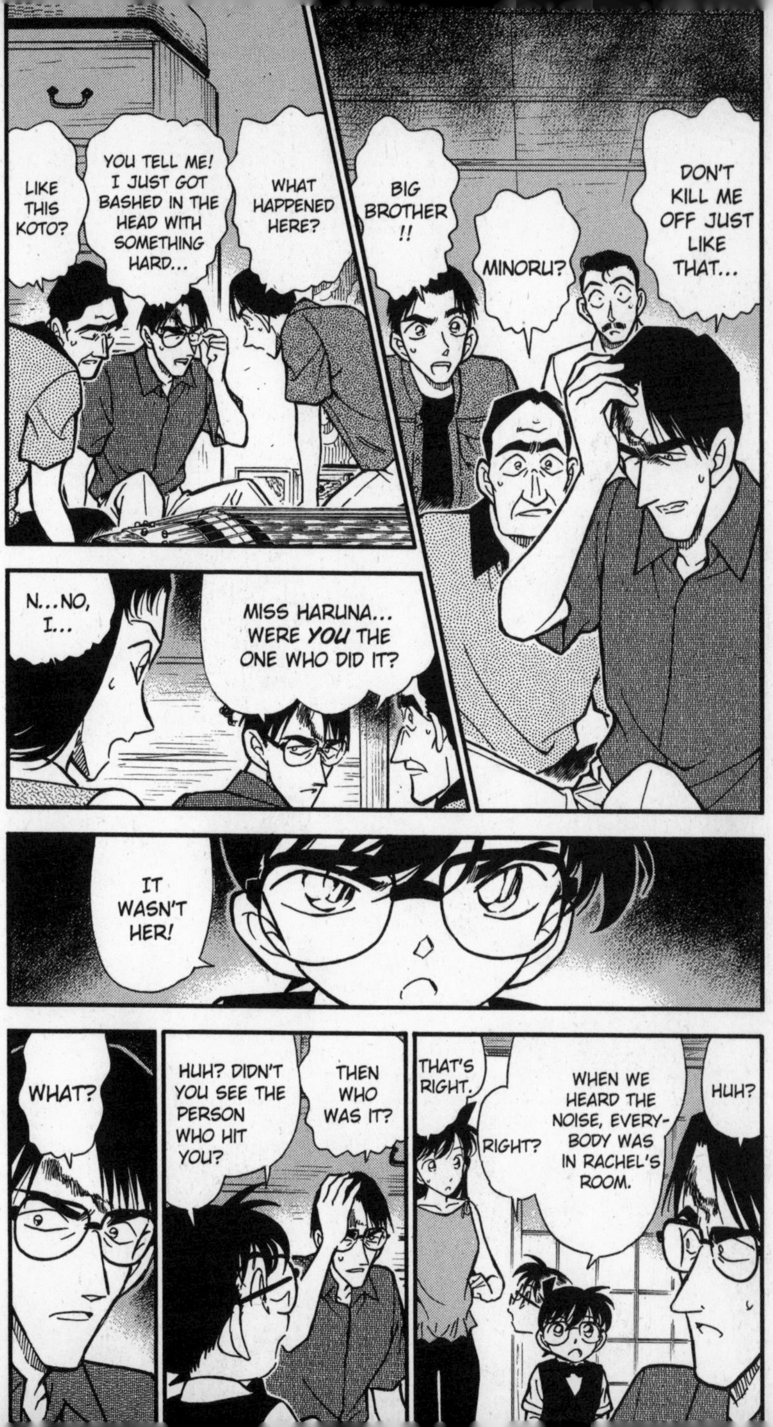
DON'T KILL ME OFF JUST LIKE THAT...
MINORU?
BIG BROTHER !!
WHAT HAPPENED HERE?
YOU TELL ME! I JUST GOT BASHED IN THE HEAD WITH SOMETHING HARD...
LIKE THIS KOTO?
MISS HARUNA... WERE *YOU* THE ONE WHO DID IT?
N...NO, I...
IT WASN'T HER!
HUH?
WHEN WE HEARD THE NOISE, EVERYBODY WAS IN RACHEL'S ROOM.
RIGHT?
THAT'S RIGHT.
THEN WHO WAS IT?
HUH? DIDN'T YOU SEE THE PERSON WHO HIT YOU?
WHAT?

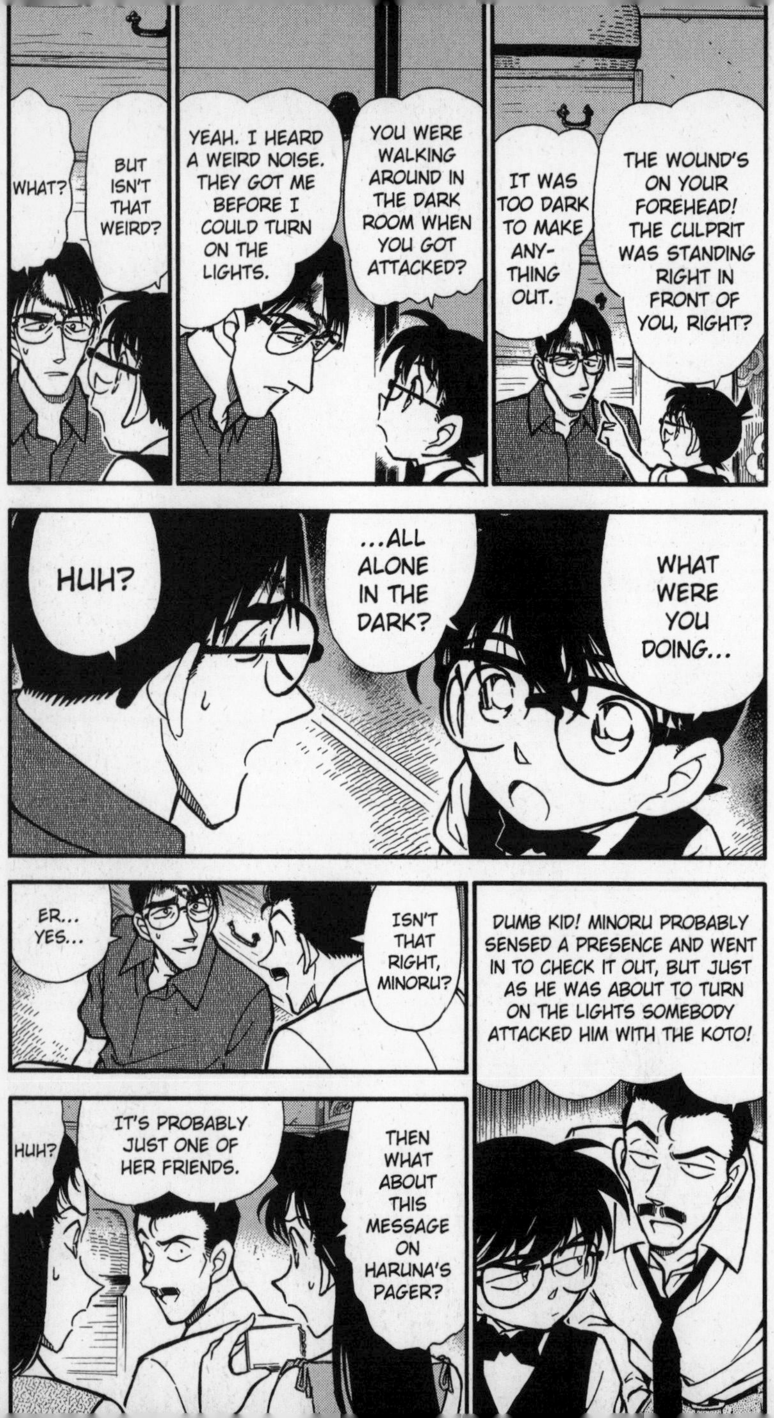
THE WOUND'S ON YOUR FOREHEAD! THE CULPRIT WAS STANDING RIGHT IN FRONT OF YOU, RIGHT?
IT WAS TOO DARK TO MAKE ANY-THING OUT.
YOU WERE WALKING AROUND IN THE DARK ROOM WHEN YOU GOT ATTACKED?
YEAH. I HEARD A WEIRD NOISE. THEY GOT ME BEFORE I COULD TURN ON THE LIGHTS.
BUT ISN'T THAT WEIRD?
WHAT?
WHAT WERE YOU DOING...
...ALL ALONE IN THE DARK?
HUH?
DUMB KID! MINORU PROBABLY SENSED A PRESENCE AND WENT IN TO CHECK IT OUT, BUT JUST AS HE WAS ABOUT TO TURN ON THE LIGHTS SOMEBODY ATTACKED HIM WITH THE KOTO!
ISN'T THAT RIGHT, MINORU?
ER... YES...
THEN WHAT ABOUT THIS MESSAGE ON HARUNA'S PAGER?
IT'S PROBABLY JUST ONE OF HER FRIENDS.
HUH?

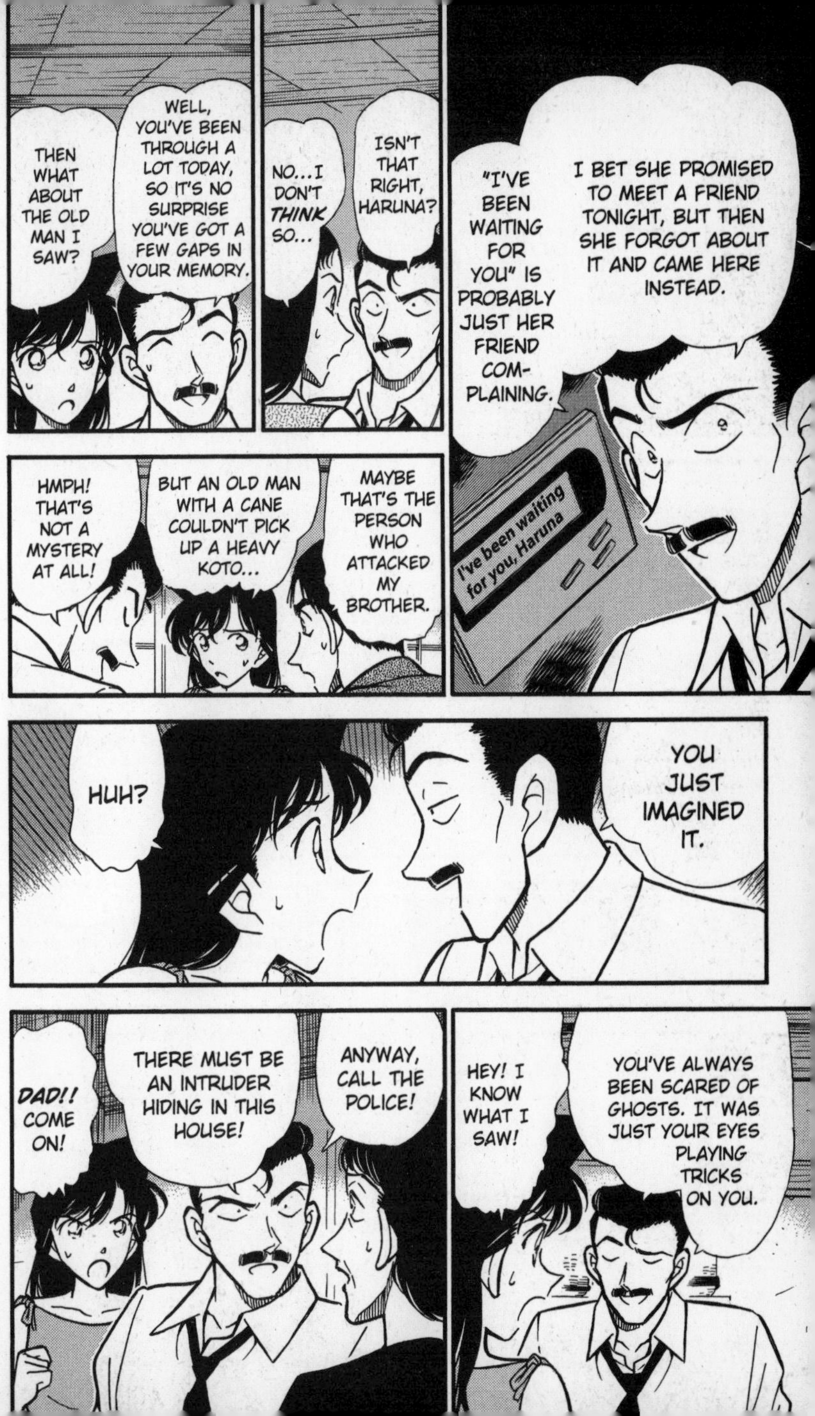
I BET SHE PROMISED TO MEET A FRIEND TONIGHT, BUT THEN SHE FORGOT ABOUT IT AND CAME HERE INSTEAD.
"I'VE BEEN WAITING FOR YOU" IS PROBABLY JUST HER FRIEND COM-PLAINING.
I've been waiting for you, Haruna
ISN'T THAT RIGHT, HARUNA?
NO...I DON'T *THINK* SO...
WELL, YOU'VE BEEN THROUGH A LOT TODAY, SO IT'S NO SURPRISE YOU'VE GOT A FEW GAPS IN YOUR MEMORY.
THEN WHAT ABOUT THE OLD MAN I SAW?
MAYBE THAT'S THE PERSON WHO ATTACKED MY BROTHER.
BUT AN OLD MAN WITH A CANE COULDN'T PICK UP A HEAVY KOTO...
HMPH! THAT'S NOT A MYSTERY AT ALL!
YOU JUST IMAGINED IT.
HUH?
YOU'VE ALWAYS BEEN SCARED OF GHOSTS. IT WAS JUST YOUR EYES PLAYING TRICKS ON YOU.
HEY! I KNOW WHAT I SAW!
ANYWAY, CALL THE POLICE!
THERE MUST BE AN INTRUDER HIDING IN THIS HOUSE!
DAD!! COME ON!

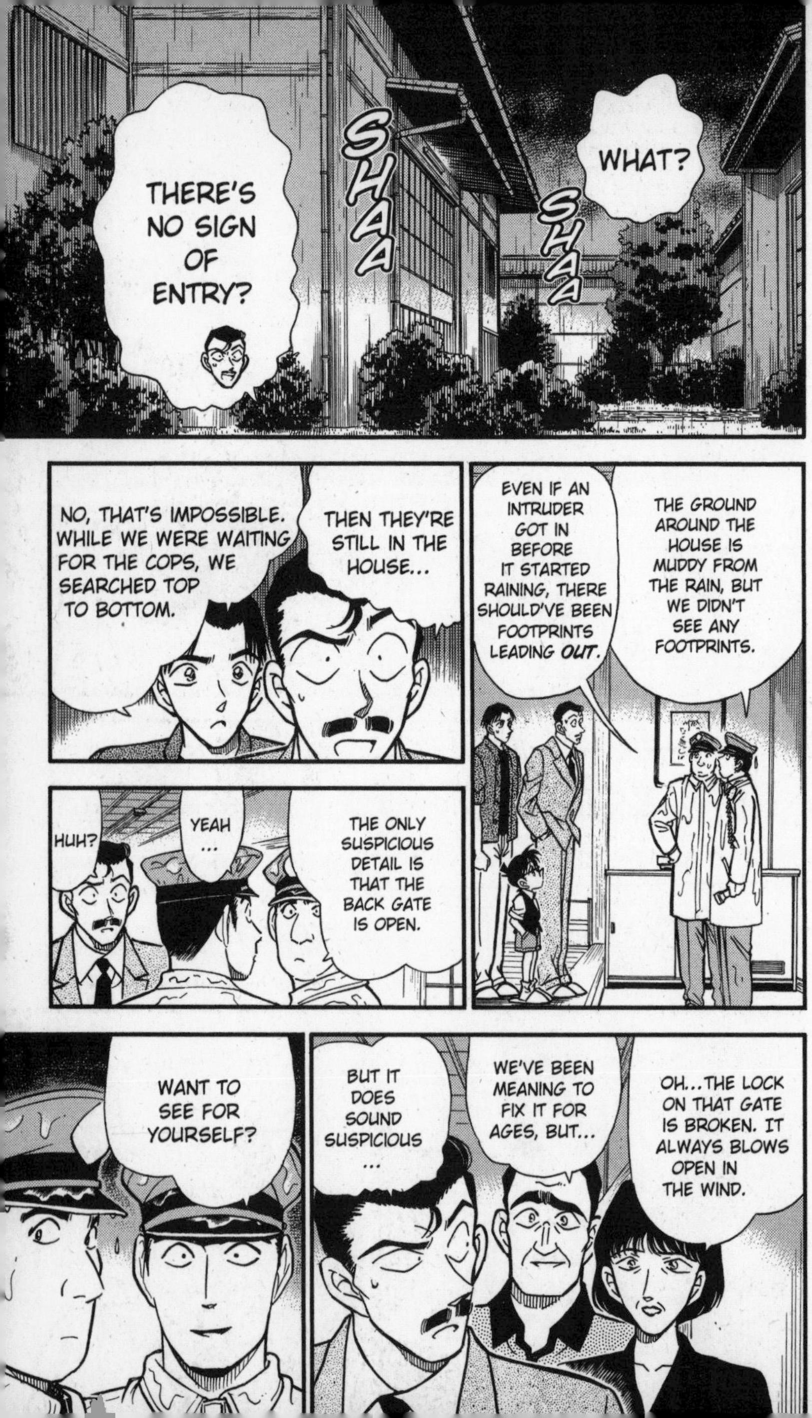
WHAT?
SHAA
SHAA
THERE'S NO SIGN OF ENTRY?
THE GROUND AROUND THE HOUSE IS MUDDY FROM THE RAIN, BUT WE DIDN'T SEE ANY FOOTPRINTS.
EVEN IF AN INTRUDER GOT IN BEFORE IT STARTED RAINING, THERE SHOULD'VE BEEN FOOTPRINTS LEADING *OUT*.
THEN THEY'RE STILL IN THE HOUSE...
NO, THAT'S IMPOSSIBLE. WHILE WE WERE WAITING FOR THE COPS, WE SEARCHED TOP TO BOTTOM.
THE ONLY SUSPICIOUS DETAIL IS THAT THE BACK GATE IS OPEN.
YEAH...
HUH?
OH...THE LOCK ON THAT GATE IS BROKEN. IT ALWAYS BLOWS OPEN IN THE WIND.
WE'VE BEEN MEANING TO FIX IT FOR AGES, BUT...
BUT IT DOES SOUND SUSPICIOUS...
WANT TO SEE FOR YOURSELF?

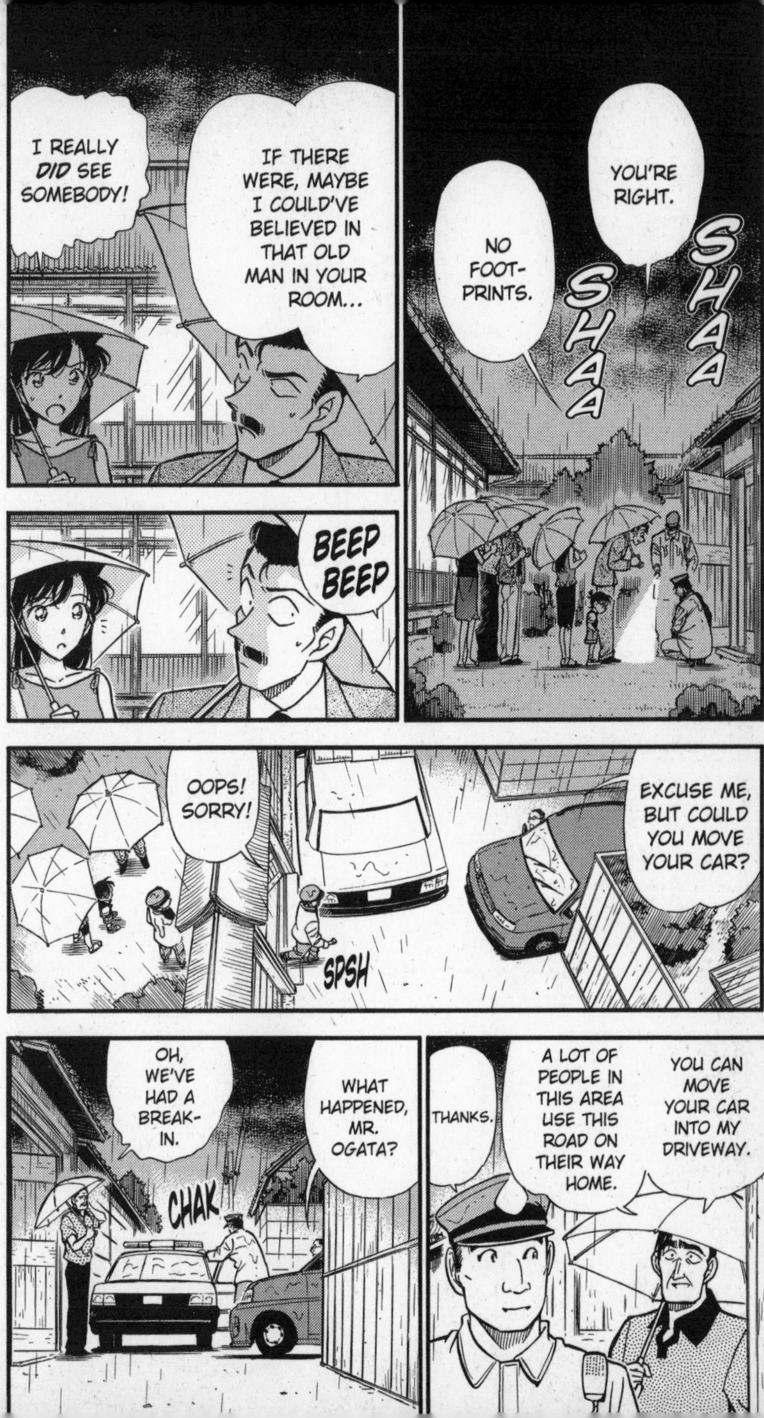
YOU'RE RIGHT.
SHAA
NO FOOT-PRINTS.
SHAA
IF THERE WERE, MAYBE I COULD'VE BELIEVED IN THAT OLD MAN IN YOUR ROOM...
I REALLY *DID* SEE SOMEBODY!
BEEP BEEP
EXCUSE ME, BUT COULD YOU MOVE YOUR CAR?
SPSH
OOPS! SORRY!
YOU CAN MOVE YOUR CAR INTO MY DRIVEWAY.
A LOT OF PEOPLE IN THIS AREA USE THIS ROAD ON THEIR WAY HOME.
THANKS.
WHAT HAPPENED, MR. OGATA?
OH, WE'VE HAD A BREAK-IN.
CHAK

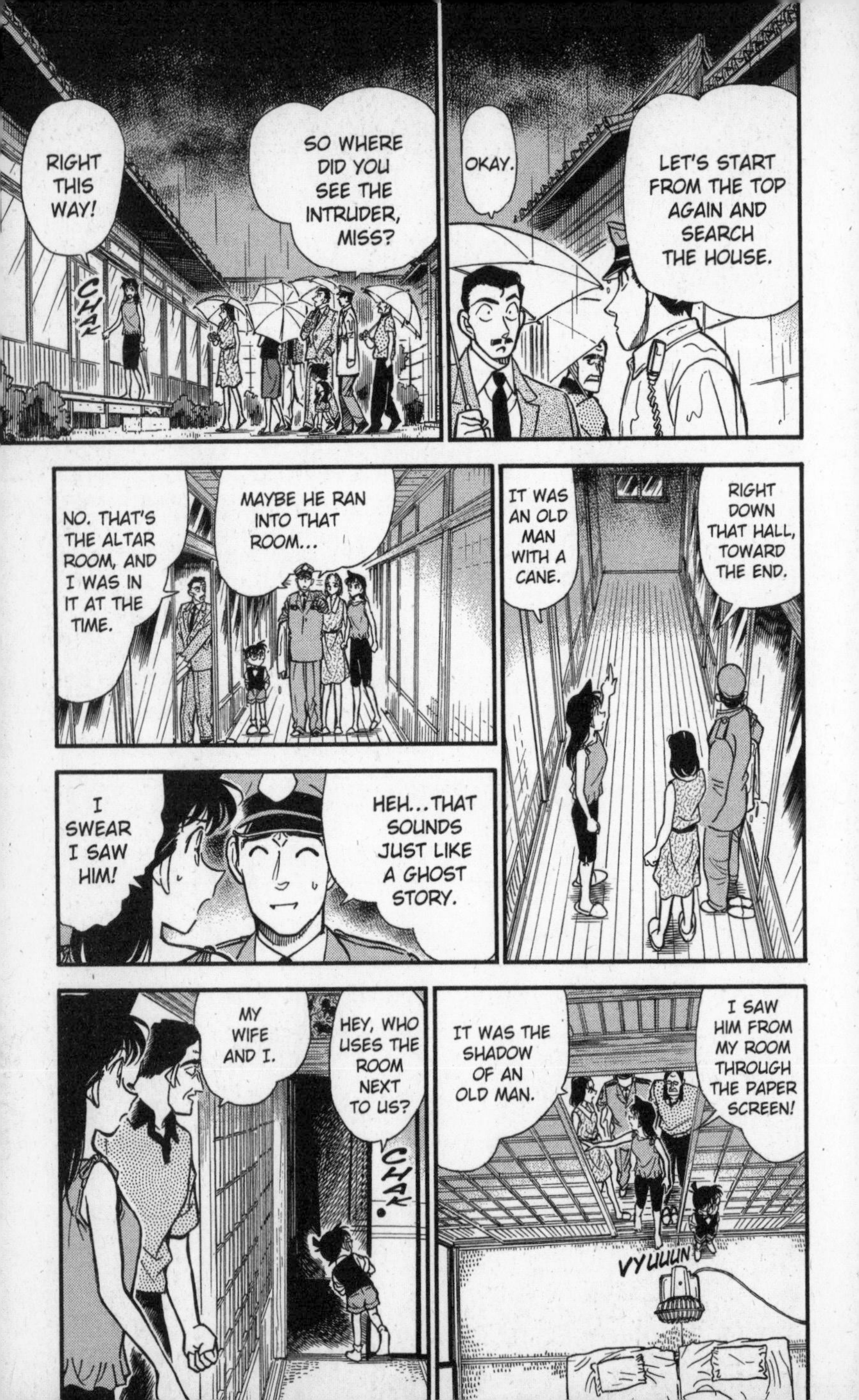
LET'S START FROM THE TOP AGAIN AND SEARCH THE HOUSE.
OKAY.
SO WHERE DID YOU SEE THE INTRUDER, MISS?
RIGHT THIS WAY!
CHAK
RIGHT DOWN THAT HALL, TOWARD THE END.
IT WAS AN OLD MAN WITH A CANE.
MAYBE HE RAN INTO THAT ROOM...
NO. THAT'S THE ALTAR ROOM, AND I WAS IN IT AT THE TIME.
HEH...THAT SOUNDS JUST LIKE A GHOST STORY.
I SWEAR I SAW HIM!
I SAW HIM FROM MY ROOM THROUGH THE PAPER SCREEN!
IT WAS THE SHADOW OF AN OLD MAN.
VYUUUN
HEY, WHO USES THE ROOM NEXT TO US?
CHAK
MY WIFE AND I.

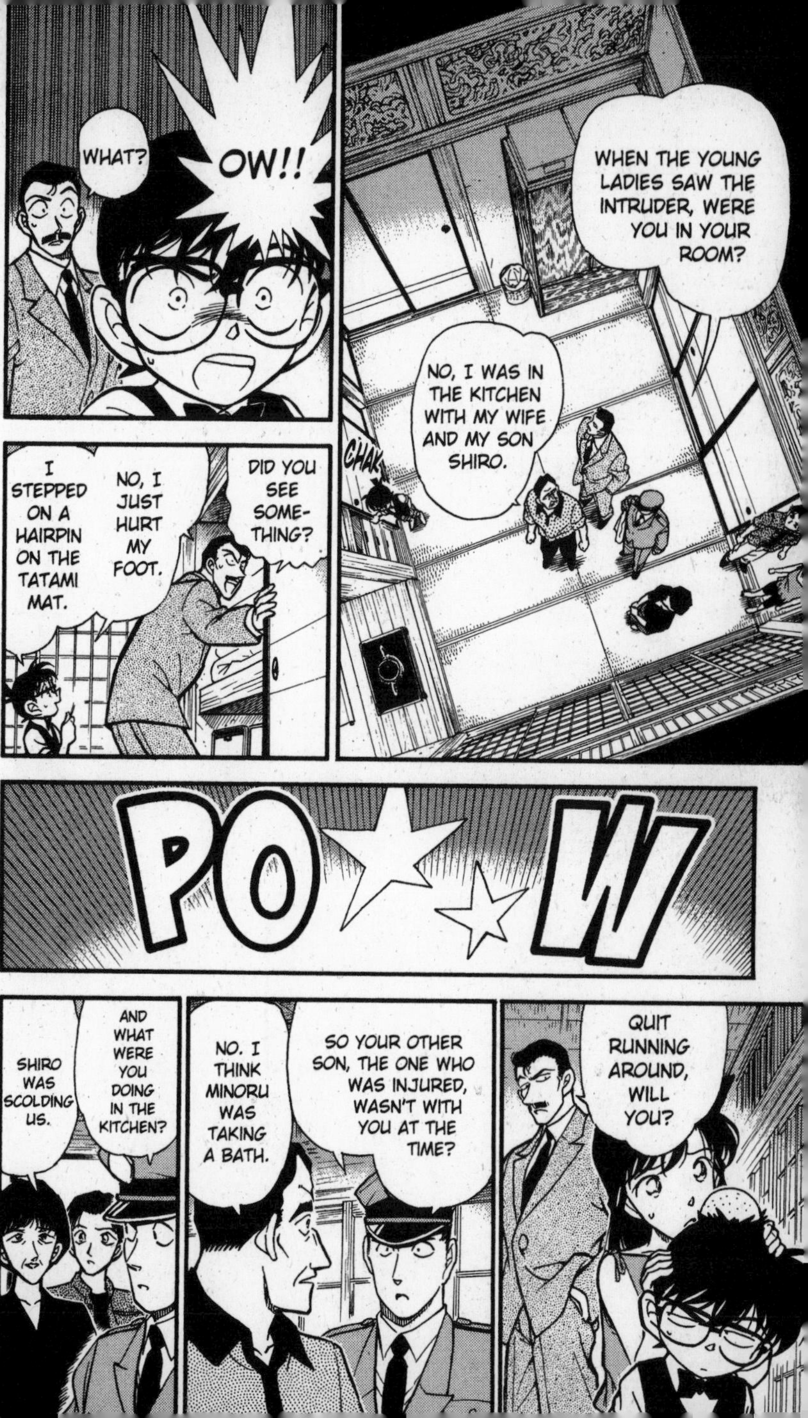
WHEN THE YOUNG LADIES SAW THE INTRUDER, WERE YOU IN YOUR ROOM?
NO, I WAS IN THE KITCHEN WITH MY WIFE AND MY SON SHIRO.
CHAK
OW!!
WHAT?
DID YOU SEE SOME-THING?
NO, I JUST HURT MY FOOT.
I STEPPED ON A HAIRPIN ON THE TATAMI MAT.
POW
QUIT RUNNING AROUND, WILL YOU?
SO YOUR OTHER SON, THE ONE WHO WAS INJURED, WASN'T WITH YOU AT THE TIME?
NO. I THINK MINORU WAS TAKING A BATH.
AND WHAT WERE YOU DOING IN THE KITCHEN?
SHIRO WAS SCOLDING US.

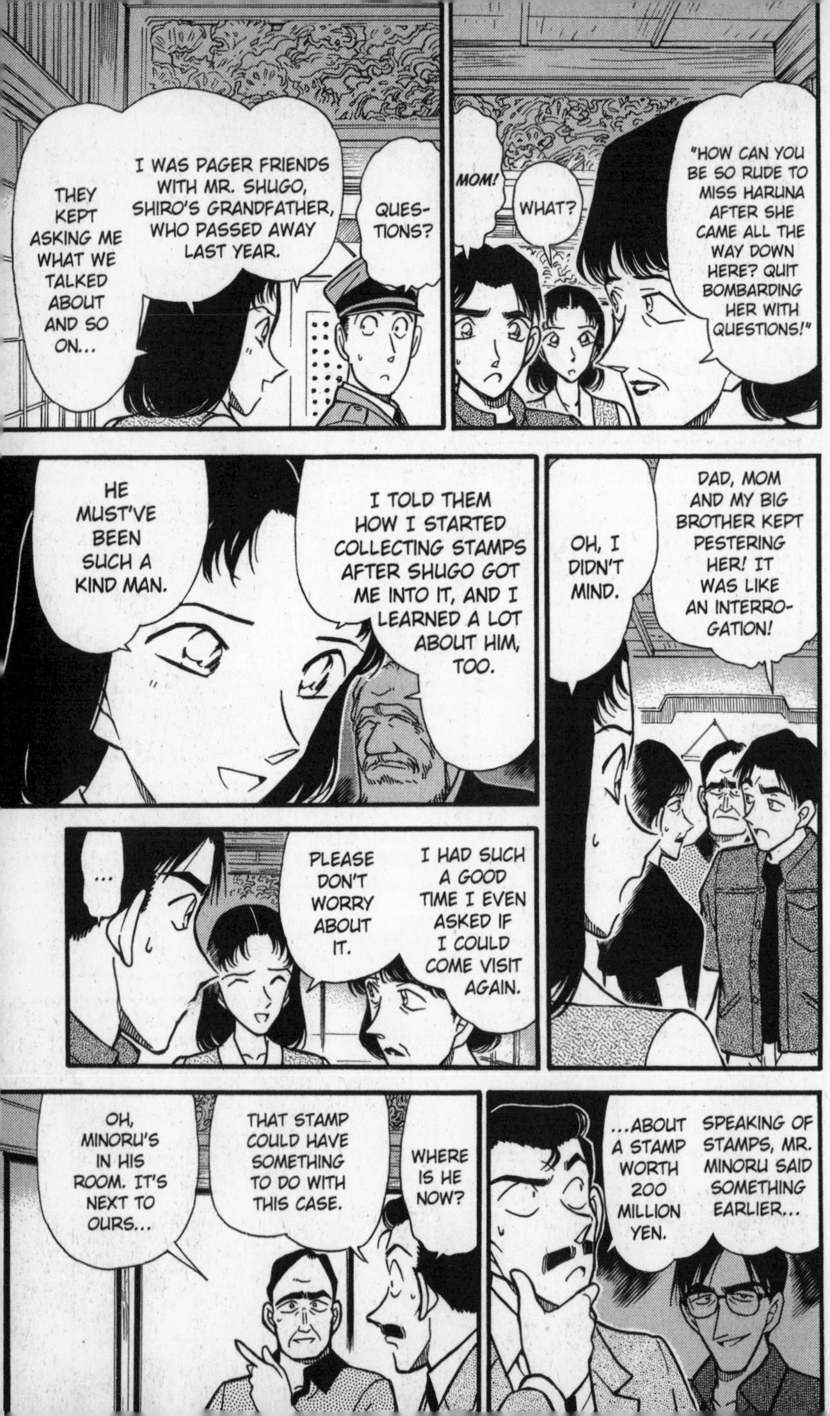
"HOW CAN YOU BE SO RUDE TO MISS HARUNA AFTER SHE CAME ALL THE WAY DOWN HERE? QUIT BOMBARDING HER WITH QUESTIONS!"
WHAT?
MOM!
QUESTIONS?
I WAS PAGER FRIENDS WITH MR. SHUGO, SHIRO'S GRANDFATHER, WHO PASSED AWAY LAST YEAR.
THEY KEPT ASKING ME WHAT WE TALKED ABOUT AND SO ON...
DAD, MOM AND MY BIG BROTHER KEPT PESTERING HER! IT WAS LIKE AN INTERROGATION!
OH, I DIDN'T MIND.
I TOLD THEM HOW I STARTED COLLECTING STAMPS AFTER SHUGO GOT ME INTO IT, AND I LEARNED A LOT ABOUT HIM, TOO.
HE MUST'VE BEEN SUCH A KIND MAN.
I HAD SUCH A GOOD TIME I EVEN ASKED IF I COULD COME VISIT AGAIN.
PLEASE DON'T WORRY ABOUT IT.
...
SPEAKING OF STAMPS, MR. MINORU SAID SOMETHING EARLIER...
...ABOUT A STAMP WORTH 200 MILLION YEN.
WHERE IS HE NOW?
THAT STAMP COULD HAVE SOMETHING TO DO WITH THIS CASE.
OH, MINORU'S IN HIS ROOM. IT'S NEXT TO OURS...

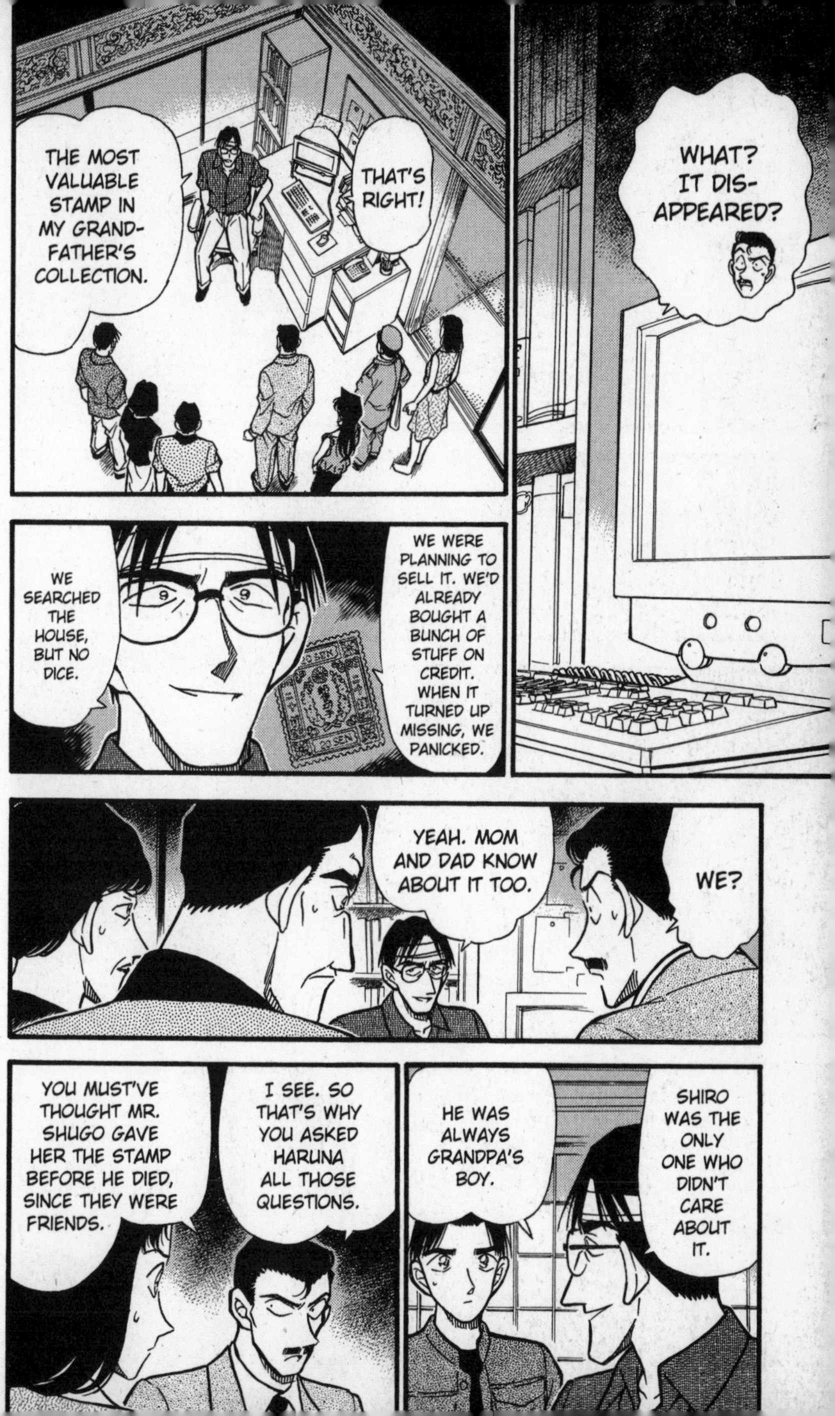
WHAT? IT DIS-APPEARED?
THAT'S RIGHT!
THE MOST VALUABLE STAMP IN MY GRAND-FATHER'S COLLECTION.
WE WERE PLANNING TO SELL IT. WE'D ALREADY BOUGHT A BUNCH OF STUFF ON CREDIT. WHEN IT TURNED UP MISSING, WE PANICKED.
WE SEARCHED THE HOUSE, BUT NO DICE.
WE?
YEAH. MOM AND DAD KNOW ABOUT IT TOO.
SHIRO WAS THE ONLY ONE WHO DIDN'T CARE ABOUT IT.
HE WAS ALWAYS GRANDPA'S BOY.
I SEE. SO THAT'S WHY YOU ASKED HARUNA ALL THOSE QUESTIONS.
YOU MUST'VE THOUGHT MR. SHUGO GAVE HER THE STAMP BEFORE HE DIED, SINCE THEY WERE FRIENDS.

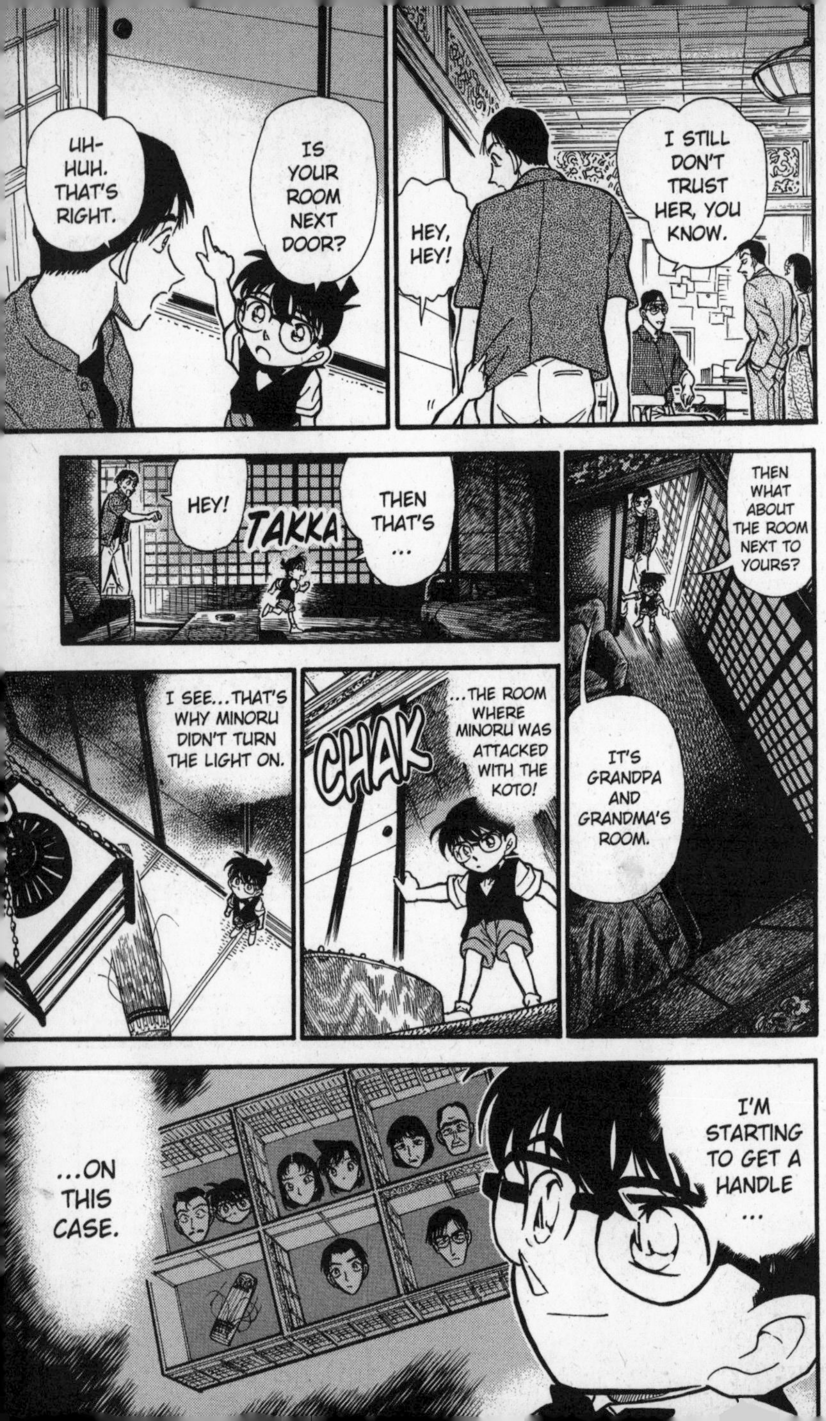
I STILL DON'T TRUST HER, YOU KNOW.
HEY, HEY!
IS YOUR ROOM NEXT DOOR?
UH-HUH. THAT'S RIGHT.
THEN WHAT ABOUT THE ROOM NEXT TO YOURS?
IT'S GRANDPA AND GRANDMA'S ROOM.
THEN THAT'S ...
TAKKA
HEY!
...THE ROOM WHERE MINORU WAS ATTACKED WITH THE KOTO!
CHAK
I SEE...THAT'S WHY MINORU DIDN'T TURN THE LIGHT ON.
I'M STARTING TO GET A HANDLE ...
...ON THIS CASE.

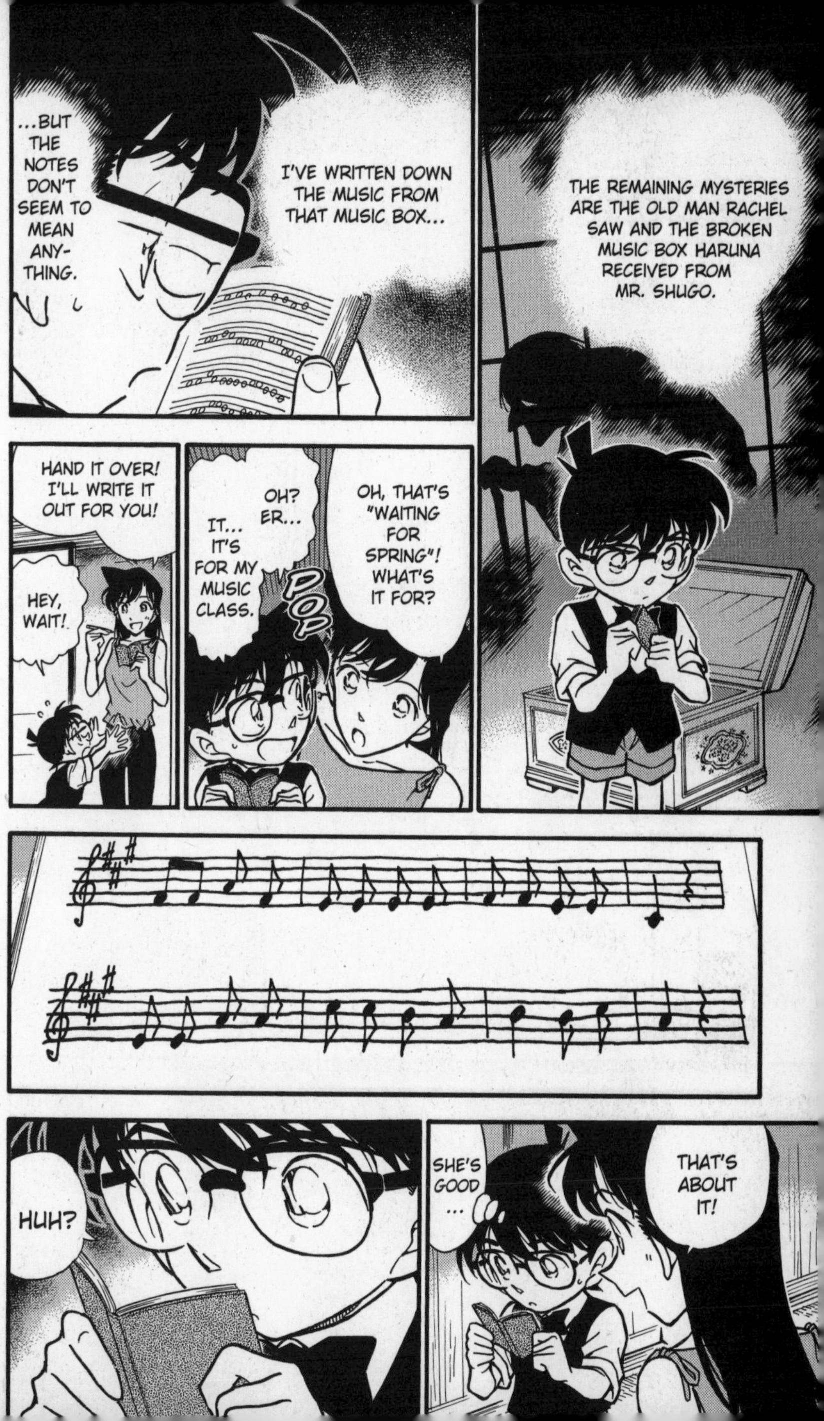
THE REMAINING MYSTERIES ARE THE OLD MAN RACHEL SAW AND THE BROKEN MUSIC BOX HARUNA RECEIVED FROM MR. SHUGO.
I'VE WRITTEN DOWN THE MUSIC FROM THAT MUSIC BOX...
...BUT THE NOTES DON'T SEEM TO MEAN ANY-THING.
OH, THAT'S "WAITING FOR SPRING"! WHAT'S IT FOR?
OH? ER...
IT... IT'S FOR MY MUSIC CLASS.
POP
HAND IT OVER! I'LL WRITE IT OUT FOR YOU!
HEY, WAIT!
THAT'S ABOUT IT!
SHE'S GOOD ...
HUH?

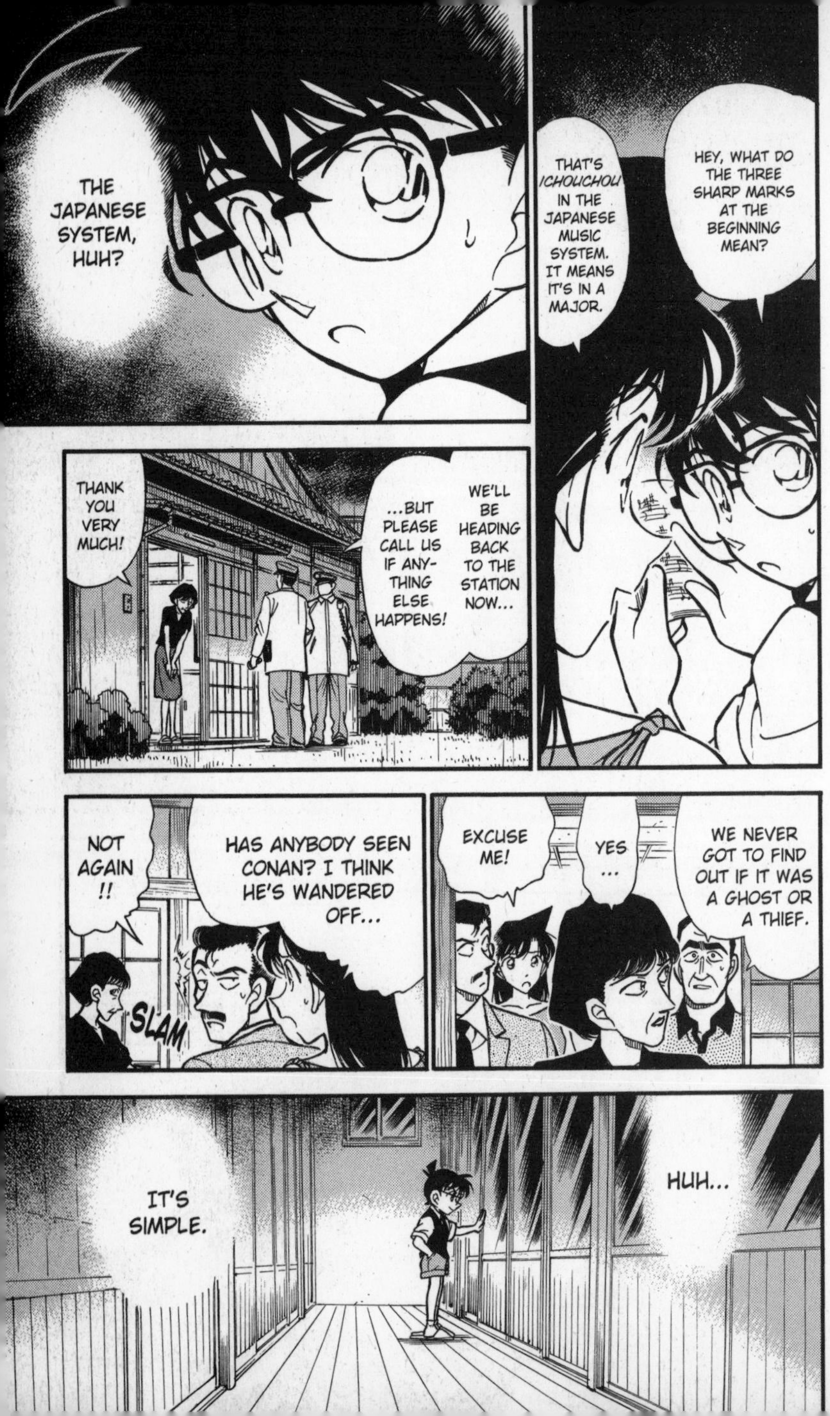
HEY, WHAT DO THE THREE SHARP MARKS AT THE BEGINNING MEAN?
THAT'S *ICHOUCHOU* IN THE JAPANESE MUSIC SYSTEM. IT MEANS IT'S IN A MAJOR.
THE JAPANESE SYSTEM, HUH?
WE'LL BE HEADING BACK TO THE STATION NOW...
...BUT PLEASE CALL US IF ANY-THING ELSE HAPPENS!
THANK YOU VERY MUCH!
WE NEVER GOT TO FIND OUT IF IT WAS A GHOST OR A THIEF.
YES ...
EXCUSE ME!
HAS ANYBODY SEEN CONAN? I THINK HE'S WANDERED OFF...
SLAM
NOT AGAIN !!
HUH...
IT'S SIMPLE.

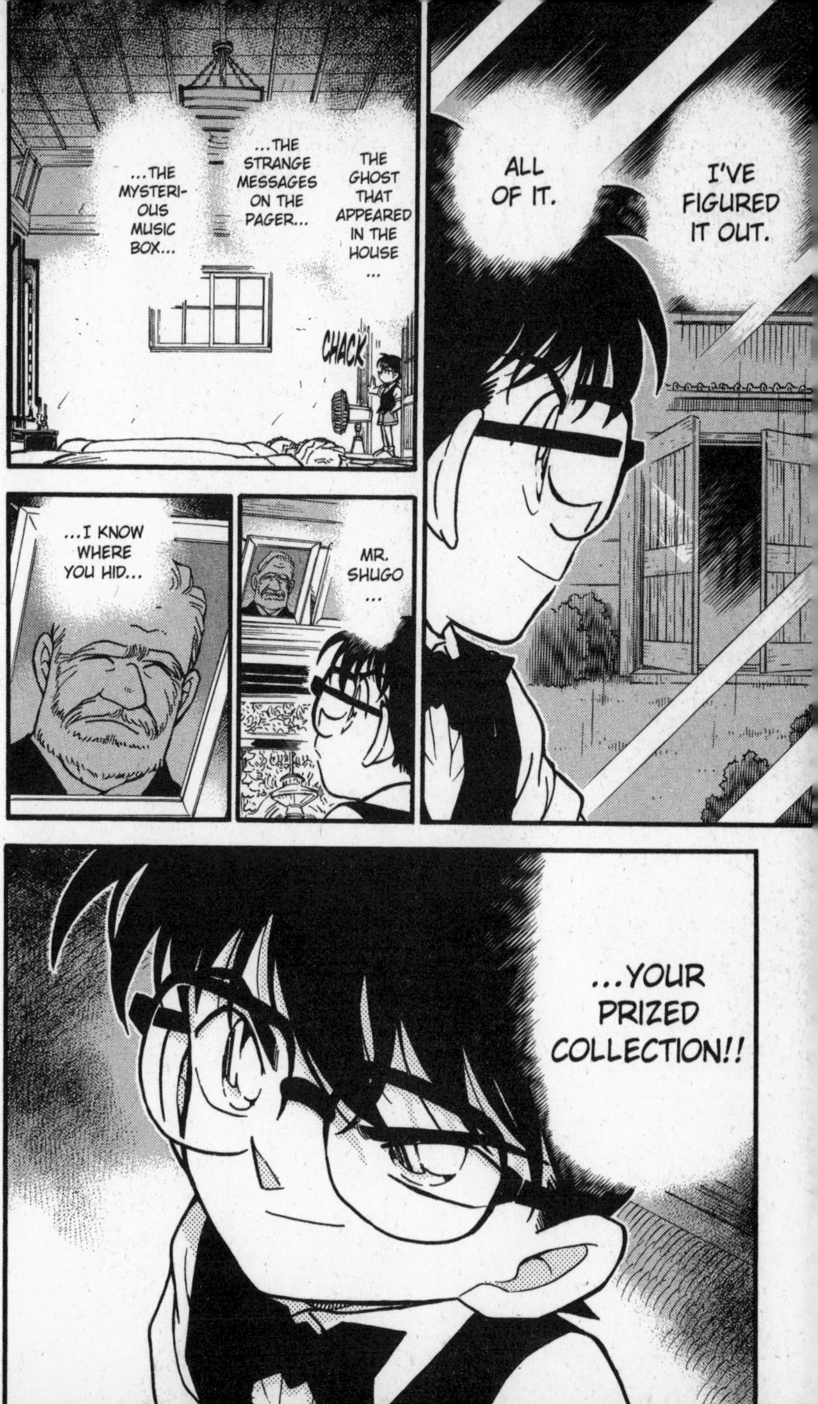
I'VE FIGURED IT OUT.
ALL OF IT.
THE GHOST THAT APPEARED IN THE HOUSE ...
...THE STRANGE MESSAGES ON THE PAGER...
...THE MYSTERI-OUS MUSIC BOX...
CHACK
MR. SHUGO ...
...I KNOW WHERE YOU HID...
...YOUR PRIZED COLLECTION!!

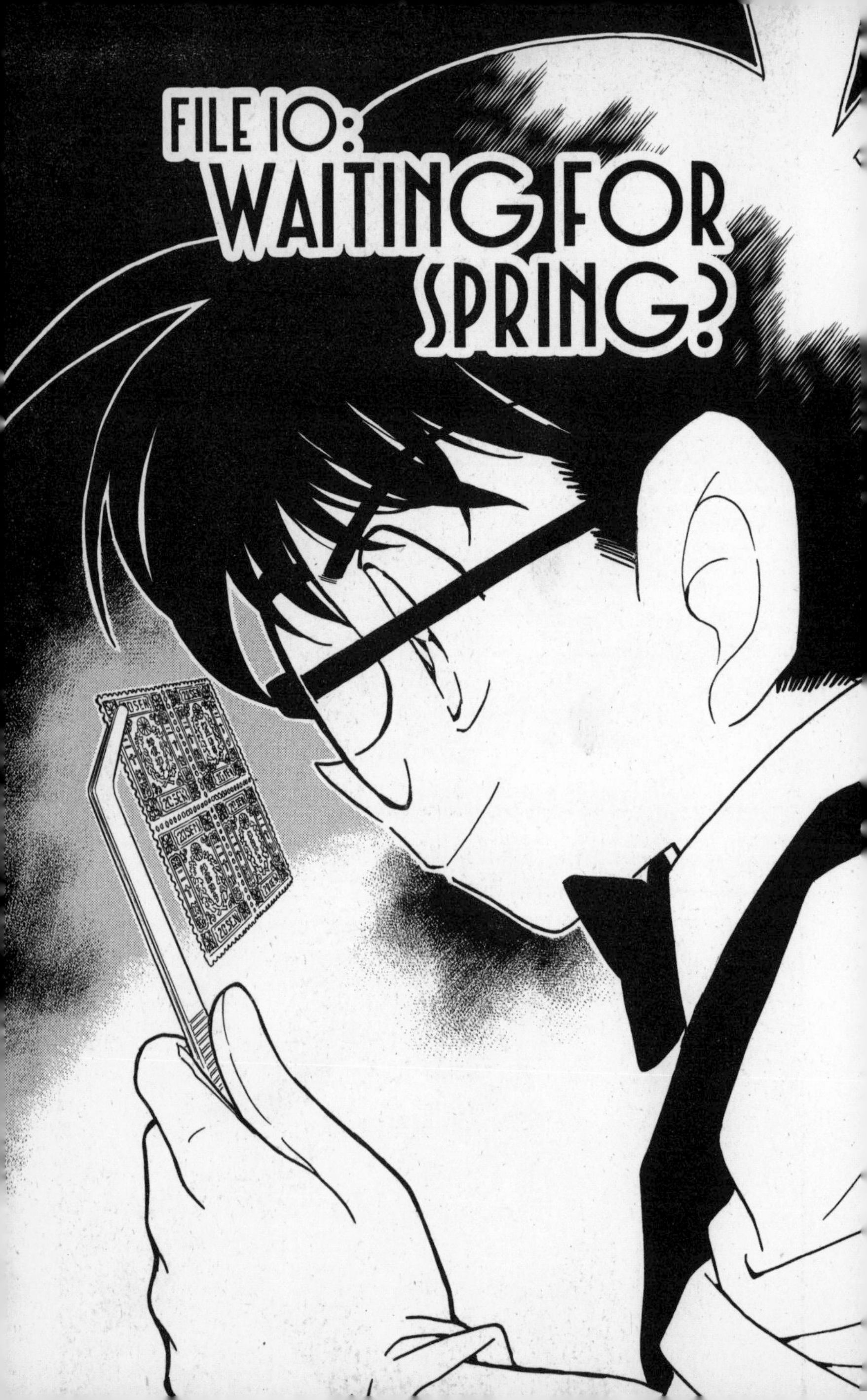
FILE 10:
WAITING FOR SPRING?

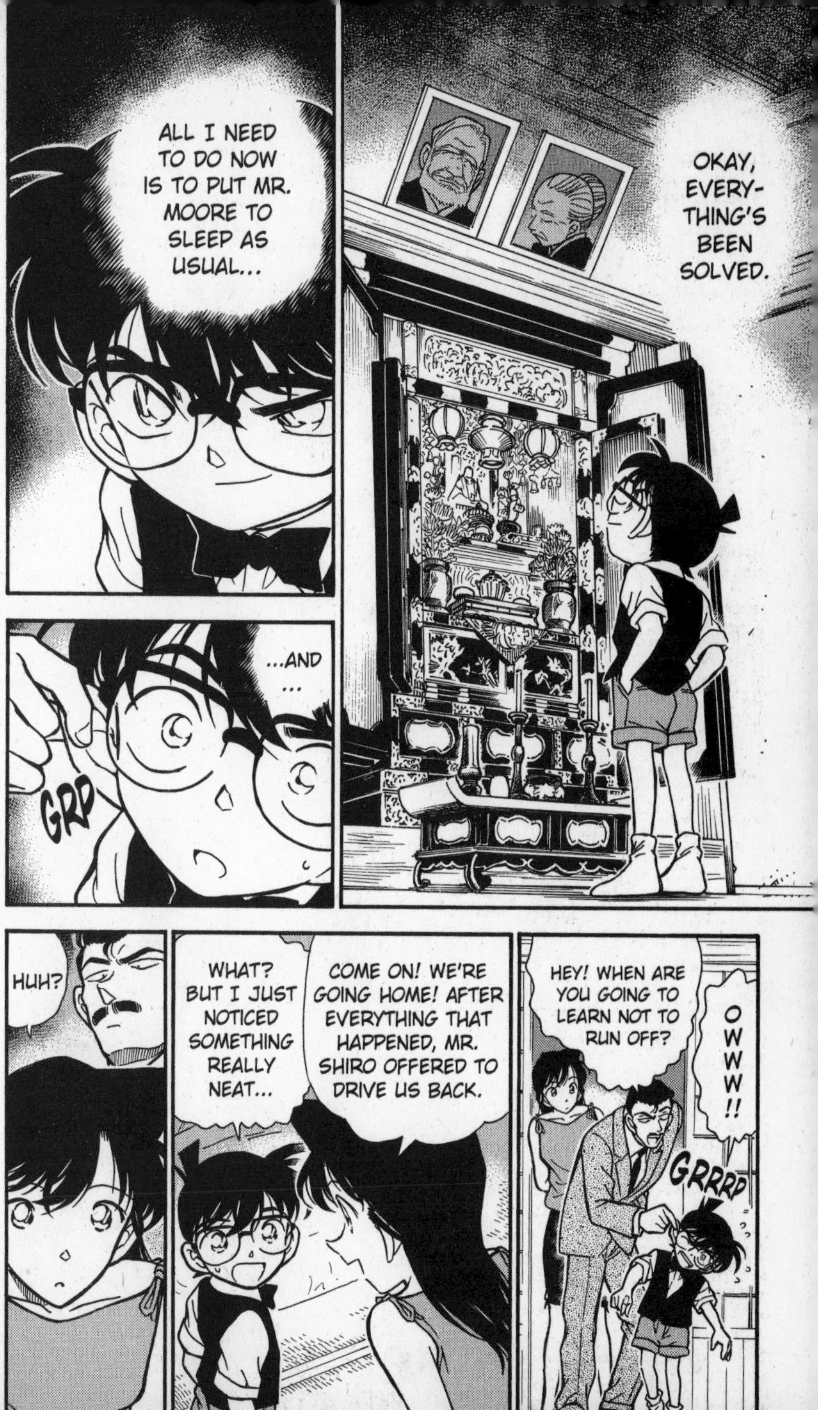
OKAY, EVERYTHING'S BEEN SOLVED.
ALL I NEED TO DO NOW IS TO PUT MR. MOORE TO SLEEP AS USUAL...
...AND ...
GRP
HEY! WHEN ARE YOU GOING TO LEARN NOT TO RUN OFF?
OWWW!!
GRRRP
COME ON! WE'RE GOING HOME! AFTER EVERYTHING THAT HAPPENED, MR. SHIRO OFFERED TO DRIVE US BACK.
WHAT? BUT I JUST NOTICED SOMETHING REALLY NEAT...
HUH?

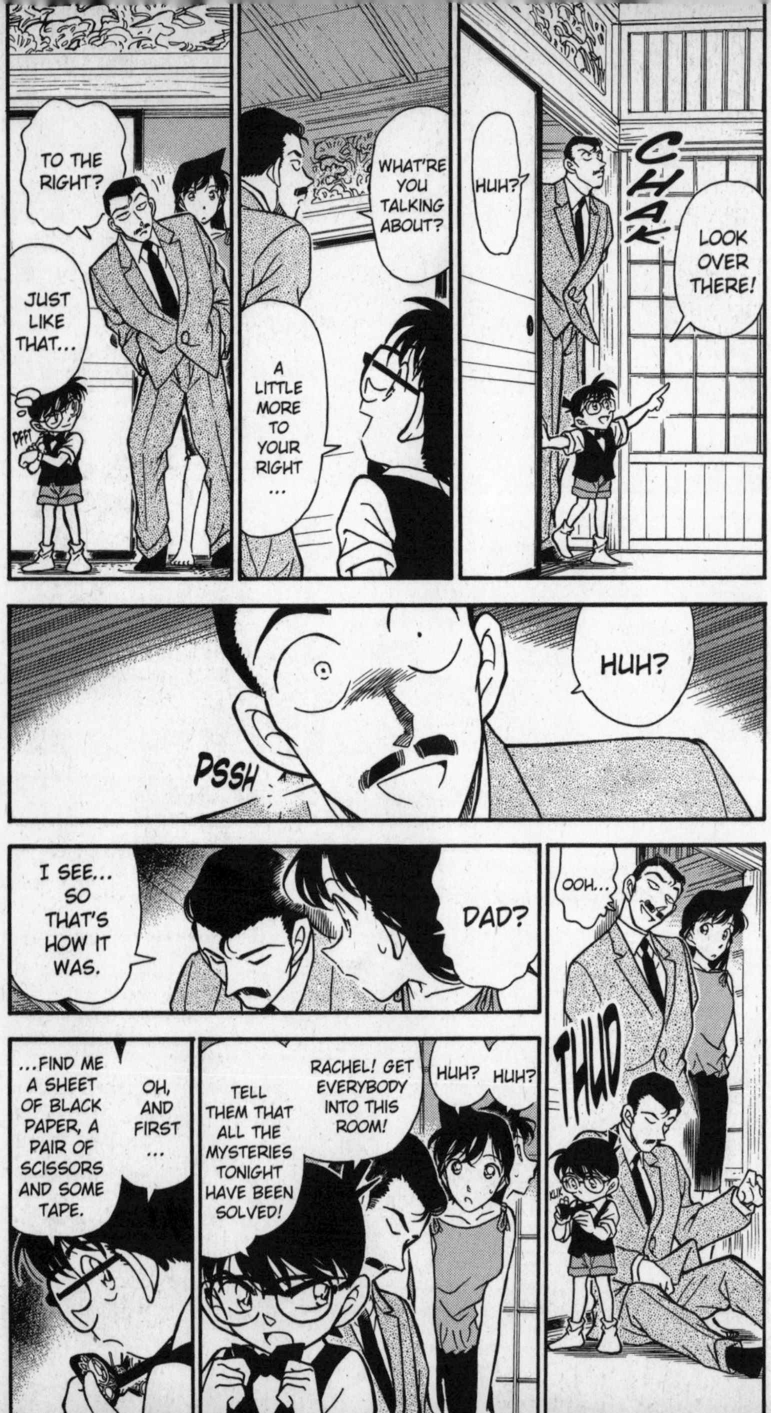
CHAK
LOOK OVER THERE!
HUH?
WHAT'RE YOU TALKING ABOUT?
A LITTLE MORE TO YOUR RIGHT ...
TO THE RIGHT?
JUST LIKE THAT...
PFFT
HUH?
PSSH
OOH...
THUD
KLIK
DAD?
I SEE... SO THAT'S HOW IT WAS.
HUH? HUH?
RACHEL! GET EVERYBODY INTO THIS ROOM!
TELL THEM THAT ALL THE MYSTERIES TONIGHT HAVE BEEN SOLVED!
OH, AND FIRST ...
...FIND ME A SHEET OF BLACK PAPER, A PAIR OF SCISSORS AND SOME TAPE.

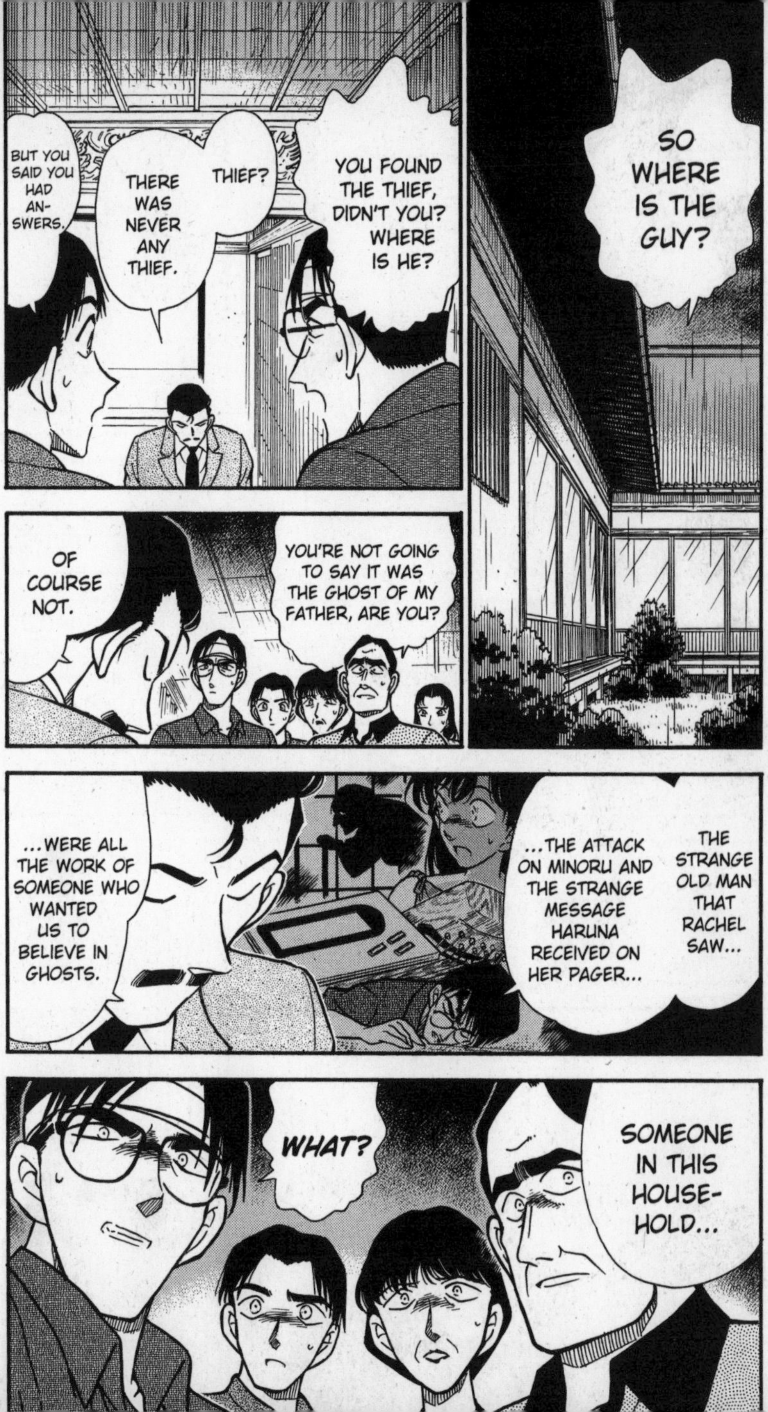
SO WHERE IS THE GUY?
YOU FOUND THE THIEF, DIDN'T YOU? WHERE IS HE?
THIEF?
THERE WAS NEVER ANY THIEF.
BUT YOU SAID YOU HAD AN-SWERS.
YOU'RE NOT GOING TO SAY IT WAS THE GHOST OF MY FATHER, ARE YOU?
OF COURSE NOT.
THE STRANGE OLD MAN THAT RACHEL SAW...
...THE ATTACK ON MINORU AND THE STRANGE MESSAGE HARUNA RECEIVED ON HER PAGER...
...WERE ALL THE WORK OF SOMEONE WHO WANTED US TO BELIEVE IN GHOSTS.
SOMEONE IN THIS HOUSE-HOLD...
WHAT?

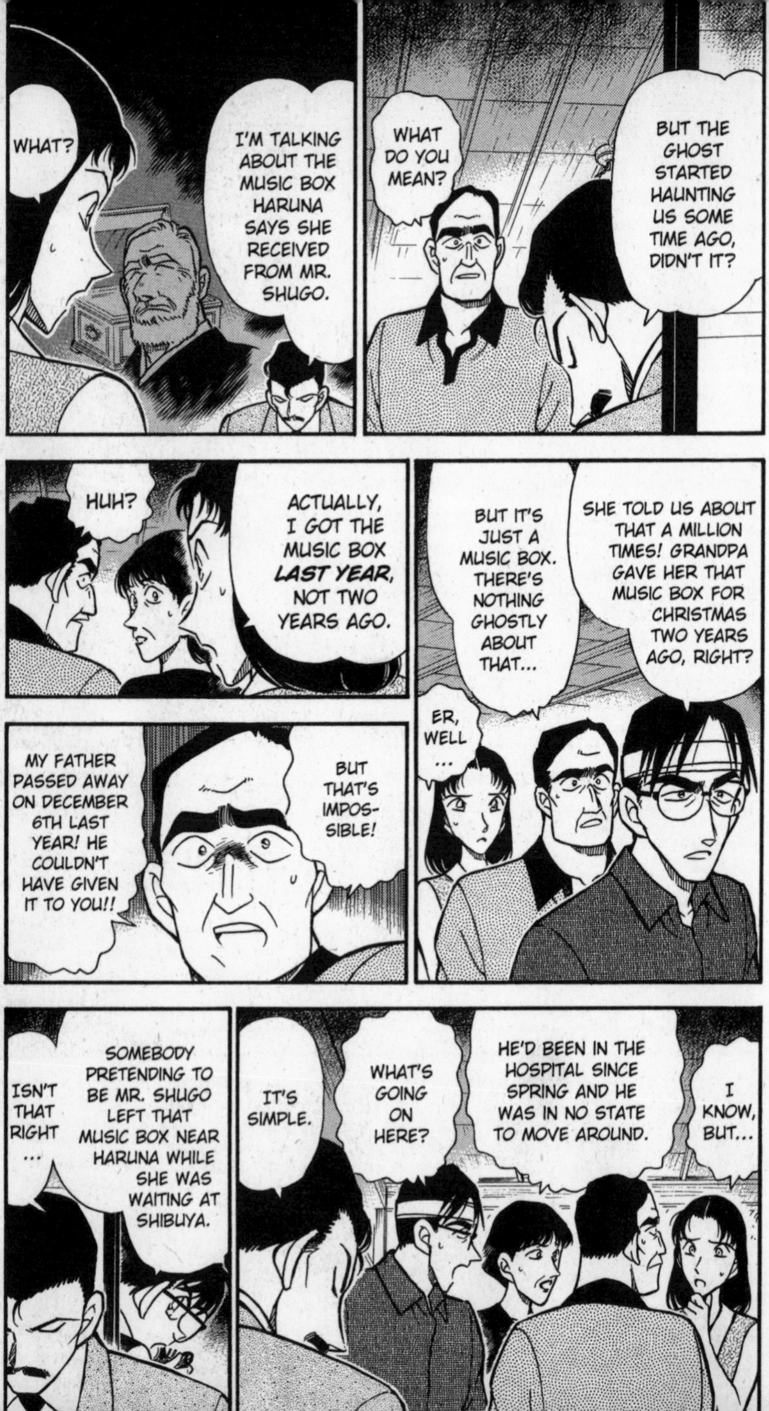
BUT THE GHOST STARTED HAUNTING US SOME TIME AGO, DIDN'T IT?
WHAT DO YOU MEAN?
I'M TALKING ABOUT THE MUSIC BOX HARUNA SAYS SHE RECEIVED FROM MR. SHUGO.
WHAT?
SHE TOLD US ABOUT THAT A MILLION TIMES! GRANDPA GAVE HER THAT MUSIC BOX FOR CHRISTMAS TWO YEARS AGO, RIGHT?
BUT IT'S JUST A MUSIC BOX. THERE'S NOTHING GHOSTLY ABOUT THAT...
ER, WELL ...
ACTUALLY, I GOT THE MUSIC BOX ***LAST YEAR***, NOT TWO YEARS AGO.
HUH?
BUT THAT'S IMPOSSIBLE!
MY FATHER PASSED AWAY ON DECEMBER 6TH LAST YEAR! HE COULDN'T HAVE GIVEN IT TO YOU!!
I KNOW, BUT...
HE'D BEEN IN THE HOSPITAL SINCE SPRING AND HE WAS IN NO STATE TO MOVE AROUND.
WHAT'S GOING ON HERE?
IT'S SIMPLE.
SOMEBODY PRETENDING TO BE MR. SHUGO LEFT THAT MUSIC BOX NEAR HARUNA WHILE SHE WAS WAITING AT SHIBUYA.
ISN'T THAT RIGHT ...

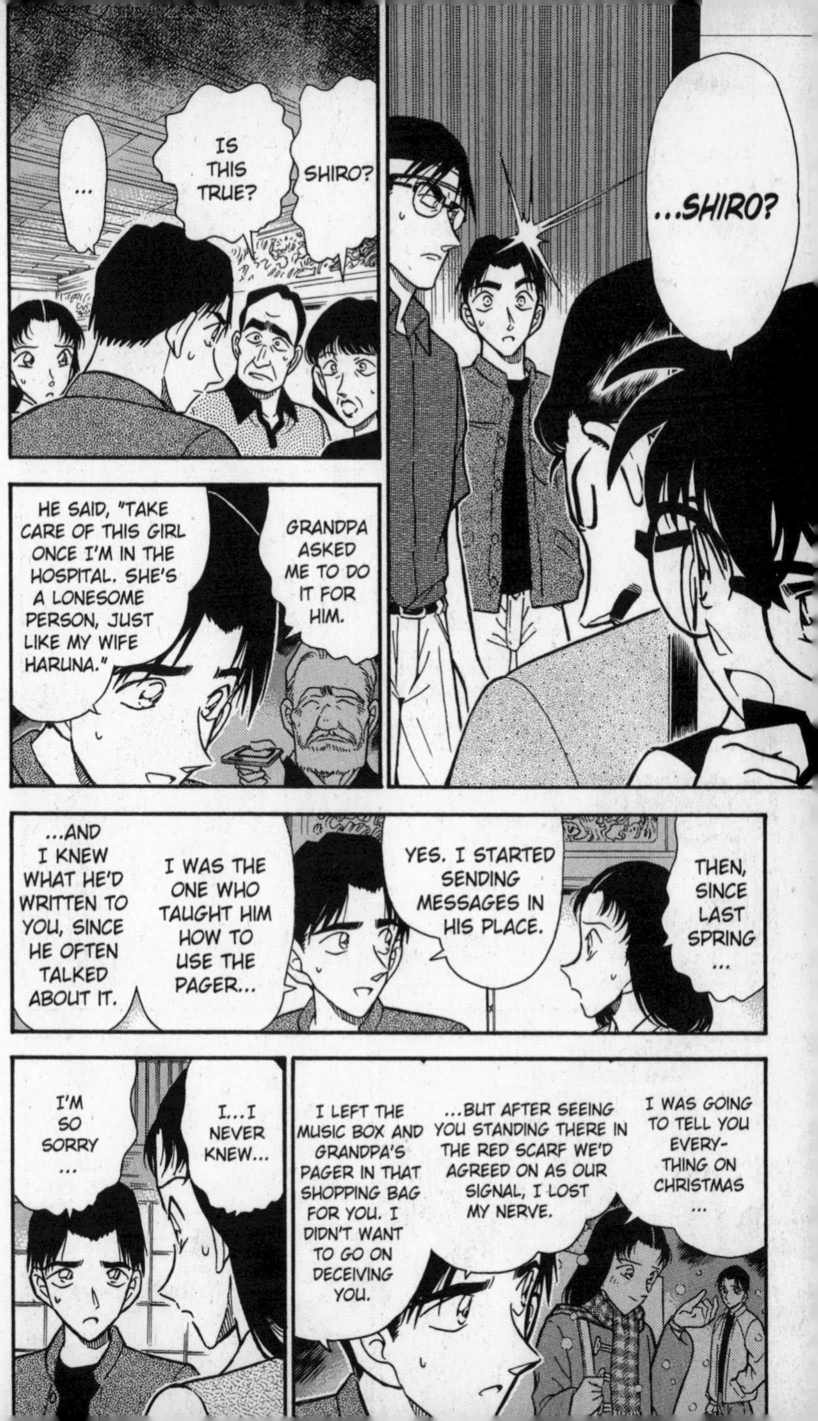
...SHIRO?
SHIRO?
IS THIS TRUE?
...
GRANDPA ASKED ME TO DO IT FOR HIM.
HE SAID, "TAKE CARE OF THIS GIRL ONCE I'M IN THE HOSPITAL. SHE'S A LONESOME PERSON, JUST LIKE MY WIFE HARUNA."
THEN, SINCE LAST SPRING ...
YES. I STARTED SENDING MESSAGES IN HIS PLACE.
I WAS THE ONE WHO TAUGHT HIM HOW TO USE THE PAGER...
...AND I KNEW WHAT HE'D WRITTEN TO YOU, SINCE HE OFTEN TALKED ABOUT IT.
I WAS GOING TO TELL YOU EVERY-THING ON CHRISTMAS ...
...BUT AFTER SEEING YOU STANDING THERE IN THE RED SCARF WE'D AGREED ON AS OUR SIGNAL, I LOST MY NERVE.
I LEFT THE MUSIC BOX AND GRANDPA'S PAGER IN THAT SHOPPING BAG FOR YOU. I DIDN'T WANT TO GO ON DECEIVING YOU.
I...I NEVER KNEW...
I'M SO SORRY ...

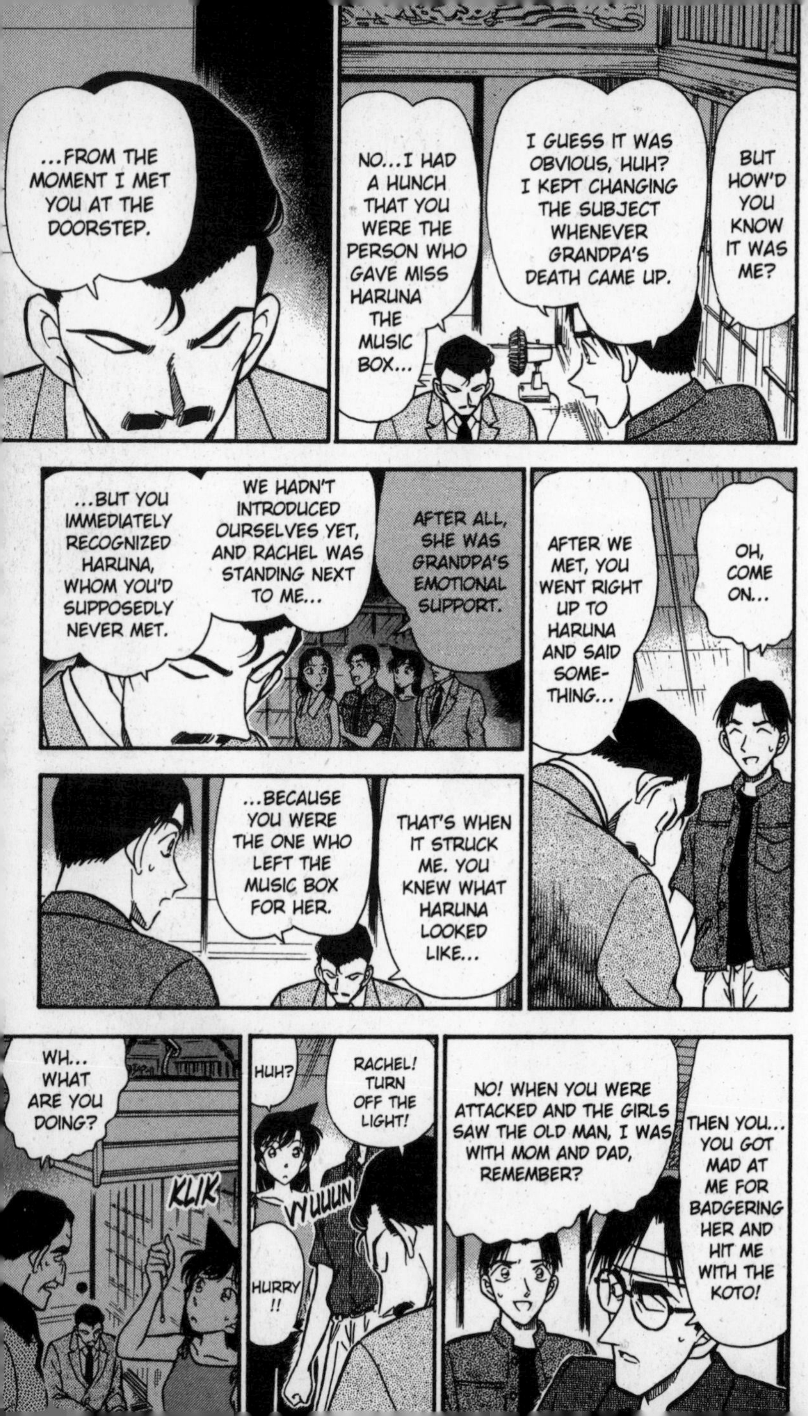
BUT HOW'D YOU KNOW IT WAS ME?
I GUESS IT WAS OBVIOUS, HUH? I KEPT CHANGING THE SUBJECT WHENEVER GRANDPA'S DEATH CAME UP.
NO...I HAD A HUNCH THAT YOU WERE THE PERSON WHO GAVE MISS HARUNA THE MUSIC BOX...
...FROM THE MOMENT I MET YOU AT THE DOORSTEP.
OH, COME ON...
AFTER WE MET, YOU WENT RIGHT UP TO HARUNA AND SAID SOME-THING...
AFTER ALL, SHE WAS GRANDPA'S EMOTIONAL SUPPORT.
WE HADN'T INTRODUCED OURSELVES YET, AND RACHEL WAS STANDING NEXT TO ME...
...BUT YOU IMMEDIATELY RECOGNIZED HARUNA, WHOM YOU'D SUPPOSEDLY NEVER MET.
THAT'S WHEN IT STRUCK ME. YOU KNEW WHAT HARUNA LOOKED LIKE...
...BECAUSE YOU WERE THE ONE WHO LEFT THE MUSIC BOX FOR HER.
THEN YOU... YOU GOT MAD AT ME FOR BADGERING HER AND HIT ME WITH THE KOTO!
NO! WHEN YOU WERE ATTACKED AND THE GIRLS SAW THE OLD MAN, I WAS WITH MOM AND DAD, REMEMBER?
RACHEL! TURN OFF THE LIGHT!
HUH?
VVUUUN
HURRY !!
WH... WHAT ARE YOU DOING?
KLIK

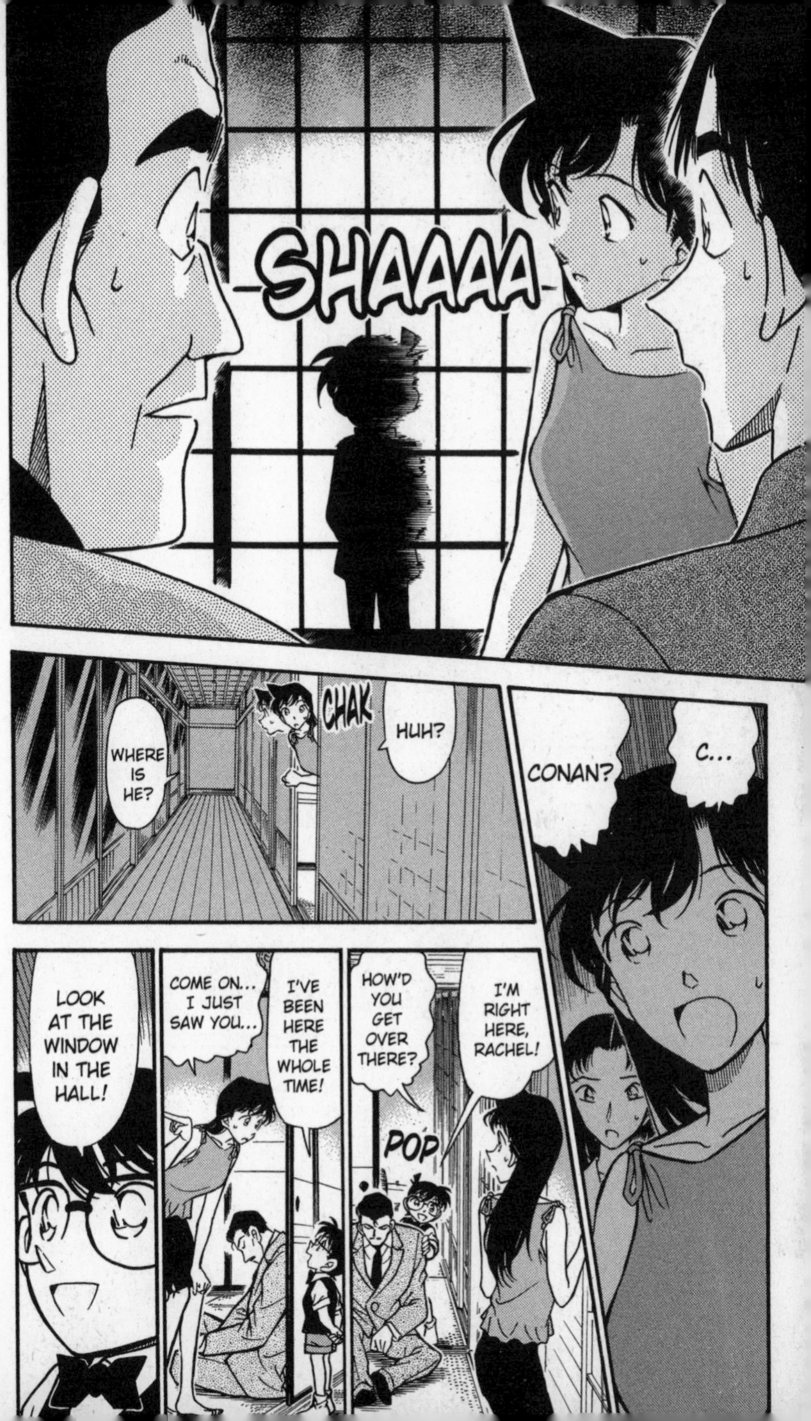

SHAAAA
C...
CONAN?
HUH?
CHAK
WHERE IS HE?
I'M RIGHT HERE, RACHEL!
HOW'D YOU GET OVER THERE?
POP
I'VE BEEN HERE THE WHOLE TIME!
COME ON... I JUST SAW YOU...
LOOK AT THE WINDOW IN THE HALL!

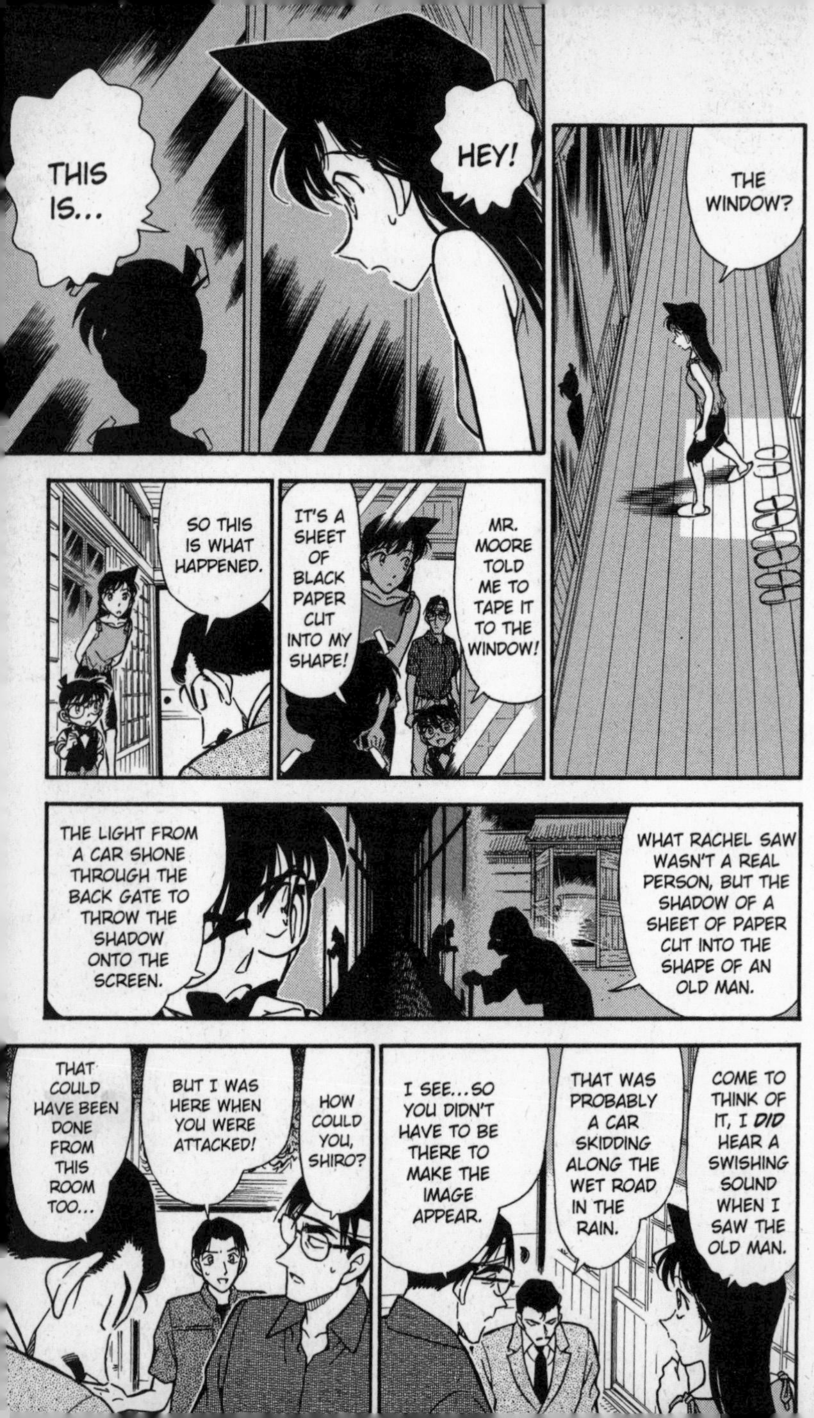
THE WINDOW?
HEY!
THIS IS...
IT'S A SHEET OF BLACK PAPER CUT INTO MY SHAPE!
MR. MOORE TOLD ME TO TAPE IT TO THE WINDOW!
SO THIS IS WHAT HAPPENED.
WHAT RACHEL SAW WASN'T A REAL PERSON, BUT THE SHADOW OF A SHEET OF PAPER CUT INTO THE SHAPE OF AN OLD MAN.
THE LIGHT FROM A CAR SHONE THROUGH THE BACK GATE TO THROW THE SHADOW ONTO THE SCREEN.
COME TO THINK OF IT, I *DID* HEAR A SWISHING SOUND WHEN I SAW THE OLD MAN.
THAT WAS PROBABLY A CAR SKIDDING ALONG THE WET ROAD IN THE RAIN.
I SEE...SO YOU DIDN'T HAVE TO BE THERE TO MAKE THE IMAGE APPEAR.
HOW COULD YOU, SHIRO?
BUT I WAS HERE WHEN YOU WERE ATTACKED!
THAT COULD HAVE BEEN DONE FROM THIS ROOM TOO...

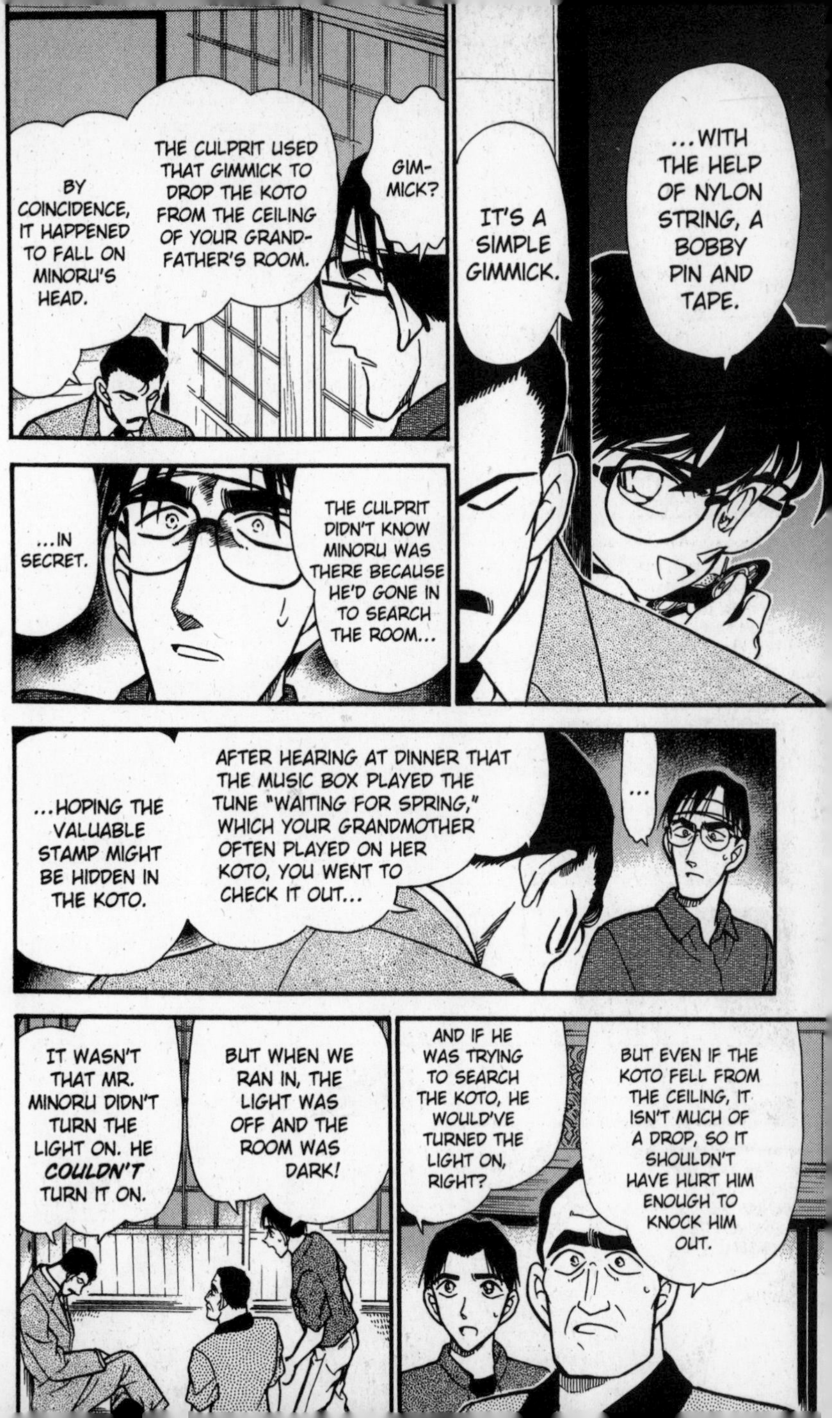
IT'S A SIMPLE GIMMICK.
...WITH THE HELP OF NYLON STRING, A BOBBY PIN AND TAPE.
GIM-MICK?
THE CULPRIT USED THAT GIMMICK TO DROP THE KOTO FROM THE CEILING OF YOUR GRAND-FATHER'S ROOM.
BY COINCIDENCE, IT HAPPENED TO FALL ON MINORU'S HEAD.
THE CULPRIT DIDN'T KNOW MINORU WAS THERE BECAUSE HE'D GONE IN TO SEARCH THE ROOM...
...IN SECRET.
...
AFTER HEARING AT DINNER THAT THE MUSIC BOX PLAYED THE TUNE "WAITING FOR SPRING," WHICH YOUR GRANDMOTHER OFTEN PLAYED ON HER KOTO, YOU WENT TO CHECK IT OUT...
...HOPING THE VALUABLE STAMP MIGHT BE HIDDEN IN THE KOTO.
BUT EVEN IF THE KOTO FELL FROM THE CEILING, IT ISN'T MUCH OF A DROP, SO IT SHOULDN'T HAVE HURT HIM ENOUGH TO KNOCK HIM OUT.
AND IF HE WAS TRYING TO SEARCH THE KOTO, HE WOULD'VE TURNED THE LIGHT ON, RIGHT?
BUT WHEN WE RAN IN, THE LIGHT WAS OFF AND THE ROOM WAS DARK!
IT WASN'T THAT MR. MINORU DIDN'T TURN THE LIGHT ON. HE *COULDN'T* TURN IT ON.

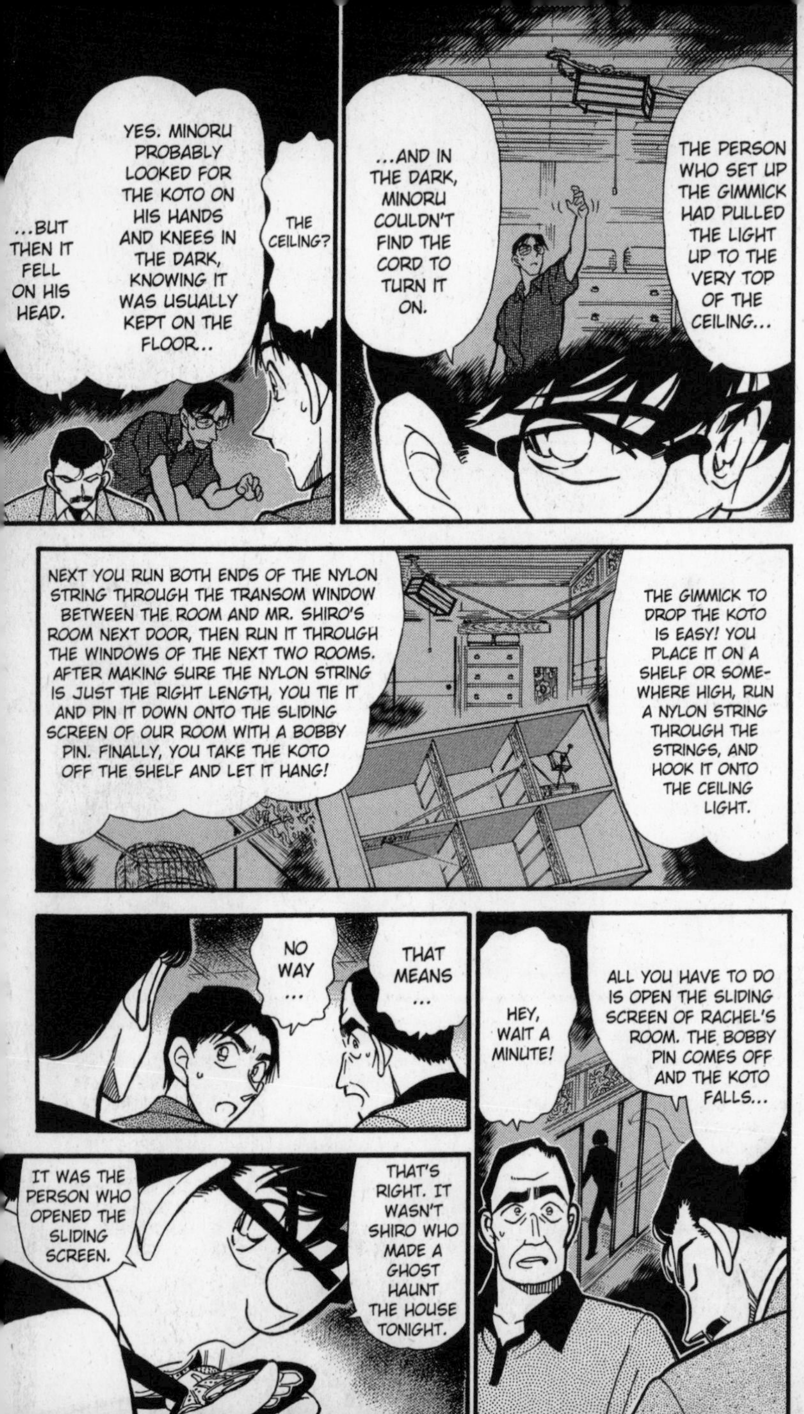
THE PERSON WHO SET UP THE GIMMICK HAD PULLED THE LIGHT UP TO THE VERY TOP OF THE CEILING...
...AND IN THE DARK, MINORU COULDN'T FIND THE CORD TO TURN IT ON.
THE CEILING?
YES. MINORU PROBABLY LOOKED FOR THE KOTO ON HIS HANDS AND KNEES IN THE DARK, KNOWING IT WAS USUALLY KEPT ON THE FLOOR...
...BUT THEN IT FELL ON HIS HEAD.
THE GIMMICK TO DROP THE KOTO IS EASY! YOU PLACE IT ON A SHELF OR SOME-WHERE HIGH, RUN A NYLON STRING THROUGH THE STRINGS, AND HOOK IT ONTO THE CEILING LIGHT.
NEXT YOU RUN BOTH ENDS OF THE NYLON STRING THROUGH THE TRANSOM WINDOW BETWEEN THE ROOM AND MR. SHIRO'S ROOM NEXT DOOR, THEN RUN IT THROUGH THE WINDOWS OF THE NEXT TWO ROOMS. AFTER MAKING SURE THE NYLON STRING IS JUST THE RIGHT LENGTH, YOU TIE IT AND PIN IT DOWN ONTO THE SLIDING SCREEN OF OUR ROOM WITH A BOBBY PIN. FINALLY, YOU TAKE THE KOTO OFF THE SHELF AND LET IT HANG!
ALL YOU HAVE TO DO IS OPEN THE SLIDING SCREEN OF RACHEL'S ROOM. THE BOBBY PIN COMES OFF AND THE KOTO FALLS...
HEY, WAIT A MINUTE!
THAT MEANS...
NO WAY...
THAT'S RIGHT. IT WASN'T SHIRO WHO MADE A GHOST HAUNT THE HOUSE TONIGHT.
IT WAS THE PERSON WHO OPENED THE SLIDING SCREEN.

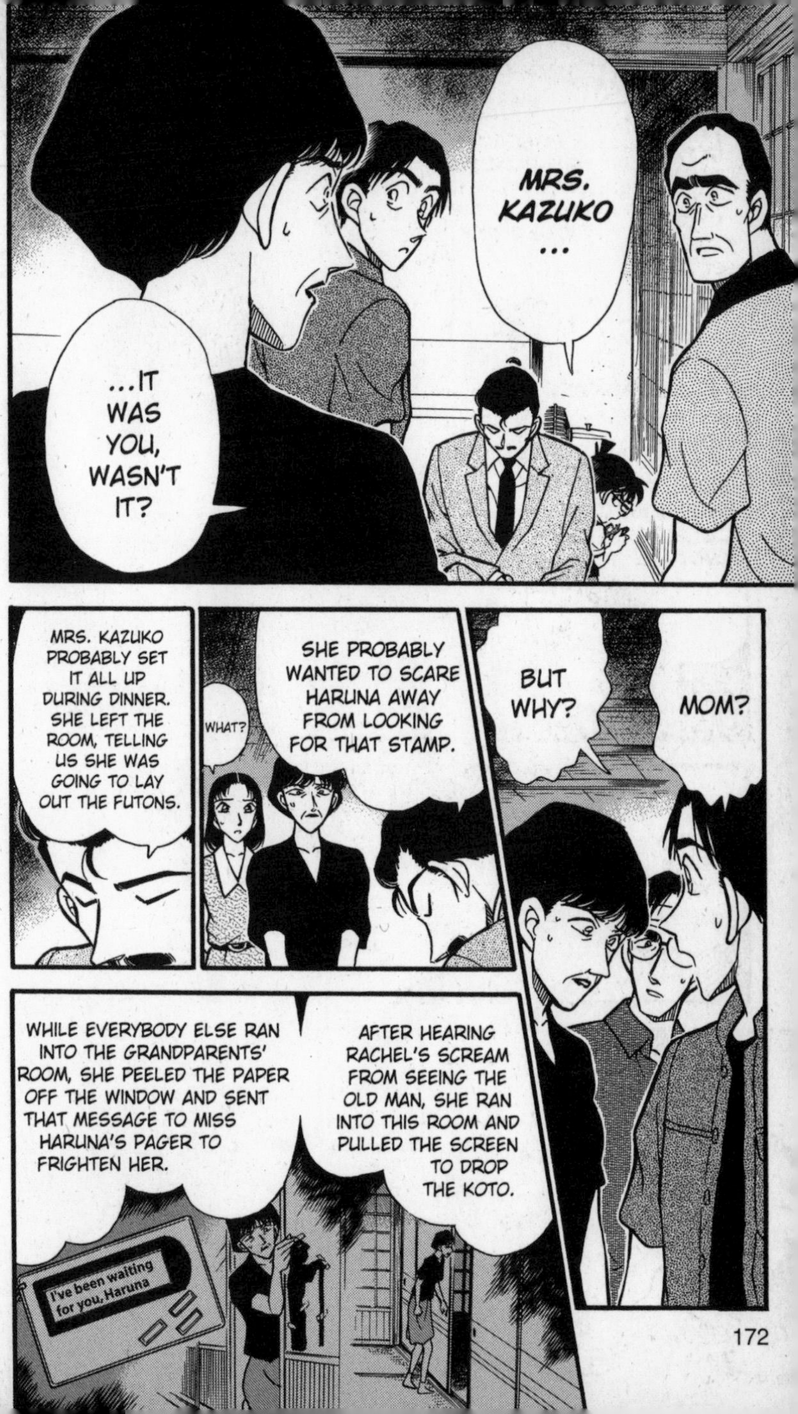
MRS. KAZUKO ...
...IT WAS YOU, WASN'T IT?
MOM?
BUT WHY?
SHE PROBABLY WANTED TO SCARE HARUNA AWAY FROM LOOKING FOR THAT STAMP.
WHAT?
MRS. KAZUKO PROBABLY SET IT ALL UP DURING DINNER. SHE LEFT THE ROOM, TELLING US SHE WAS GOING TO LAY OUT THE FUTONS.
AFTER HEARING RACHEL'S SCREAM FROM SEEING THE OLD MAN, SHE RAN INTO THIS ROOM AND PULLED THE SCREEN TO DROP THE KOTO.
WHILE EVERYBODY ELSE RAN INTO THE GRANDPARENTS' ROOM, SHE PEELED THE PAPER OFF THE WINDOW AND SENT THAT MESSAGE TO MISS HARUNA'S PAGER TO FRIGHTEN HER.
I've been waiting for you, Haruna

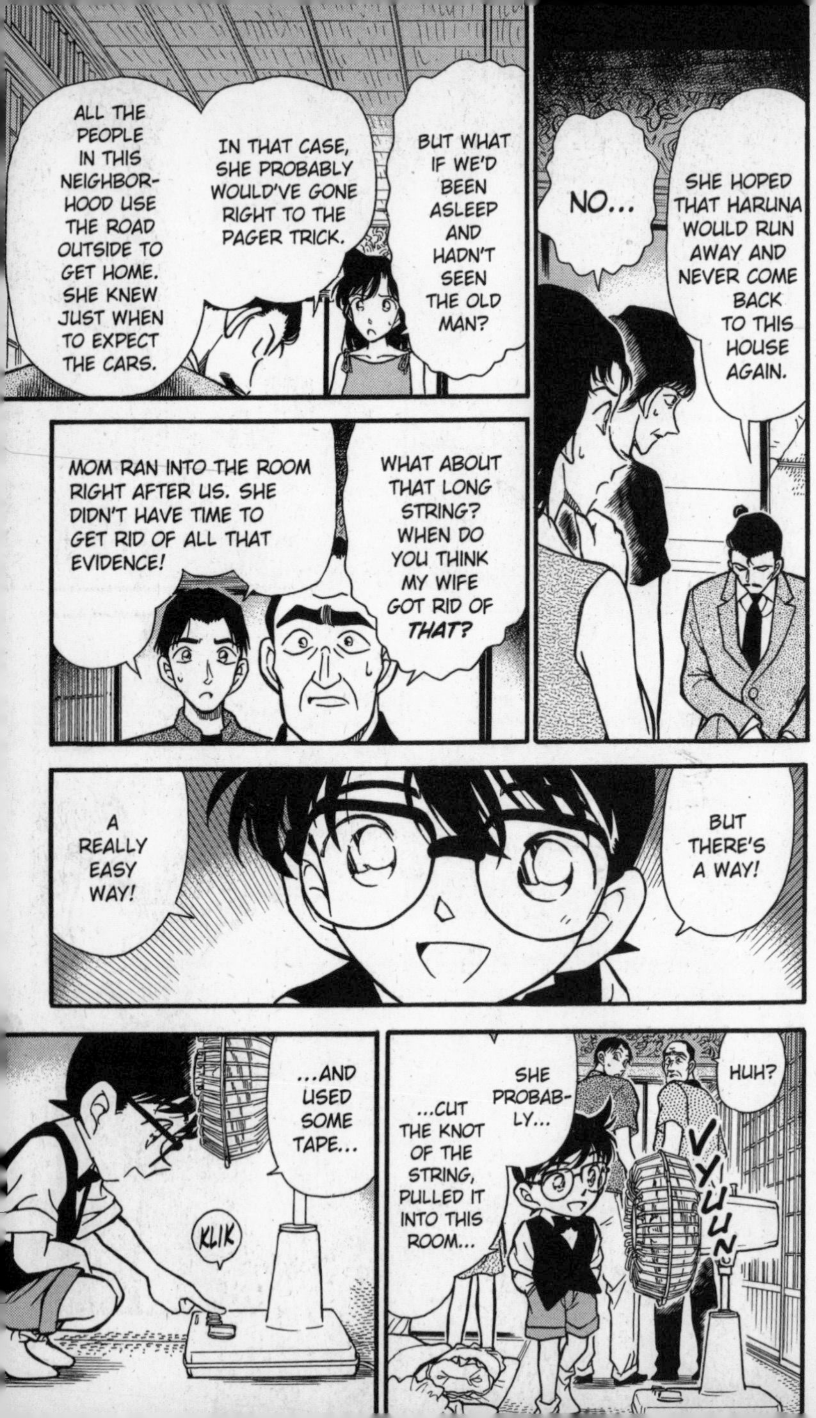
SHE HOPED THAT HARUNA WOULD RUN AWAY AND NEVER COME BACK TO THIS HOUSE AGAIN.
NO...
BUT WHAT IF WE'D BEEN ASLEEP AND HADN'T SEEN THE OLD MAN?
IN THAT CASE, SHE PROBABLY WOULD'VE GONE RIGHT TO THE PAGER TRICK.
ALL THE PEOPLE IN THIS NEIGHBOR-HOOD USE THE ROAD OUTSIDE TO GET HOME. SHE KNEW JUST WHEN TO EXPECT THE CARS.
WHAT ABOUT THAT LONG STRING? WHEN DO YOU THINK MY WIFE GOT RID OF *THAT?*
MOM RAN INTO THE ROOM RIGHT AFTER US. SHE DIDN'T HAVE TIME TO GET RID OF ALL THAT EVIDENCE!
BUT THERE'S A WAY!
A REALLY EASY WAY!
HUH?
VYUUN
SHE PROBAB-LY...
...CUT THE KNOT OF THE STRING, PULLED IT INTO THIS ROOM...
...AND USED SOME TAPE...
KLIK

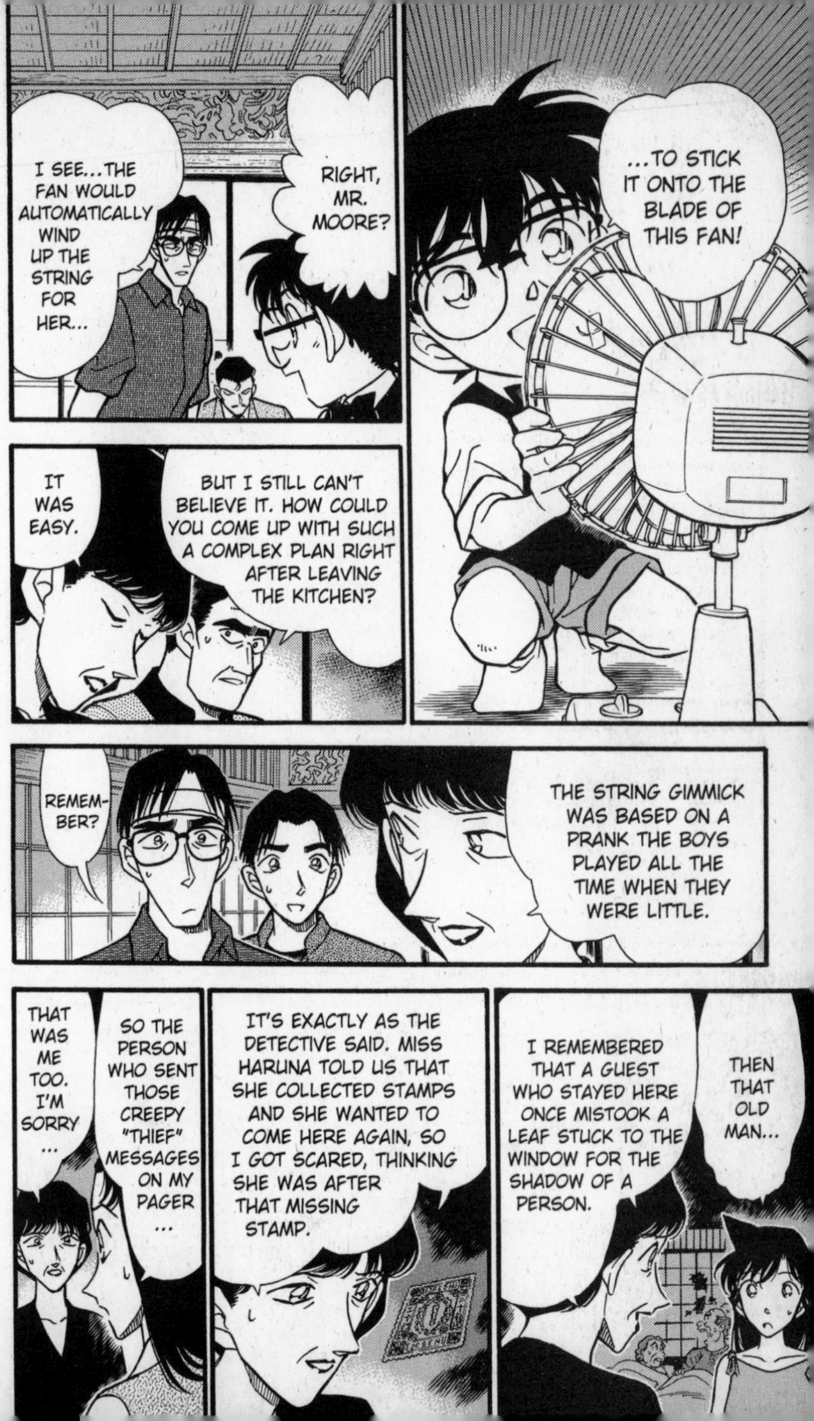
...TO STICK IT ONTO THE BLADE OF THIS FAN!
RIGHT, MR. MOORE?
I SEE...THE FAN WOULD AUTOMATICALLY WIND UP THE STRING FOR HER...
BUT I STILL CAN'T BELIEVE IT. HOW COULD YOU COME UP WITH SUCH A COMPLEX PLAN RIGHT AFTER LEAVING THE KITCHEN?
IT WAS EASY.
THE STRING GIMMICK WAS BASED ON A PRANK THE BOYS PLAYED ALL THE TIME WHEN THEY WERE LITTLE.
REMEM-BER?
THEN THAT OLD MAN...
I REMEMBERED THAT A GUEST WHO STAYED HERE ONCE MISTOOK A LEAF STUCK TO THE WINDOW FOR THE SHADOW OF A PERSON.
IT'S EXACTLY AS THE DETECTIVE SAID. MISS HARUNA TOLD US THAT SHE COLLECTED STAMPS AND SHE WANTED TO COME HERE AGAIN, SO I GOT SCARED, THINKING SHE WAS AFTER THAT MISSING STAMP.
SO THE PERSON WHO SENT THOSE CREEPY "THIEF" MESSAGES ON MY PAGER...
THAT WAS ME TOO. I'M SORRY...

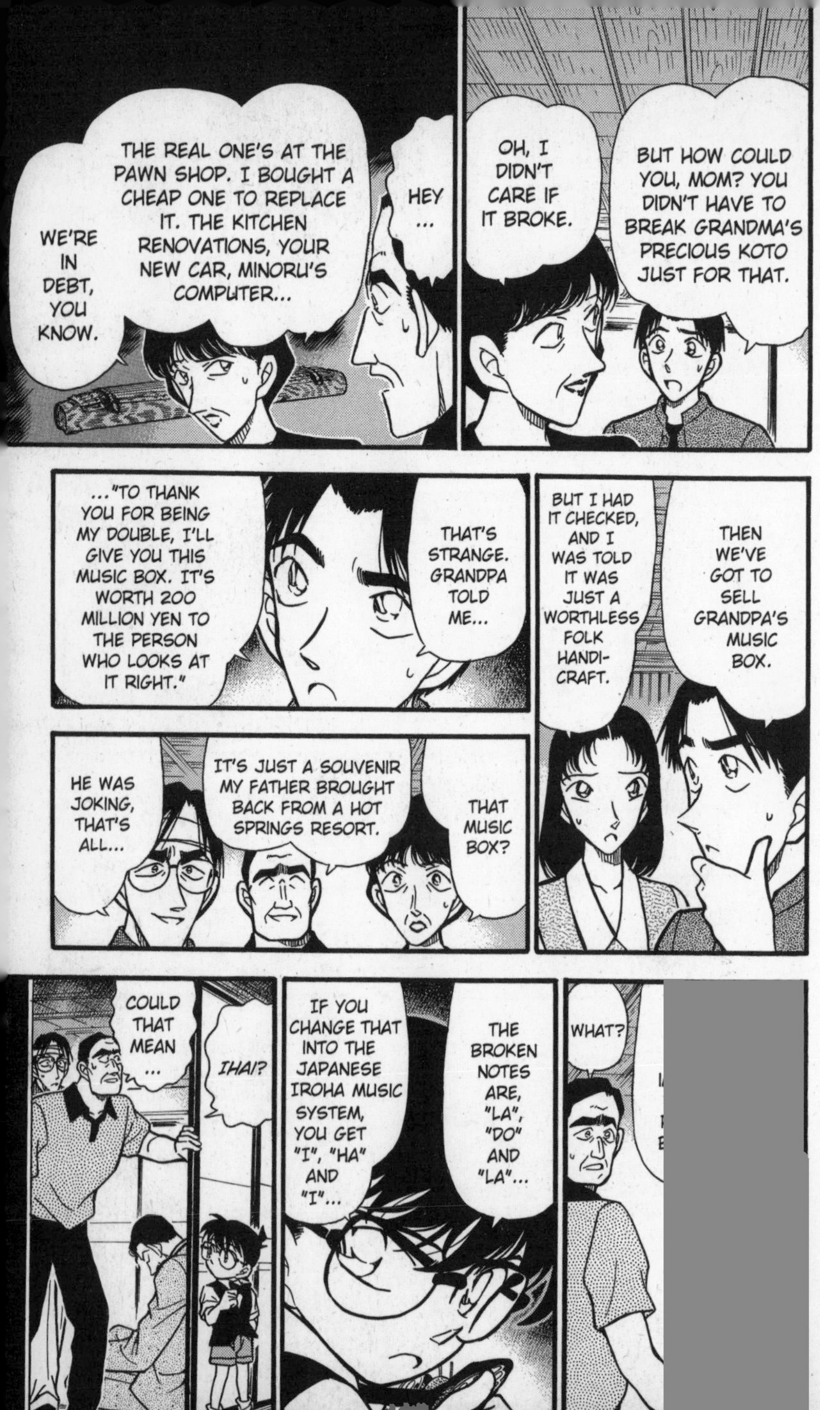
BUT HOW COULD YOU, MOM? YOU DIDN'T HAVE TO BREAK GRANDMA'S PRECIOUS KOTO JUST FOR THAT.
OH, I DIDN'T CARE IF IT BROKE.
HEY ...
THE REAL ONE'S AT THE PAWN SHOP. I BOUGHT A CHEAP ONE TO REPLACE IT. THE KITCHEN RENOVATIONS, YOUR NEW CAR, MINORU'S COMPUTER...
WE'RE IN DEBT, YOU KNOW.
THEN WE'VE GOT TO SELL GRANDPA'S MUSIC BOX.
BUT I HAD IT CHECKED, AND I WAS TOLD IT WAS JUST A WORTHLESS FOLK HANDI-CRAFT.
THAT'S STRANGE. GRANDPA TOLD ME...
..."TO THANK YOU FOR BEING MY DOUBLE, I'LL GIVE YOU THIS MUSIC BOX. IT'S WORTH 200 MILLION YEN TO THE PERSON WHO LOOKS AT IT RIGHT."
THAT MUSIC BOX?
IT'S JUST A SOUVENIR MY FATHER BROUGHT BACK FROM A HOT SPRINGS RESORT.
HE WAS JOKING, THAT'S ALL...
WHAT?
THE BROKEN NOTES ARE, "LA", "DO" AND "LA"...
IF YOU CHANGE THAT INTO THE JAPANESE IROHA MUSIC SYSTEM, YOU GET "I", "HA" AND "I"...
IHAI?
COULD THAT MEAN ...

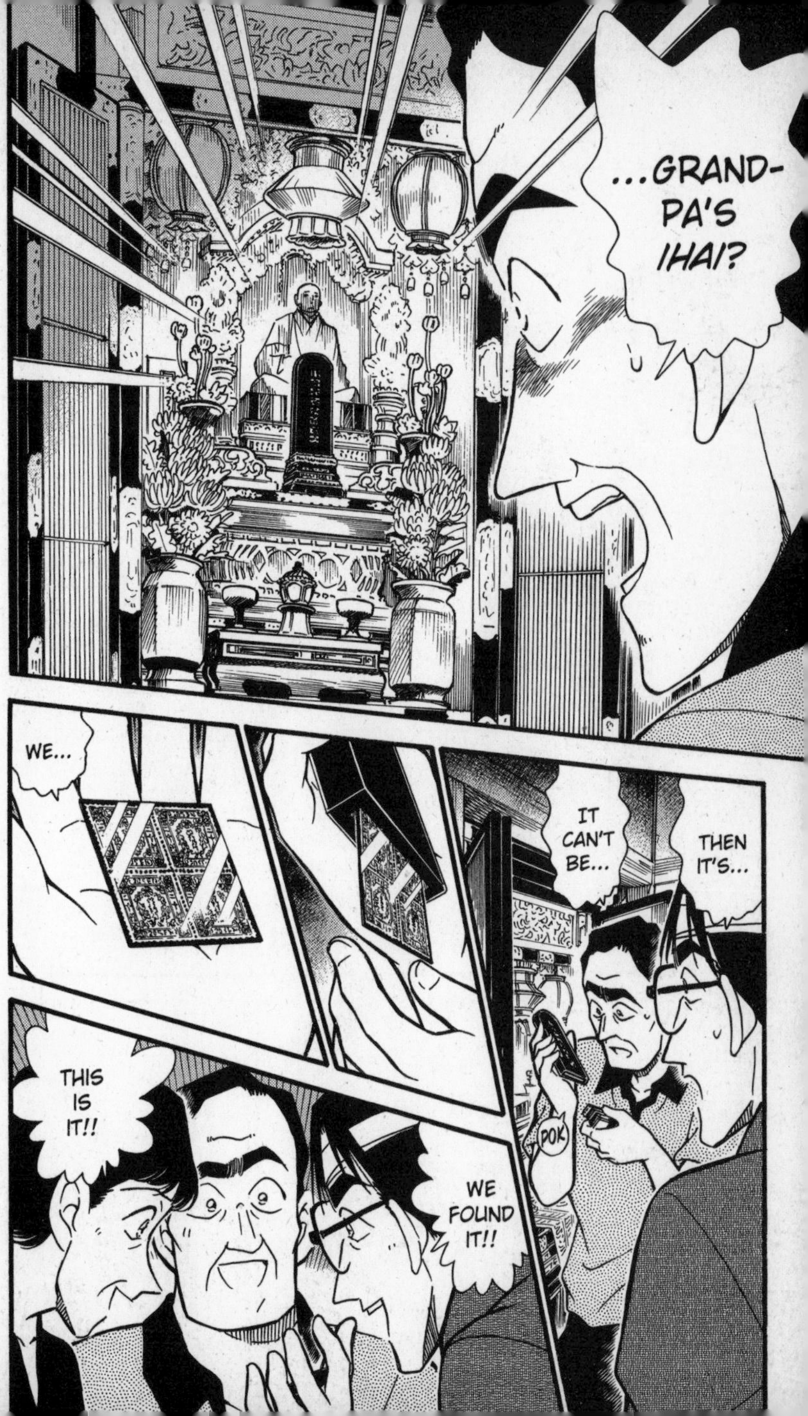
...GRAND-PA'S IHAI?
THEN IT'S...
IT CAN'T BE...
WE...
THIS IS IT!!
WE FOUND IT!!
POK

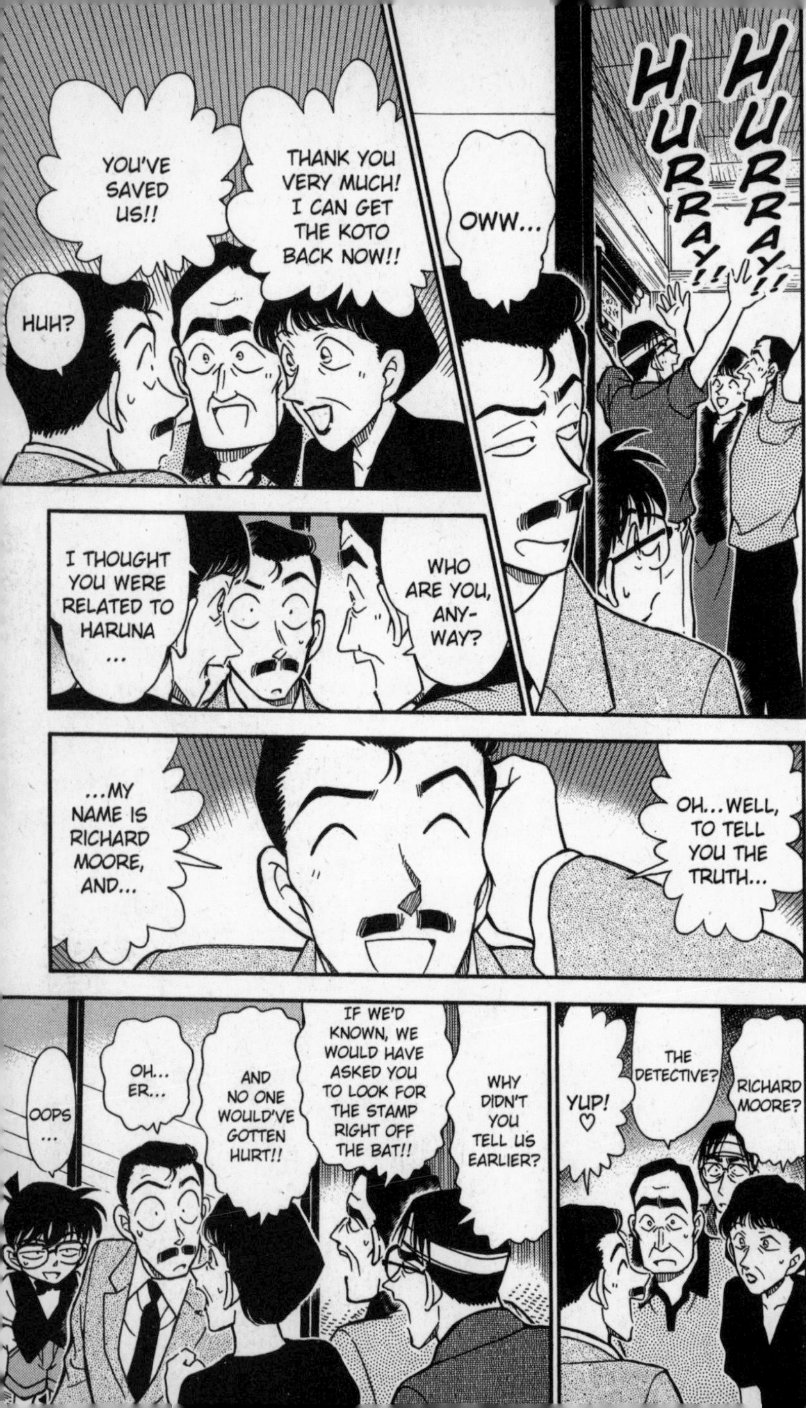
HURRAY!!
HURRAY!!
OWW...
THANK YOU VERY MUCH! I CAN GET THE KOTO BACK NOW!!
YOU'VE SAVED US!!
HUH?
WHO ARE YOU, ANY-WAY?
I THOUGHT YOU WERE RELATED TO HARUNA ...
OH...WELL, TO TELL YOU THE TRUTH...
...MY NAME IS RICHARD MOORE, AND...
RICHARD MOORE?
THE DETECTIVE?
YUP! ♡
WHY DIDN'T YOU TELL US EARLIER?
IF WE'D KNOWN, WE WOULD HAVE ASKED YOU TO LOOK FOR THE STAMP RIGHT OFF THE BAT!!
AND NO ONE WOULD'VE GOTTEN HURT!!
OH... ER...
OOPS ...

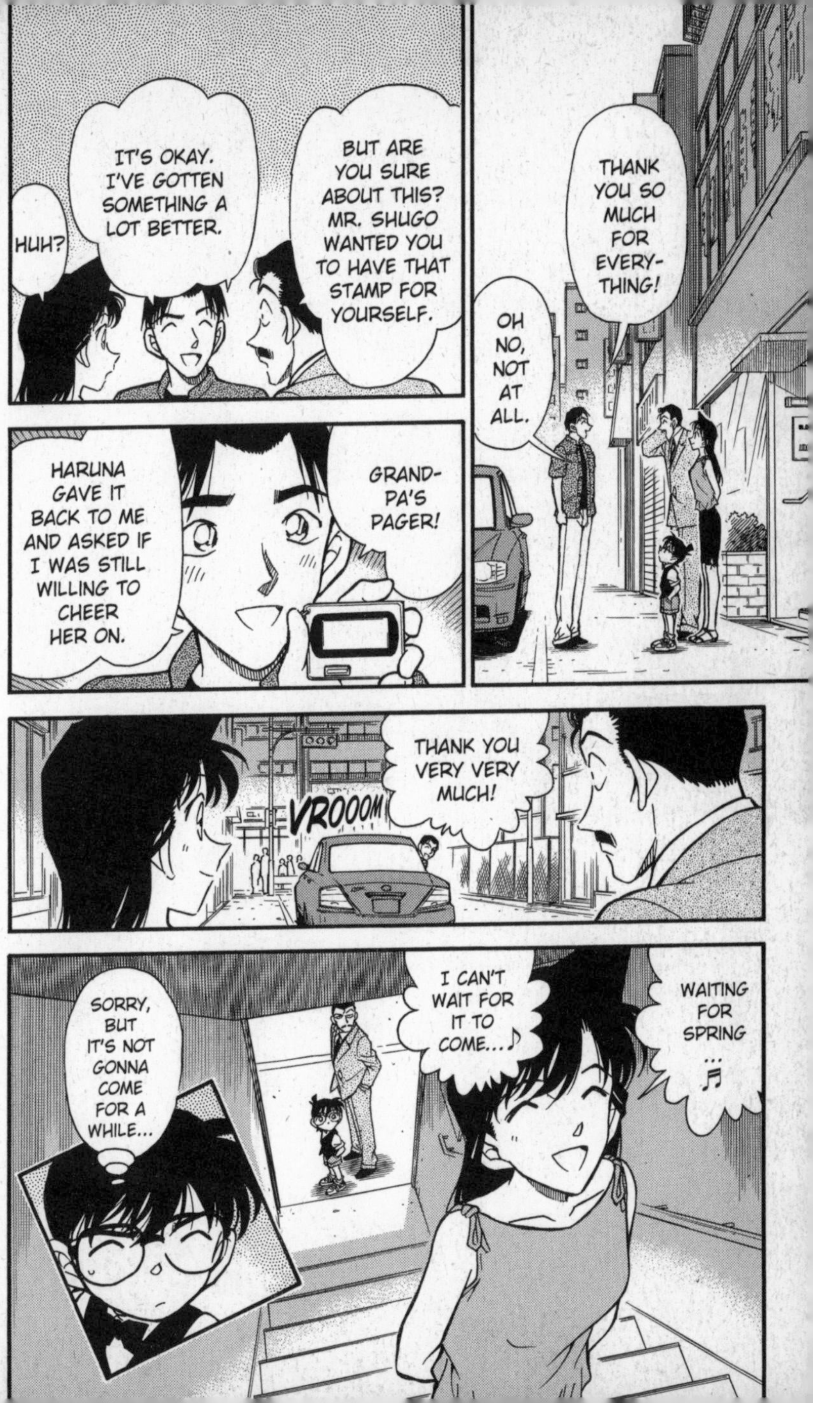
THANK YOU SO MUCH FOR EVERY-THING!
OH NO, NOT AT ALL.
BUT ARE YOU SURE ABOUT THIS? MR. SHUGO WANTED YOU TO HAVE THAT STAMP FOR YOURSELF.
IT'S OKAY. I'VE GOTTEN SOMETHING A LOT BETTER.
HUH?
GRAND-PA'S PAGER!
HARUNA GAVE IT BACK TO ME AND ASKED IF I WAS STILL WILLING TO CHEER HER ON.
THANK YOU VERY VERY MUCH!
VROOOM
WAITING FOR SPRING ...♬
I CAN'T WAIT FOR IT TO COME...♪
SORRY, BUT IT'S NOT GONNA COME FOR A WHILE...

Hello, Aoyama here.

The year 2000 is finally here!

Looks like the world survived the Y2K bug, but my Gosho computer malfunctioned and Jimmy escaped from the comic! I had to redraw the panel he came out of, so it's different from the version in the magazine. See if you can find it. ❤

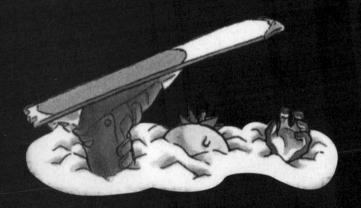

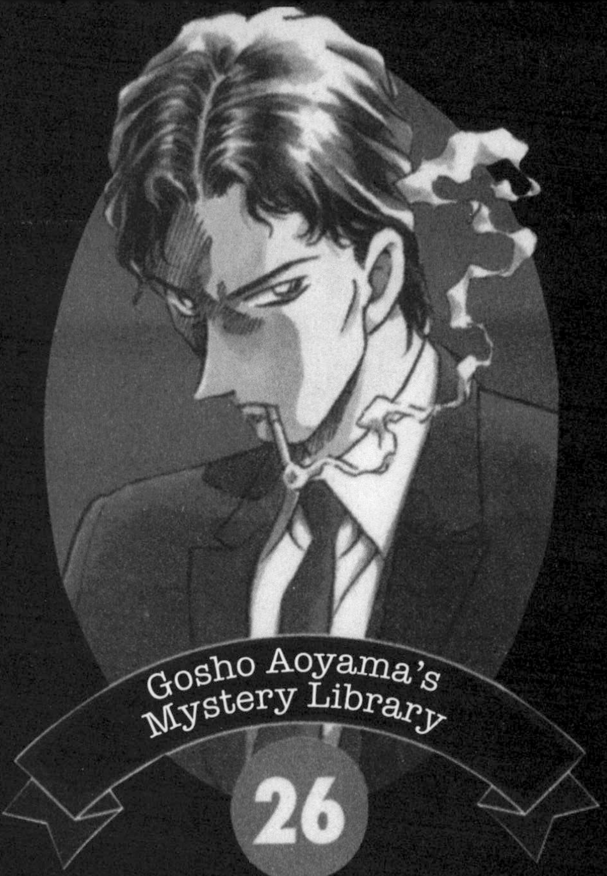
Gosho Aoyama's
Mystery Library
26

INSPECTOR SAMEJIMA

Solitude comes naturally to a hard-boiled detective, but this man is a lone wolf even while working in a big police force. He's Inspector Samejima, aka "The Shinjuku Shark," created by Arimasa Osawa! Samejima is 36 years old, but he looks younger thanks to the long hair flowing past his neckline. He's an elite career officer and has passed the advanced exam for national public officials, so he should be at least a commissioner. But because of a certain case he was involved in years ago, not to mention the strong sense of justice which often inspires him to rebel against the police organization, he's not on good terms with his superiors. He currently works in the crime prevention department of Shinjuku Police Station. He usually works on investigations alone and has an unbelievable arrest rate in high-crime areas. He'll come up to crooks without a sound, then suddenly bite... hence his nickname, "The Shinjuku Shark"! His only comfort and weak spot is his girlfriend Sho, a rock singer. I'd love to have a weak spot like her too. ❤

I recommend *Dokuzaru* (The Poisonous Ape).

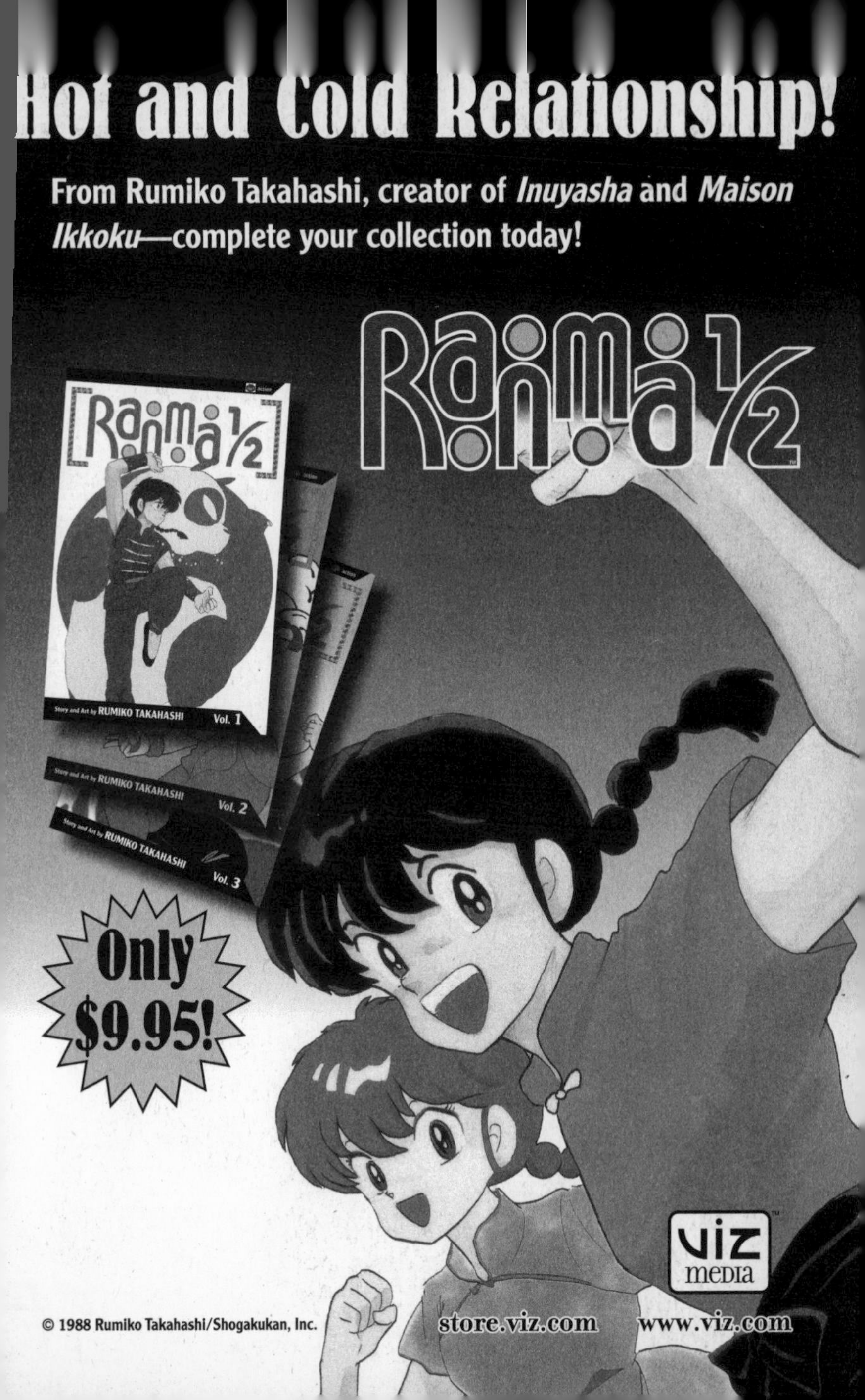

Hot and Cold Relationship!
From Rumiko Takahashi, creator of *Inuyasha* and *Maison Ikkoku*—complete your collection today!
Ranma 1/2
Ranma 1/2
Story and Art by RUMIKO TAKAHASHI Vol. 1
Story and Art by RUMIKO TAKAHASHI Vol. 2
Story and Art by RUMIKO TAKAHASHI Vol. 3
Only $9.95!
VIZ MEDIA
© 1988 Rumiko Takahashi/Shogakukan, Inc.
store.viz.com
www.viz.com

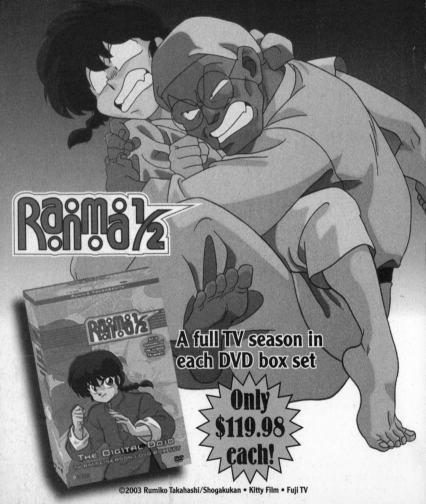

LOVE MANGA?

LET US KNOW WHAT YOU THINK!

NOW
E VISIT:
EY

HELP US MAKE THE MANGA
YOU LOVE BETTER!